WHAT GENDER IS MOTHERHOOD?

D1570861

GENDER AND CULTURAL STUDIES IN AFRICA AND THE DIASPORA

Series Editor: Oyèrónké Oyěwùmí, Stony Brook University

Series Advisers:

Adeleke Adeeko, Ohio State University
N'Dri Assié-Lumumba, Cornell University
Ayo Coly, Dartmouth College
Carolyn Cooper, University of Western Indies, Mona
Godwin Murunga, University of Nairobi
Filomina Steady, Wellesley College

This book series spotlights the experiences of Africans on the continent and in its multiple and multilayered diasporas. Its objective is to make available publications that focus on people of African descent wherever they are located, targeting innovative research that derives questions, concepts, and theories from historical and contemporary experiences. The broad scope of the series includes gender scholarship as well as studies that engage with culture in all its complexities. From a variety of disciplinary, interdisciplinary, and transdisciplinary orientations, these studies engage current debates, address urgent questions, and open up new perspectives in African knowledge production.

PUBLISHED BY PALGRAVE:

Spatial Literacy: Contemporary Asante Women's Place-making
by Epifania Akosua Amoo-Adare

Folklore, Gender, and AIDS in Malawi: No Secret Under the Sun
by Anika Wilson

Democracy at Home in South Africa: Family Fictions and Transitional Culture
by Kerry Bystrom

What Gender is Motherhood?: Changing Yorùbá Ideals of Power, Procreation, and Identity in the Age of Modernity
by Oyèrónké Oyěwùmí

WHAT GENDER IS MOTHERHOOD?

CHANGING YORÙBÁ IDEALS OF POWER, PROCREATION, AND IDENTITY IN THE AGE OF MODERNITY

Oyèrónkẹ́ Oyěwùmí

WHAT GENDER IS MOTHERHOOD?
Copyright © Oyèrónkẹ́ Oyěwùmí 2016
Softcover reprint of the hardcover 1st edition 2016 978-1-137-53877-2

All rights reserved. No reproduction, copy or transmission of this publication may be made without written permission. No portion of this publication may be reproduced, copied or transmitted save with written permission. In accordance with the provisions of the Copyright, Designs and Patents Act 1988, or under the terms of any licence permitting limited copying issued by the Copyright Licensing Agency, Saffron House, 6-10 Kirby Street, London EC1N 8TS.

Any person who does any unauthorized act in relation to this publication may be liable to criminal prosecution and civil claims for damages.

First published 2016 by
PALGRAVE MACMILLAN

The author has asserted their rights to be identified as the author of this work in accordance with the Copyright, Designs and Patents Act 1988.

Palgrave Macmillan in the UK is an imprint of Macmillan Publishers Limited, registered in England, company number 785998, of Houndmills, Basingstoke, Hampshire, RG21 6XS.

Palgrave Macmillan in the US is a division of Nature America, Inc., One New York Plaza, Suite 4500, New York, NY 10004-1562.

Palgrave Macmillan is the global academic imprint of the above companies and has companies and representatives throughout the world.

ISBN: 978-1-349-58051-4
E-PDF ISBN: 978–1–137–52125–5
DOI: 10.1057/9781137521255

Distribution in the UK, Europe and the rest of the world is by Palgrave Macmillan®, a division of Macmillan Publishers Limited, registered in England, company number 785998, of Houndmills, Basingstoke, Hampshire RG21 6XS.

Library of Congress Cataloging-in-Publication Data

Names: Oyěwùmí, Oyèrónkẹ́, author.
Title: What gender is motherhood? : changing Yorùbá ideas on power, procreation, and identity in the age of modernity / by Oyèrónkẹ́ Oyěwùmí.
Other titles: Gender and cultural studies in Africa and the diaspora.
Description: New York : Palgrave Macmillan, 2015. | Series: Gender and cultural studies in Africa and the diaspora | Includes bibliographical references and index.
Identifiers: LCCN 2015023978
Subjects: LCSH: Motherhood—Nigeria. | Ifa (Religion) | Gender identity—Nigeria. | Oyo (African people)
Classification: LCC HQ759 O95 2015 | DDC 306.874/308996333—dc23
LC record available at http://lccn.loc.gov/2015023978

A catalogue record for the book is available from the British Library.

In Praise of Iya

Mo f 'ire fún Ọ̀ṣun
Mo f 'ire fún Ọ̀ya
Mo fọ ire fún gbogbo àwọn ìyá
Afimọ̀ f 'obìnrin, Iye wa táa pé nímọ̀
Afimọ̀ jẹ t'Ọ̀ṣun o, Iye wa táa pé nímọ̀
Ǹjẹ́, ẹ jẹ́ ká wólẹ̀ f 'obìnrin
Obìnrin ló bí wa
Ka wa to dènìyàn
Ẹ jẹ́ ká wólẹ̀ f 'obìnrin
Obìnrin ló b'Ọba
K'Ọ́ba ó tó d'Òrìṣà

CONTENTS

ACKNOWLEDGMENTS

The completion of this book represents another stage in my intellectual journey. During the long process of producing it, I drew on the generosity and support of a number of individuals and institutions. First, I want to thank my colleague Adélékè Adéèkó for reading drafts of the evolving manuscript from the very beginning of the project to its completion. He has always patiently read anything I sent him, and his comments prompt me to refine my ideas. I am especially grateful to him for making available to me his expertise in Yorùbá language, offering his translations of words and phrases and applying diacritical marks to my Yorùbá-language texts.

I thank Tolulope Idowu, my friend from youth, who read numerous versions of the manuscript from the very beginning of the process. She was always willing to read the crudest of my drafts, offering helpful suggestions and applying her strong editorial skills. My friend Diana Cassells listened patiently on a daily basis to my ideas, read various parts of the manuscript, and was especially helpful in providing insightful comments about the Yorùbá Diasporic experiences in Cuba and Brazil.

I am grateful to Filomina Steady, friend, mentor and colleague, who read a draft of the manuscript and shared her considerable knowledge and experience unstintingly throughout the writing process. In addition, the following friends and colleagues read all or parts of the manuscript and offered useful comments: Tushabe Tushabe, Abosede George, Abena Asare, Olakunle George, and Marame Gueye. Olasope Oyelaran also gave me the benefit of his knowledge of Yorùbá society and letters. My colleague Akintunde Akinyemi drew my attention to recent studies on oriki and Oyo oral traditions including his own. Thank you for your insights and the book. Farooq Kperogi and Muhammad Shakir Balogun read chapters of the manuscript, shared their extensive knowledge of Islam, and gave insightful comments on the impact of Islam on the naming practices of various ethnic communities in Nigeria including Hausa, Yorùbá, and Batonum. To them both, I offer my gratitude.

I owe a load of thanks to my friend and colleague Jimi Adesina for his encouragement and unwavering support over the years. I appreciate my *sista* and colleague Cheryl Sterling for her encouragement and willingness to share her knowledge of the workings of the academy.

It is a compliment to a scholar when another scholar takes up his or her work and looks at it critically. It is in that spirit that I hope my examination of the work of intellectuals writing on Yorùbá culture will be taken. In this regard, I wish to thank Toyin Falola for responding by email to my questions about aspects of his writings on Samuel Johnson, the pioneer Yorùbá local historian. I am also grateful to him for lending books and documents from his formidable library when I could not get them anywhere else.

I cannot thank enough my research assistants Titilayo Halimat Somotan and Emma Wilhelmina Parker Halm, and Ademide Adelusi-Adeluyi, who put in an inordinate number of hours in preparing the manuscript for publication. I am especially indebted to Ademide who dropped everything and came to the rescue at the last minute, solving technical glitches as we adhered to the publisher's guidelines. To my long-standing editor extraordinaire and friend Lindsey Reed, I have benefitted from your ideas and skill over many years, and this book is no exception. I am deeply appreciative of your efforts.

I would like to acknowledge a series of grants from the Stony Brook University: The Provost's Fine Arts, Humanities and Social Science (FAHSS) initiative. These grants supported me over three summers, allowing me to go to Ogbomoso, Nigeria, to conduct research.

I must acknowledge the *babalawo* in Ogbomoso, who gave generously of their time and knowledge, contributing significantly to the quality of my work. In this regard, I cannot thank enough babalawo Chief Akalaifa and his son Olayode Akalaifa (now deceased), who gave many hours of their time and knowledge to educate me about Ifa and Orisa Devotion. Olayode introduced me to an Orisa Devoted congregation in Ogbomoso named Ijo Elesin Ifa Adimula, Irunmole Parapo. It was on my visit to this house of worship that the 15-year-old girl Fafunso Oyetayo explained the procedure of the religious service to me. I appreciate them all. Chief Olagoke Adio Akanni, Araba Oluawo Ogbomoso, the head of the Babalawo in the town, granted me many interviews. He answered my numerous questions and also shared numerous Ifa verses. I am grateful.

Special thanks to the anonymous reviewers whose comments and questions prodded me to refine the manuscript.

This book is about motherhood. My gratitude must start with my very own *iya*, Igbayilola, the model of matripotency, who showed me the way, and from whom I gained much knowledge and experience. I am grateful to my children Olasunbo, Akinboye, and Mapate for choosing me and making me their mother. My *omooya* are always there to support me. I appreciate them all: Bolanle, Aderemi, Ademola, Oyewole, and Oyekemi for their encouragement. *Eku oro iya o.* I am appreciative of my father, His Royal Majesty Oba Oladunni Oyewumi, Laronke, and *awon iya* in the palace, who were always ready to entertain my questions, share their knowledge and experiences: most especially Iya Saki. Over the years, Soun's Palace has been a superb space for apprehending "culture" for a culture fiend like me.

I must not forget my aunt Nkanlola, who always accompanied me on my interview rounds with babalawo. Finally, I appreciate my friends Bose Afolabi and Olajide Bello for their unwavering support. I was especially encouraged by their rapt attention whenever I discussed my visits to the babalawo.

I take full responsibility for the content of this book.

A NOTE ON ORTHOGRAPHY

Yorùbá is a tonal language, with three underlying pitch levels for vowels and syllabic nasal: the low tone is marked with a grave accent; the midtone is unmarked; and the high tone is marked with an acute accent. I have used tonal accents and subscript marks (e.g., ẹ, ọ, ṣ). Some syllables require two diacritics, as in my last name, Oyěwùmí, where an acute accent joins with a grave accent over the *e* to form a *v*. As to the subscript marks: the ẹ is approximately equivalent to the *e* in the English word "yet"; the ọ is close to the sound in "dog"; and the ṣ is close to the English "sh" sound. I have used tonal marks on the Yorùbá words and names that are part of my text. However, there are many Yorùbá names, especially of scholars, that remain unmarked because up to this point, the tendency has been to discount the diacritics in African languages. Yet, without the diacritics, those words do not make sense.

INTRODUCTION

EXHUMING SUBJUGATED KNOWLEDGE AND LIBERATING MARGINALIZED EPISTEMES

Societies that have experienced colonization have suffered many ill effects, some psychological, some linguistic, and some intellectual. But none have perhaps been less studied than how colonization subjugates knowledge and marginalizes local epistemes. This book aims to take endogenous categories and epistemologies seriously, focusing on the production of knowledge in the Yorùbá society of southwestern Nigeria and exploring the extent to which indigenous concepts, ideas, and language are taken into account in academic research. Paying close attention to language, endogenous discourses, and local knowledge systems, I hope to provide a new understanding of a number of important institutions and social practices such as *Ifá*, motherhood, marriage, and family. This study draws on data collected over a long period of time, starting with my dissertation research in Ibadan and Ogbomoso in the 1980s and continuing to the present. Significantly for this book, I also conducted interviews with diviners in Ogbomoso.

This volume develops themes first presented in my book *The Invention of Women: Making an African Sense of Western Gender Discourses* (1997), in which I exposed gender as a historically recent category in Yorùbá culture, one that emerged with European colonization of both the society and its knowledge systems. Concomitantly, I demonstrated that prior to colonization, endogenous Yorùbá hierarchies were based on seniority gained through age, rather than on gender, which, I argued, was a Western patriarchal value. I posited that gender is a colonial category.

One of the themes that emerged from my investigation of gender in Yorùbá society is the role of writing and scholars in interpreting and therefore representing the culture. All too often, I found, research betrayed a glaring lack of understanding of local realities. In fact, many researchers who had written about gender in Yorùbá culture did not recognize—indeed never even did a systematic analysis of—current, everyday, every time, gender-neutral categories of kinship and the related seniority-based organization of families and social groups. For so many academics, both local and foreign, indigenous categories and experiences did not seem to drive their work, at least not in the first instance. From the perspective of knowledge making, Yorùbá categories of knowledge—the ways in which the culture codified and organized information—tended in the main not to influence scholarly claims and conclusions.

In the current book *What Gender Is Motherhood? Changing Yorùbá Ideals of Power, Procreation, and Identity in the Age of Modernity*, then, questions of knowledge and gender and the role of intellectuals take center stage. In exploring the intersections of knowledge making and gender, I focus on *Ifá*, the most important endogenous system of knowledge. My interest in *Ifá* stems from its significance in the culture—its historical depth and its continuing resonance in postcolonial society. Taking seriously the traditional Yorùbá nongendered ontology, I explore how gender is implicated in interpretations of the *Ifá* knowledge system, as social and ritual practice, and as a cultural institution in a changing world.

At the center of this book is a discussion of the institution of *Iya* (motherhood), historically the most consequential category in social, political, and spiritual organization. The objective is to document the indigenous epistemology that has been shunted aside as the new gender-saturated colonial epistemology gains ever-deeper resonance in the culture. The argument here is that the category *Iya* is not originally a gender category. It is this chapter that informs the title of the book: *What Gender Is Motherhood?* I introduce the concept of "matripotency"—supremacy of motherhood—as a lens through which to appreciate and understand the discounted Yorùbá epistemology. More than anything else, the different construction of motherhood demonstrates the seismic epistemic shift occasioned by European colonization and policies, the establishment of notions of individualism, Christianization, Islamization of the culture, and globalization.

The global context for knowledge production is crucial to understanding the origins and trajectory of academic research and knowledge production on Yorùbá society. Therefore, in this introduction, I wish to use the concept of the coloniality of power to unpack the culture and practices of institutions of higher learning and the ways in which the race and gender identities of intellectuals enable or disable their quest to contribute to the wealth of human knowledge.

The Coloniality of Power, Gender, and Knowledge

The global hierarchies that we inhabit today are the legacy of a process that started in 1492, involving what Peruvian sociologist Anibal Quijano calls the "coloniality of power," a system that defines modernity. At the core of Quijano's articulation of the coloniality of power is the idea that the racial superiority of Euro/Americans was constituted during this period, and most importantly, that their dominance over other groups, whom they racialized, was deemed to be natural. The notion that white racial superiority is inherent in the human condition was offered as an explanation of why Europeans dominate other groups, an idea that displaced the earlier belief that control of subordinated groups was based on force. Quijano described the ways in which racialized colonial domination influenced both knowledge making and the power embedded in it:

> Repression fell, above all, over the modes of knowing, of producing knowledge, of producing perspectives, images and systems of images, symbols, modes of signification, over the resources, patterns, and instruments of formalized and ob- jectivised expression, intellectual or visual. It was followed by the imposition of the use of the rulers' own patterns of expression, and of their beliefs and images with reference to the supernatural. [...] The colonizers also imposed a mystified image of their own patterns of producing knowledge and meaning.[1]

It was the global imposition of Eurocentric patterns of organizing knowledge that my earlier book *The Invention of Women: Making an African Sense of Western Gender Discourses* challenged. In that volume, I exposed gender as a colonial category, calling into question the idea that gender categories are natural, universal, and inherent in the way in which human communities organized and thought about themselves. In this manner, my work dovetails with some of the issues raised by Quijano, although his focus is on race. But race and gender are inseparable, as we have learnt from intersectional theory and the fact that there is a matrix of domination in human social organization. Maria Lugones writes about the need to incorporate gender in comprehending the coloniality of power. She is essentially correct when she states that "colonialism did not impose precolonial, European gender arrangements on the colonized. It imposed a new gender system that created very different arrangements for colonized males and females than for whites."[2]

Gender, then, is a category central to the construction and organization of knowledge in our time. My research showed that in Yorùbá society in the past, gender was not a factor for classifying information. Hence, I pointed out that the idea in Western feminist discourses that the social category woman and her subordination are universals contradicts another passionately held feminist tenet that gender is socially constructed. I argued that if gender is socially constructed, then there must have been a time during which it was not constructed. I posit therefore that if the constitution of gender as a social category is a product of culture (space), it must also be recognized to be a product of history (time). *Invention* traces the emergence of gender categorization in Yorùbá society of southwestern Nigeria to European imperialism of body, mind, and knowledge. Drawing evidence from family organization, language, the division of labor, religion, and oral traditions, I show that unlike in the West, gender was not originally part of the Yorùbá conceptual framework for making sense of the social world. Instead, British colonization, which was both a racial and gendered process, was instrumental in the establishment of the existing gender systems in this region.

Thus the study concludes that gender, as a mode of organizing society, is simply not inherent in human nature. Although currently gender has become universal, I assert that this development must be understood in historical terms. The groundbreaking book *Invention* inaugurated a paradigm shift in the understanding of gender as a social construct by insisting that our investigations should not take gender for granted but must ask questions about how it is constituted and when, where, and how it came into being in a given locality. The thesis put forth in my work denaturalized and deuniversalized gender, a construct that Euro/Americans are able to impose around the world, given their global power. To borrow Historian Dipesh Chakrabarty's apt phrase, *Invention* sought to "provincialize the West"[3] to recognize that the West is but one region of the geographical and social world, and therefore its institutions, practices, and ways of being do not represent a universal human norm.

In much of Africa, provincializing the West is an epic struggle, given the erasure of African cosmologies, demonization of indigenous religion, destruction of institutions, Othering of persons, and the epistemicide that resulted from colonial conquest. Attempts at decolonization of spaces, bodies, and minds have had little impact, because Africans tend to misunderstand the phenomenon itself. They are like their white colonizers, who self-interestedly think that the removal of white bodies from the polity (aka independence) necessarily "decolonizes." But this is not so, as historian Sabelo Ndlovu-Gatsheni explains. And it is especially not so as regards knowledge production in Africa, which he describes as being "deeply ensnared within the colonial matrix of power and reproduces Western ideational domination on the African continent."[4]

The depth of the problem faced by Africa having passed through European colonization is captured by the distinction that is made between coloniality and colonialism. Following Nelson Maldonado-Torres, Ndlovu-Gatsheni writes:

The concept of coloniality is different from colonialism as it refers to long-standing patterns of power that emerged from colonialism and continue to define culture, labor, intersubjective relations and knowledge production long after the end of direct colonialism. It is that continuing dominating phenomenon that survived colonialism. It is hidden in discourses, books, cultures, common sense, academic performances, and even self images of Africans...Africans have breathed and lived coloniality since their colonial encounters and it continues to shape their everyday life today.[5]

For the purposes of this introduction, I would like to single out the prevailing cultural pattern undergirding systems of knowledge through a recent experience. In January 2015, I was one of the panelists at a conference in a college in Massachusetts, United States. During one of the plenary sessions, I heard the chairperson advise participants from the floor to say their names and the preferred pronouns with which they are to be addressed, as they stood up to ask questions of the panelists. The chairperson was not a comedian, nor was her statement nonsensical, as it would seem to the uninitiated. Rather, it was a response to the challenge that transgender persons pose to English-speaking historically women's colleges in particular, and other human communities more generally.

An article in the *New York Times* sums up the salient points associated with the changing notions of gender and gender identity through the story of a student at the University of Vermont:

Gieselman dumped the girlie name bestowed at birth, asked friends and teachers to use Rocko, the tough-sounding nickname friends had come up with, and told people to use "they" instead of "he" or "she." "They" has become an increasingly popular substitute for "he" or "she" in the transgender community, and the University of Vermont, a public institution of some 12,700 students, has agreed to use it...The university allows students like Gieselman to select their own identity—a new first name, regardless of whether they've legally changed it, as well as a chosen pronoun—and records these details in the campuswide information system so that professors have the correct terminology at their fingertips.[6]

At the conference that evening, I was not so certain that I would be able to keep up with the customized pronouns that my student-audience would conjure, but I was amused at the very idea of choosing one's own personal pronoun. What a pity, I thought. Learn to speak Yorùbá! North Americans would not have to reinvent the wheel if they adopted Yorùbá, one of the many African languages whose pronouns and personal names do not "do gender."

In a similar vein, I was reminded of anthropologist Ifi Amadiume's statement many moons ago about the antics of Western feminists "European feminists...seek possible ways out of their historically oppressive patriarchal family structure...inventing single-parenthood and alternative affective relationships...In the African case we do not need to invent anything."[7]

In any case, Yorùbá do not need to invent a new language, new pronouns, or new names, because their language is not organized on the basis of gender categories; hence there are no gendered pronouns, no gendered names, or gendered kinship categories. If Geiselman and other transgendered persons operated in Yorùbá language, they would not have had to invent any new vocabulary to express their identity. So the Western colonizers who would "civilize" the natives were actually imposing on Africans their own crude languages with their gendered preoccupations, gender binaries, and gender discriminatory and male-dominant ideologies. Unfortunately, given the global hierarchy that is a hallmark of modernity, learning is unidirectional: Africans must learn from Europeans and Americans (including their pathologies); Africans, on the other hand, are not perceived to have anything of value that they could teach the West. Thus the original nongenderness of Yorùbá language becomes invisible as native speakers adjust their vocabulary to model the English language.

Language, however, is only the tip of the iceberg when it comes to the institutions imposed by colonial modernity. Unfortunately, we have to qualify Amadiume's notion that Africans don't need to invent anything, because the African elite have been so schooled in Western race and gender primitivism that today many fail to recognize that African societies had their own spiritual identities and distinct ways of thinking and organizing before European conquest. They are so entrenched in Western ways that they must relearn local languages and even names—if they care enough to do so. On the huge significance of colonial languages anthropologist Maxwell Owusu reminds us,

> one of the subtler and more effective weapons of imperial supremacy was the European language. Subject peoples were obliged to adopt and use it if they wished to succeed in the colonial world. In time the colonized African was made to believe that anything written in a colonial language is sacrosanct, infallible and beyond question.[8]

Marginalization of endogenous languages, erasure of memory, jettisoning of episteme, othering of cultures and bodies, demonizing of the Gods and ancestors, and destruction of social institutions are some of the key elements associated with Africa's experience of colonialism.

What Gender Is Motherhood?

In my previous book, *Invention*, I wrote about the epistemic shift occasioned by the imposition of gender and male dominance on Yorùbá society by the European colonizers: colonial officials and missionaries. In the current book, *What Gender Is Motherhood? Changing Yorùbá Ideals of Power, Procreation, and Identity in the Age of Modernity*, I name the exact nature of the shift as a move away from the indigenous seniority-based matripotent ethos to a male-dominant, gender-based one. In this study, I am concerned with the intersections of power, gender, history, and knowledge making, and the role of intellectuals in the process. In exploring the intersections of knowledge and gender, I focus on *Ifá*, the most important endogenous system of knowledge and divination. In the first two chapters of the book, I apply the finding of a nongendered ontology to the institution of *Ifá* and explore how gender is implicated in interpretations of the knowledge system, as social and ritual practice, and as a cultural institution in a changing world. In this chapter, I examine what I call "the man question" in *Ifá*, as opposed to the standard Eurocentric "woman question," as the most apposite way of analyzing gender in *Ifá* texts.

Chapter 2 interrogates the work of a group of scholars who have imposed gender binaries on *Ifá*. These authors consciously write about women in *Ifá* and Yorùbá society in general, seemingly in response to the worldwide development of gender and feminist studies, disciplines that in the past four decades have insisted on the importance of the category in contemporary life. Some of these writings respond to my own earlier work questioning the imposition of male dominance on primordial Yorùbá institutions.

Chapter 3 is on the all-important institution of *Iya*. The chapter documents the indigenous epistemology that has been shunted aside as the new gender-saturated colonial epistemology gains ever-deeper resonance in the culture. I posit that the category *Iya* is not originally a gender category. It is this chapter that informs the title of the book: *What Gender Is Motherhood?* I introduce the concept of "matripotency"—supremacy of motherhood—as a lens through which to appreciate and understand the marginalized Yorùbá epistemology. More than anything else, the different construction of motherhood demonstrates the seismic epistemic shift in thinking occasioned by European colonization and policies, the establishment of notions of individualism, Christianization, Islamization of the culture, and globalization.

The title-question "What Gender Is Motherhood?" is posed against the background of the fact that in Western discourses that determine intellectual concepts and theories, motherhood is a paradigmatic gender category. However, gender is a social and historical construct; thus we must not impose Euro/American categories on Yorùbá unquestioningly. As I showed in *Invention*, Yorùbá society ontologically did not operate on the basis of gender. Without gender, what then is the traditional Yorùbá understanding of procreation and the institution of motherhood? What meanings are attached to the events and processes associated with human reproduction and attendant social reproduction? And what are the implications of these ideas for the organization of society, concepts of identity, and spirituality?

In chapter 4, continuing with the spotlight on intellectuals, I consider the historical place of writing and the gendered status of literate persons in the culture. *Akòwé*, a word for literate Yorùbá that originated in the nineteenth century, was applied to males only, despite the obvious presence of females who were literate. I explore the relationship between the gender identity of pioneering, local, nonacademically trained writers, and the academics that followed them. This analysis sets the stage for considering the work of two prominent scholars of Yorùbá religion and their writings on gender in chapter 5.

The last three chapters, 6–8, are strongly interconnected and are a work of historical sociology. Through a study of Yorùbá names, naming systems, and social change, I investigate the emergence of gender markers in society. Starting from the nineteenth century as a period of great ferment and social change, I examine new names, new institutions, new practices, and an emergent gender consciousness. What these emerging categories tell us about the historicity of gender in Yorùbá society is one of the driving questions of this chapter and indeed of the project as a whole. Fundamentally, what does the construction of gender in Yorùbá society tell us about the same process in other societies.

Throughout the text, although I refer to Yorùbá people, my primary focus is on the Oyo-Yorùbá, which is a dominant subgroup of the nationality. As I noted in *Invention*, my primary focus is on Oyo-Yorùbá history and culture. That said, it should be noted that those cultural specificities were more pronounced before the sweeping changes that occurred in the civil war and the post-nineteenth-century periods—I should add that language is central to my study, and my engagement is with the Yorùbá language as spoken by the Oyo initially but much of which became universalized as the language was standardized through writing.

The terms "Global North" and "Global South" have become current in designating what was once known as the "First World" and "Third World" countries, respectively. The Global North is also increasingly used to designate the West or the Western world comprising countries in Western Europe and North America (excluding Mexico). In this book, I have chosen to retain the West as my preferred designation of these societies.

CHAPTER 1

DIVINING KNOWLEDGE: THE MAN QUESTION IN *IFÁ*

The primordial Yorùbá[1] social organization was a seniority-based system. In the society, the main principle of social relations was seniority defined by relative age. Thus the older person in any social interaction or institutions that are deemed to be of older vintage are privileged in the culture. As an institution, seniority is socially constructed and chronological age is not its only feature. In other contexts, chronology is reckoned differently. For example, in the case of twin births, the first infant to emerge from the birth canal is regarded as the junior and the second is the privileged senior, a convention encapsulated in their names: Táíwò for the junior and Kẹ́hìndé for the senior. In the culture, the belief is that Táíwò, the àbúrò (junior), came out of the birth canal first because Kẹ́hìndé, the ẹ̀gbọ́n (senior), had sent her on an errand to go to the world first and ascertain if it is a hospitable place. Another context in which the seniority hierarchy exposes a different form of accounting than chronological age is its usage in families. In patrilocal marriages, the in-marrying bride is regarded as junior to all the members of the groom's lineage no matter their biological age. In this instance, the seniority ranking is predicated on when each and every member of the lineage entered the patrilineage whether through marriage or through birth. The chronology of brides entering the family through marriage is reckoned from the day they married into the family and not the day they were born. The juniorizing of brides in the families into which they are married does not take away from their chronological age-based positions in the families of their birth or in the society as a whole. The fundamental fact that originary Yorùbá social relations are based on seniority was laid bare in my book *The Invention of Women: Making an African Sense of Western Gender Discourses.*[2]

Concomitantly, the thesis in the book challenged the idea that gender categorization is natural and universal to the human condition. I showed that gender is not ontological to the Yorùbá ethos, and thus the presence of identifiable gender constructs in the language, history, and social institutions is at best evidence of recent social change and at worse confirmation of an alien imposition. The most important point is that the seniority-based system does not draw attention to the anatomy or genitalia as gender systems do. Seniority privileges social relations rather than the type of the body. Therefore, a seniority-based system is fluid and more egalitarian given that each person in society can be junior or senior in interactions depending on the situation. Seniority, unlike gender, is relational and speaks to the collective ethos rather than to individual identity. Thus, I concluded that the current presumption of gender and attendant male dominance in the interpretation of endogenous Yorùbá institutions, social practices, and values represents an epistemological shift away from the seniority-based system.

In this chapter then, my objective is to interrogate the ways in which gender constructs have been imposed on *Ifá* and the implications of this for understanding the institution in particular, and the society as a whole. Ifá is a knowledge system. It occupies an important place in the culture, lives, and imagination of the people, and as such investigating the role of gender and male dominance in this venerable institution is necessary. Although I made references to Ifá at various points in *Invention*, I centered my analysis on other social institutions such as lineage, marriage, the economy, and language. In this chapter and the next, I aim to do a focused analysis of Ifá as an institution, using gender as probe. My goal is to investigate and expose the ways in which Ifá has been imprinted with gender, represented as a male-dominant institution, and in the process create further understanding of the ongoing institutionalization of male dominance in the culture as a whole.

Academic discussions of gender in Ifá are usually framed around the "woman question," a question that does not originate from the seniority-based system. Approaches to gender constructs, expressed as male dominance in these writings, are of the "images of women" variety. Two papers, for example, "The Image of Women in Ifá Literary Corpus"[3] and "Images of Women in the Ifá Literary Corpus,"[4] make exactly this point. Two problems are immediately apparent with this orientation: academic writings on gender in Yorùbá society do not problematize gender categories but assume them to be natural and integral to the culture and knowledge system. Second, no matter how many images of women these authors present, their approach exhibits an inherent antifemale bias, because in searching for images of women in Ifá, they have already defined it as a man's world. In these representations, men are the normative category, and women then are treated as the subsidiary to the putative male world. Because primordial Yorùbá society was seniority and not gender-based, the woman question is an invalid premise from which to start analysis of its social institutions.

Of course social institutions do evolve, but research must take history into account. Thus I propose that the "man question"[5] instead is the more apposite perspective from which to understand contemporary Yorùbá society and its cultural institutions. I use the man question to encapsulate ideas of male dominance and male privilege that have come to define societies around the globe especially following European and American conquests. Yorùbá society has not escaped Western domination and European predilection for using gender constructs to organize and interpret the universe and the social world.

Thus the man question represents an attempt to ask why Yorùbá society is increasingly a gendered and male-dominant world. When and how did this happen? The point is that we cannot take male dominance for granted given the original seniority-based system; its presence demands explanation. The normative categories man and woman are marked by their origins from a gender system. In a gendered dispensation, "man," an anatomical biological entity, is regarded as dominant and superior, in opposition to woman, another category, which is considered inferior and subordinate. Although, man/male and woman/female are used to express the biological distinction between the two types of anatomy, the categories go beyond mere distinction but contain social baggage in which one category is deemed to be worthier than the other. In Western culture, ultimately, these anatomies symbolize social and moral attributes.

Dominant Western gender categories and the hierarchies they represent did not exist in the original Yorùbá seniority-based system. In the seniority-based arrangement, the human anatomy or genitalia does not express any distinct social or moral attributes. Thus the Yorùbá categories okùnrin (usually translated as male/man/boy) and obìnrin (usually translated as woman/female/girl) represent mistranslation in that they introduce gender hierarchy where there was none.[6] Elsewhere, I have demonstrated that the Yorùbá distinctions are superficial and are merely expressing anatomic difference without any social or moral connotations. As a result of this finding I introduced two concepts: anatomic male and anatomic female, which I abbreviated to anamale and anafemale as the correct translation of Yorùbá categories okùnrin and obìnrin. Anamale and anafemale better express the meaning of Yorùbá classification of the human body as one in which the categories in and of themselves do not constitute any social hierarchy.[7]

It is clear that the standard woman question that studies of postcolonial African societies so easily utilize in their research is an imposed question that derives from European colonization and the current dominance of Western epistemologies in the constitution of knowledge worldwide. Consequently, a brief genealogy of the woman question is necessary. In the nineteenth century, the woman question was articulated by women's rights activists in England and the United States as an interrogation of the nature and role of women in society as English and white American women started to agitate for political rights and challenge their gender subordination. In these societies, as far back as they could tell, men were the dominant gender. Privileged politically, and socially regarded as the norm, the male was universalized as representing the human. Taken for granted, the dominance of men in Western societies was believed to be universal and therefore natural. Thus in much of feminist writings even when they questioned the naturalness of male dominance, its universality was never in question. But this was erroneous, imperialistic, and self-aggrandizing thinking on the part of Europeans and Americans because there were many cultures around the world in which gender categorization and male dominance were absent originally. Yorùbá culture was one of these: the central principle of social ethos was seniority. Nevertheless, with the conquest of Africans by Europeans, there was a wholesale forcing of Western values, social institutions, and practices on the colonized. Language was one of those institutions whose imposition profoundly affected the colonized and continues after the end of formal colonialism. In the next section, I consider the implications of using the English language to represent and interpret Ifá, an endogenous knowledge system.

What Is Ifá?

Ifá is a system of knowledge that was transmitted orally originally. Structured into the institution are a set of procedures that facilitate the retrieval of information on all aspects of Yorùbá life past, present, and future. This knowledge is made accessible through a system of divination, a process that generates stories, myths, and narratives that profess to be God send, and which make assertions about anything and everything in Yorùbá life. As literary scholar Adélékè Adéẹkọ́ puts it, Ifá narratives claim "divine origins and expressly assert the authority to make proclamations regarding the essential being of every object and idea, from the beginning of time and extending into the limitless future."[8] Thus Ifá is seen as a comprehensive record of Yorùbá culture providing historical precedents for events and conduct, and guidance for the future. Ifá is not the only system of divination in Yorùbá society, but it has garnered hegemonic importance vis-à-vis other forms of divination as a result of the interest in it on the part of the Westernized Yorùbá elite and Western scholars.[9] Consequently, our understanding of the place of Ifá in the culture has not been immune from social change attending colonization.

Before the twentieth century, Ifá and other divination systems were hugely important in Yorùbá life. Throughout the life cycle of individuals, families, and sociopolitical entities (states), in times of joy and in times of trouble, people would consult Ifá diviners to make sense of their lives and destiny. One of the most significant rituals performed when a child is born is to consult a *babaláwo* (Ifá diviner) to decipher aspects of the child's destiny, especially as it relates to which Òrìṣà (deity, God) presides over his or her fate. We see a description of this ritual practice in the work of anthropologist William Bascom, who produced one of the first scholarly documentation of Ifá. In his tome *Sixteen Cowries: Yorùbá Divination from Africa to the New World*, researched in the 1930s, we learn that Salako, an anamale diviner of Ẹ́ẹ̀rìndìnlógún, another divination system who worked with the anthropologist, described his visit as an infant to Ifá diviners so that they could perform the customary àkọsẹ̀jáyé (deciphering baby's first earthly steps). Bascom writes about Salako: "Shortly after his birth he was taken to an Ifá diviner and his foot was placed on the divining tray; the diviner consulted Ifá and confirmed that he belonged to Orishala."[10]

Consulting Ifá represents a central part of the ceremonies marking rites of passage. In pre-Islamic and pre-Christian Yorùbáland, every individual had to memorize what was called ọwọ́ Ifá kan—one hand of Ifá—units of verses and narratives of Ifá. This mass training represented schooling in Yorùbáland at the time.[11] It is no wonder, then, that much of the language of Ifá is so familiar to the Yorùbá ear: many of the figures of speech (parables, metaphors, similes) in everyday language come directly from Ifá narratives. But of course one could also interpret this as a sign that Ifá narratives are a product of persons albeit knowledge makers who are a part of the culture. Ifá was venerated in the society and even today, despite the fact that Islam and Christianity have become dominant religions in the culture, the phrase ó gbọ́n bi'fá—as wise as Ifá—is still used for complimenting intellectual achievement.

Ifá is a divination system, and such systems are by definition modes of seeking knowledge. There are quite a number of divinatory systems in Yorùbáland, but Ifá and Ẹ́ẹ̀rìndínlógún, which are closely related, are widely recognized as the most important. Ifá divination is presided over by diviners called *babaláwo*, a professional guild of practitioners. When a client consults them, they manipulate a divining chain (ọ̀pẹ̀lẹ̀) or sixteen ritually blessed palm nuts (*ikin*) a number of times, which eventually leads to recitation of a specific *odù* (chapter), which tell a story that is deemed appropriate to the situation of the client who is seeking knowledge about a particular predicament or issue. These stories are regarded as precedents. *Babaláwo* have spent many years memorizing the Ifá corpus that is the basis of their profession. This corpus is large, consisting of 256 chapters, but the number of verses present in each chapter is undetermined.

Traditionally, the way to access Ifá knowledge was through divination presided over by *babaláwo*. Today, there are other ways to access the information: through divination that customizes the information to an individual situation, through interviews with diviners, or through reading scholarly books that have sought to compile the *odù* or chapters of Ifá knowledge. Bascom's *Ifá Divination: Communication between Gods and Men in West Africa* was the first academic treatment of Ifá in the English-speaking world. Before this publication, there had been studies of aspects of Ifá by Yorùbá Christian missionaries in Yorùbá language, with various degrees of sophistication. There had also been studies by French scholars researching in West Africa and still more studies in Spanish and Portuguese based on the Yorùbá Diaspora in the Americas. Two decades after his first book, Bascom published *Sixteen Cowries: Yorùbá Divination from Africa to the New World.* Wande Abimbola published his dissertation *Ifá: An Exposition of Ifá Literary Corpus* and has subsequently published additional books on Ifá. Other book-length studies of Ifá have been written more recently, including *Ifá: The Ancient Wisdom* by Afolabi A. Epega, *Ifá Festival* by Abosede Emmanuel, and *Ifá: A Complete Divination* by Ayo Salami.

Ifá also constitutes part of òrìṣà devotion, which is the endogenous religion of the Yorùbá people. In this tradition, the God Ọ̀rúnmìlà is the owner of the divination system. Sometimes Ifá and Ọ̀rúnmìlà are used synonymously; however, in this study, Ifá will refer to the divination system, and Ọ̀rúnmìlà will refer to the deity who presides over it. My focus on Ifá draws from the divination system, the diviners, scholars and their writings, and my own research and interviews I conducted with diviners in Ogbomoso at different times between 2007 and 2012.

The Language of Translation[12]

The majority of Yorùbáland[13] was formally colonized by the British (1852–1960) as part of the colony that they named Nigeria. During the colonial period, male dominant institutions, laws, and policies were imposed extensively on the society. These developments in turn have had an untold impact on endogenous institutions and social practices.[14] One notable institution that has an immediate relevance for our discussion of Ifá—the indigenous knowledge system—is the English language. Under British colonization, English was imposed as the official language of the country and this has remained so ever since. Thus, despite the fact that the original language of Ifá is Yorùbá, much of the scholarship on it has been conducted in English, essentially through translation. This fact of constantly translating from Yorùbá into the English language, coupled with the reality that the primary audience for such writings is an English-speaking one, has enormous consequences for how Ifá is written about and interpreted, and for the type of "knowledge" generated. A basic contradiction apparent in these translations is that English, the target language, is a gendered language in which the male category is privileged, and Yorùbá, the source language, is a seniority-based one in which social categories did not indicate the type of anatomy. To illustrate this significant point, there are no gendered names, pronouns, or kinship categories in Yorùbá language. Hence words denoting son, daughter, brother, or sister are not part of the indigenous vocabulary. Instead the principle underlying Yorùbá kinship categories is seniority. The kinship categories *ẹ̀gbọ́n* (older sibling) and *àbúrò* (younger sibling) and the third person pronouns *ó* (singular) and *wọ́n* (they, formal) demonstrate the seniority hierarchy. This significant point is lost on many translators of Yorùbá who inadvertently introduce gender into social life and erase the indigenous values merely through translation. This point is easily demonstrated with the imposition of English gendered pronouns through what elsewhere I have called the ubiquitous "he." This process is clear in the following poetry and its translation taken from the Wande Abimbola's book *Ifá: An Exposition of Ifá Literary Corpus.*[15]

1. *Ó ní*
2. *Oníkékẹ́ logún;*
3. *Alágbàjà logbọ̀n;*
4. *Oníkolo làádọta;*
5. *A díá fún Ọdúnm̀bákú*
6. *Tí í sọmọ bíbí inú Àgbọnnìrégún.*
7. *Wọ́n ní ó rúbọ nítorí Ikú.*
8. *Ó ṣe é,*
9. *Ikú ò pa á.*
10. *Ọdún m̀bá kú,*
11. *Ejié ti gb'ádìẹ̀ mi lọ.*
12. *Adìẹ̀ mi,*
13. *Adìeerànà,*
14. *Tí mo fi'ílẹ̀*
15. *Lejié gbé lọ.*[16]

1. One who has (my translation because Abimbola did not translate this line)
2. He who has *kẹ́kẹ́* facial marks has twenty markings;
3. He who has *àbàjà* facial marks has thirty markings;
4. He who has *kolo* facial marks has fifty markings;
5. Ifá divination was performed for Ọdúnm̀bákú
6. Who was the son of Àgbọnnìrègún.
7. He was asked to perform a sacrifice.
8. In order to avert imminent death,

9. He was asked to offer sacrifice of one ìrànà hen.
10. He did so,
11. He did not die.
12. He started to dance,
13. He started to rejoice,
14. He started to praise his Ifá priest
15. While his Ifá priest praised Ifá.[17]

I numbered the lines for ease of analysis. Two problems are immediately apparent in this translation: "Ó," the Yorùbá third-person pronoun that Abimbola translates as "he" in lines 2–5, 7, 8, 10–12, and 14, indicate that the speaker is referring to someone who is their age mate or junior to them. The Yorùbá pronoun does not disclose the type of genitalia the subject has. By introducing the pronoun "he," Abimbola has masculinized the subject. The best translation of the subject in these lines is "one who has" as I have translated it in line 1, which Abimbola excluded from his translation. In line 5, we are given the name Ọdúnmìbákú, in keeping with Yorùbá tradition in which proper names rarely indicate gender, and does not tell us the anatomic body type of the subject. But we see Abimbola's intention very clearly when in line 6, he tells us that Ọdúnmìbákú is the son of Àgbọnnìrègún. There is no justification whatsoever in translating ọmọ in line 6 into the gender-specific "son," because in the Yorùbá original, "ọmọ" simply means to be the biological child of Àgbọnnìrègún. Àgbọnnìrègún can be called a "he" because from other sources, we know that it is another name for Ọ̀rúnmìlà, the divination deity who in many sources is said to be anamale. There is nothing inherent in "Àgbọnnìrègún" that tells us it is the name of an anamale parsonage. There are no words for son or daughter in Yorùbá, and thus Abimbola's introduction of son is one of imposing the male-privileging values of the English language. Curiously, in one footnote, Abimbola himself tells us that Ọdúnmìbákú is the name of a person, but he does not claim that it is the name of a male person.[18] The net effect of this kind of translation, which is typical of the rendering of Ifá texts in this book and others written by him and many other Ifá scholars, is to present a world that is almost exclusively male, a claim that is not supported by reality.

Nevertheless, Yorùbá language, society, and culture remain a different domain from the culture of the colonizers, and as such, it behooves us to consider it on its own terms. Because Yorùbá culture, unlike the dominant West, was traditionally a seniority-based culture, it is clear that the most appropriate gender debate in the Ifá world must upend the conventional trend and instead pose what I call the "man question." Simply put, the man question is an attempt to historicize, account for, and challenge the processes by which a seniority-based ethos, as expressed in institutions and social practices including Ifá, is being increasingly rendered into a male-dominant system of knowledge that distorts the tradition and discriminates against anafemales. The man question as applied to the Yorùbá universe aims to interrogate how male privilege is being naturalized and universalized as the order of things in the culture. Male dominance and Western dominance in Yorùbá society are entwined.

Furthermore, the man question is postulated to recognize the specific problem that interpreters of Ifá generate when they impose male dominance on Ifá and the culture as a whole. My discussion will be multi-faceted, considering gender questions in relation to forms of divination, the gender of both Western-trained scholars and endogenous diviners, the language of divination in relation to the language of scholarship, how assumptions about gender have shaped scholarly interpretations of the odù or chapters of Ifá, and indeed of the diviners themselves. Finally, an analysis of some of the odù that are assumed to have dealt with gender questions more directly will be conducted. Given that Ifá has become[19] a hugely important system of knowledge in Yorùbá culture, it seems to me to be the logical place to go to make enquiries about any particular developments in Yorùbá society. Thus, my goal in this chapter is to investigate what studies of Ifá can tell us about the seniority-based system and the newly imposed gender arrangement. The question of what Ifá says about gender did not arise from the knowledge system itself, but is a result of the preoccupation with gender in modernity and the gender discrimination that resulted from it.

Divining Scholars

Perhaps the most significant claim about Ifá, and one that has had a major impact on defining the knowledge system as existing in a male-dominant world, is the notion that only males can be babaláwo, despite evidence to the contrary—the existence of female Ifá diviners. I will focus on the very influential work of two Ifá scholars, Bascom and Abimbola, to illuminate this discussion. Bascom's book *Ifa Divination* first published in 1969 is the first academic study of Ifá in English. The bulk of the data for the book was accumulated during fieldwork in Ile-Ife in 1937–1938. Preceding Bascom's research however are commentaries by all and sundry European and American missionaries, slave traders, explorers, and adventurers who had made pronouncements about various aspects of the Ifá divination system as they traveled through the West African region in the nineteenth and twentieth centuries.

Bascom's is a relatively sophisticated account of Ifá very much aware of variation in Ifá worship and divination practice in different towns based on information he gathered during his fieldwork, although his focus was on Ile-Ife. On Ifá diviners, Bascom writes, "Ifá diviners are most commonly called *babaláwo* 'or father has secrets'...or simply awo, secrets or mysteries...Only men can become *babaláwo.*"[20] One thing that never varied in Bascom's account even as he alludes to differences in Ifá practice in the towns he visited is the fact that *babaláwo* are men. It is curious that the anthropologist does not give an explanation as to why women are excluded from Ifá priesthood. There is no record of the questions he asked his informants, and more significantly, there is no reference to a follow-up question to the informant who claimed Ifá priesthood as male-only territory, or any explanation of the reasons that women are excluded from presiding over Ifá divination. The positivist or empiricist is quick to add that because the anthropologist saw only male Ifá diviners and was not aware of female *babaláwo*, then it was within his purview to confirm the male-exclusive claims of his informants. It is not clear however from his account that any informant stated such a claim categorically. Bascom presented this male-exclusive claim to Ifá priesthood as merely a matter of fact, a part of the order of things. But whose order does this derive from? Certainly not the Yorùbá epistemic order. In Ifá texts, diviners are referred to as *awo* or *babaláwo*, which like most Yorùbá nouns are not gendered or gender-specific.

Bascom, like many pioneering male anthropologist, hardly, if ever, had female informants.[21] Most significantly, he did not apply his keen sense of the changes taking place in the Yorùbá social and religious landscape following the spread of Christianity and Islam to ideas about male privilege in Ifá worship. For example, commenting on the declining numbers of babaláwo of a certain rank in Ile-Ife in 1937, he writes: "Although alien religious influences have had less effect on Ifa than on some Yoruba cults, there has still been considerable attrition, because men who would normally have filled these posts have given up Ifa in favor of Christianity and Islam."[22]

I am suggesting that the invisibility of females among the ranks of babaláwo is a negative consequence of the impact of the world religions and other changes that were being put in place in a colonial society. A number of European observers such as Bernard Maupoil considered babaláwo a male cult but did point out that they met one or two female babaláwo.[23] As a result, it seemed justified to them based on statistical "evidence" of the paucity of female babaláwo that this is proof positive of a male exclusive cult and that any identifiable female babaláwo is an exception that proves the rule. In my discussion of what I call "statistical gendering" or categoricalism in a previous work,[24] I expose a number of scholarly assumptions that lead to erroneous conclusions about gender in the society under study. In this instance, the making of the categories female babaláwo and male babaláwo already presupposes a worldview and social landscape in which these gender divisions exist. The statistic then only validates such a worldview. Hence, it is not the statistic that constitutes evidence for postulating the male privileged worldview; rather it is the worldview of the researcher that in the first place led to constituting knowledge in the form of gendered statistics. In other words, it is not the statistic that constitutes evidence of gender distinctions; it is the gendered lens that is brought to the situation by the researcher that produces the statistics. Statistics about the gender of babaláwo and the distribution of male and female diviners is an effect of viewing the society through a gender lens. It is an epistemological question relating to world-sense and what the social categories of knowledge are in the particular society. In the Yorùbá world in which the categories male and female were not divisions involving social valuation, such a statistic would be meaningless. This is not an argument about numbers, but one about how information is organized and understood. Thus beyond what the anthropologist saw or did not see, we have to pay attention to other factors to explain claims of male privilege in Ifá that is assumed in the writings of scholars such as Bascom.

Perhaps because Ifá was a much revered divination system in Yorùbá culture, and its babaláwo were very influential and much respected, to the Western mind such a profession would have to be male-exclusive. In fact, there is information about what sociologist John Peel calls "grudging reverence" for Ifá by Christian missionaries (both Yorùbá and European) and Qur'anic scholars in Yorùbá towns in the nineteenth century. Peel, interpreting the Church Missionary Society (CMS) papers documenting the experiences of Christian missionaries at the time of initial Christian evangelization of the society, noted: "It is hardly surprising that the babaláwo, as a body of male religious professionals, won a degree of respect, refused to the possession-priests of other orisa, from the two other bodies of male professionals who offered themselves as interpreters of God's will in nineteenth-century Yorubaland."[25]

Peel was referring to "Christian pastors" and Muslim clerics all of whom were inevitably male given the requirements of these world faiths. Peel's statement raises the intriguing question as to which came first: the reverence for Ifá because it was perceived to be a male province, or the definition of Ifá as a male province because of the reverence for it. Peel's quote also focuses our attention on the role of Christianity and Islam, the world religions in introducing male-exclusive institutions and patriarchal values into the society. I will discuss these issues later.

In regard to Bascom, apart from his Western mindset, I am exposing multiple sources of gendering and male dominance that seemed to have influenced his writings on Ifá. First, he approached the knowledge system from his knowledge of it in the Yorùbá-Cuban Diaspora, where he claims

Ifá is "little known" and it is represented as a male-exclusive cult. In fact, this reliance on Cuba becomes more apparent in *Sixteen Cowries*, his second major study of Yorùbá divination. Bascom explains that Ẹẹ̀rìndínlógún, the sixteen cowries divination system is more widespread in the Americas because "it can be practiced by both men and women, who outnumber men in these cults, whereas only men can practice Ifá."[26] Because from his Cuban experience, the anthropologist already understood Ifá to be a male-only club, he did not find it necessary to question that claim further when he researched Ifá in its original home in Nigeria. Second, Bascom was only falling in line with a procession of Western commentators like the Baptist missionary T. J. Bowen, who reported that "the worship of Ifá is a mystery into which none but men are initiated,"[27] or Pierre Bouche, who wrote that "*Ifa est l'oricha des sorts et de la divination. Ses prêtres sont des devins: on les appelle babbalawo, pères du secret, du mystère (awo)*" (Ifá is the oricha of fate and divination. His priests are diviners: they're called babbalawo, fathers of the secret and mysterious).[28] I quote the French writer because this is the first translation of babaláwo that I have seen that renders it as "fathers of the secret," a mistranslation of the word.

A close reading of Bascom's analysis of the nature of Ifá priesthood suggests that Bascom's summation that only males can be diviners may not be based on information gathered from a "native informant" but are a result of his own (and Bouche's) linguistic analysis of the meaning of the word *babaláwo*. They translate *babaláwo* into "father has secrets," or "father of the secret." By translating "baba" as father, they assume gendered meaning where it is not necessarily the case. The crucial translation of "baba" into father in this instance is erroneous because despite the fact that baba is an equivalent of the English father, or the French *pères*, it is also a word that means mastery, expertise, or leadership. Thus the *baba* in *babaláwo* is the equivalent of the English "expert in" or "master of." Thus the word *babaláwo* simply means "expert in the realm of *awo*." The *baba* in *babaláwo* alludes to the expertise or mastery of the Ifá corpus that *babaláwo* must attain before they are admitted into the order of Ifá diviners. Consequently, the word *babaláwo* is not gendered male, and in actuality, the term is used to refer to both male and female diviners, all of whom have gone through the rigorous and lengthy training to become Ifá diviners and have been inducted into the Ifá order. *Babaláwo* is a mark of intellectual distinction and not gender division.

Perhaps it is also pertinent to point out that the terms *ìyá*, often translated as mother, and *bàbá*, translated as father, in Yorùbá usage do not always attach to anatomy. Thus one may refer to any male or female relatives of one's mother as mother because they are seen as representing the matrikin in one's life regardless of their body type. The Burkinabe shaman Malidoma Somé describes a similar concept in Dagara culture drawing from his own personal experience: "I learned later that Nyangoli was my male mother's son, that is, the son of my mother's brother, my uncle…It is as though the father must at some point efface himself for the son to survive, and this is when the male mother becomes useful. The feminine in the male—the mother in the man—is an energy that can be triggered into wakefulness only by a male directly associated with the mother. The male mother is therefore thought of as someone who 'carries water,' the energy of peace, quiet, reconciliation and healing."[29] Although in the Dagara example, Somé cast this relationship in gendered terms, what I want to draw attention to is the fact that these kinship categories in African cultures are collectively derived and not constructed as individual identity. The same logic applies to male and female relations of one's father, who may be called father in situations where they are seen to be representing the patrician of a particular person. These conceptualizations of family relationships suggest caution in the imposition of gender identity constructs onto the Yorùbá world. It is also true that *baba* and *ìyá* can also imply dominance, priority, and privilege and are markers of seniority.

In many English translations, the preference for *awo* as secret instead of mystery is also suggestive. Samuel Johnson, the pioneering Yorùbá local historian, writes about "mysteries of Ifá worship," and the authoritative Yorùbá dictionary defines *awo* as one versed in mystery. It seems to me that the emphasis that you see on *babaláwo* as purveyors of secrecy in missionary and anthropological writings is an attempt to reduce what is actually a learned society to a secret cult. Early Yorùbá Christian missionaries such as Bishop Phillips saw divination stories as mind control and as a result "recommended print dissemination of these narratives as a means of freeing the critical faculty of non-Christians from the shroud of secrecy (*awo*) with which Ifá priests deceived Yorùbá people through the ages."[30] At another level missionaries found *babaláwo* distasteful because they considered them to be purveyors of "fake" knowledge, which they used to defraud their clients, many of whom were seen as gullible women. Daniel Coker, another nineteenth-century Yorùbá missionary, wrote of women in Ido near Lagos in 1873: "The women worship Songo and Agba, they are more ignorant than the men. The men do not worship any God, they hold Ifa in great reverence."[31] Assumptions about women's exclusion from cults and male-only clubs are very much linked to ideas about secrecy. It is such a cast of mind that makes it easy to mistranslate *babaláwo* as father of secret. The labeling of Ifá as a secret cult may be tied up with assumptions about male superiority and the exclusion of women.

Scholar of religion Oyeronke Olajubu discusses *awo* in the context of hierarchies of knowledge in Yorùbá religion. She points out that "*awo*" are those with the secret, who are imbued with power and authority; and "*ọ̀gbẹ̀rì*" are the novices. She continues: "some have argued that secret knowledge is hidden from women because they are unable to keep secrets. Empirical analysis, however, negates this stance; as women are part of these secret groupings, in some cases have access to and control of powers that are unavailable to men."[32] Olajubu identified the *Ìyá'mi* group as a secret society of powerful women. It is regrettable that Olajubu assumes gender constructs as natural to Yorùbá and does not provide any insight into the identity of those "who have argued that secret knowledge is hidden from women." [33] What is discernible here is the clash of two worldviews. In the worldview that came with Christianity and Islam, females are marginalized in the religious sphere. In contrast, in the Yorùbá world-sense, it is inconceivable that anafemales can be excluded from mystical power, which is regarded as the basis of all power including political power. In chapter 3, I analyze the powers associated with procreation and show why a reading of the institution of *ìyá* (procreator) as gendered endowment is erroneous. *Ìyá* are at the center of Yorùbá spirituality and the *Ìyá'mi* cult alluded to by *Olajubu* is based on this understanding. I will discuss this institution in chapter 3.

Despite the labeling of Ifá as a secret cult by various Christian missionaries and scholars, for the *babaláwo* and the society in general, Ifá diviners were seen first and foremost as a professional, learned guild and not a secret society. Their rigorous and lifelong training is seen as evidence of their discipline, dedication, and accomplishment. In the culture, in discussions of *babaláwo*, one thing that is often emphasized is their long training, which means that they are considered a learned group; an accomplishment that is revered. We see a facet of this kind of reverence displayed in Bascom's account of how his Yorùbá servants who saw themselves as more modern and enlightened because of their literacy responded to the old diviner Salako although he was not even a diviner of Ifá, who had come to recite divination verses for the anthropologist in Ile-Ife, in 1951. "At first our servants looked down on Salako as a rustic (*ara oke*) and a person out of the pagan, oral past. But when they had had a chance to hear the verses he was reciting, their attitude changed to one of respect, and they would gather at the recording sessions in their free time to listen to him with delight."[34] It is instructive that "Ifá is commonly called alákọ̀wé, the scribe or literate one- and not a seance or other kind of intuitive, magical, or 'gifted' fortune telling."[35] When literary anthropologist Karen Barber found a female *babaláwo* in Okuku and using the Western gender-based lens wondered how a female could have become an Ifá diviner, her Yorùbá informants replied, "She [the female diviner] learnt Ifá. If a woman goes to school she becomes an educated person; if she learns Ifá, she becomes a *babaláwo*."[36] These Yorùbá commentators were clearly not aware that in the Western dispensation, if a woman goes to school, she may become educated but remains an inferior being—a woman—by definition. With scholar of religion Wande Abimbola, a different facet of the gendering of the babaláwo is apparent. In *Ifá: An Exposition*, Abimbola writes that the Ifá cult is essentially a male cult.[37] However, over the years, in more recent publications, he has repudiated this stance, although he still introduces and elaborates gender divisions that are not supported by evidence. Furthermore, because Abimbola is popularly associated with Ifá, his earlier work has been so influential that it has produced a male-dominant Ifá ethos that requires a lot of work to undo. In *Ifá Will Mend Our Broken World*, a more recent book geared toward Òrìṣà practitioners, he makes the following claims in response to a question comparing the practices of Ifá practitioners in Cuba to those of Ifá practitioners in Yorùbáland, which is the original home of the knowledge system.

> As far as we [Yorùbá] are concerned, we don't make a distinction between men and women, both can study Ifá ...Women who are Ifá diviners in Africa are called ìyánífá, but they function as babaláwo. There are not many of them. But ìyánífá may not see Odù ...Not all babaláwo have Odù. There are very few who have Odù.[38]

Despite his correct assertions that Yorùbá "don't make distinctions between men and women in the study of Ifá," a fact that is clear from investigation and analyses of Yorùbá institutions, social practices, and social organization, he immediately contradicts himself by making some gender distinctions of his own. Let us examine these claims. First, the idea that there is gendered language for naming Ifá diviners is not borne out in Ifá texts, which name Ifá diviners as babaláwo or awo. There is no mention of Ìyánífá in the Ifá corpus. Second, his claim that the word ìyánífá is the designation of female Ifá diviners is ahistorical. French anthropologist Bernard Maupoil mentions several cases of female babaláwo.[39] Traditionally and currently, following Ifá texts, both male and female diviners are called babaláwo or awo. In my own conversations with male babaláwo, I am told that both males and females are babaláwo. Karin Barber writes about a female babaláwo in Okuku, a Yorùbá town. In her discussion about Sangowemi, a professional performer, Barber writes: "Her mother was a fully-qualified practising babaláwo, the only female one Okuku remembers ...She traveled for long periods performing divination for clients and adding to her knowledge of Ifá."[40] Today, female babaláwo are relatively few.

It is also true that currently Ìyánífá is a name that is increasingly used to refer exclusively to female Ifá diviners in some parts of Yorùbáland. Olajubu agrees with Abimbola and writes, "Females who practice Ifá are known as *Ìyánífá* as opposed to male practitioners who are called *Babaláwo*."[41] However, this claim is ahistorical. The gendered distinction in naming of male and female diviners must be historicized; I am suggesting that the word *Ìyánífá* is of recent coinage. *Ìyánífá* is an elision of *Ìyá nínú Ifá* meaning master or expert in Ifá, which is identical to the meaning of *babaláwo*. In Ọ̀yọ́-Yorùbá speech, *Ìyánífá* is routinely elided further as Ìyáń'fá (an observation I made in my oral interviews with a number of *babaláwo* in Ogbomoso), which shows that the meaning of it is "expert in Ifá" rather than "mother has Ifá." In my interviews with male diviners and lay people alike in Ogbomoso, there were many references to a particular *Ìyáń'fá* who was revered for her knowledge of Ifá and known as the leader of Ifá diviners in the town in the 1970s and 1980s.[42] The term *ìyáń'fá* is gaining currency in certain circles as the accepted mode for referring to female Ifá diviners but knowledge of the word is hardly widespread. Because the term *Ìyánífá* is absent in Ifá texts, and therefore not as widely known in the society as the word *babaláwo*, I would postulate that it is of more recent coinage, a necessary development in reaction to the increasing gendering of *babaláwo* as male and a deepening awareness of gendered language since many Yorùbá today use English as well as Yorùbá to communicate on a daily basis. This unfortunate occurrence has had the effect of eclipsing the historical role, if not erasing anafemale diviners in a field that is regarded as learned and highly accomplished. The trend to create gendered vocabulary in Yorùbá is an interesting one, and may be a practical solution to female marginalization as Yorùbá social categories are increasingly interpreted according to the-male-as-norm standards of the dominant colonial language—English.[43] The implications of creating new gendered nouns only applicable to females are far reaching, and it is actually a solution that may be reinscribing the problem of female marginalization and exclusion it seeks to solve and more. At the very least, by assuming that awo and babaláwo refer only to male persons, it excludes females from original sacred texts.

From the foregoing, it is clear that scholars are not merely recording or observing social institutions like Ifá, they are also actively framing and reframing them. The original impetus for the kind of male-dominant thinking exhibited by both Bascom and Abimbola is rooted in the idea that gender constructs are a natural way of organizing society and codifying knowledge, the ultimate manifestation of which is male privilege. Researchers often transfer their own biases to their subjects or the issue under consideration at many levels; most notably in drawing up research questions and creating knowledge by default through unasked questions. We see another aspect of the issue of gendering by scholars demonstrated in the case of Barber, who, after calling Ifá "the man's world," was surprised to find a practicing female *babaláwo* in Okuku, a Yorùbá town. Barber promptly labels the situation extraordinary and the female diviner an exception to the male norm. Clearly there is a gap in thinking between Barber's orientation and the orientation of the culture that created Ifá, and indeed, Barber's informants in Okuku. As I pointed out elsewhere, Barber's presentation of the female diviner as an exception is founded on the Western rule of male exclusivity in religious leadership. In Yorùbáland, no such exclusion existed, and Barber's informants were quick to educate her on that when she inquired about the diviner's "extraordinary behavior." This is what they said, as reported by Barber herself:

> She [the female diviner] learnt Ifá. If a woman goes to school she becomes an educated person; if she learns Ifá, she becomes a *babaláwo*. Her father was a *babaláwo*, so was her husband, so she picked it up little by little from them. There was never a time when the association of *babaláwo* said she had no right to participate in their activities. She would go to the cult house and participate in meetings just like the others. They would ask her about a certain verse of Ifá: if she answered correctly, they would accept that she was a *babaláwo*. The verses she learnt were the same as those of other *babaláwo*. Once she learnt them, she was a *babaláwo*. Then she also had the right to examine other people on their knowledge, just as they had examined her. Both men and women would come as clients to consult her.[44]

For the research informants, the behavior of the diviner was neither extraordinary nor outside the Yorùbá social norm. We must, however, commend Barber the researcher for asking more questions that have illuminated the nature of training and the role of *babaláwo*. The idea that divining Ifá is a male-exclusive affair may have originated from the Baptist missionary T. J. Bowen, who wrote in an 1857 book that "the worship of Ifá is a mystery into which none but men are initiated"[45]—a perception that was repeated again and again by others. In his review of studies of Ifá that preceded his own, Bascom noted the tendency in scholarship for later accounts of a study to repeat earlier errors because there is often no indication of any independent verification of the original statement.[46] Expanding on this theme, Bascom further noted: "The number of times that a statement is made is no measure of its reliability."[47] The idea that *babaláwo* is exclusively a male role is undoubtedly one of those errors that have been repeated by Bascom, Abimbola, and Barber, among many others. It is time to correct it.

Gendering Forms of Divination

Given the assumption that *babaláwo* are all males with females all but banished from the realm of Ifá diviners, it is not surprising that the entwined Ifá and Ẹ́ẹ̀rìndínlógún divination systems have acquired their own gender distinctions and hierarchies. Ifá is said to have been founded by Ọ̀rúnmìlà—a male deity—and Ẹ́ẹ̀rìndínlógún is owned by Ọ̀ṣun—a female deity—who was also at one time Ọ̀rúnmìlà's wife. It is instructive that all practitioners of Ẹ́ẹ̀rìndínlógún, male or female, are regarded as ìyàwó or wives of Ọ̀ṣun, a standard way of designating devotees of different Òrìṣà in Yorùbá indigenous religion. Elsewhere, I have argued that the word ìyàwó, usually translated as wife in the English accounts, is a nongendered term because it refers to both males and females and is usually an expression of order of seniority in relation to a particular space, or an indicator of a patron-client relationship.[48]

Despite the similarities and apparent common origin of the two divination systems, in the gendered framing, Ifá is presented in the literature as the superior male institution, while Ẹ́ẹ̀rìndínlógún is represented as the female and secondary one.[49] The fact that Ẹ́ẹ̀rìndínlógún diviners include women is seen as one point of its distinction from Ifá. For example, Bascom writes that, in Cuba "it can be practiced by both men and women, who outnumber men in these cults, whereas only men can practice Ifá."[50] The fact that Ẹ́ẹ̀rìndínlógún diviners are not all female, and that this divination system is not a female-exclusive province has not stopped writers from viewing it as such. Because Ifá is erroneously presented as a male system, it is not surprising that Ẹ́ẹ̀rìndínlógún is seen as the female inferior half. From the male-dominant stance from which many scholars approach the culture, gender exclusion only applies to females whose participation in an institution is deemed to be restricted; often the idea that males could be excluded from anything is not entertained because being male is perceived to be inherently powerful and therefore a mark of privilege, if not license.

In his study of Ẹ́ẹ̀rìndínlógún divination system *Sixteen Cowries* Bascom explicitly brings together the divination practices of Yorùbá and its Cuban Diaspora. The word "Ẹ́ẹ̀rìndínlógún" is literally the number sixteen in Yorùbá and this is also the name of the divination system. In fact, the anthropologist's interest in Ẹ́ẹ̀rìndínlógún seemed to have originated in his experience in Cuba, where he claims it is more widely known than Ifá. In Cuba he tells us, Ẹ́ẹ̀rìndínlógún is called "*dilogun or los caracoles*"[51] and furthermore, "It is simpler than Ifá divination…and can be practiced by both men and women."[52] Bascom also made the interesting observation that in the period during which he was writing, there were a great many studies of Ifá divination in Africa, but very few that make Ẹ́ẹ̀rìndínlógún their subject matter. He concludes that this development is due to the lack of esteem that Yorùbá scholars attach to the Ẹ́ẹ̀rìndínlógún system. I concur with Bascom's conclusion and point out that seven decades later, there are still very few studies of Ẹ́ẹ̀rìndínlógún, whereas research on Ifá is ever increasing. In contrast to scholarly interest, however, scholar of religion David Ogungbile tells us that "the Ẹ̀ẹ̀rìndínlógún system today is the most popular, reliable, and commonly used form of divination among Òrìṣà devotees. This system is the form practiced in some places in the Americas and most significantly Brazil where it is called Dilogun Ifá."[53]

Furthermore, Ogungbile writes, "The role of women as diviners in Ẹ̀ẹ̀rìndínlógún is immense...Ẹ̀ẹ̀rìndínlógún is woman-centered."[54] In light of the fact that Ẹ̀ẹ̀rìndínlógún is perceived to be a female province, it is ironic that Bascom's Ẹ̀ẹ̀rìndínlógún study, which remains the only comprehensive one on the divination system, is a collection of narratives that is the product of a five-and-a-half hour recitation by Salako, a male Ẹ̀ẹ̀rìndínlógún diviner in the cult of orishala at Ọ̀yọ́. According to this awoloriṣa (Ẹ̀ẹ̀rìndínlógún diviner), "shortly after his [Salako] birth he was taken to an Ifa diviner and his foot was placed on the divining tray; the diviner consulted Ifa and confirmed that he belonged to Orisala. He was not initiated until he was fifteen...When she was nineteen years of age, Adeyoyin, his younger sister by the same mother, was also initiated."[55]

In his attempt to decipher when one divination system is employed over the other, Bascom introduces another level of difference between Ifá and Ẹ̀ẹ̀rìndínlógún, one that has further gender undertones:"I believe that when affairs of state are to be settled, Ifá divination is employed...; But when the personal religious matters of kings or chiefs are involved, they may rely on sixteen cowries if they are worshippers of Orishala, Shango, or the other deities in whose cults this form of divination is employed."[56] Present in this distinction is a public/private dichotomy of Western thinking represented in that public affairs are associated with the male, here represented by Ifá and the private, represented by Ẹ̀ẹ̀rìndínlógún as female. In my conversation with babaláwo, Chief Olagoke Akanni in Ogbomoso he drew attention to another kind of distinction: not between the two divination systems but within Ifá divining itself pointing to the meaning of different implements of the ritual practice. The babaláwo said that in divination practice, for matters of state, the divining implements must be the ritual palm nuts (ikin) and not ọ̀pẹ̀lẹ̀ (the divining chain), which are the two possible implements employed by babaláwo in the divination process. Since the only implements used in Ẹ̀ẹ̀rìndínlógún are cowries, is this then a statement that Ẹ̀ẹ̀rìndínlógún is not as expedient for matters of state? Furthermore, he pointed out that divining with ikin speaks to the urgency of the problem that needs to be resolved. Once the ikin has been used to divine, he continued, the required ritual offering (ẹbọ) must be carried out within 24 hours. If the state or monarchy finds it necessary to consult babaláwo on account of a collective problem, then the state, unlike an individual, must have the resources to fulfill the demands of the consultation. The fact that state matters command Ifá divination with the ritual palm nuts is an indication of the urgency of such matters. This form of divination is chosen more because of the availability of the resources needed to fulfill the ritual offerings than because Ifá is a public (and therefore masculine) divination process. The distinction therefore is not between personal (private) and state (public) matters but rather has to do with the urgency of resolving a crisis and the availability of resources necessary to complete the sacrifices in a timely manner.

Similarly, if a rich private individual insists on *ikin* divination in a consultation for her own personal problems, as long as she has the resources to pay for the needed sacrifice the same day, then there is no restriction on such an Ifá consultation. In fact, there is no particular restriction on *ikin* divination at all, other than one's ability to complete the sacrifice within a day. Because sacrifice[57] is central to the divination process, usually, after an individual consults a diviner, she may need time to accumulate the items required for sacrifice. Making a ritual offering of a goat or chicken, for example, requires an outlay of cash that many people do not have readily in hand. The distinction here is between the two instruments used for Ifá divination and does not involve Ẹ́ẹ̀rìndínlógún. However, it is pertinent to ask whether Ẹ́ẹ̀rìndínlógún system can be used when a matter needs urgent resolution.

Thus we can ask the question what evidence is provided for the gendered reading of the nature and practice of these two divination systems— Ifá and Ẹ́ẹ̀rìndínlógún. If anything, what is striking is their similarity, which not a few researchers have noted. Bascom, for one, points out: "Like the Ifá diviners, all Orishala [Ẹ́ẹ̀rìndínlógún] priests are herbalists...Salako knew that some of his verses are the same as those in Ifá divination. He described his work as similar to that of an Ifá diviner, but different."[58] In a more recent study, anthropologist Niyi Akinnaso provides a comparative summary of the two systems, drawing our attention to the similarities:

> Ifá and ẹ́ẹ̀rìndínlógún are similar (indeed identical in some respects), *one Ẹ́ẹ̀rìndínlógún) being, in fact, a mythological, historical and structural derivative of the other.* To a great extent, Ifá and ẹ́ẹ̀rìndínlógún texts share similar myths, stories and themes and employ similar methods of acquisition and performance. Together they constitute a specialized body of knowledge...employing relevant historical and mythological precedents contained in the special divination corpus to be recited, chanted, or sung (as appropriate) by the diviner.[59]

Nevertheless, one cannot deny their points of distinction, one of which is indicated by the fact that they have different names. Some of the basic differences are in the size of the corpus to be memorized by the diviners, the appellation of the diviners, and the instruments and methods of divination. Undoubtedly, these differences are of degree and not of kind. Significantly, anatomic sex is not a point of difference in the Yorùbá social organization.

The gender division of practice that has been imposed by some scholars on
Ẹ́ẹ̀rìndínlógún and Ifá as representing separate female and male provinces
is alien to Yorùbá conception: in reality one system appears to derive from
the other. In fact, one seems to be an expansion or extended version of
the other. The fact that there are both male and female diviners practicing in the two traditions and a diverse group of clients consulting all kinds
of diviners reinforces this point. Given Akinnaso's observation that one of
them derived from the other, we can ask the question what is the line of
derivation or descent? Without debating the issue, Akinnaso assumes that
Ẹ́ẹ̀rìndínlógún derives from Ifá. His approach is in line with the tendency
to treat Ifá as the original, and Ẹ́ẹ̀rìndínlógún as the less comprehensive and
underdeveloped copy.

    Conversely, recent scholarship, responding to the challenge of studies
like *The Invention of Women*, which questioned the wholesale imposition of
male dominance on Yorùbá religion and culture, has suggested an opposite
line of descent, shedding further light on issues that in the past scholars
had taken for granted. In a paper on Ọ̀ṣun and the origins of Ifá divination, Abimbola calls into question the received idea that Ọ̀ṣun came to Ifá
divination through her husband Ọ̀rúnmìlà. Sifting through multiple and
often contradictory evidence from several narratives of Ifá regarding Ọ̀ṣun's
involvement with Ifá and Ẹ́ẹ̀rìndínlógún divination systems, Abimbola
draws two conclusions: first, that Ọ̀ṣun may well have been the discoverer of
Ifá, given the story from *odù ọ̀kànrànsodè* in the Ifá corpus; and second, that
Ẹ́ẹ̀rìndínlógún appears to be antecedent to Ifá and therefore Ifá is derived
from it. Abimbola reasons that:

> When one takes a look at the Odù of *Ẹ́ẹ̀rìndínlógún* and those of Ifá, it would
> seem that the Odù of Ifá are based on those of *Ẹ́ẹ̀rìndínlógún*, and not the
> other way round. *Ẹ́ẹ̀rìndínlógún* is based on sixteen single signs of Ifá such as
> Òdí, Ìròsùn, Ọ̀wọ́nrín, et cetera; except Èjì Ogbè, which is coupled in the
> case of Ifá. Ifá, however, does not make use of single signs (even though Ifá
> literature refers to it). All the signs are coupled either as *ojú odù* (major Odù)
> or as *ọmọ odù* (minor Odù). It stands to reason to say that a single sign such as
> Òdí must exist in reality or at least in the mind before it is coupled to become
> Òdí Méjì (two Odi).[60]

Here Abimbola's gives credence to Ọ̀ṣun as should be because the Òrìṣà
is one of the most important in the religion and even in Ifá itself as I will
show in the next chapter. In addition, what the above quotation also shows
very clearly is the gender discrimination that has been imported into the
discourses of Ifá and Ẹ́ẹ̀rìndínlógún especially on the question of authorship. It is significant that the idea of gender is so blatantly imposed on a
Yorùbá epistemology that did not divide the social world of which Ifá

and Ẹ̀ẹ́rìndínlógún is a part into male and female. Equally intriguing in these discussions is the entwinement of the Yorùbá seniority-based system (which is prior) with the newly imported gender-based system touting inherent male superiority. The initial idea that Ifá is the original—which came first—and therefore the privileged senior may have formed the basis of why contemporary scholars could only think of it as a male province or vice versa. It may also explain why the anafemale deity Ọ̀ṣun was deauthorized by contemporary scholars. Priority as seniority and superiority is highly valued in Yorùbá culture but in the research on divination systems, it is used as a tool to automatically ascribe privilege to what is deemed male, a move that actually overrides the Yorùbá ethos. What is clear and enduring is that the two divination systems are entangled and seemed to have one original source. The next section analyzes further the entwinement of the two systems.

In 2009, I conducted an interview[61] in Ogbomoso with Chief Òrìṣàrínú Ogala, a male awoolórìṣà (diviner of Ẹ̀ẹ́rìndínlógún) who had inherited his practice of the divination from his mother. My findings bear on a number of issues we have been addressing. When I asked him about his training as an Ẹ̀ẹ́rìndínlógún diviner, he said that divining with sixteen cowries does not involve extensive training as Ifá. What it required, he said, is a commitment and intense devotion to the Gods such as Ọ̀ṣun, Ṣàngó, Ọbàtálá, and Ògìyán who are associated with this particular divination system. Ogungbile, researching in Osogbo, another Yorùbá town, found that Ẹ̀ẹ́rìndínlógún divination requires about five years of apprenticeship. But he also noted that

> most Olorisha acquire both the practice of their òrìṣà as well as their elaborate ritual preparations from their aged biological parents with whom they spend a lot of their time. Some among the olorisha augment their acquired knowledge with apprenticeship for a period of time from a more knowledgeable eerindinlogun diviner. [In short, many acquire their initial knowledge as inheritors of a family religious tradition, a practice which is not so different from Ifá.][62]

To the question of the relationship between Ẹ̀ẹ́rìndínlógún and Ifá, Chief Ogala, the awoolórìṣà replied that Ifá is the source of Ẹ̀ẹ́rìndínlógún. He believes that Ifá is the source and a more advanced form of Sixteen Cowries. The naming of diviners in the two systems seems to confirm that Ifá is more advanced although not necessarily prior. The appellation awoolórìṣà, which is immediately applied to all the devotees who take up Ẹ̀ẹ́rìndínlógún divination, suggests little or no external bar to entry; hence such knowledge is not considered as advanced as Ifá. The emphasis in their naming is on service to the community of devotees of òrìṣà, in contrast to babaláwo, a name that is more focused on their mastery of the Ifá corpus. In my earlier discussion, I pointed out that the translation of the word *babaláwo* into English as "father of secrets" is mistaken, and is an attempt to introduce gender exclusivity to the guild. Rather, I argued that the *baba* in *babaláwo* means "mastery of *awo.*" When the two divination systems are brought together, the meaning of *babaláwo* is more fully appreciated in distinction to *awoolórìṣà*. It becomes clear that the distinction that *babaláwo* sought to make is not between *ọ̀gbèrì* (novice/lay people) and Ifá diviners, but between *awoolórìṣà* (the divination generalist) and *babaláwo* (divination specialist) who have devoted years of their lives studying Ifá and have graduated with an initiation ceremony. It is possible that some *babaláwo* started as *awoolórìṣà* and then decided to enter the longer and rigorous training that Ifá divination, unlike Ẹ́ẹ̀rìndínlógún, requires. At one level, the distinction between Ẹ́ẹ̀rìndínlógún and Ifá is akin to the one between a bachelor's degree and the more specialized doctor of philosophy (PhD) degree in that being initiated as a *babaláwo* is like being admitted into a learned society.

The point I am making here is that at one time all the diviners who made use of odù (unit of verses) were originally all *awoolórìṣà* because the specialization of Ifá had not yet been developed. But as the system evolved, a specialized branch called Ifá emerged requiring longer training periods because of the need to memorize expanding numbers of chapters. Subsequently, those who took on this training and succeeded through initiation were recognized as *baba nínú awo*—masters of knowledge. It is also instructive that both Ifá diviners and Sixteen Cowries diviners are also called *awo* for short. In the Ifá narratives *awo* is one of the recurrent names used for diviners.

Abimbola raises a number of important issues in his paper on Ẹ́ẹ̀rìndínlógún, and I want to focus on two of them that have a direct bearing on the issue of male dominance in Yorùbá studies. If indeed, as Abimbola suggests, both the divinity Ọ̀ṣun and Ẹ́ẹ̀rìndínlógún their crea- tion have been given short shrift, on whom or what should we lay blame? One answer is suggested by Abimbola when he states cryptically, "I will make the claim that Ọ̀ṣun has much more to do with the origins of Ifá divination than the *babaláwo* (Ifá priests) *are ready to admit.*"[63] At the very least, the statement implies that the male diviners are sexist and do not want Ifá, their divination system, to be associated with a female founding deity. Abimbola's remarks here about endogenous custodians of Ifá is reminiscent of historian Robert Smith's statement about the *Arókin* (indigenous custo- dians of history) and their acceptance (or lack thereof) of the existence of female rulers, in Old Ọ̀yọ́. According to Smith: "This account of the mil- itary success of Orompoto's [female ruler] reign…confirmed reluctantly by the authorities at New Ọ̀yọ́, that the warlike Orompoto was a woman,

[a] sister and not [a] brother of Egunoju."[64] The suggestion from these two Western-trained scholars is that the local custodians of knowledge that are perceived to be closer to indigenous values are predisposed to gender discrimination: refusing to grant females authority, marginalizing and stripping them of their leadership positions and accomplishments. Neither Abimbola nor Smith present any evidence to support the view that the local keepers of tradition are sexist or more sexist than the academics. A careful reading of the Western-generated literature including the accounts of Abimbola, Smith, and Bascom and my own research does not support the view that endogenous practitioners of knowledge such as babaláwo exhibit stronger patriarchal values than the academic scholars. If anything, what my research shows is the degree to which Yorùbá male dominance has been manufactured since the nineteenth century from the writings of various literate and Western-educated African and European personnel. The simplest and most incontrovertible evidence is in their unconscious use of the English language to exclude, to marginalize, and to turn seniority-based positions and non-gender-specific persons and practices into males thereby grafting a male-dominant system on one that originally eschewed gender.

As part of the ritual of sacrifice to the Gods following a divination consultation, Oseetura, the divination narratives that are said to be very specific to the deity Ọ̀ṣun, are always recited by a babaláwo at the end of each and every sacrificial offering. The babaláwo Akalaifa whom I interviewed[65] in Ogbomoso informed me about this ritual practice and pointed out that it is a sign of the importance of Ọ̀ṣun to òrìṣà devotion and Ifá practice. If the male diviners do not have much regard for Ọ̀ṣun, why is the Odù Oseetura the one that must be recited at the end of every sacrifice? Given the ubiquity of sacrifice in òrìṣà worship, Ọ̀ṣun is venerated in every divination process. There is no other òrìṣà, apart from Èṣù and Ọ̀rúnmìlà, who is called upon in Ifá so continuously and constantly. Furthermore, given the Eurocentric male-dominant ethos of our times, as I have shown repeatedly, Western-trained scholars are often vectors of genderism (the idea that male dominance is inherent in human organizations) and sexism (gender discrimination), as is easily evident in the sorts of questions they ask and most significantly, in the questions they *do not* ask of their informants, the traditions, and texts.

Decoding Genderism and Sexism in the Content of Ifá Corpus

Thus far I have been focusing on published Ifá Divination texts as documents produced by Western-oriented scholars, whilst at the same time documenting their genderist and sexist interpretations of the corpus. I have not directly engaged with Ifá texts as creations of diviners. Am I arguing that gender distinctions, male dominance, and antiwomen utterances are absent from the Ifá corpus in and of themselves? In the next section, I will inter-rogate the role of the diviners in the creation of Ifá; second, I will decode the multilayered gendering that Ifá is subject to and the meanings attached to them. Because the Ifá corpus is a product of Yorùbá society, it is part and parcel of the culture, and therefore its content is a reflection of the Yorùbá ethos. It is a wonderful source of knowledge of the issues that people face in their everyday lives and their values. It is also a good recorder of historical developments, reflecting the concerns of the society.

As a result of this, Ifá is often treated by diviners, clients, as well as schol-ars as a timeless document. As Bascom puts it, some people treat it as "the unwritten scriptures" of Yorùbá people.[66] But the Ifá corpus is not time-less. It is clear that not all odù were authored at the same time, a fact that is apparent in the references that are made to contemporary events, places, and products in some of them. The most notable is Odù Ìmàle,[67] which is about the coming of Islam to Yorùbáland, and other verses that make reference to Ibadan and Abeokuta, two Yorùbá polities that were founded only in the nineteenth century. Consequently, we can say that Ifá's content is open in the sense of not being settled, but subject to editing and further expansion. The constant in Ifá are the signs that lead to a particular recitation of unit of verses. There are 256 of them, and they are also called "odù."

What are the implications of the openness of Ifá and of its historical nature for our understanding of gender categories, themes of male domi-nance, and the antiwomen stance of some of its chapters? Odù are creations of diviners, and the presence of current events in Ifá demonstrates that diviners are not immune or impervious to what is going on in society. Hence their reaction codified in the appearance of Islam in the society, for example. I could not agree more with anthropologist Niyi Akinnaso when he writes:

> Although a diviner is defined by society and by anthropologists (as a diviner or as a ritual specialist), principally in reference to his ritual knowledge and role, it should be borne in mind that, in the course of divination, diviners typically appropriate and incorporate other forms of knowledge as if they all derived from the same transcendental source.[68]

It is not surprising, then, that we find references to gender and antiwomen stances in some of the odù, given the gender-saturated and sexist age in which we live. The issues of gender and patriarchy are even more intensi-fied in religious discourses because of the assault of Christianity and Islam on the culture in the past two centuries, at least. Christian patriarchy is widely evident in the colonizers' descriptions of Yorùbá divinities. One of the most devastating is the rechristening of Olódùmarè (a noncorporeal, nonhuman entity) as a male, equivalent to the Christian God, with all the

damning exclusions that this implies for females. We also see Christian practices of demonization, coupled with European traditions of witch hunting,
as Yorùbá converts absorb the values of their new religions and act on them.
With regard to the practice of divination, it is not farfetched to suppose
that some diviners are sexist in their orientation, just like some academic
scholars, and may then interpret Ifá verses in this light in a current world
in which male superiority and female derogation are institutionalized and
widespread. We must not forget that diviners do not merely report the
words of Òrúnmìlà, the divination God; they interpret and comment on
these messages as well. Besides, divination is an interactive process in which
the client not only brings her *orí* (agency) to the consultation but also is
expected to use her experience and knowledge to decipher which odù is
applicable to her situation as the diviner recites various narratives. In short,
in a society in which gender discrimination is increasingly widespread and
has become a fact of life, it would be surprising if it were not reflected
in Ifá.

Nonetheless, this deepening of gender thinking and its expansion does
not nullify the fact that originally, the Yorùbá world was not divided into
male and female, and that gender categories and subsequent male dominance
are a result of modernity. We cannot exaggerate the fact that Westernization,
Islam, and Christianity continue to be sources of male dominance in Yorùbá
religion, culture, and society. Gender as category, source of identity, and
factor of social organization emerged only recently in Yorùbá thinking and
behavior. The implication of this, then, for our purposes of understanding
Yorùbá culture is that when we look at oral traditions such as Ifá and find
references to gender, it becomes apparent that either the poems and narratives have a recent publication date, or they have been subject to more
recent review and editing. It should be clear that Yorùbá oral traditions
that display gender markings were not composed in antiquity. In sum, I
am arguing that in the Yorùbá world, the presence of a gender practice is
an indication that a particular practice or discourse is of more historically
recent vintage.

CHAPTER 2

(RE)CASTING THE YORÙBÁ WORLD: *IFÁ, ÌYÁ*, AND THE SIGNIFICATION OF DIFFERENCE

In the previous chapter I focused on the writings of scholars who discuss different aspects of gender issues in *Ifá*, a Yorùbá knowledge and divination system. William Bascom and Wande Abimbola, the two main scholars that I interrogate extensively, did not set out consciously in their major works to make gender claims in the first instance. The gender statements they make are a by-product of their attempts to develop a comprehensive understanding of the Ifá world through the collection, analysis, and interpretation of all aspects of the system, including diviners, divination practice, and the content of Ifá and its place in Yorùbá culture and imagination. One could have explained their silence on gender as a sign of the nongendered quality of the Yorùbá ethos that they are attempting to elucidate. This line of thinking becomes untenable, however, because these Ifá scholars specifically mapped female exclusion, male dominance, and patriarchal values into the knowledge system by assuming a male-dominant lens from the get-go. They did not display any consciousness that they needed to account for male superiority and female deauthorization as they depicted cultural institutions and social practices.

In this chapter, I will continue my interrogation of the claims of scholars who inflict gender dichotomies and male privilege on Yorùbá culture. I will also examine work by gender-conscious authors who have explicitly located women in Ifá. These authors, including the "later"[1] Abimbola, consciously write about women in Ifá and Yorùbá society in general, seemingly in response to the worldwide development of gender and feminist studies, which have in the past four decades insisted on the importance of the category in academic writing and contemporary life. Some of these writings respond to my own earlier work questioning the imposition of male dominance on Yorùbá institutions. As I pointed out earlier, these writings disregard the seniority-based Yorùbá episteme; they fail to problematize gender categories but assume it to be an ontological and integral part of the culture and knowledge system. Furthermore, despite the fact that a number of scholars have pointed out that the Ifá corpus is not timeless, the fact that researchers still approach categories mentioned in Ifá as if they have all remained the same since the dawn of time invalidate this important understanding. This chapter just like the previous one aims to historicize Ifá knowledge and to raise questions about gender constructs and patriarchal values that are projected on it in scholarly circles and some popular understandings of the corpus.

My goal, then, is to interrogate the ways in which gender issues have been articulated in the Ifá universe and how assumptions about gender have shaped interpretations of the *odù* (chapters) on the part of academic scholars and indeed some diviners themselves. Finally, informed by the Yorùbá world-sense and social practices, I offer my own interpretation of some of the *odù* and of the social categories that have been the currency for promoting a gendered, if not a male-dominant, reading of Ifá. But such awareness has not been the norm among those who have sought to record and translate Ifá; inevitably many have infused it with their own gender predilections. Many researchers have come to Ifá with preconceived notions of the existence of gender categories and the male privilege that is the raison d'être of colonial categories. Indeed, the default position that is assumed in the interpretation of Yorùbá life including Ifá is that the male is the norm and privileged whether we are talking about the divination form itself, the diviners, the clients, or the interpretations of the narratives themselves, as I demonstrated in the previous chapter. Added to this is the incommensurability of Yorùbá categories and English-derived ones.

Seeing Gender through Borrowed Eyes

In her paper "Seeing through a Woman's Eye: Yorùbá Religious Tradition and Gender Relations," Oyeronke Olajubu, a scholar of religion, uses gender constructs to analyze some Yorùbá religious texts, including a number from the Ifá corpus. This paper is particularly obtuse in the ways in which she simplistically deploys proverbs and sayings as evidence of one kind of gendered social practice or the other. For example, she cites the saying "*bi o nidi obìnrin ki je kumolu*," meaning "If there is no special reason, a woman would not be named Kumolu,"[2] as evidence that females are not normally leaders in the society. She claims that this name signifies that the family has no male heir to be lineage head/leader (Olu); therefore they must make do with an emergent female who is an exception to the rule of male headship. Olajubu's assertion that leadership in Yorùbá culture is a male prerogative is contradicted by the fact that historically and currently there are female lineage heads and female ọba (monarchs). The gendering of Olú as male by the creator of the proverb and Olajubu's unquestioning acceptance of its sexist meaning despite evidence to the contrary are the problem. In fact, some oral traditions portray the Yorùbá progenitor Odùduwà as female, a mother.[3] Contrary to Olajubu's uncritical pronouncements, this saying is merely a restatement of the Yorùbá naming principle that primary names (àbísọ) are meaningfully derived from the circumstances of birth and often tell a story. In the case of Kumolu, which means "death has taken the leader/ the first born/the most accomplished," there is no reason why such a name should be assumed to refer only to females who succeed departed males, because leaders, firstborns, and the most accomplished departed member of the family that is being commemorated in such a name are not by defini-tion male.[4] Since the proverb does express gender preference, the question is where does it come from and when was it constructed? Commonplace sayings such as this one cannot in and of themselves constitute evidence of the antiquity of gender discrimination. Cited unreflectingly in the way in which Olajubu has done, they constitute a propagation of sexism and a reading of it back into history. Because such sayings cannot be dated, they have no provenance or pedigree, and therefore they cannot in and of themselves be used to fix the antiquity of a particular social practice or the other.

Next, Olajubu uses stories from Ifá to postulate an ontology of gender in Yorùbá religious tradition. Here is the first odù (in translation, her trans-lation) she used to make her argument:

Ha! An elder who misbehaves has to be disgraced
Ifa was divined for Odu
When she arrived on Earth
She was advised to control her passion
Odu did not heed advice
She was asked to sacrifice she refused
She sacrificed to appeal to Olódùmarè to grant
Her power instead
She wished to use the power for a long time
But she did not sacrifice to prevent people from
Knowing the secret
She entered the sacred grove of eégún one day and
Came out as a masquerader
Ha! So it is to Odu that Olódùmarè gave the power
Over all of the world said Obarisa (the archdivinity)
Obarisa went to Orunmila to consult Ifá
Orunmila asked him to sacrifice and he obeyed

Orunmila gave the necessary remedy
But warned that he had to be patient
To become the ruler of the world
One day Odu invited Obarisa to a discussion
She said, as colleagues, they should be more
Familiar with each other
Odu and Obarisa then moved closer, living together
Obarisa gave Odu the snail fluid that was
Part of his diet
And Odu liked it and promised to always drink it
Odu then invited Obarisa to come along
And he followed her to the sacred grove of *eégún*
She put on her *eku* (costume) and came out a masquerader
They came out from the grove together
When they returned to the grove
And Odu removed the *eku*
Obarisa moved closer and inspected the *eku*
He renovated it by putting on a net to cover his face
Any masquerader's outfit without a net is an ordinary costume
After reaching home
Obarisa entered the *eégún* shrine and turned
Into a masquerader
He held a whip
He changed his voice to that of an *eégún*
To disguise himself
When Odu saw the *eégún* in the new guise she was afraid
This was how men cunningly overpowered women.[5]

The objective of her paper is to demonstrate that gender constructs in the form of what she calls "gender complementarity" and "gender balance" have always been part of Yorùbá institutions. Ironically, the first odù she presents tells a story of how women lost their control of the *eégún* (ancestral cult) and were subsequently barred from participating in it. Despite the fact that this odù explicitly challenges Olajubu's thesis about the gender complementarity of Yorùbá social relations, she writes, "The gender complementary roles implicit in Yoruba life notwithstanding, a tension is apparent here between male and the female in a power struggle. As a liberating narrative, the story challenges men's desire to tame women's powers."[6] The first problem is that she assumed gendered social categories of men and women. She takes for granted that there was gender complementarity without any evidence. Yet her assumption of gender harmony is immediately challenged by the gender tension and conflict in the story. Olajubu is correct about the tension and gender struggle central to the story; however, she does not account for the said desire of men to tame women. Where does this

desire come from? Is it natural? Again, who are the men and women represented in the story, given the absence of such social categories historically
in the Yorùbá world. Olajubu does not define her categories; neither does
she explain the imputed desire of males to dominate. From a Yorùbá perspective, an account of these developments is necessary, because the social
categories and the practice of seniority integral to social hierarchy do not
support the idea that the male is superior. Rather than imposing gender
categories, Olajubu needs to explain why she assumes gender division as
normative in Ifá in particular and in the society at large. Here is the second
Ifá chapter she proffers:

> It is the Agbagiwo who is the chief priest of divination
> In the heavenly abode
> Ifá said "look" at Orunmila
> The day he was coming to the earth from heaven
> They told him he would marry a woman
> They said the woman would deliver children
> Two children in a day
> Just as Ifá predicted
> Orunmila had a wife
> She was pregnant and delivered twins
> One was male while the other is female
> From the tender age, they both
> Watched their father in the act of divination
> Just as the male could divine
> So could the female
> When human beings go to the earth
> To live with the diviners
> One individual said, you Awawonlaseri (a human character)
> Your child does not practice Ifá
> Awawonlaseri answered, she is female
> They told him that is not taboo.[7]

Equally ironic is the fact that the second odù to which she draws our attention also documents male attempts to exclude women from the profession
of diviners even as Olajubu insists on "gender balance," which she does not
define. Yet she presents these two odù as evidence of the complementarity
of genders founded on "gender balance" in Yorùbá society. Since she is cit-
ing these odù as evidence of gender in historical Yorùbá dispensation, one
must question her apparent lack of awareness that Ifá is not a timeless document. As oral tradition transmitted over long periods of time, the chapters
may be the work of a multiplicity of authors composing them in different times and places, and some quite recently; therefore, using such stories
uncritically as evidence of a primordial Yorùbá gendered universe is not

justifiable. As I established earlier, the appearance of gender constructs in some Ifá verses suggests a contemporary development, signaling the emergence of a gendered and increasingly male-dominant ethos in the society. In fact, the two odù that Olajubu presents run counter to her claims of gender harmony, the romance of Odù (the character in the story) and Obarisa notwithstanding. What these poems show is the developing tension and conflict between anamales and anafemales in the society at a point in time. The first story is designed to account for the disenfranchisement of females and their apparent exclusion from the ancestral cult. The second story documents a process by which a charter is provided for females to practice Ifá divination at a time in which their right to be diviners was under assault. It is a document of resistance.

Given the fact that gender is not ontological to Yorùbá world and recognizing the reality that even now both males and females participate in the two institutions[8] described in these stories, what these verses do is record the emergence of gender division in the society. What these myths speak to is the fact that Ifá registers perturbations in the society, and the emergence of male dominance, just like the coming of Islam, for example, were major events of seismic proportions that the diviners who authored the odù could not ignore. I submit that the two myths presented by Olajubu encapsulate a gendered struggle at the point at which patriarchal values were beginning to be ascendant in the society, and the resistance that anafemales were mounting against such developments. What is remarkable is the ability of females to prevail sometimes in spite of the obstacles and resources arrayed against them. The ways in which male dominance and female exclusion are being put in place is well documented in my previous work.[9]

With this in mind, it would be useful to examine some of the odù that have become vehicles for gendering the Ifá corpus. In the Western tradition, gender is the paradigmatic sign of difference and hierarchy written on human bodies. In Yorùbá society, on the contrary, hierarchy is not marked on different body types. Rather, the principle of seniority/priority—who came first—was the basis of social hierarchy. We see this principle expressed in Ifá in the ranking of the 16 principal odù (deities). Èjì Ogbè is ranked as the leader because s/he was the first to cross the frontier gate separating *orun* (abode of the Gods) and *aye* (earth). The other deities subsequently followed and are rank ordered in a descending hierarchy according to who crossed the gate first.[10]

Oṣun: The Signification of Difference?

Perhaps if there is one chapter of Ifá that is used to argue for ontological gender in Yorùbá life and discourses, it would be the seventeenth odù called

Oseetura. It is no exaggeration to say that this chapter is represented as the preeminent gender chapter. Feminist scholars have especially projected it as providing a charter for women's equality in Yorùbá culture. A roll call of scholars have used the chapter to establish and underscore original gender basis of Yorùbá culture. But we must ask: Is odu Oseetura odù Jenda (a story about gender)? Or is it Odù'yá (a story about the powers of the *Ìyá*, the procreator)? Because not all odù were authored in the dawn of time, and given the fact that historically the corpus is open and subject to revision, any reference to gender institutions, personalities, and constructs invites interrogation.

The odù Oseetura is a myth of origin that deals with Yorùbá primordiality in the dawn of time. Many versions of this story have been published with varying degrees of gendering and sexism. The anthology *Ọ̀ṣun across the Waters: A Yorùbá Goddess in Africa and the Americas* was published in 2001. The collection contains 17 essays on Ọ̀ṣun, easily the iconic Yorùbá *Òrìṣà* today both in Africa and the Yorùbá Diaspora in the Americas. Writing about Ọ̀ṣun, who is a female god,[11] became for many of the contributors to the volume an occasion for engaging with issues of gender in Yorùbá religion, cultures, and societies. This rich collection of original studies of different aspects of the deity becomes for me an opportunity to elucidate issues of gender in the culture and the role of scholars in constructing a male-dominant ethos. I aim to do this by analyzing two papers in the anthology that focus on Oseetura, the Ifá narrative that is closely associated with Ọ̀ṣun. This piece of oral tradition has been the preeminent vehicle for incorporating gender constructs deep into Yorùbá ontology. It has been interpreted by various scholars as a documentation of a gender struggle among the primordial *òrìṣà* in which Ọ̀ṣun, the only female deity among them, triumphed.

But first here is a summary of the basic elements of the myth of Oseetura. The primordial òrìṣà (*Irúnmọlẹ̀*) came to earth from their otherworld abode (orun) because Olódùmarè (the Supreme Being) had given them the task of making the earth livable for humans. There were 17 deities in the party, and Ọ̀ṣun, the seventeenth one, was *different*. When they got to earth, the 16 Odù went about the business of making the world habitable but did not consult with Ọ̀ṣun, the seventeenth one. They ignored Ọ̀ṣun[12] and continued with their own business. But alas, they did not succeed in their endeavors. Whatever plans they made, and whatever tasks they set their hands to, did not succeed. Things got really bad: the earth had been turned upside down and there was no normalcy. They were perplexed by this turn of events and at the end of their ropes when they went back to Olódùmarè to lament their failure to accomplish the mission on earth. Olódùmarè then asked, "How many of you are here?" They answered 16. Then Olódùmarè, who is regarded as the Supreme Being, questioned them further, "When you were leaving the other world, how many were you?" They replied that they were 17. On hearing this, Olódùmarè admonished them for being troublemakers, and said, "That one you left behind, if you do not bring her here, there will be no solution to your problem. If you continue this way, you will always fail." So they went back to earth, made peace with Ọ̀ṣun and addressed her as "Mother, the preeminent hair plaiter with the coral-beaded comb."[13]

All the scholars, feminist and otherwise, who have interpreted the struggle between the 16 Odù and the "seventeenth one" have characterized it as a gender struggle in which the seventeenth triumphed. The only anatomic sex reference that is obvious and named in this story is that of Ọ̀ṣun: the seventeenth deity who is named *Ìyá* (procreator). In some versions there is nothing that tells us that all of the other 16 deities are males. However, current interpretations of the story concludes with more gender constructs in that Ọ̀ṣun is said to have given birth to a male child who will then belong with the group of 16, thereby implying that what defines the cohort is their maleness.[14] Despite the inconclusive anatomic identity of the group of 16, all the interpreters of this story that I have come across have represented the group with varying degrees of gender awareness and sexism, as a brotherhood. Feminist scholars such as Deidre Badejo, among others, have advanced Oseetura as a charter for women's equality in traditional Yorùbá culture. Summing up the story told in this Ifá chapter, Badejo writes:

> Olódùmarè's [Supreme Being] inquiry "What about *Osun?*" subtly questions the male *orisa*'s denial of *Osun*'s role in the cosmic order, and their affront to the Supreme Being who has designated her role as critical to the human and spiritual order. The *odu Ifa* acknowledges the presence of sexism but does not condone it. By their actions, the male *orisa* undermine the decision of *Olódùmarè* to empower *Osun* in the first place, and Olódùmarè humbles them before her.[15]

This myth has been presented by an array of scholars, each version characterized by overt and subtle differences in translation, use of words, and interpretation of events. Here I present two different versions of the myth in translation by the authors. Subsequently, I analyze what appears to be the imposition of a male-dominant ethos on the story. This sexism and genderism exhibited by the interpreters of Ose Tura notwithstanding, everyone agrees that this is a story of Ọ̀ṣun's triumph—the victory of a female over her male adversaries. If we take the gendered reading seriously, the question then is this: how is Ọ̀ṣun—the excluded female—able to win even in the modernist dispensation in which patriarchal values have come to dominate? This is the same question I raised earlier in regard to the oral tradition presented in Olajubu's work positively sanctioning female "Ifá diviners."

The following are the two versions of Ose Tura. The first one is culled from the paper by art historian Rowland Abiodun, titled "Hidden Power: Ọ̀ṣun, the Seventeenth Odù":

It was divined for the sixteen Odù
Who were coming from heaven to earth
A woman was the seventeenth of them.
When they got to earth,
They cleared the grove for Oro,
Oro had his own space.
They cleared the grove for Opa,
Opa's abode was secure.
They prepared the grove for Eégún,
Eégún had a home.
But they made no provision for Ọ̀ṣun,
Also known as "Seegesi the preeminent hair-plaiter with the coral-beaded
    comb."
So, she decided to wait and see
How they would carry out their mission successfully;
Osun sat quietly and watched them.
Beginning with Eji-Ogbe and Oyeku meji,
Iwori meji, Odi meji, Irosun meji
Owonrin meji, Obara meji, Okanran meji,
Ogun-da, Osa, Orangun meji and so on,
They all decided not to countenance Ọ̀ṣun in their mission.
She, too, kept mute,
And carried on her rightful duty,
Which is hair plaiting.
She had a comb.
They never knew she was an "àjé."
When they were coming from heaven,
God chose all good things;
He also chose their keeper,
And this was a woman.
All women are àjé.
And because all other Odu left Osu out,
Nothing they did was successful.
They went to Eégún's grove and pleaded with him,
That their mission be crowned with success.
"Eégún, it is you who straightens the four corners of the world,
Let all be straight."
They went to Adagba Ojomu
Who is called Oro
"You are the only one who frightens Death and Sickness.
Please help drive them away."

Healing failed to take place;
Instead epidemic festered.
They went to Ose and begged him
To let the rain fall.
Rain didn't fall.
Then they went to Osun
Osun received them warmly,
And entertained them,
But shame would not let them confide in Osun,
Whom they had ignored.
They then headed for heaven
And made straight for Olódùmarè,
Who asked why they came
They said it was about their mission on earth.
When they left heaven,
And arrived on earth
All things went well;
Then later things turned for the worse,
Nothing was successful.
And Olódùmarè asked
"How many of you are here?"
They answered, "Sixteen."
He also asked, "When you were leaving heaven, how many were you?"
They answered, "Seventeen."
And Olódùmarè said, "You are all intriguers.
That one you left behind
If you do not bring her here,
There will be no solution to your problem
If you continue this way,
You will always fail."
They then returned to Osun,
And addressed her, "Mother, the preeminent hair-plaiter with the coral-
    beaded comb.
We have been to the Creator
And it was there we discovered that all Odu were derived from you [Ọ̀sun],
And that our suffering would continue
If we failed to recognize and obey you [Ọ̀sun]."
So, on their return to the earth from the Creator,
All the remaining Odu wanted to pacify and please Osun.
But Osun would not go out with them.
The baby she was expecting might go out with them,
But even that would depend on the gender of the baby
For she said that if the baby she was expecting
Turned out to be male,
It is that male child who would go out with them
But if the baby turned out to be female,

She [Ọ̀ṣun] would have nothing to do with them.
She said she knew of all they [the Odu] had eaten and enjoyed without her,
Particularly all the delicacies and he-goat they ate.
As Osun was about to curse them all,
Ose covered her mouth
And the remaining Odu started praying
That Osun might deliver a male child.
They then started to beg her.
When Osun delivered
She had a baby boy
Whom they named Ose-Tura.[16]

Abiodun's interpretation of the Odù is very much aware of the male dominance that is taking over present-day society. At the very beginning of his essay he states, "Even though much of the traditional political power in Yorùbáland today seems to be located in the domain of men, Yorùbá oral traditions and visual art do not provide much authority for assuming that has always been the case."[17] Abiodun clearly has a sense of history: even though he is genderist in that he assumes gender categories to be the basis of social organization and therefore natural. Abiodun's interpretation is not sexist because he does not assume, like many scholars, that male dominance is a natural expression of gender divisions. Given his orientation, he draws our attention to what he sees as Ọ̀ṣun's female and superior power, which was able to counteract that of the male Òrìṣà. He concludes: "It is conceivable that the àṣẹ (powers) of female òrìṣà is inherently different from the male òrìṣà, and perhaps even antagonistic when they compete, with one (presumably the female àṣẹ) neutralizing the other (that is, the male àṣẹ), as appears to be the case in the story."[18] Abiodun then goes on to develop ideas about Ọ̀ṣun's power and female power in general as inherent in their role as Ìyá.

Be that as it may, my concern remains not only the imposition of patriarchal values on Yorùbá oral traditions, but also the imposition of gender concepts where there had been none. We see this problem in Abiodun's "alternative" interpretation of Oseetura, in which he postulates a domain of men and women and a Yorùbá tradition in which "women are thought to be indispensable to men as Ọ̀ṣun was to the sixteen male Òrìṣà or odù at the time of creation."[19] In this reading men are presented as the norm. But if males were superior, then Ọ̀ṣun would not be the vital source and the supreme power that the god is said to be. If indeed there is a domain of women, then there is no reason why we cannot ask that question of dispensability differently: Are men thought by women to be necessary to women or to human existence? Abiodun's initial reading, in which he recognizes the expanse of Ọ̀ṣun's power, is the correct one:

In the divination verse above the Creator-God has placed all good things on earth in Ọṣun's charge, making her "the vital source" as her name suggests. Without Ọṣun's sanction, no healing can take place, no rain can fall, no plants can bear fruit, and no children can come into the world.[20]

Where is the gender dichotomy here? There is no limit to Ọṣun's domain, it extends to the whole world; there are no two domains here, let alone a gender dichotomy. The key to understanding this divination verse is the sociospiritual category of *Ìyá*, a concept I will bring to bear following my discussion of the second version of Oseetura, presented here.

The second version of Oseetura presented here is by David Ogungbile, a scholar of comparative religion. It is taken from his paper "Eerindinlogun: The Seeing Eyes of Sacred Shells and Stones":

Their diviner in the town of Ado;
Their diviner in Ijesa kingdom;
The-crab-is-in-the-river
And-crawls-in-extremely-cold-ground;
They all divined for the sixteen principal divinities
On the day they were descending from heaven
To the planetary earth.
They arrived in the world,
They cleared Oro grove,
They cleared Opa grove.
They planned,
They never consulted with Osun,
They tried to maintain the world,
There was no order in the world.
They rose up immediately
And went to Olódùmarè.
Olódùmarè greeted them
And asked of their seventeenth person.
Olódùmarè asked them "Why
Don't you often consult with her?"
They replied, "It was because she was only female among us."
Olódùmarè said, "No, it should not be so!
Osun is a manly woman."
Olódùmarè said,
"Boribori, their diviner in Iragberi,
Is a divination apprentice of Ọṣun.
Egba, their diviner in Ilukan,
Is a divination apprentice of Ọṣun ...
These divinities,
They allow a person to trade,
They allow a person to make gains,

But they do not allow
The person to carry the gain home."
Olódùmarè said,
"What you are ignorant of
Is what you now know.
Go back into the world
And consult with Òṣun
In whatever you embark upon,
Whatever then you lay your hands on
Will continue to prosper."
When they got into the world
They now continued to call Òṣun
And praise Òṣun thus;
One who has a store for brass in a big shelf;
One who generously appeases her children with brass.
My mother, she who accepts corals for ritual offerings.
Ota! Omi! Agbaja!
The ever-present counselor at their decision-making meetings!
Ladekoju! The Gracious Mother, Osun![21]

Unlike Abiodun, Ogungbile's interpretation of the myth is unabashedly sexist and genderist. In this scholar's hands, Oseetura becomes a vehicle for creating a gender-dichotomized world in which males and females are essentially different, with males dominating. The Òṣun that emerges from his account is a "manly woman," endowed with "masculinity, bravery and prowess," whose powers can only be accounted for by her association with men, and infused with a good dose of masculinity.[22] For example, the Éérìndínlógún divination system, which in many different genres of oral traditions is said to have been authored by Òṣun, is attributed here to Òrúnmìlà, who is said to have invented it and subsequently "approved and authorized its use by Òṣun."[23] Recognizing that his interpretation contradicts the depiction of Òṣun in Oseetura as the all-powerful òrìṣà, Ogungbile had to introduce a qualifier to his earlier statement that Òṣun is not the author of Éérìndínlógún. "This story shows, despite the negative gender bias, that the woman in this spiritual realm has the capability and competence to make great achievements in a way that will surpass the man's."[24] But whose "negative gender bias" is Ogungbile referring to other than his own? In Oseetura, it is obvious that Òṣun's powers surpassed those of all the other 16 divinities; yet he writes: "Olódùmarè affirmed that Òṣun as a female has been endowed with power as essential as her male counterparts."[25] Similarly, in the same volume, another scholar opines that "according to God, she should be involved because she was as powerful as men."[26] Olódùmarè did no such thing: the Supreme Being did not compare Òṣun to the rest; this deity was above them all; Ọ̀sun was the one in charge, and they needed to venerate the deity if normalcy was to return to earth. Ọ̀sun's power is not just essential but vital. Even in Ogungbile's own male-biased and gender-saturated reading of the odù, this specific lowering of Ọ̀sun to the level of the group of 16 is absent:

> Olódùmarè said,
> "What you are ignorant of
> Is what you now know.
> Go back into the world
> And consult with Osun
> In whatever you embark upon,
> Whatever then you lay your hands on
> Will continue to prosper."[27]

And in Abiodun's account:

> And Olódùmarè said, "You are all intriguers.
> That one you left behind
> If you do not bring her here,
> There will be no solution to your problem
> If you continue this way,
> You will always fail."
> They then returned to Ọ̀sun,
> And addressed her, "Mother, the preeminent hair-plaiter with the coral-
>   beaded comb.
> We have been to the Creator
> And it was there we discovered that all Odu were derived from you [Ọ̀sun],
> And that our suffering would continue
> If we failed to recognize and obey you [Ọ̀sun]."[28]

Ogungbile's gender-fixated and male-dominant reading of Oseetura, among other oral traditions, is much more in line with that of other scholars than Abiodun's account, which is more gender modulated. The most striking difference in Abiodun's presentation and translation of the Odù is the dialogue between Olódùmarè and the group of 16 deities as to why the seventeenth was not present at the return meeting to the otherworld. He writes:

> And Olódùmarè asked
> "How many of you are here?"
> They answered, "Sixteen."
> He also asked, "When you were leaving heaven, how many were you?"
> They answered, "Seventeen."
> And Olódùmarè said, "You are all intriguers.

That one you left behind."[29]

We see that there is very little use of gender identification here, more faithful to the Yorùbá nongendered language except of course that Olódùmarè is immediately turned into male by the English gendered pronoun "he," which is absent in Yorùbá. Recall my discussion of the "ubiquitous he" and its effect of creating gender categories and male-centeredness where there is none in the source language. In contrast, Ogungbile's account brooks no subtlety; his record of the scene is a monument to gender concepts and patriarchal values:

> Olódùmarè asked them "Why
> Don't you consult with her?"
> They replied, "It was because she was only a female among us."
> Olódùmarè said, "No, it should not be so!
> Osun is a manly woman"[30]

Ogungbile's task, it would seem, is to bring Òṣun down to the level of the novices. My own interpretation of Ose Tura is twofold: first, taking the gendered translations and readings at face value, I see it as a modernist fable of gender struggle. As I established earlier, the appearance of gender constructs in some Ifá texts suggests a contemporary development, signaling the emergence of a gendered and increasingly male-dominant ethos in the society. What these divination verses show is the tension and conflict between males and females in the society—a veritable battle of the sexes even among the òrìṣà. As Deidre Badejo accurately demonstrated, Oseetura documents a process by which a charter is provided by Olódùmarè for females to reclaim their power at a time when it was increasingly being challenged by males. Like the earlier chapters culled from Olajubu's paper, which reiterated the female's right to preside over Ifá divination, Oseetura documents resistance and female triumph. In spite of the fact that this Ifá narrative most explicitly is supposed to be about creation at the dawn of time, the gendered reading would place contemporary scholars not outside of the text but very much inside of it, as participants in the documented gender conflict. The struggle continues, as oral traditions and history are now being rewritten and re-presented in the male-dominant world that we all live in today.

Taking seriously the original seniority-based epistemology, social organization and social relations, the odù Oseetura originally had nothing to do with gender; however, with the emergence in the society of gender as a mark of difference, hierarchy, and exclusion, the Oseetura narrative was imprinted with the new male-dominant gender norms, and the challenges mounted against it, reflecting the times. If the Yorùbá ethos had been truly gendered in the beginning of time, then the question of why there is only 1 female in relation to 16 males would be a pertinent one. The ratio 1 female to 16 males contradicts commonly held gender-based ideas expressed in the Judeo-Christian edenic Adam and Eve, ideas about gender complementarity, notions of gender balance, or even the organization of the Western nuclear family, which is used as a model of gender relations. All of these ideas and institutions are expressions of gender thinking alien to Yorùbá worldsense. Interestingly enough, none of the interpreter-scholars of Oseetura addressed the apparently gender-skewed ratio of 16:1 except Olajubu,[31] who despite the female victory felt that the statistic favored males.

It is apparent that the only plausible way in which we can understand gender constructs in the text is as new insertions by some diviners and scholars, a sign of the contemporary male-dominant ethos. Recall how Ogungbile even puts the words "manly woman"—whatever that means—in the pronouncements of Olódùmarè, the Supreme Being. It is only Abiodun who comes close to recognizing the nontimeless nature of male-dominant categories in Ifá, and indeed in Yorùbá society, although he took the inherent nature of society as divided by gender for granted. All of the scholars including Badejo are mistaken that the gender dichotomy they introduce through various devices such as gender balance, male/female principle, and male dominance are inherent in the Yorùbá world; they are in fact a product of historical change and their own worldview embedded in the present epoch.

As I mentioned earlier, what Ifá divination texts do, among other things, is provide a record of perturbations in the society, and the emergence of gender constructs and male dominance are certainly seismic events that threw the world upside down, as the Oseetura story attests. What is remarkable, however, is that Òṣun prevails: the deity's power and authority are reinforced in spite of the formidable obstacles arrayed against the God. How do we account for this triumph despite the relentless assault on females in all spheres of society and their increasing subordination? This question is at the heart of my reading of Oseetura, interpretations that reject gender constructs, but insist that we take off the imposed gender lens and analyze Yorùbá institutions on their own terms and in historical perspective.

The most important piece of information in the Oseetura myth is not that Òṣun is anafemale but that Òṣun is Ìyá. Hence the God is oldest and senior one in the group and must be respected. Subsequently, I use the pronoun they for Òṣun and Ìyá, which is that of reverence and formality in Yorùbá as a way of minimizing the unrelenting gendering accomplished by the use of the English language. When the 17 Irúnmọlè (primordial deities) came to earth, the difference between Òṣun, the seventeenth, and the group of 16 is the distinction between Ìyá and their children. There is no dispute that the most significant representation of the deity in the text is as *Ìyá*. The uniqueness of Ọ̀ṣun within the group is that Ọ̀ṣun is *Ìyá*, the procreator. Here are a few illustrations from the text: "We have been to the Creator and it was there we discovered that all Odu were derived from you [Ọ̀ṣun]," "she was an àjẹ́." The group of 16 addressed Ọ̀ṣun as "Mother, the preeminent hair-plaiter with the coral-beaded comb."[32] There is no dispute among scholars and indigenous intellectuals that Ọ̀ṣun's power is founded on the deity's role in procreation and as *Ìyá*. Ọ̀ṣun is the primordial *Ìyá*.

Thus the basis of the conflict in Oseetura is the failure of the 16 Odù to recognize Ọ̀ṣun as *Ìyá*, implying that they not only disrespected the seventeeth one, but also insulted the God by their behavior. Although a number of translators of Oseetura have described Ọ̀ṣun as "peer" of the other Odù because they are part of the group that Olódùmarè sent to earth suggesting that all members of the group were all the same except that the seventeenth deity was female. This is incorrect since in Yorùbá culture, the normative mark of status is seniority. Due to the dominant social principle of seniority in the Yorùbá ethos, misrecognition of Ọ̀ṣun as something other than *Ìyá* amounts to an insult. Such an act that does not accord Ọ̀ṣun the civilities due to a senior, especially the one that gave birth to them. Ọ̀ṣun was certainly one of the party but the *Òrìṣà* was not their peer in terms of status and standing. Ọ̀ṣun was superior not only relatively (due to age) but qualitatively because the deity gave birth to them. The 16 *Òrìṣà* may have arrived on earth at the same time as Ọ̀ṣun but the seventeenth one was not their *ẹgbẹ́* (age-mate). In keeping with the Yorùbá world-sense in which seniority and age are a mark of social status, a common way of reiterating the seniority principle and establishing one's higher social standing in social relations is the statement *"mi ò kì ńṣe ẹgbẹ́ rẹ"* (I am not of your [lower] rank). This reading is also reinforced by the fact that even after the 16 had reconciled with the deity, Ọ̀ṣun "would not go out with them. The baby she was expecting would go out with them."[33] In essence Ọ̀ṣun is saying that the baby is their peer—of their level—a truth underscored by the fact that the baby in the womb indeed would be their sibling since they were all the children of Ọ̀ṣun, the primordial *Ìyá*.

Is it surprising then that chaos ensued because of the transgression against Ọ̀ṣun? As we are told in Oseetura, this was a breach of the social order so egregious that it turned the world upside down. Consequently, "Ọ̀ṣun was about to curse them all," but "Ose covered her mouth" so that *Ìyá* would not pronounce the *àṣẹ* (power of the word) on them.[34] It is very clear now that Ọ̀ṣun was not only their *Ìyá* in a social or symbolic sense, but was their birth *Ìyá*, and they were the children (*ọmọ bíbí inú rẹ̀*). Ose, one of the 16, like any culturally conscious Yorùbá, recognized that they were in real trouble and their lives would be inevitably destroyed if their *Ìyá*, the seventeenth

Odù, were to turn on them using the àṣẹ of the procreator. In the Yorùbá belief system, the curse of Ìyá of their birth children is the most efficacious kind of malediction. A negative àṣẹ pronounced on them by their Ìyá would inevitably destroy them. Ose promptly covered Òṣun's mouth to stem the utterance of the curse, because beyond intention, it is the voicing of àṣẹ that packs the most power. As rude as Ose's move to cover Òṣun's mouth may appear to be, it is understandable given the calamity that was about to befall them if Òṣun acted on the God's inclination to utter a curse using the *ase abiyamo* (power of the word deriving from the fact of procreation); the children were in mortal danger.

There is no question that scholarly interpretations of Oseetura clearly recognize Òṣun as Ìyá, and correctly so, that this identity is foundational to the God's exercise of power and authority. Where these interpretations fail, however, is in the conflation of Ìyá (of the seniority-based Yorùbá ethos) with woman—a historically recent category emanating from the newfangled postcolonial gender system. In so doing, they transform the category Ìyá into a gender category, as if it has a male equivalent. It does not. Gender by definition is a binary, the categories often defined in opposition to each other. But there is only one Ìyá. Despite the fact that there is no basis in the text of transforming Ìyá into woman the counterpart of man in the colonial tradition, it did not stop the interpreters from importing gender concepts. Consider the following gender statements from various academics: "while completing the male-female principle among the spiritual beings, Òṣun"[35] and "women are thought to be indispensable to men as Òṣun was to the sixteen male òrìṣà."[36] Feminist scholar Olajubu writes, "Òṣun's position among the Irunmole...represents both the female principle and women in the cosmic enterprise,"[37] and for Badejo, "Òṣun symbolizes woman power."[38] But in Oseetura, the story itself, there is no "man power" or male principle in sight! The other 16 members of the cohort that came to earth were children of Ìyá. There is no male counterpart to Òṣun! There is only one source of power on earth, one kind of power, Òṣun's power over the rest of the Irúnmọlẹ̀ and everything else on earth, because the deity is the one and only source. Òṣun, as the name suggests, is the "Source."[39] By imposing gender constructs, these scholars have overwritten the indigenous seniority-based, spiritually centered episteme and in so doing distort reality and obfuscate knowledge about what is at the core of the society.

At the center of the seniority-based system is Ìyá, who symbolizes what I describe as the matripotent principle. Matripotency refers to the powers, spiritual and otherwise, deriving from Ìyá's procreative role. Its efficacy is most pronounced when Ìyá is considered in relation to their birth children. The matripotent ethos expresses the seniority system in that Ìyá is the venerated senior over the children. Since all humans have an Ìyá, we are all born of an *Ìyá*, no one is greater, older or more senior to *Ìyá* in society.[40] As the odù Oseetura shows, the originator of human society, the founder is *Ìyá*, the most fundamental social unit is matricentric, consisting of *Ìyá* and their children. The relationship between iya and the procreator's children is sacred.

Against this backdrop what Ọ̀ṣun manifests in the myth of Oseetura is the matripotent principle of the Yorùbá ethos. It is not gendered because there is no corresponding male in *ọ̀run* (otherworld) where the *Irúnmọlè* were coming from, or *ìsálayé* (earth), which was to become their new abode. Ọ̀ṣun is founder, a position only open to *Ìyá*. There are no founding fathers in the Oseetura, a story of origin. There is no dichotomy, no duality, nor are there notions of yin and yang in the ontology.

In Oseetura, Ọ̀ṣun is also the sign of difference. In addition, this deity is the essence of the story. The fact that Ọ̀ṣun is the seventeenth Odù is equally important to our understanding of the deity's position and role. Ọ̀ṣun's position as seventeenth here is not a rank order, as we can see that the procreator outranks all the *Irúnmọlè*:. one with the higher social status as senior, and as *Ìyá*. It is common everyday practice for *Ìyá* to walk behind their children. Furthermore, the apparent contradiction between Ọ̀ṣun's seventeenth position on the journey to earth, and the role of *Ìyá* as author of the whole process of making earth livable for humans is a function of the limitation of language use. The procreator's social position outranking all the other deities as the most senior, is reminiscent of the status of second twin to emerge from the birth canal, who is regarded as the senior. Ọ̀ṣun's rank and status are also apparent in the fact that the Odù tells us that this deity has acolytes:

Olódùmarè said,
"*Boribori*, their diviner in Iragberi,
Is a divination apprentice of Osun.
Egba, their diviner in Ilukan,
Is a divination apprentice of Osun.[41]

This verse also underscores Ọ̀ṣun's vocation as a diviner. As discussed in the previous chapter, Ọ̀ṣun is recognized as the originator of Ẹ́ẹ̀rìndínlógún— the 16 cowries divination system that is similar to Ifá but prior to it, and probably its source. Perhaps, Ọ̀ṣun named the original divination system Ẹ́ẹ̀rìndínlógún (16) in honor of the deity's 16 offspring.

The number 17 in Oseetura has symbolic significance. It implicates the numerology of Yorùbá spirituality, wonderfully expressed in Ifá divination with the 17 sacred *ikin* (palm nuts used in divination). The number 16 is loaded with meaning, but other scholars have noted that it is the "remainder" that signifies what the whole process is about. Abiodun draws our attention to the position of Ọṣun in the text as parallel to the position of the seventeenth *ikin* in Ifá divination. "In a different but related instance, Ọṣun, identifiable as the seventeenth *ikin* in the *Ifá* divination system, takes charge of, and directs, all *Ifá* procedures."[42] In a similar vein, literary scholar Adéẹ̀kọ́, in a paper on "'Writing' and 'Reference' in Ifá Divination Chants," reminds us "the Odù writing practice is literally operated by remainders; in the palm nut divination system, for example, only remainders express portentous inscription."[43] Much as I appreciate the analyses by Abiodun and Adéẹ̀kọ́ emphasizing the significance of Ọṣun's role and identity in the *Ifá* world, their conceptualization of the role as that of a "remainder" seem to contradict that intent. The word remainder suggests irrelevance, marginalization and disposability. Its synonyms are leftover, remnant, surplus and excess. In this context, all these terms seem to negate the very essence of Ọṣun's role in Oseetura and the ultimate ikin in the divination process. Consequently, I propose a different metaphor for both the ultimate ikin in the divination system, and Ọṣun in relation to the 16 deities who made their way to earth. A better image is of a dramatic stage and its lights: each ikin in the divination system and each odu in the Oseetura myth has a role to play: each of them takes their turn in the spotlight, and then disappears from view. It is only Ọṣun or the portentous ikin that is left standing. Ọṣun is the One as in Numero Uno. Ọṣun is the quintessence of Oseetura.

What I have been exposing and analyzing in this chapter and the previous one is the process by which one set of ideologies gained ascendancy and then were used to reconstruct the past and remake Ifá into a male-dominant knowledge system. The dominance of Western ideas about gender and modes of thinking among local and sundry intellectuals leaves no room for considering an alternate episteme such as the Yorùbá one, at the inception of any investigation. The problem is compounded most especially in gender discourses in that gender constructs are assumed to be natural and universal. Fundamentally, my narrative is about the subjugation of knowledge, which is an important and effective strategy in establishing and maintaining domination. George Bond and Angela Gilliam have considered the practical consequences of such subjugation when they write: "They provide justifications and rationalizations for social and intellectual hierarchies, imperial conquests and the exclusion and subjugation of populations."[44] The male domination that is apparent is not the whole story; it is anchored first and foremost by racial and cultural domination of the West, and Western ideas about the nature of humans embedded in the learned intellectual tradition.

Nevertheless, reality is more complex than a black/white picture of colonial values sweeping away endogenous ones tout de suite. It bears repeating that in the Oseetura myth as relayed by different scholars, no matter the depth of male bias in the accounts, Ọṣun still triumphs over adversity and emerges as the leader, progenitor, and Ìyá of all the deities. The question then arises as to why Ọṣun remains victorious even in these days of deepening patriarchy? We are left with a conundrum. A cynical response goes as follows: Oseetura is the Yorùbá story of creation, but ironically, it has been effectively replaced in our social discourse, thinking, and imagination by the Judeo-Christian male-dominant story of Adam and Eve. The biblical narrative of origins from the Book of Genesis establishes a charter for female subordination and male dominance. In postcolonial society, it is the Jewish story of creation that we learn in school, in church, and in everyday life as part of our induction into modernity. It is now presented as a universalist tale, a myth about the origins of human society not specifically Judaic or pertaining to Christendom. T. M. Aluko, a novelist, captures this perceived change in African ancestry brilliantly in his novel *One Man, One Wife* set in a colonial Yorùbá town. In a dialogue between two male characters, one of them sums up the character of a woman and extend this to womanhood in general: "This woman, Sister Rebecca, is a good woman. But you cannot always rely on the evidence of a woman…Daughter of Eve, Tempter of Adam—Jeremiah dug up woman's unenviable ancestry."[45] Yèyé Ọ̀ṣun, the primordial Ìyá and the ancestor of Yorùbá, has disappeared, replaced by Eve and foreign Gods and even as the children have been given new names like Rebecca and Jeremiah. The question, therefore, is this: does Ọṣun's triumph in Oseetura matter in the contemporary period when foreign Gods and institutions dominate everyday life, and the African imagination?

Alternatively, a more complex analysis is necessary to draw out the enduring nature of matripotency and the continuing significance of Ìyá personally, symbolically, and in foundational social institutions in the society. In this regard, Ìyá remains supreme. In the next chapter, I do a comprehensive analysis of matripotency and Ìyá as institution with continuing significance and resonance.

CHAPTER 3

MATRIPOTENCY: *ÌYÁ* IN PHILOSOPHICAL CONCEPTS AND SOCIOPOLITICAL INSTITUTIONS*

Afimò f'obìnrin, Iye wa táa pé nímò
Afimò jẹ t'Osun o, Iye wa táa pé nímò
Ñjé, ẹ jẹ́ ká wólẹ̀ f'obìnrin
Obìnrin ló bí wa
Ka wa to dènìyàn
Ẹ jẹ́ ká wólẹ̀ f'obìnrin
Obìnrin ló b'Ọba
K'ọ́ba ó tó d'Òrìṣà (excerpt of Oseetura)[1]

We give knowledge to the female, our *Ìyá* who incarnate knowledge
We call Ọṣun Knowledge, our *Ìyá* who incarnate knowledge
Let us submit to *Ìyá*
It is *Ìyá* who gave birth to us
Before we became human beings
Let us submit to *Ìyá*
The Female gave birth to the sovereign
Before the sovereign became a God. (My translation)

I n my analysis of Oseetura, a chapter of Ifá and a myth of origin, I began to articulate Yorùbá epistemology through the category of *Ìyá*. But because the theoretical categories employed to discuss society derive from Western social sciences, deeply rooted in a eurocentered culture, the challenge of writing about an endogenous African epistemology is apparent. For a start, the words *Ìyá* or *Yèyé* are normally glossed as the English word "mother." This translation is highly problematic because it distorts the original meaning of *Ìyá* in the Yorùbá context failing to capture the core meaning of the term because dominant theoretical approaches to motherhood—feminist and nonfeminist alike—have represented the institution as a gendered one.

In Western societies, focusing on the sexual dimorphism of the human body, gender constructs are introduced as the fundamental way in which the human anatomy is to be understood in the social world. Hence, gender is socially constructed as two hierarchically organized, binarily opposed categories in which the male is superior and dominant, and the female is subordinated and inferior. From this perspective then, motherhood is a paradigmatic gendered institution. The category mother is perceived to be embodied by women who are subordinated wives, weak, powerless, and relatively socially marginalized. Yorùbá understanding of the sociospiritual category of *Ìyá* is different because in origin it did not derive from notions of gender as I showed in the last chapter. In my discussion, I will maintain the concept *Ìyá* in the original language because of my insistence on taking Yorùbá ethos seriously. I will avoid using the gendered English pronouns she and her and instead use they or them to refer to *Ìyá* because it mimics the Yorùbá practice of using the senior/formal pronoun *awon* and *won* to denote seniority and indicate respect. The meanings attached to *Ìyá* that I present in this chapter are current, accessible, and still important to the culture in spite of the ascendancy of colonial gender categories.

Analyzing the sociospiritual category *Ìyá* as a social institution is important because the central argument of my work is that the introduction of gender into Yorùbá society, systems of knowledge, and thought created an opening for an epistemological shift from a nongendered world-sense to an increasingly gendered worldview. In my previous book *The Invention of Women: Making an African Sense of Western Gender Discourses*, I showed systematically the impact of gender on Yorùbá society. In this chapter then, my goal is to describe methodically the indigenous episteme that was imposed upon by Euro/American ways of viewing and organizing the world. I identify important philosophical concepts and social institutions central to the Yorùbá world and locate their relationship to the institution of *Ìyá*. By the end of the chapter, I remind readers that significant understanding of *Ìyá* in postcolonial society derives from the gendered episteme of modernity in which *Ìyá* is a subordinated category in official narratives. The inroad of exogenous ideas on the construction of the social category of *Ìyá* notwithstanding, Yorùbá understandings of this venerable institution continue to resonate in many areas of life.

At the core of the seniority-based system is *Ìyá*, who symbolizes what I describe as the matripotent principle. Matripotency describes the powers, spiritual and material, deriving from *Ìyá*'s procreative role. The efficacy of *Ìyá* is most pronounced when they are considered in relation to their birth children. The matripotent ethos expresses the seniority system in that *Ìyá* is the venerated senior in relation to their children. Since all humans have an *Ìyá*, we are all born of an *Ìyá*, no one is greater, older or more senior to *Ìyá*.

The procreator is the founder of human society as indicated in Oseetura, the Yorùbá founding myth. The most fundamental social unit in the Yorùbá world is *Ìyá* and child/ren. Because it is only anafemales who procreate, the original construction of *Ìyá* is not gendered because its rationale and meaning derive from *Ìyá's* role as comaker with *Ẹlẹ́dàá* (the Creator) of humans... *Ìyá* is also a singular category without compare to any other. Furthermore, both anamale and anafemale children spiritually choose their *Ìyá* in the same way, and *Ìyá* are connected to all their birth children similarly without any distinction made of the type of genitalia they may have. Perhaps the place to start this exposition of Yorùbá ideas and imagination about *Ìyá* is with *orí* and the related concept of *àkúnlẹ̀yàn* because they lead us directly to procreation highlighting the relationship between *Ìyá* and their children, and consequently humanity, given that all humans are born of *Ìyá*. The idea that *Ìyá* is a nongendered category should not be difficult to understand if we proceed from the premise that the concept emanates from a different episteme than the universalized Euro-American gender-saturated one.

Orí and Àkúnlẹ̀yàn: Choosing Ìyá

Perhaps the most important concept in articulating the Yorùbá world sense is *orí*. Like everything else in Yorùbá life, Ifá addresses the meaning of *orí* in a number of *odù*. *Orí* literally means head. It has two interdependent distinctions: *orí-inú* (inner head) and *orí-òde* (outer head). *Orí* is elaborated as the seat of individual fate or destiny. Therefore destiny and fate are two synonyms for *orí-inú*. In ordinary Yorùbá life *orí-inú* is referred to merely as *orí*, and I will follow that usage. In the cosmology, the most important task facing *ènìyàn* (humans) in their pre-earthly guise is to choose an *orí* in *òrun* (otherworld) before making the journey to earth. In matters concerning human life, there is a preoccupation with choosing the right *orí* in order to have a good destiny on earth. In Ifá we also learn that *Orí* is a deity in its own right. *Orí* is thus a personal God. An Ifá chapter tells us that the most faithful and therefore the most important divinity for any individual's well-being is their *orí*. Hence the injunction that the propitiation of one's *orí* should precede any entreaties to other Gods, for there is nothing that other divinities can do for an individual without the consent of their *orí*.

It is *Orí* alone
Who can accompany his devotee to any place
Without turning back
If I have money,
It is my *Orí* I will praise

My *Orí*, it is you
If I have children on earth,
It is my *Orí* to whom I will give praise
My *Orí*, it is you
All good things I have on earth,
It is *Orí*, I will praise
My *Orí*, it is you.[2]

Another Odù underscores *Orí*'s importance as mediator between the individual and other Òrìṣà (Gods), because without *Orí*'s due sanction, no requests to other Òrìṣà will be countenanced:

No god shall offer protection
Without sanction from *Orí*
Orí, we salute (you)
Whose protection precedes that of other *òrìṣà*
Without sanction from *Orí*
Orí, we salute (you)
Orí that is destined to live
Whosoever sacrifice *Orí* chooses to accept,
Let him rejoice.[3]

The process by which pre-earthly souls acquire their destiny is called *àkúnlèyàn* (the act of kneeling down to choose), because humans are said to kneel before the maker to choose their fate—preordained prospects in life—before coming to earth. These concepts have been well researched by scholars of Yorùbá culture, but many have failed to recognize the distinctive place of *Ìyá* in the sociospiritual world, which is necessary if we are to comprehend the individual destinies of humans—*Ìyá*'s children. Philosopher Segun Gbadegesin appropriately draws attention to the interconnectedness of human destinies when he writes: "For the child whose destiny is to die in infancy is born to a family whose destiny it is to mourn its child. Therefore, one can assume that each of the parents must also have chosen (or received) a related destiny."[4] His analysis is highly problematic, however, because he assumes that the interconnection of the destiny of *Ìyá* and child is no more privileged than that of a father and child, or even of other members of a particular community and the child. Gbadegesin's mistake stems from his narrow focus on the fact that babies are born into families. Of course, babies are physically born into families, but in the Yorùbá tradition, they are first and foremost born to their *Ìyá*, spiritually and physically, hence, they are their *Ìyá*'s children in the first instance, most fundamentally. The bonds between *Ìyá* and a particular offspring are seen to be strong and of a different order than any other kind of ties. The *Ìyá*-child dyad is perceived as predating the earthly appearance of the child and therefore predates marriage and all other familial relations. Another name for Ìyá in Yorùbá is Iye or Yèyé, which means "the one who laid me (yé) like an egg."[5] In Yorùbá discourses of reproduction, one often gets the impression that Ìyá makes babies through a process of parthenogenesis. This is not surprising, because for Yorùbá it is fundamentally a spiritual process in that Ìyá is the entity who incubates and gives birth to an already existing soul. The process is understood to be more spiritual than biological. The rituals surrounding the birth of twins are a good illustration of the bonds, rights, and responsibilities of Ìyá. Twins are considered spiritually extraordinary babies whose continuous survival demands special rituals from Ìyá.[6] There's no corresponding demands on the father, which is understood as a social and not a spiritual category in the first instance. Fatherhood in the tradition is socially established and need not be biological. The Ìyá-child relationship, however, is constructed as longer, stronger, and deeper than any other. The relationship is perceived to be pre-earthly, pregestational, lifelong, and even persisting into the afterlife in its vitality. In his discussion of aroya, conceptual portraits that are commissioned as shrine figures in memorials to the dead, art historian Babatunde Lawal points out that one of the functions of this art form is to provide a visual metaphor encapsulating a message. For example, he writes, "the motif of [Ìyá] and child reminds a female ancestor of her maternal duties as a provider and nurturer."[7] The aroya portraits that are commissioned for fathers are of the subject alone; they do not include the picture of the child, since the connections between father and child are not seen as direct and unmediated, and are therefore of a different order. It is marriage that connects father to child; their bond is not seen as visceral in the same way that the Ìyá/child bond is perceived.

The social context of Ìyá and the meanings attached to birthing events are a good starting point for appreciating the connectedness of Ìyá's orí and that of their child. At the moment of birth, two entities are born—a baby and an Ìyá. This construction underscores the individual nature of the Ìyá-child relationship regardless of whether a particular Ìyá is a first time Ìyá or not. The term abiyamọ (birth Ìyá) is often paired with the term ìkúnlẹ̀ (kneeling), referring to the preferred birthing position in the culture. Thus ìkúnlẹ̀ abiyamọ refers to the kneeling of an Ìyá in the pains of labor. The day a particular Ìyá gives birth is ọjọ́ ìkúnlẹ̀ (day of birth, birthday). There are as many "birth days" as there are children. It is interesting that in the Western tradition now adopted the world over, each person has only one birthday, but for Ìyá, the birthday of each child is also the Ìyá's ọjọ́ ìkúnlẹ̀ (literally day of kneeling in labor). References to particular ọjọ́ ìkúnlẹ̀ are usually an occasion to meditate on the wonders, dangers, and miracle of childbirth in relation to the Ìyá. Importantly, àkúnlẹ̀yàn (the moment of pre-earthly creation in which individuals choose their destiny) and *ìkúnlẹ̀ abiyamọ* (the kneeling of *Ìyá* in labor pains) are often conflated and are therefore regarded as one and the same. This fusing of events suggests an integration of the *orí* of the *Ìyá* with that of the child. The image is readily depicted in art and the female in the *ìkúnlẹ̀* pose (the kneeling female) is one of the most prevalent icons of Yorùbá art. Though the two moments are separated temporally, they are visually represented by *ìkúnlẹ̀ abiyamọ*. Art historian Abiodun explains the significance of this image:

> A kneeling nude woman figure holding her breast, symbolises humanity choosing its destiny in heaven ...To the Yorùbá, this choice of destiny is probably the most important creation of man [humans], and it is significant that woman has been chosen to handle the assignment. The woman uses *ìkúnlẹ̀-abiyamọ* "the kneeling with pain at child-birth," often regarded as the greatest act of reverence that can be shown to any being, to appease and "soften" the gods and solicit their support.[8]

In this tradition, then, the *Ìyá* figure is representative of humanity—they are the archetypal human being from which all humans derive. Socially, *ìkúnlẹ̀ abiyamọ* is invested with much meaning. In the cosmology, *Ìkúnlẹ̀* recalls *àkúnlẹ̀yàn* (the pre-earthly act of kneeling before the Creator to choose one's *orí*). It is significant that the most fateful choice any individual makes at this crucial pre-earthly moment is the selection of one's *Ìyá*. Apart from the fact that *Ìyá* is the one who introduces a person into earthly life, there is the added fear that one might mistakenly choose *Ìyá* who has a short lifespan. Such a choice is likely to result in tragedy, because an infant or child without *Ìyá* is highly vulnerable and unlikely to survive. The saying *omo k'oni ohun o ye, ìyá ni ko je e*—a child survives and thrives only at the *Ìyá*'s will—suggests the critical role that *Ìyá* plays in the child's welfare. *Ìyá* is not only the birth giver; *Ìyá* is also a cocreator, a life giver, because *Ìyá* is present at creation. The role of *Ìyá* is regarded as a lifelong vocation. As ancestors, *Ìyá* are *primus inter pares* among the departed, first in line to be propitiated by their children, to seek their benevolence and blessings in order for their progeny to have trouble-free and successful lives. *Ìyá*'s relationship with their child is considered to be otherworldly, pre-earthly, preconception, pregestational, presocial, prenatal, postnatal, lifelong, and posthumous. Thus relationship between *Ìyá* and child is timeless. The *ìkúnlẹ̀* moment is both a moment in which *Ìyá* is at their most human because of the vulnerability attending childbirth, and it is also a moment in which *Ìyá* is transcendental.

Ìyá is a lifelong commitment, and one remains a child to one's *Ìyá* regardless of one's age. The importance of having an *Ìyá* who has a long lifespan cannot be overemphasized. It is understood that one needs one's *Ìyá* at every turn in life, and most especially through rites of passage including the birth of one's own children. Until the very recent past, an expectant *Ìyá* normally had her first child with their own *Yèyé* in attendance. As soon as a young bride was in her sixth month of pregnancy, *Ìyá* would insist that the expectant mother leave their marital home and come back to their natal home so that they could be properly looked after and ushered successfully through what is regarded as a dangerous and life-threatening process. Even today, the first Yorùbá prayer uttered as greeting after a baby is born is *ẹ kú ewu ọmọ*—greetings for surviving the dangers of childbirth. T. A. A. Ladele et al. paints a memorable scene of the day in which the expectant *Ìyá* goes into labor:

> *Tí inú ìkúnlè abiyamọ bá ń tẹ obìnrin, àwọn òbí rẹ̀ yóò téní sí yàrá fún un. Wọn yóò kó àkísà aṣọ tí wọ́n ti lò sí itòsí, wọn yóò wá mú ọsẹ abíwẹ́rẹ̀ tí wọ́n ti gún pamọ́ fún un, yóò lọ fiwẹ̀ ní ẹ̀hìnkùlé. Lẹ́hìn èyí, yóò wọ iyàrá, yó wà lórí ìkúnlè sórí ẹní. Ìyá rẹ̀ yóò máa kù wọlé, kù jáde.…Ńṣe ni yóò máa mú igbá tí yóò máa mú àwo;. Ẹ̀kọ̀ọ̀kan ni iyá yìí yóò máa lọ wo ọmọ rẹ ní iyàrá, tí yóò máa bẹ orí, bẹ òrìṣà pé kí Ọlọ́run yọ òun.*[9]

(When the expectant mother is in labor, the parent will gather scraps of cloth or other disused clothing nearby and she will be provided with a piece of *abiwere* soap [formulated to facilitate the birthing process] that had been prepared beforehand. She will proceed to take a bath. Afterwards, she will return to the room, kneeling on a mat in what is the [Yorùbá] cultural birthing posture. [Meanwhile,] her restive mother will be pacing up and down, going in and out of the house…Once in a while, she will check on her daughter in the room, invoking her *orí*, entreating *òrìṣà* that the Lord of the Heavens will pull them through.[10])

This passage captures the drama and the spirituality associated with giving birth, and the responsibility of *Ìyá* in relation even to an adult child, in this case another *Ìyá*-in-making. The quotation also conveys the anxiety-producing nature of the moment, with the expectant grand *Ìyá* one of two protagonists in the cycle of procreation. In invoking *orí* the senior *Ìyá* would appeal to both their own *orí*, and the expectant *Ìyá's orí*; but at one level their destinies are perceived to be inseparable—they are one and the same. It is important to note that appeal to *orí* is regarded as the key prayer in time of crisis, superseding entreaties to the other deities.

Invocations of *orí*, prayers to *Òrìṣà*, and entreaties to God do not separate the expectant *Ìyá's destiny* from that of *Ìyá àgbà* (older *Ìyá*). In moments of danger, the first deity to be invoked is one's *orí*, followed by an appeal to the *orí* of one's *Ìyá*. *Orí'yàámi gbà mí o* (my *Ìyá's orí*, please save me) is the ultimate prayerful cry of alarm, fear, or sorrow uttered by anyone in distress.

The utterance expresses the close identification of child with the *Ìyá*. In the culture at large and more specifically for expectant *Ìyá*, there is no moment of greater danger than the birthing of a child. Hence pregnancy is a period during which the *orí* is constantly invoked by family members and well-wishers alike. It is no wonder, then, that if indeed the worst were to occur, that is the death of an *Ìyá* in childbirth, the older *Ìyá* would be regarded as the primary bereaved, even ahead of the husband of the expectant *Ìyá*. There is no greater tragedy in Yorùbá society than the death of an *Ìyá* in childbirth. Whenever this unfortunate event does occur, the graphic images used to describe the calamity are telling enough: *ilè wo*—the community is threatened with destruction; or *ilè bàjé*—the death is regarded as pollution, the despoiling of the land that presages the unhinging of the world.[11] Such a death calls for elaborate and costly cleansing rituals.

The birthing process is invested with so much significance that birth *Ìyá* are perceived to have mystical powers, especially over their offspring. In a certain sense, each birthing moment produces its own baby, its own *Ìyá*, and the special bonds between them. Growing up in a Yorùbá world, one learns to respect the potency of the *Ìyá's* words and the efficacy of their prayers. Children are told that the only curse that has no antidote is the malediction directed by an *Ìyá* and toward their own child. In Oseetura, which I discussed in the last chapter, we see how afraid Òṣun's children were when the primordial *Ìyá* threatened to curse them. It is common knowledge that *Ìyá* have a special *àṣẹ* (power of the word) to which they routinely draw attention when they must have their way with any of their children; they invoke *ìkúnlè abiyamọ* (the pain of childbirth) and the spiritual and social values associated with these concepts. These ideas are well expressed in this passage taken from the novel *One Man, One Wife* by T. M. Aluko, set in Idasa, a Yorùbá town. Here we see an *Ìyá* try to "persuade" their daughter, Toro, to yield to the wishes of *Ìyá* by marrying the groom they have chosen for her:

> Toro, I enjoin you to marry Joshua. By the womb in which I carried you for ten moons; by the great travail I underwent at your birth; by these breasts, now withered, on which I suckled you when you were helpless, by this back on which I carried you for nearly three years ...In the name of motherhood I command you to marry Joshua.[12]

Given the mystical powers associated with it, it is clear that *ìkúnlè abiyamọ* embodies the *àṣẹ* of the *Ìyá* institution. The concept of *àṣẹ* is equally central to Yorùbá spirituality and has been variously analyzed by scholars. *Àṣẹ* translates as power, authority, command. According to Abiodun, *àṣẹ* "can be understood as 'power,' 'authority,' 'command,' 'scepter,' the 'vital force' in all living and nonliving things; or a coming-to-pass of an utterance."[13] There are undoubtedly different sources of àṣẹ, but the àṣẹ of Ìyá derives from their singular role in procreation. John Pemberton and Funso Afolayan describe it as the "hidden, procreative power, a power that can give birth but can also be used to deny others their creative power."[14] It was Olódùmarè (the Supreme Being) who gave "awon ìyá" (plural of Ìyá) power and authority over all their children—humanity. We are reminded once again of Oseetura, where Òṣun is given àṣẹ by Olódùmarè over all the other 16 divinities who had journeyed with Yèyé Òṣun to earth. They are Òṣun's children and therefore must respect and obey the Ìyá.

In his analysis of the Church Missionary Society (CMS) papers documenting the experiences of Christian missionaries both native and foreign in nineteenth-century Yorùbáland, sociologist John Peel draws our attention to the fact that the anxieties created by the cataclysmic disruptions may have heightened the need for "portable devices" for individual (spiritual) protection. Women especially relied on the "cult of Orí or personal destiny, whose icon was a small circular box (igbá Orí)."[15] One missionary account stated that "a woman once interrupted an evangelist's outdoor preaching in Ibadan, to say that even if they forsook the rest of their òrìṣà, they would still keep 'Orí the head,' for it was 'their god and maker.'"[16] These quotations underscore the colossal role of Ìyá in Òrìṣà devotion and everyday worship, in which they have not only to propitiate their own orí and protect themselves, but must also protect their children: consulting babaláwo, offering sacrifice, propitiating orí, and constantly praying for their progeny. On a daily basis, Ìyá also invoked oríkì (literally head praise) of their children.

During my research and numerous conversations with Yorùbá persons over the years, I heard many versions of the following story expressing anxieties associated with being away from home and the comfort that they derive from the thought of just having a mother. On the occasion of leaving home (for work, study, marriage) their Ìyá said, "whenever you think of me, just say amen because I am constantly praying for you." This statement expresses very well the way in which many Yorùbá think of Ìyá as their spiritual protector, greatest ally, and cheerleader. This does not mean that fathers do not influence their children's lives, but their role is perceived differently. The mystical resources that Ìyá are believed to be able to martial on their children's behalf are without compare. Because Yorùbá religion is a practice-based one, devotees of the Òrìṣà are engaged constantly in practices to honor, entreat, and propitiate the Gods on behalf of their children. This spiritual practice was Ìyá responsibility par excellence, deriving from their unique role in making, nurturing, and preserving humanity. Another way in which the importance of Ìyá's presence in a person's life is seen is captured by notions that the true translation of "orphan" in Yorùbá culture is *omoalainiya* (motherless child) and not *omoorukan* (orphan—fatherless and motherless—in the English sense of the word).

In the light of the foregoing, it is clear that *Ìyá* is not a gender category, not least because gender was not ontological in the Yorùbá world. Yet scholarly writings and depictions of *ìyá* as we have seen from many of the quotations that I cite from other scholars of Yorùbá society present *Ìyá* as a gendered category, the other half of fatherhood, the male category. It is unconscionable to represent *Ìyá* as a gendered category in opposition to father, a superior male category based on a Western model deriving from Judeo-Christian cultures. Intrinsic to the category mother in the Western tradition is the idea of nurturing. While nurturing is part of what *Ìyá* does in Yorùbá society, the core meaning of *Ìyá* is cocreator of the child and its welfare and preservation through life depends on *Ìyá's* physical and spiritual vigilance. *Ìyá* in the Yorùbá dispensation is a mystical identity that is not comparable to any other in the society. There are no such mystical powers associated with fatherhood in that regard, since they were not present at creation. Recall that a pre-earthly soul at the moment of making their destiny choose *Ìyá* who is part of that destiny and would make possible the realization of such. Hence, in relation to children, the roles of *Ìyá* and fathers are not comparable, for the many reasons I have been elucidating. The connection between *Ìyá* and *omo* (child) is sacred. By equating father and *Ìyá*, which is what imposing gender does, *Ìyá's* pre-earthly and mystical roles, which are the very essence of their identity and *àṣẹ*, are abrogated. Such a move is contrary to the endogenous Yorùbá ethos. The imposition of gender constructs overturn Yorùbá world-sense and put *Ìyá* and father in the same box—an imported box. In the nineteenth century, as we can see especially through Christianity, those boxes were already present in the society, and many Yorùbá were already availing themselves of the new dispensation. I discuss this at length in the next chapter.

Ọnàyíya: The Life-Giving Artist called Ìyá

The relationship between *Ìyá* and art in the Yorùbá imagination is compelling, as we have seen with the iconic sculptures of *ìkúnlè abiyamọ*, an eloquent case of word and image coming together. At another level, creativity (making art) and procreativity (forming babies) are linked and portrayed as rooted in the same source. *Ìyá* is at the center of both. Art historian Babatunde Lawal comments on the connection between art and the institution of *Ìyá*:

> Yorùbá identify a work of art as *ọnà*, that is, an embodiment of creative skills, implicating an archetypal action of Ọbàtálá, the creativity deity and patron

of the Yorùbá artist. The process of creating a work of art is called *onayiya*
(literally, ọnà, art, and *yiya,* creation or making), a term implicated in the—
prayer to the expectant mother [*Ìyá*] ...*Ki òrìṣà ya ọnà re koni.* (May the *Òrìṣà*
[Obatala] fashion for us a good work of art).[17]

He continues, explaining that "the fact that the female body mediates
Obatala's creation has led some to translate the word *ìyá*... as 'someone
from whom another life is fashioned' or the body from which we are created."[18] Lawal, however, portrays the role of *Ìyá* in procreation as passive
bystanders (vessels) than cocreators of the child with the deity Obatala. The
greeting to an expectant *Ìyá* (may *Òrìṣà* fashion for us a good work of art)
refers not only to Obatala (the creator deity), but it is also directed at the *Orí*
(personal god) of the hopeful *Ìyá.* The greeting is an invocation to the *Orí*
of the expectant *Ìyá* to support and bless them through the arduous process
of birthing a child, as I discussed earlier. No prospective *ìyá* can give birth
without the support of their very own *orí,* which is a personal god. Thus
Ìyá's agency in procreation cannot be discounted as the bystander approach
is designed to do.

The connectedness of the *Ìyá* institution and aesthetics continues
through the physical birthing process and postpartum care of the infant.
All these processes are regarded as *ọnàyiya*—making art—among other
things. Postpartum care of the infant in the first months of life requires
continuous molding (analogous to the molding of clay) of the head into
a beautiful shape. But of course, the most aesthetically pleasing sight is
the child in and of itself. *Ọmọlẹwà* (a child is beauty) is a common personal name and often included in *oríkì* performances. At another level,
Ìyálẹwà (Ìyá makes beauty) would be an appropriate name because *Ìyá*
not only form babies; they are also the source of babies who by definition
are beautiful creatures who inherently make human existence beautiful.
Having children is considered the ultimate blessing from the *Òrìṣà* and
ancestors.

We see another link between aesthetics and *Ìyá* in Abiodun's description
of the *epa* masks of northeastern Yorùbáland:

> In the helmet masks of north-eastern Yorùbá (sometimes known as *elefon*
> or as *epa*), a common theme in the superstructure is that of a kneeling
> woman with two children, sometimes called *Otonporo.* During a festival at
> Ikerin it is singled out for praise. Hailed as *Otonporo niyi Elefon* "Otonporo,
> the pride of Elefon," she is an embodiment of all that can be considered
> beautiful in Yorùbá context. Beauty in this context includes the gift of chil-
> dren, which most women pray for during the festival. *Otonporo* is painted
> with black, red, yellow and white colours to make her beauty visible even
> at a distance.[19]

Children are emblematic of beauty in Yorùbá representations, and Ìyá as cocreators of these beauties have a unique role to play in the life of their children, and hence the community. The vagina is also called Ìyámàpó, a name that arises from its creative role in making and molding babies as works of art. Among the divinities, there is one named Ìyámàpó. Her role as Ìyá and artist are wonderfully linked. We see this in the yearly festival of Ìyámàpó, a rock-dwelling deity in the town of Igbeti. At the festival, "the worshippers sang a song of prayer to the Great Mother [ÌYÁ] that she might never lose the tie [òjá] that fastens her children, the townspeople, securely on her back." Ìyámàpó is regarded as the "tutelary deity of craftswomen particularly of potters and dyers."[20]

Thus far, we have been considering Yorùbá elaboration of the aesthetic functions of iya institution, and the role of Ìyá in the creation of living art, also known as children. But the culture also recognizes the role of Ìyá in the production of both visual and verbal art. The impetus for visual and the verbal arts is one and the same: these beautiful creations represent adornments for the Òrìṣà, and herald the celebration of their greatest gift to humans— children. Because Ìyá are central to the process of creation and procreation, it is not surprising that their artistry often flows from it. Because each and every one of us is born of Ìyá, no one, anamale or anafemale, is excluded from participating or enjoying the inheritance of the Ìyá, including their artistry.

But it is not only in the visual arts that Ìyá and her artistry are present; in fact Ìyá's role is dominant in the verbal arts, most notably oríkì. Oríkì is poetry recited and directed at a particular person or subject. Oríkì (literally head praise) commonly called praise poetry is what literary anthropologist Karin Barber who studied the genre calls a "master discourse" because of its ubiquity and the many uses to which it is put in daily life.[21] Most other genre are made of oríkì, even as oríkì is a genre in its own right. All things in Yorùbá life have their own oríkì, which in a sense is an extended definition of the thing; oríkì encapsulates essence. To perform the oríkì of a person is to name, rename, and pile up more names. Oríkì, simply put, is name calling in the most literal sense of the term. Barber draws our attention to the fact that through oríkì, "the essential attributes of all entities are affirmed, and people's connection with each other, with the spiritual universe, and with their past are kept alive and remade."[22] The performance of oríkì by professionals at public celebrations (rites of passage ceremonies, title taking, marriage, funerals, etc.) is one thing, but I contend that the dominance of anafemales in the making of oríkì stems from their unique role as Ìyá. In its origins and its everyday uses, it is part of the daily work of nurturing life that Ìyá does.

In my own personal experience growing up in a Yorùbá family, every morning when each of the children knelt before our Ìyá in greeting, her greeting for me started with Àníkẹ́ (which is my personal praise name), followed by Ọ̀kín, which is my father's lineage *oríḷè* (totemic appellation). My *Ìyá* would, usually recite a few stanzas of our *oríkì oríḷè* (lineage poetry). Even now, when I have been away from home, and they have not seen me for a while, for example, when I return home to Ogbomoso on visits from the United States (where I now live), following her utterance of Àníkẹ́ Ọ̀kín, *okọ mi* (my "husband," a sign that they recognize that I am a member of their marital lineage), *Ìyá* then launches into a full-blown recitation of the *oríkì oríḷè* of my patrilineage, at different points slicing in some units from her own family *oríkì oríḷè*. I gather from these performances that such moments are occasions to reconnect me with *Ìyá*, home, family, ancestors, and even family Òrìṣà. My father, too, welcomes me home with Àníkẹ́ Ọ̀kín; however, he rarely if ever, adds a few lines of *oríkì oríḷè* to the address. The effect on a subject of the recitation of the *oríkì* is intense pleasure, due to the heightened sense of recognition and bonds of belonging that are invoked. Barber, commenting on public performance of *oríkì*, totally understands this when she writes:

> Uttering a subject's *oríkì* is thus a process of empowerment. The subject's latent qualities are activated and enhanced. This is true of all subjects. A living human being addressed by *oríkì* will experience an intense gratification. He or she has associated *oríkì* since earliest childhood with affection, approval and a sense of group belonging...The recipient of an *oríkì* performance is deeply moved and elated...To describe the experience, people say *Orí mi wú*, "My head swelled"—an expression used to describe the thrill and shock of an encounter with the supernatural, for instance if you meet a spirit on a lonely path. *Oríkì* arouse the dormant qualities in people and bring them to their fullest realization.[23]

It is no wonder then that *Ìyá* continuously recite the *oríkì* of their children to raise self-esteem and goad them to better heights especially at such moments when it is required. In my family, even days that we had scheduled school examinations were days that demanded a few more lines of our *oríkì oríḷè*. It is also for these reasons that in times of danger and distress, such as when one's child is going through labor pains, part of the job of the *Ìyá* is to minister to the expectant *Ìyá*, reminding *Ìyá*-to-be of who they are, reinforcing a sense of belonging, and overriding a sense of isolation that could emerge in the birth-giving process. All these efforts are directed to arouse the *Ìyá*-to-be to put forth their best. In chapter 5, I discuss the origins and meanings of personal *oríkì* names and their implications in social change. In Yorùbá society, beauty and being are not separate as expressed in the saying *ìwàlẹwà* variously translated as beauty is character, and beauty is being. To exist is to be beautiful. *Ìyá* makes existence possible. I hereby introduce the concept, *Ìyálewa*—our beauty and existence derives from *Ìyá*—as a good summary of the significance of *Ìyá*.

As I have written elsewhere, *Ìyá* is not merely a body since the spiritual understanding of their identity is paramount in the Yorùbá construction. One cannot overemphasize the notion of pregestational *Ìyá*hood; the immediate impact of recognizing a pre-earthly role for *Ìyá* is to deepen temporally and widen spatially the scope of the institution. The Yorùbá world is experienced as consisting of the unborn, the living, and the dead, and the *Ìyá* institution is present in all these realms. An *aboyún* (pregnant female) is understood to exist vicariously in two realms: the world of the unborn and that of the living. All spiritual and medicinal efforts made during the periods of gestation and parturition are designed to keep the expectant *Ìyá* firmly planted in the world of the living at the end of this life-transforming and indeed community-transforming process. Consequently, because the whole community is naturally invested in it, there is no greater public institution than *Ìyá*. *Ìyá* is the procreator of humanity.

Ọmọọyá: Matrifocality and Multiplying Community

In the anthropological literature, the characterization of kinship ties in linear terms inevitably misconstrues what is at the core of African understanding of family systems. The reduction of family ties to patrilineal is especially distorting, because it displaces the consanguinal principle (as opposed to the conjugal) as the dominant idiom of family relations. Because many African communities privilege blood over conjugal ties, a number of African and African American scholars have drawn attention to the matrifocal or matricentric nature of families regardless of which "lines" are drawn over them.[24] Elsewhere, I have shown that *Ìyá* is at the heart of Yorùbá family systems regardless of marriage residence and assumed lines of descent.[25] The most fundamental social relationship is the one between *Ìyá* and child; it is the bloodiest relationship, if you will. Flowing from this dyadic connection are the bonds between and among siblings—uterine or womb siblings. Earlier in my discussion of the concept of *orí*, I exposed the fact that the *orí* of the child(ren) and *Ìyá* are believed to be conjoined. I also pointed out that the relationship between *Ìyá* and offspring is perceived to be metaphysical, long, and enduring given the fact that it predates even conception.

Against this background it is clear that the *Ìyá*/child dyad is the nucleus[26] of family relations and indeed human society. The story of origin told in Oseetura, which I analyzed in the previous chapter, shows the beginnings of human society as one comprising a founding *Ìyá* and their children. This notion corresponds to the *kikuyu* myth of origin in which Moombi, the founding mother, and her nine daughters represent the nucleus of human society.[27] These African understanding of origins of human society bear no relation to the portrayal of Western nuclear family as the natural human state or the Judeo-Christian Adam and Eve story of origin both of which disregard motherhood but promote male dominance. The conceptualization of the Ìyá/child dyad as the nucleus of human relations and by extension family ties places Ìyá in a position of seniority, an elder, whose presence is prior to anyone else because every human is born of Yèyé (as stated in the lines from Oseetura cited at the beginning of this chapter). The same idea is expressed in the Asante saying "even the king has a mother" and thus no one is prior to, superior to, or greater than their Ìyá.[28] Consequently, we see how the matricentric ethos is very much tied up with the seniority-based system.

A related aspect of the Yorùbá seniority-based social system is elegantly demonstrated in the organization of the family. The foundational organizing principle within the family is seniority, based on relative age. Seniority is the social ranking of persons based on their chronological ages. In keeping with this orientation, kinship categories encode seniority, in that the words ègbón refers to the older sibling and àbúrò to the younger sibling of the speaker. This seniority-based organization is dynamic, fluid, and egalitarian in that all members of the lineage have the opportunity to be senior or junior depending on the situation. The seniority-based categories are relational and do not draw attention to the body. This is very much unlike gender or racial hierarchies, which are rigid, static, and exclusive in that they are permanently promoting one category over the other.

Before the modern period, marriage residence in Yorùbá society was a mixed bag. However, by the early twentieth century, patrilocal marriage residence seemed to have come to dominate marriage organization, a development that I analyze in chapter 6. Thus, on marriage the bride moves into the patrilineage of the groom. Within the patrilineage, the category okọ, which is usually glossed as the English husband, is a term of seniority ranking that does not discriminate on the basis of anatomy. The corresponding term ìyàwó[29] or aya, glossed as wife in English, refers to in-marrying anafemales. Both okọ and aya are relational and not individually based, self-contained identities similar to all other Yorùbá kinship categories. The distinction expressed in the terms okọ and ìyàwó is between those who are born into the lineage and those members who enter it through marriage. The difference expresses a hierarchy in which the okọ position is ranked above ìyàwó in the seniority system. This hierarchy is not a gender hierarchy, because even anafemale okọ are ranked higher than anafemale ìyàwó in family ranking. Outside of the family, in the society at large, the category of ìyàwó include both anamale and anafemale in that devotees of the Òrìṣà are called ìyàwó òrìṣà, a point that underscores the fact that conceptualization of *ìyàwó*'s position is not about her anatomy but the chronology of her entrance into the lineage space. As I have written elsewhere about seniority, it

> is best understood as an organization operating on a first-come-first-served basis. A "priority of claim" was established for each newcomer, s/he entered the lineage through birth or through marriage. Seniority was based on birth order for *ọmọ-ilé* and on marriage order for *aya-ilé*. Children born before a particular *aya* entered the lineage were ranked higher than she was. Children born after an *aya* born into the lineage were ranked lower.[30]

There exists therefore a single chronological ranking of all members of the lineage regardless of how they entered it. Relationships are dynamic, continuously ranking individuals depending on the situation.

With the understanding of the entwinement of the *Ìyá* and child, we can appreciate the ways in which this dyadic bond structures lineage relations. Within the household, members are grouped around different *Ìyá*-child units described as *ọmọọ̀yá* (womb/uterine sibling unit). It is a unit of affection, production, consumption, and inheritance. *Ìyá* is the pivot around which familial relationships are delineated and organized. *Ọmọọ̀yá* is the ultimate term of solidarity within and without the family. The relationship among womb siblings is based on an understanding of common interests borne out of a shared experience of children choosing the same *Ìyá* in the pre-earthly moment of choosing their destiny, an act that binds them in loyalty and unconditional love to *Ìyá* and to one another. *Ọmọọ̀yá* locates a person within a socially recognized grouping and underscores the significance of the *Ìyá*-child ties in delineating and anchoring a child's place in the family and the world. Thus *ọmọọ̀yá* relationships are seen as primary and privileged, and one that should be protected above all others.

The ideology of maternal dominance that *ọmọọ̀yá* represents in social and spiritual lives is ubiquitous in many West African cultures. *Ọmọọ̀yá* is a term of solidarity that is invoked in spheres beyond the family. For instance, in the *Ogboni* cult that venerates Ilẹ̀, the earth, which is an anafemale god, "all *Ogboni* members regard themselves as *Omo Ìyá*, "children of the same mother,"[31] and continuously invoke the sweet taste of the *Ìyá*'s sacred milk (*omu'ya*) as a fundamental shared experience. Furthermore, invocations of unity among groups are expressed through this maternal ideology. For example, the anatomic sex of *Odùduwà*, the progenitor of the Yorùbá, is said to be indeterminate because in some traditions s/he is depicted as male and in some other localities they are called *Ìyá*. Given the overwhelming meaning of *Ìyá* as a foundation for unity and solidarity, I believe that *Odùduwà* as *Ìyá* makes more sense. The value of unity dominates Yorùbá articulations of identity, and the ways in which they see themselves rests on notions of the shared destiny of *ọmọọyá*. This is in stark contrast to constructions of children who share the same father (*omo baba*) but different *Ìyá*, which point in the direction of division, competition, and rivalry. When there's a conflict between two *ọmọọyá*, onlookers would express shock and dismay at such a development by saying, "*ọmọọyá láì ṣ'ọmọ bàbá*" (why is your relationship so conflictual given that you are *ọmọọyá* and not *ọmọ bàbá* (half-siblings, who share only a father). Such a pronouncement immediately has the effect of making the two parties rethink their conflict, if not abandon it altogether, and make peace as a sign of *ọmọ Ìyá* (maternal bonds). Children born of the same *Ìyá* but different fathers are not regarded as half-siblings because the *orí* of the *Ìyá* that joins them is indivisible. The relationship between father and child does not, however, implicate *orí* in the spiritually dense and special way in which the *Ìyá*/child dyad is constructed in the culture. *Ẹ kú oro Ìyá* (greetings in the name of maternal bonds) is a favorite greeting among uterine siblings, especially during those shared rites of passage that families go through. The *oro Ìyá* extends to all of one's maternal kin and their children way beyond the patrilineage or any other place of residence (household) incorporating adult siblings who may have different residence and each of their children as sharing unshakeable bonds between and among them. Thus matrilateral cousins are one's *ọmọọyá* and are perceived to be closer family members than half-siblings with whom one shares the same father.

In Yorùbá self-representation of ethnonational identity, they see themselves as children of one *Ìyá* named *Odùduwà*. *Ìyá* is the source, and in chapter 2 I discussed another story of origin in which Ọ̀sun is the *Ìyá*, the Source. Similarly, lineages always imagine themselves as unified and seek to present this face of unity to the world. But as Nkiru Nzegwu writes in the context of Onitsha Igbo, "The ideology of motherhood is what gives siblings and lineages a close-knit sense of loyalty and unity. Although a lineage consists of children of several different mothers, the cement that binds these siblings together is not the paternal tie, as some would like to believe, but the mother or the maternal ideology of the founding ancestor."[32] Similarly, in regard to Yorùbá thinking, I have written that there is no notion of solidarity without the appeal to *Ìyá*.[33]

Iṣẹ́ Ìyá: The Work of Providing for Children

The necessity of *Ìyá* to their children's welfare is metaphysical, emotional, and practical. One of the responsibilities of *Ìyá* to their children is to provide for them materially. The most immediate effect of having a child is that *Ìyá*'s position in relation to other members of the marital family rises in patrilocal marriage settings. This is because this *ìyàwó who has become Ìyá* is on their way on the ladder of seniority, but most importantly, they have produced a child, another human being, a member of the lineage for which *Ìyá* is the be-all and end-all in the first few years of life. This does not mean that *Ìyá* alone is in charge of the child, but the society recognizes that *ọmọ o ni ohun o ye ìyá ni ko je*—the child survives and thrives only at the will of the *Ìyá*. Their paramount unconditional love for the child and the entwinement of the interest of the *Ìyá*-child dyad or *orí* is what is registered in this saying. But the joy of successfully navigating the dangers of childbearing and having a baby to show for it is coupled with an acute awareness of the responsibility to nurture it and to provide for it. It is interesting to note that Ọ̀ṣun, the primordial *Ìyá* as the Odù Oseetura tells us, is honored by their devotees not only because they give children but also because the deity provides for them. These sentiments are repeated again and again in the *oríkì* of Ọ̀ṣun and songs dedicated to the deity.[34]

Thus Yorùbá *Ìyá* are noted for their industry and labor on behalf of their progeny. The basis of their occupational engagement is to provide for their children. Thus, if an *ìyàwó* (bride) has not started trading before she has a child, she would start a trade as soon as the baby is born and the 40-day period of maternity seclusion is ended. Rather than being an instrument of domestication, as many Western feminists have argued, *Ìyá*hood in Yorùbá society was the impetus to go out and even further afield, to find gainful employment for the purpose of fulfilling this singular responsibility. The fact that babies are carried on the backs of *Ìyá* meant that for newborns and toddlers, the question of finding childcare did not arise: all they needed was that utilitarian piece of cloth called *ọ̀já*—a sash used to strap the baby on the back. The use and meaning of *Ọ̀já* is apparent in the prayer by the people of Igbeti to Ìyámàpó, a deity who is known for their creativity as artist, and as *Ìyá* may "the Great mother [*Ìyá*] never lose the tie [*ọ̀já*] that fastens her children."[35]

By the time a cash economy had developed, it became the duty of the marital family to contribute monies, capital to new *Ìyá*, so that they can fend for themselves and their children regardless of what the individual *ọkọ* contributes to the upkeep of the family. It is noteworthy that Ọ̀ṣun the primordial Ìyá is recognized as having three professions: diviner, hairdresser, and food seller. Yorùbá *Ìyá* value their autonomy and believe that it is the height of insult for an adult female to have to ask anyone for money to buy things like salt and sundry; it would just invite disrespect, they say. More significantly, the period following the birth of a child is especially enriching for *Ìyá* because the whole community gives gifts for the nurturing of the baby, and today, the most valued and necessary present is money. The wealth generated during this period is then combined with whatever else the family has contributed to form the capital for trade. In my own experience growing up in a Yorùbá community, my own Ìyá always said that it is acceptable to give gift items for newborn babies, but it is even more important to give money. Therefore if you present diapers or a suit of clothes for the baby, you must always top it up with some cash because the needs of a newborn are endless. These sentiments are expressed in the common saying, "Show me your newborn is another way of saying I want to give you some money." This practice also underscores the collective nature of childrearing—the proverbial African village, the support of which it takes to rear a child. The emphasis on cash is a reflection of the deepening of cash transactions in a domestic but urban economy.

Because Yorùbá communities are resident in *ìlú*—relatively large urban settlements—in which the farmlands were miles away, the agrarian economy had a strong trading component in which traders sold food, foodstuff, and craft products in local markets and distant central markets in even bigger towns. Anafemales have been associated with trade and *oja* (the market space) in which trading took place has been labeled by some scholars as the quintessential "women's space."[36] Representation of *oja* and the social division of labor have been gender dichotomized in some writings, suggesting that only males farmed, and that they, and not females, traveled back and forth from towns to their farms during the planting and harvesting season, while females on the other hand remained in towns to trade in goods. The anafemale god, the deity Àjé, presides over trade. Thus trading and farming are portrayed as binarily opposed occupations. Both the market then and the larger space of the *ìlú* (urban settlement) have been designated in the literature as "women's space." In an earlier work[37] I contested the imposition of gender constructs on Yorùbá institutions, social spaces, and social practices. From the perspective of the culture, the *ìlú* and the *oko* are indeed opposed: the farmlands contrasted with the urban space where people had their *ilé* (lineage compounds). The farmland was primarily a place of work, in contrast with *ìlú*, which was seen as a place of rest, belonging, civic engagements, enjoyment, and self-affirmation. Everyone belonged in *ìlú*. Within towns, both males and females traded various goods, much of which was foodstuff procured from farms. Anafemales farmed as well, and carried foodstuff to towns. The *ojà* itself was an important institution, always situated right next to another great institution, the *ààfin* (Oba's palace). *Ìyá* are everywhere in the marketplace; however "the reduction of the most public and the most inclusive space in the society to a gender-specific, exclusive 'women's space' constitutes a gross misrepresentation."[38] The market was the most open realm in town and identified with no single group: all comers including even unseen spirits were understood to be present at this crossroad. Besides, markets were not just for trading: they were social centers in which people celebrated important occasions, including reenactments of historical rituals of state. There were always drummers, dancers, and sundry performers on hand. There was no ideology in the society that precluded anyone from one space or another or one occupation or the other. The preoccupation of *Ìyá* was to fend for their children in whatever endeavor proved most productive given the resources available to them. Here, I am reminded of Scottish traveler Clapperton's description of a market scene in Old Ọ̀yọ́ in 1826:

> In returning we came through the market which though nearly sunset was well supplied with raw cotthon [*sic*], Country cloths provision[s] and fruit such as oranges, limes, plantains, bananas,& vegetables such as small onions, chalotes pepper & greens for soups also boiled yams and Acusson—here the crowd rolled on like a Sea, the Men jumping over the provision baskets—the boys diving under the stalls, women baweling and saluting them looking after their scattered goods.[39]

Boiled yams and "acusson" are among the foods available in markets. Selling cooked food in local markets and on the streets of towns is very much a feature of the landscape, providing many an *Ìyá* a livelihood. Elsewhere I have exposed the fundamental implication of the fact that a sizable percentage of meals consumed by families were bought from anafemale food vendors.

> This was no doubt one of the factors that shaped not only the family division of labor but also the economy. The professionalization of cooking not only provided an occupation for some but also freed many mothers [*Ìyá*] from cooking so that they could go to the local markets or engage in farming and long distance trade.[40]

The selling of street food appears to be an old practice, probably a result of the urban settlement pattern in which thousands of people lived in delineated polities. One of the remarkable experiences that Richard Lander and Clapperton detail in their travel tales is the range of foods they were able to buy and enjoy as they moved through this region; one could almost taste the "palaver soup" that they described with such relish. The profession of food vendor is very well documented in Ifá verses such as this one:

> Ifá divination was performed for *Aduke*,
> Offspring of kind-hearted people of ancient times,
> Who cooked maize and beans together in order to live a better life.
> She woke up early in the morning
> Weeping because she lacked all good things.
> *Aduke* was told to perform sacrifice,

And she did so.
After she had performed sacrifice,
She became an important person.
She had money.
All the good things that she sought after
Were attained by her ...
When we cook maize and beans together,
All the good things of life fill our home.[41]

The role of the food vendor in the urban settlements is not without some mytho-historical significance. One of the legends associated with the role of *Ìyá* as food vendor is documented by religion scholar Jacob Olupona. He writes that in the nineteenth century when parts of Yorùbáland was threatened by Muslim invaders, their advance was stopped dead in Osogbo thanks to the intervention of the Yèyé Ọ̀ṣun, the original *Ìyá*, who is the tutelary deity of the town. We are told that the Primordial *Ìyá* "turned herself into a food-vendor [and] sold poisoned vegetables (*efo Yanrin*) to the Muslim Fulani soldiers. The Jihadists instantly developed uncontrollable diarrhea; in their weakened state, they were routed out of Osogbo."[42]

Sacred Monarchy and Matripotency

Historically, the society was a hierarchical one, at the top of which is the *Ọba* (monarch or sovereign). Traditions of monarchy are deep, wide, and enduring in Yorùbá society and imagination. It is ironic that the Yorùbá word for government and even democratic systems of government today is *ìjọba*, meaning the *Ọba*'s community. *Ọba* are sacred because they are representatives of the *Òrìṣà* on earth. The first greeting that must be addressed to a monarch is *Kábíyèsí o, aláṣẹ, èkejì Òrìṣà—Kabiyesi*, the owner of *àṣẹ*, second only to the *Òrìṣà*. In many writings in English, Yorùbá rulers have been labeled kings, suggesting and reinforcing the erroneous but dominant notion that the rulership of a polity was the preserve of males of the royal family. A slew of researchers have documented the existence of female monarchs in various Yorùbá polities at different times in the past, and even more recently. However, the prevailing attitude is that only males are authorized to be monarchs. What is clear is that one of the immediate impacts of the ideology of male dominance in the modern period is the almost complete abrogation of female presence in positions of rulership, a terrible development that is being read back into history as if it had been the norm of the traditional order.[43] Thus my insistence on the gender-neutral term "monarch" or "sovereign" to designate *Ọba*, which in Yorùbá is a non-gendered construct. The translation of the word *Ọba* as king is not only male privileging but inaccurate. As I have noted consistently, one must be mindful of how language creates its own gender patterns and hierarchy. My interest in this section is to look at the ways in which *Ìyá* and the ideologies emanating from the *Ìyá* institution are a central feature in the construction of sacred monarchy and religion.

In the writings of religion scholar Oyeronke Olajubu, she sets up a gender division of labor in the realm of politics and governance when she writes: "while men in principle held political offices and authority, women controlled the ritual base that made political rule possible."[44] While it is true that anafemales are central to the ritual base of the monarchy, the idea that they were excluded from rulership is untenable because there were females who occupied thrones as *Ọba*, too. In fact, a number of old Yorùbá polities such as Kétu and Ọ̀ràngún were said to have been founded by anafemales, offspring of Odùduwà, the Yorùbá progenitor who in many traditions is described as *Ìyá*.[45] The inherent *àṣẹ* possessed by *Ìyá* undoubtedly was drafted in the service of the monarchy, and we see the open acknowledgment of this arrangement in the words of Ọ̀ràngún (*Ọba*) of Ìlá, who said, "Without the mothers, I could not rule."[46] The recognition of *àṣẹ* of *ìyá*hood is visually represented in the birds that are mounted on the beaded crown of the Ọba. In the iconography, birds are the emblem of the power of *Ìyá*. The local historian Samuel Johnson identified a coterie of *Ìyá* officials who exercised executive powers as part of the monarchical system in Old Ọ̀yọ́. They included *Ìyá Kere* "who wields the greatest power in the palace" and had the charge of the King's treasures."[47] Next came *Ìyá Naso* who "has to do with the worship of Ṣàngó" the official religious cult of the monarchy.[48] Other *Ìyá* officials in the service of the monarchy included *Ìyá-Monari, Ìyá-Fin-Iku, Iyalagbon,* the *Orun-kumefun,* and the *Are-orite* to mention a few. There were many more especially in priestly roles and as ritual specialists.

The meaning of *Ìyá* is very much tied up with inherent metaphysical power that the *Ìyá* personifies. Hence Ìyá are also known as *àjé*. In the odù Oseetura we see that *Ìyá* are characterized as *àjé*, and Ọ̀ṣun the sovereign *Ìyá* is the head of the *àjé* as discussed in chapter 2. The harmonious functioning of any Yorùbá community rests on the *àṣẹ* of the *Ìyá* that has been given to them by Olódùmarè. Consequently, it is understood that nothing can be achieved without their consent and participation; hence the awe and reverence in which *Ìyá* were held. *Ìyàmi,* a cult of powerful anafemales, is one of the recognized organizations necessary to the functioning on the polity.[49]

Ìyálóde: The Political Diminution of *Ìyá*

Easily, the most important ways in which gender and power has been addressed in the literature is through the chieftaincy title of Ìyálóde. This chiefly position gained prominence in the nineteenth century in Ibadan and Abeokuta, two newly founded polities. Historian Bolanle Awe in her classic study "The Iyalode in the Traditional Political System of Yoruba" explored the origins, function, and meaning of the institution and came to the conclusion that the woman who occupied this position represented the voice of women in government.[50] In *Invention* I did a comprehensive critique and challenged the claims that were being made about the office. My earlier critique remains valid. Here, I merely want to refine and add to my arguments. I questioned two main assertions: first, that the title was "traditional" to Ọ̀yọ́-Yorùbá political system; second, that the position was constituted in order to give a constituency called "women" representation in politics. The evidence that Awe herself presents contradicts the title of her paper that the Ìyálóde chieftaincy is "traditional" (pre-nineteenth century). She writes that among the Alafin's palace staff were "the royal mothers and royal priestesses. These were very powerful women. They were in charge of the different compounds in the large palace of Ọ̀yọ́; some of them were also priestesses of the most important cults, such as that of Ṣàngó, the god of thunder, which was the official religious cult of the kingdom. They were in positions to wield great influence because they had the most direct access to the king."[51] Most significantly she continued, "Far from being representatives of the women in Oyo, they constituted part of the system used by the Alafin to strengthen his position *vis-a-vis* his chiefs."[52] One can deduce from this that Old Ọ̀yọ́ did not have an Ìyálóde among its chiefly officials. Clearly, there was no homogenized group or political constituency called "women" that was to be represented by an Ìyálóde or any other titleholder. Notwithstanding the references to the king, kingdom, and the like, what Awe, following Johnson, has described here is the traditional Ọ̀yọ́ monarchical system in which the basis of leadership was not gender based. Even the ruler was a monarch and not a king (gendered male) because traditionally as I have repeatedly noted, there were anafemale monarchs. Awe too acknowledged as much when she stated: "Oral traditions record the existence of a few female rulers."[53] It would appear that the intellectual context, in which the paper was written, the late twentieth century in which Western feminist were preoccupied with gender concepts, and their search for subordinated and marginalized women in Africa unduly shaped Awe's interpretation of the Ọ̀yọ́ traditional monarchical system. In an earlier work, I concluded that "a gendered framework of analysis is an imposition" and misrepresents the traditional political system as a gender-based one."[54]

But the Ìyálóde chieftaincy did have a place in the newly emerging political system of the state of Ibadan, a successor to Ọ̀yọ́. The title emerged out of the political and social reconfigurations of the polities of Ibadan and possibly Abeokuta in the nineteenth century. The new polity of Ibadan had thrown up a republican system of government and jettisoned the traditional hereditary monarchy typified by Old Ọ̀yọ́.[55] This is how Awe characterized the Ibadan revolution in governance: "One aberration within this Ọ̀yọ́-Yorùbá system is to be found in the comparatively new settlement of Ibadan, which in the nineteenth-century threw overboard the idea of hereditary government and chose chiefs on merit. This same system of appointment was extended to the Ìyálóde title."[56] She is correct about the Ibadan rejection of tradition but why would the Ìyálóde title be an exception, given her summation that it is an import from the past? Many of Ibadan chieftaincy titles such as Mógàjí, and the innovation of appending Ọ̀tún (the right of) and Òsì (the left of), to titles such as Àrẹ-ọ̀nà-Kakaǹfò and later on to the apex title Olúbàdàn itself are well recognized as new inventions.[57] Ìyálóde was no exception. I contend that it too was equally newly invented, not traditional. Reviewing the Ibadan chieftaincy system of the early period, historian Ruth Watson writes:

> The number of positions in use was not constant. New offices were adopted on particular occasions, while others were dropped, sometimes to be revived later. There was, nonetheless, a steady increase in the number of titles made available through the course of the nineteenth century. To generalize, it appears that there were four main lines by the 1850s. Titles in those of the *Balogun, Seriki,* and *Bale* were taken by male *ologun* ("brave warriors"). The *Iyalode* was a successful female trader.[58]

Since the business of the state of Ibadan was war making, the Ìyálóde just like the male chiefs "contributed her own quota of soldiers to Ibadan's *ad hoc* army whenever there was warfare."[59]

The Ìyálóde title was obviously within the purview of Ibadan chieftaincies. Many of the scholars who claim traditional (pre-Ibadan) for the Ìyálóde title should explain why the female chieftaincy has a different provenance than other chieftaincy titles in this new republic whose raison d'etre was to overturn tradition. In fact, the creation of an Ìyálóde as only one chieftaincy title open to women did overturn the tradition of nongender-based politics that was the hallmark of Ọ̀yọ́ monarchical system. Although the existence of a female chieftaincy is treated as evidence of women's access to politics, I want to suggest to the contrary that what it represents is the emergence of the new factor of gender in politics and the institutionalization of male privilege: a novel approach that effectively abrogated female access to rulership, and reduced their space for representation. In traditional Yorùbá monarchy as it is well documented, male or female anatomy was not a perquisite to Obaship; in Ibadan's republicanism, anatomy became a precondition to rulership and the newly constituted political category called

women were excluded from the apex title, and were limited merely to one
chiefly position of Ìyálóde.[60] The Ìyálóde title may have been the only position open to females in
Ibadan political system; however, the idea that she represented only women
is not supported by the evidence. As we already noted that like the male
chiefs, she also contributed to Ibadan warring campaigns. Besides, what was
this "women's affairs" that she was in charge of? Awe noted, "Information
about what these matters are is scanty."[61] What is apparent is that there is
a tendency to reduce the range of authority of this chief subsuming her
under various gender regimes. Some of these efforts rely very much on the
literal translation of the word "Ìyálóde" as "mother in charge of external
affairs"[62] or as Johnson says, "Through the Iyalode, the women can make
their voices heard in municipal and other affairs."[63] But as literary critic
Adéẹ̀kọ́ concluded after a survey of the translations and mistranslations of
the word "Ìyálóde":

> We rarely pause to consider how the language of theorizing and reporting
> discoveries overwrites observable colloquialisms of [cultural] difference. My
> extended discussion of the (un)translatability of Ìyálóde is meant to highlight
> the grossly inequitable, but inadequately interrogated, linguistic and discur-
> sive environments in which terms of Africa gender are constructed. As the
> examples discussed above illustrate, the necessary translation decisions that
> scholars must make for the sake of intelligibility usually defer to the interests
> of the socially dominant and intellectually prestigious target languages of
> reporting, such as English.[64]

There is a tendency among scholars to interpret the keyword òde that is
attached to the all-important Ìyá as a spatial concept. True, òde could be
translated as public space but I aver that a deeper understanding of òde in
Yorùbá is a reference to people, multitudes. The idea of public in Yorùbá
refers to people not space; there is no empty òde. It is people who constitute
a Yorùbá public. Thus Ìyálóde is better understood as Ìyá of the people, Ìyá
of humanity, a name that unconsciously reinscribes the matripotent ethos.
Incidentally, in Abeokuta, another newer Yorùbá polity that boasts a tradition of Ìyálóde, there is an ìta Ìyálóde in the town. Ìta is correctly a spatial
concept and ìta Ìyálóde refers to the Ìyálóde's square or designated space.[65]

In nineteenth-century Ibadan, the creation of a women's only chieftaincy title signaled the emerging gender consciousness in a militaristic and
increasingly diverse polity in which you had persons from different ethnic
groups, Yorùbá people from varied towns, Muslims, Christians, Western-
educated, captives and free, missionaries, and even a few white people like
Mr. and Mrs. Hinderer.[66] Besides, the British had already taken over Lagos,

making their presence felt and they were certainly too close for comfort. There was little that was traditional in the organization of Ibadan. Increased gendering of institutions was not an exception as Ibadan had embarked on its journey into colonial modernity.

Ìyàmi: Misrecognition, Demonization, and Modernity

Ìyàmi or àwọn Ìyá is a secret society of powerful women whose power is thought to derive from the procreative role. In spiritual terms, the deity Òṣun presides over the group. They are also known as àjẹ́. In Oseetura, Òṣun's Odù, analyzed in chapter 2, we gather that another name for Yèyé Òṣun is àjẹ́, an appellation that is central to the interpretation of this myth of origin. But we are told that the group of 16 deities who journeyed with Òṣun to earth, initially "never knew she was àjẹ́."[67]

> They never knew she was an "àjẹ́."
> When they were coming from heaven,
> God chose all good things;
> He also chose their keeper,
> And this was a woman.
> All women are àjẹ́.
> And because all other Odù left Òṣun out,
> Nothing they did was successful.[68]

The fellow travelers had misrecognized the deity: they did not see Yèyé Òṣun as their Ìyá, and their birth Ìyá at that—a grave error that almost cost them their lives. This is the height of misrecognition. In not knowing who Òṣun really was, they could not recognize even themselves. Consequently, they were incapable of realizing their purpose on earth until they gained knowledge of Òṣun as their Yèyé, and were then able to perceive their own self-identities. Apparently, the misrecognition of àjẹ́ by the group of 16 is just the tip of the iceberg—misrecognition, demonization, and persecution have attended the category of àjẹ́ in colonial and postcolonial society.

In Yorùbá traditions as encapsulated in Oseetura, àjẹ́ is a synonym for Ìyá. The often cited chapter continues, "all women are àjẹ́" (ibid.) who is a spiritually powerful and gifted being. But the word has been translated into English as "witch," and in many parts of Yorùbá society today, the category has been demonized: being called àjẹ́ is a prelude to persecution in a society saturated with Christian, Western, and Islamic notions of appropriate religion and spirituality. The mistranslation and misapprehension of àjẹ́ as "witch" has resulted in gender dichotomies that have placed anafemales in general and Ìyá in particular in the demon category. In the next section, I examine this transition through the writings of Fagunwa, Abimbola, and a number of writers whose work have defined *àjé* in contemporary Yorùbá culture and imagination.

The writings of D. O. Fagunwa, the preeminent Yorùbá-language creative writer, was extremely influential in shaping the cultural imagination and possibly the behavior of generations of Yorùbá. A pioneer in indigenous fiction writing, his books became a staple for children as they were adopted as school texts from the 1940s. Hence its huge impact on generations of Yorùbá people as his words became part of the fabric of language and culture. Although Fagunwa drew from folklore in writing his stories, he injected as much into this body of knowledge particularly in the use of language. In the next chapter, I draw attention to his disregard for women by excluding them from his universe of knowledgeable beings. Here, I want to concentrate on his representation of *Ìyá* and *àjé*. In his seminal novel *Ogboju Ode ninu Igbo Irunmole*, Fagunwa gives us inarguably one of the most shocking and memorable lines in Yorùbá-language narrative when the main character Akara Ogun in introducing himself declared, "*ogbologbo àjé ni ìyá mi i se.*"[69] In Soyinka's translation, Akara Ogun has just announced that his mother is "a deep seasoned witch from the cauldrons of hell" who justifiably was murdered by his father, her husband, because of her evil ways.[70] In Fagunwa's rendering, *àjé* is utter evil; there is no hint that in the original tradition, *àjé* is used as a positive term, associated with nurturing and doing good. The protagonist Akara Ogun then warns his friend, the nameless scribe, about the demonic nature of women and instructs him on what to watch out for in choosing a wife. Literary critic Olakunle George translates the passage thus:

> The important requisite is that your wife should not be prone to evil, for it is your wife who gives you meat and gives you drink and is admitted to your secrets. God has created them such close creatures that there hardly exists any manner in which they cannot come at a man; and when I tell you what my father suffered in the hands of this wife of his, you will be truly terrified.[71]

In summarizing Fagunwa's representation of females, George tellingly concludes, "Woman here is the Other."[72]

Given Yorùbá ethos, a good question flowing from these negative portrayals is when did *Ìyá* become "woman"? Another question that is of immediate concern here is under what conditions is it acceptable for a Yorùbá person to call their *Ìyá* names and declare them to be evil personified. Never. Fagunwa's depiction of an institution of such reverence in the culture in such a harsh and contrary manner leads one to ask what his motives were? The picture of *Ìyá* and *àjé* that he paints is certainly outside of traditional understandings; and may be one of the earliest documented cases of translating the category of àjẹ́ into witch, reminiscent of the way in which Èṣù, a Yorùbá deity, was transformed and renamed Satan or devil in the emerging local Christian tradition. Again, what was Fagunwa's intention? Was he ignorant of the meaning of àjẹ́ in the traditions? Probably not because Fagunwa's mother Osunyomi had been born into a family of devotees of the deity Ọ̀ṣun and his paternal grandfather was a babaláwo, and therefore his father must have been familiar with Ifá. His parents both later converted to Christianity and took the names Joshua and Rachel. It is reasonable to assume that Fagunwa was not unfamiliar with the revered place of Ọ̀ṣun, the primordial Ìyá, leader of àjẹ́, in the culture, the positive meaning of àjẹ́, and the reverence in which spiritual and embodied Ìyá were held. The answer to the earlier question of his motivation is that it was an opportunity to denigrate and demonize a category that Christian missionaries and their converts found objectionable having assimilated it to Western understandings of female power as evil in their gendered episteme.

Because of the pioneering nature of Fagunwa's writings, his use of folklore, and his command of the language, two important questions have preoccupied his critics: how close is he to tradition, and what are his sources and influences. The questions are intertwined. A study of gender categories, gender relations, and gender-associated institutions show his distance from tradition, if anything. In this regard Afolabi Olabimtan draws our attention to his Christian values and his copious use of biblical language: For example, "the injunction of the heavenly spirit to the father of Akara Ogun the protagonist of the novel, that he should not allow his wife who is a witch to live is similar to the biblical injunction: 'Thou shalt not suffer a witch to live.'"[73] During the colonial period, across the African continent, it was clear that the first-generation writers like Fagunwa were products of Christian missions: He entered St. Andrews Ọ̀yọ́ in 1916, an institution founded to produce evangelists who would help spread Christianity. Orowole, who dropped his name because it alluded to indigenous religious beliefs, adopted a new name Olorunfemi, a Yorùbá Christian name, and must have emerged from this institution a man of firm belief in Christianity, as his writings demonstrate.[74] In her study of Zimbabwean literature, sociologist Rudo Gaidzanwa noted that many authors of indigenous language writings were Christians and schoolteachers. She also pointed out that the portrayal of women in Shona- and Ndebele-language novels were more negative and stereotypical than in writings in English. Gaidzanwa suggests that this fact is partially attributable to the "differential development of prose and the novel in English than in these African languages." She goes on, "It was also a signal that the pre-independence regime had a language bureau which censored, shaped and selected writings that were simple, unproblematic (from the point of view of the colonialists) and apolitical for publication."[75] In Yorùbáland, however, not being part of a settler colony, the government did not set up such a language bureau, the missions played the part determining who and what was to be published. Recall that the Church Missionary Society mission disapproved of the fact that Johnson wrote *The History of Yorùbás* because they preferred writing that they perceived would further their evangelization.[76] A generation later, Fagunwa most certainly had mission support and more for his labors in the Christian vineyard. I would concur with Olabimtan's assessment:

> The fact that his debut novel Ogboju Òde was published by CMS and distributed to mission schools by them should not be taken lightly. It is not at all preposterous to suggest that Christian missionaries, having learnt that story telling was a traditional way of inculcating belief into young ones, encouraged the late Fagunwa to write a book with traditional background in order to teach Christian ideals, and to suppress such elements of traditional Yorùbá religion to the Christian religion.[77]

But even within the newly constituted colonial Christianity, children did not go about calling their *Ìyá*, witch, which is the most startling aspect of the protagonist's description of his mother. Such a damning pronouncement given the matripotent ethos in which children hold their *Ìyá* in reverence above everyone else. It is disturbing that in the novel, Akara Ogun the protagonist, despite the use of the possessive *Ìyá mi* (my *Ìyá*), really did not see his *Ìyá* as such; he disidentifies and disowns his *Yèyé* when he names *Ìyá* as "ìyàwó re"—his wife referring to his father.[78] His labeling of his *Ìyá* as *ìyàwó* (wife), a junior category in the lineage hierarchy, would justify his disrespect for *Ìyá* since his own position becomes superior and thus he is able to heap all sorts of abuse and indignities on the procreator. The world that Fagunwa paints is one turned upside down in which Akara Ogun not only misrecognizes his *Ìyá*, he derecognizes and demonizes them. He not only identifies with his father's murderous actions, he simply disowns his mother by demoting *Ìyá* to the level of an *ìyàwó*.

Subsequent portrayals of females in the novel is of young women in juniorized *ìyàwó* positions. This is a sure sign that Fagunwa was replacing the matripotent seniority-based episteme with a gender-based, male-dominant one. In the novel, there appears to be a patent male anxiety in depicting females in positions of authority such as *Ìyá*. Akara Ogun in describing his parents had catalogued his father's vast material resources and spiritual powers; however, in relation to his *Ìyá*, he reluctantly admits that his father is wanting. The father was so much less powerful than the *Ìyá* that *"ohun ko kapa ìyá mi"*—he is not capable of standing up to *Ìyá*.[79] That was the original sin of the protagonist's *Ìyá*: it is not so much that *Ìyá* was powerful but *Yèyé* was more powerful than the father. In a sexist society that Yorùbá society was on the road to becoming, there's anxiety over powerful females, men feel threatened and females are generally expected to be subordinate to men not just the *ọkọ* particularly in marriage, the Christian marriage. A new dispensation was being put in place. The prospect and actual situations of women refusing to accept social and sexual subordination provoke violent reactions and invite a labeling of the independent, strong-minded female as witch. Another murderous husband in the novel is a hunter named Kako who hacks his wife to death because she refused to obey his self-centered commands. As he hacks her to pieces, he declared "*iwo àjé obìnrin*"—you witch![80] With Fagunwa's writings, the position of *Ìyá* in Yorùbá society and imagination was shifting downward and the identity of *àjé* was being transformed into that of the devil incarnate.

In the next section, I will examine the work of the scholar of religion Abimbola, who has written about *Ìyá* and *àjé* in Ifá.[81] In chapters 1 and 2, I already examined some other aspects of this academic's work in relation to imposition of male-dominant ideologies on Ifá. Here, my aim is to examine his writings on the categories of *Ìyá* and *àjé* and assess his contribution to its representation. Abimbola's depictions must have benefitted from Fagunwa's earlier writings because he like generations of Yorùbá had been exposed to his novels as school texts.

The identity, role, and function of *àjé* in Ifá and Yorùbá society is at best poorly understood by many scholars who have written about it. At worst, many analyses of *àjé* betray antifemale stances, and their writings express the dominance of Christian and European values held to heart by scholar-interpreters of the Yorùbá world. In his influential treatise *Ifá: An Exposition of Ifá Literary Corpus*, published in 1976, Wande Abimbola writes that Yorùbá belief in supernatural powers are of two types, good and evil, that is, from the point of view of what they do to or for humans. He elaborates: the good supernatural beings are of two types—the *Òrìṣà* and the ancestors—and the evil supernatural forces are also of two kinds—the *ajogun* (purveyors of doom—death, disease, destruction, and loss) and *eníyán* or *eleye*, which he translates as witches. He goes on to explain that the witches are known as *eleye* because they can assume the form of birds, and most damningly the witches are said to have "no other purpose in life than the destruction of Man and his property. They are therefore the arch enemies of Man"[82] (the "inclusive man," although I think it will make better sense to read it as the exclusive man!). We notice that *àjé* are given a series of names in the Ifá verses that Abimbola chose to present: *eniyán, eleye, ajogun*. The *eleye*, we suspect, are female because of the use of the English female pronoun, a gendering that does not occur in Yorùbá language. We also gather that they are female because in some of the Ifá verses they are referred to as Ìyàmí, meaning "my Ìyá"—a name for a spiritually powerful group of anafemales that I discussed earlier. But who are the witches? Their identity is fully fleshed out in a later paper titled "Images of Women in the Ifá literary Corpus"; in it we soon discover that Abimbola's witches are women. He writes:

> As èníyàn (humans), a woman shares all the qualities of other humans. A woman while functioning at this level, is a friend, a lover, a sister a mother [Ìyá], a queen, a market woman and a wife. But as eníyán, she becomes àjé—a blood-sucking, wicked, dreadful cannibal who transforms herself into a bird at night and flies to distant places, to hold nocturnal meetings with her fellow witches who belong to a society, which excludes all men.[83]

Furthermore, Abimbola tells us that there is hardly any armor that can protect against the witches, and even the all-important sacrifice[84] cannot appease them. In Abimbola's interpretation, the elẹyẹ seem to have taken on the persona of the Christian Satan—an out-and-out evil being. What is the evidence of the unmitigated evilness of the elẹyẹ in Ifá? The evidence of their evil ways in the selected odù presented by Abimbola in this work is at best ambiguous. Two examples will suffice. In one of the Ifá myths presented,[85] the story is told that when humans and àjé were coming from the other world to earth, after due consultation with Ifá, they were told to perform sacrifice. The àjé did as they were told and performed sacrifice, but humans refused to obey the demands attending divination. As is to be expected, the humans encountered a deep crisis of survival when they got to earth. They then accused the elẹyẹ of being their undoing and finally were able to destroy the elẹyẹ only after they performed the neglected sacrifice.

In the interpretation of this myth, a number of pointers to understanding are obvious. For one thing, there is no absolute distinction made between the so-called humans and the elẹyẹ. In fact the Yorùbá term used to refer to both travelers from the other world is èníyàn (literally human), with the distinction being in the tone marks on the word. This of course raises the question of how eníyán came to be translated as "witch." By the end of this Odù, it is clear that both the "human èníyàn" and the "àjé eníyán" have more in common than the radical demonization, and that the act of lumping the àjé with the evil ajogun would suggest. The last two lines of the Odù are instructive:

> They are all Witches
> Though they are human Beings.
> The Witches prevent the Human Beings from having rest.[86]

More interesting is that at the beginning of the *Odù*, the "*àjé enìyán*" (human *àjé*) are the "good guys," in contrast to the "human *enìyàn*" (human humans). It is the spiritually conscious *àjé* who followed the religious tenets, obeyed and performed the necessary sacrifice after Ifá consultation, and subsequently reaped the benefits. The human *enìyàn* are the apostates who were promptly punished for their dereliction of duty. As philosopher Kola Abimbola reminds us, sacrifice, apart from being a religious act, is also a social act. Analyzing Ọ̀wọ́nrín Méjì, the sixth chapter of the Ifá corpus, he writes that the effective sacrifice is one in which the client shows that he or she is more other-regarding, showing concern about "the well being and welfare of others, and to give up his or her self-centred [*sic*] way of life."[87] As social beings, this was exactly how the "*àjé enìyán*" behaved; it was "human *enìyàn*" who were antisocial.

A second *Odù* that Abimbola includes suffers from the same ambiguity about the nature of *àjé*. In the second story we are told that the *àjé* were angry with, and ready to punish Yemòó, the wife of Ò̀ọ̀ṣáálá (the god of creation), who had committed a crime against them. Apparently, Yemòó had gone to the *àjé*'s brook to fetch water during the dry season when water was scarce. After getting her share of water, Yemòó promptly fouls up the pool with her menstrual cloth. Subsequently, when the *àjé* came to fetch water, the pool was red, so they asked the person who had been stationed to guard the water about the color of the water. When the guard said it was Yemòó's blood, they asked:

> Did she stab herself?
> He answered: "She did not stab herself,
> The blood was from her private part.[88]

The *Ìyàmi* (group of *àjé*) were incensed and therefore went after Yemòó and demanded restitution. But Yemòó and her husband refused to admit any wrongdoing. Thus the *Ìyàmi* took matters into their own hands and swallowed the couple. The *àjé* were finally overcome and killed by the combined efforts of *eegún* and *Orò*, who came to their rescue.

Even in the preceding excerpt, we see that *Ìyàmi* are not the aggressors, but rather Yemòó, who had committed an egregious crime and arrogantly refused to take responsibility for it. Yemòó's behavior was evil. The *Ìyàmi* are in the right, and even more so when we consider the implications of having Yemòó's menstrual blood in their drinking water, quite apart from fact that it is unhygienic. In Yorùbá culture, blood is no ordinary gene-carrying matter; it is sacred. It is perceived to be a neutralizer of *àṣẹ* and hence disempowering for anyone who gets close to it. Consequently, Yemòó's act of fouling the brook with blood can be viewed as a declaration of war. In this light, then, the reaction of the *àjé* was logical and cannot be faulted morally. If anything, what they are guilty of is that they defended themselves on their own turf.

In essence, Abimbola's interpretation of these stories is prejudiced against the *àjé*, since he does not take into consideration the extenuating circumstances of their actions. The translations of their three names in these Ifá excerpts, *Ẹlẹyẹ*, Ìyàmi, and *Eníyán*, as "witch" distorts their relationship to humans and indeed, their actions and the nature of their being. It may well be that it is this ambiguity in their behavior that led philosopher Kola Abimbola to "upgrade" their status in his book on Yorùbá culture. He removes the *àjé* from the category of the totally evil and moves them closer to Èṣù, who holds the middle but neutral ground in the Yorùbá universe of good and evil forces. According to Kola Abimbola:

> Although the àjẹ́ (witches) also straddle the two sides of the divide, they, unlike Èṣù, are not neutral. They are allies of the Ajogun. Ifá poems describe them as entities who suck human blood, eat human flesh, and they can afflict humans with various types of diseases. The Àjẹ́ are, however, sometimes benevolent.[89]

Whatever the case may be, in the hands of the two Abimbolas, *àjé* are a negative force. Other scholars have written about *àjé* in the Yorùbá world, but what is clear in these discussions is the degree to which there is deep prejudice in certain quarters about their role and place in Yorùbá life. For one thing, in these times, it has become difficult, indeed almost impossible, to have an objective discussion of *àjé*. Their representation by Wande Abimbola mirrors the image of *àjé* in contemporary popular discourse. The fact that we have what appear to be antifemale Ifá texts reminds us of the openness of the Ifá corpus and reiterates the fact that *odù* must be historicized. Some of the *odù* were produced only after large numbers of Yorùbá had imbibed Christian and Islamic ideas demonizing indigenous religion and spiritual forces. Female personages bore the brunt of this because unlike in Òrìṣà worship, the Abrahamic religions that have become the dominant religions among Yorùbá had little or no esteemed place for women, especially in leadership roles.

But the question goes beyond the presentation of selected texts; there is also the fundamental question of the logic of Wande Abimbola's categories, which he used to delineate Yorùbá world-sense. It is clear from this subsequent elaboration that Abimbola's delineation of the Yorùbá understanding of the metaphysical evil types, from the point of view of "what they do to humans," is actually a gender dichotomy in which "women" are grouped with those who do evil to "humans." But who are women? Are women

humans? Can women be classed as human beings if they are also classed
among those who do harm to human beings, defined by implication as
men? This makes no sense whatsoever, not in Ifá nor in the larger Òrìṣà traditions. Let us break it down: because the good metaphysical forces (Gods
and ancestors) also include females, because Gods and ancestors are not
gender-specified categories, and because the category ènìyàn is the designation of all humans male and female in Yorùbá language and culture, on what
basis then does Abimbola's dichotomy make sense? On what basis does this
schema work? The logical question is this: Whose perspective is used to
interpret in such a dichotomous fashion? If females are present in all these
categories, surely Abimbola's typology collapses on itself. It is obvious that
the fabricated dichotomy functions as a vehicle to impose gender, and then
to demonize anafemales as a group. This representation expresses gender
prejudice of the most virulent kind.

There are many more things to say about Abimbola's interpretation of
àjé in Ifá verses. Clearly, the evidence he presents to bolster his interpretation of àjé as evil beings is selective, but even so, the sign of their evil ways
in the Ifá texts presented by Abimbola is at best ambiguous. The biggest gap
in Abimbola's account is in the omission of copious Odù and religious texts
that celebrate the beneficence of àjé in Yorùbá culture. As we know from
Osetura, Òṣun, Iyanla, the primordial Ìyá, is the iconic àjé: she is worshiped
for her àjé powers, to give children to her devotees, and to provide the
resources to nurture them. Òṣun is the divine àjé.

In his monograph on Òrìṣà Òṣun and the worship of the deity as part
of civil religion in Osogbo in the contemporary period, Ajibade Olusola
records much evidence showing Òṣun devotees' representation of the deity
as àjé and supreme Ìyá in their songs, prayers, and rituals. We are able to see
the positive attributes of àjé even through his mistranslation of the category
as witch:

> During Òṣun festival in Osogbo, a group of women do sing songs that reveal
> Òṣun is a witch and that most of the women if not all of them, who are her
> devotees, are witches as well. There are devotees of Òṣun who sing on the
> grand finale of the Òṣun festival. One of their songs says:..."the group of
> Òṣun witches are the owners of children, Follow Òṣun, so that you will be
> blessed with children to dance with." The point of emphasis by this women
> group is that, Òṣun is a witch who uses her power to bless people with chil-
> dren and riches.[90]

Although he discusses Òṣun, Abimbola does so in a section of his paper
called "Images of Women," in which he presents "women as ìyá," and leaves
the iconic àjé out in the section in which he writes about "women as àjé."

The reason is obvious: in order to maintain his representation of *àjẹ́* as evil, he could not include Ọ̀ṣun who, being one of the primordial deities in Ifá and Òrìṣà worship, is recognized widely for their goodness and benevolence. This is what Abimbola says about Ọ̀ṣun:

> One of the most prominent images of woman as mother [Ìyá] is that of
> *Ọ̀ṣun* ... Ọ̀ṣun is fondly remembered as *Oore Yeye* (the generous mother [Ìyá]).
> Up till today when one mentions the name of *Ọ̀ṣun* among the Yorùbá, people salute her with a shout *Oore yèyé o!*[91]

Abimbola's characterization of *àjẹ́* as evil leads me to conclude that he has turned Yorùbá *àjẹ́* into the European witch, after which he gives the b/ witch a bad name and hangs her!

The gendering of *àjẹ́* as female is also problematic, considering that in Yorùbá traditions and social practices *àjẹ́* encompasses both anamales and anafemales. In everyday Yorùbá usage, *àjẹ́* is not a gender-specific category, although it is increasingly associated with females in contemporary popular stereotypical discourse. In interviews I conducted in Ogbomoso, one diviner[92] told me that *àjẹ́* is not a gender-specific term, and *àjẹ́* actually denotes a gifted person, a person of extraordinary talent and powers. The word *àjẹ́* literally means one who is efficacious; the verb *jẹ́* speaks to efficacy and the ability to be effective and make things happen. In their studies of knowledge, belief, and witchcraft in Yorùbá society, Barry Hallen and J. O. Sodipo[93] expose a distinction between contemporary popular stereotypes of *àjẹ́*, in contrast with the views of knowledgeable sages like the *oníṣègùn*, with whom the two scholars engaged in philosophical discussions. According to the *oníṣègùn*, àjẹ́ are not just women, and in fact some of them insisted that there are more male *àjẹ́* than female.[94] The Hallen and Sodipo study deals comprehensively with some of the questions I raised earlier about Abimbola's representation of *àjẹ́*; the conclusion of Hallen and Sodipo's study is worth quoting:

> We conclude by asserting that "witch" is not a representative translation of
> "*àjẹ́*." *Àjẹ́* are men. *Àjẹ́* is not quintessentially evil. *Àjẹ́* does make use of
> medicine. And, most importantly, *àjẹ́* may be a good person—intentionally
> benevolent, using their extraordinary talents for the welfare and benefit of
> mankind.[95]

If the view of the *oníṣègùn* in this study that male *àjẹ́* are more prevalent than female ones (at least at the point in time of the study) is correct, then why *àjẹ́* has come to be closely associated with females in many people's minds needs further interrogation. Two issues come to mind: First, *àjẹ́* is about power and authority and in contemporary society, the idea that females are powerful and have authority is being challenged and delegitimated. Thus it may be less risky for males to claim and wear their spiritual power more publicly than females. We know of many instances when females have been attacked, abused, and killed after having been labeled àjé. The category of àjé in many religious circles have become conflated with "witches" of the Western and Christian traditions whose norms and practices became internalized following European colonization of Yorùbá religious and secular life.

Nevertheless, Yorùbá representation of Ìyá as àjé as we discussed in the case of Òrìṣà Òṣun remains resonant and speaks to the understanding of procreation and the attendant spiritual powers that are said to flow from it. To be able to procreate is considered a gift, a spiritual gift. One intriguing question remains: Why is it that Odù such as Ose Tura that recognize and celebrate matripotency continue to resonate in the era of the ascending male dominance in which we live today? I believe that this Ìyá worship is a result of the overwhelming importance and continuing significance of the institution socially and spiritually.

CHAPTER 4

WRITING AND GENDERING THE PAST:
AKỌ̀WÉ AND THE ENDOGENOUS
PRODUCTION OF HISTORY

In the first two chapters of this book, I concentrated on the role of intellectuals in the explication of Ifá as both institution and social practice. Beginning in the middle of the nineteenth century, the first generations of literate Yorùbá sought to document history and culture. It was within this group of what I call the "writing class" that the Yorùbá language was "reduced"[1] to writing and the orthography developed.[2] It is important to clarify what sorts of people were considered to be members of the writing class. In this chapter, I refer to early generations of literate persons as *akọ̀wé*, a word that literally means one who writes or writer. Before literacy became widespread in the society, *akọ̀wé* was the term for the Western-educated individual, whose education was perceived to flow from learning the Roman script. The word *akọ̀wé* was not universally applied to all literate persons, however. Those literate in the Arabic script[3] did not seem to qualify to be *akọ̀wé*, and neither did women, regardless of what kind of literacy they had acquired. As I have shown in my earlier work, these early Yorùbá, mostly Christian-identified intellectuals such as the famous Samuel Johnson, were largely responsible for representing Yorùbá culture as gendered and male dominant.

My objective in this chapter, then, is to look at the enduring role of knowledge-makers or the intelligentsia in the imposition of male dominance on Yorùbá history, traditions, religion, and culture—a theme that has animated my earlier writings. Here, I focus on the continuity between the pioneering work of nonacademically trained local historians and the work of academically trained historians who followed them. I concentrate on historical writing because of the importance of the past in the constitution of both collective and individual identities. In the first part, I discuss the gendered nature of the group of first generations of *akòwé* through the lives and work of a male-only club in early-twentieth-century Ibadan. Second, I spotlight Samuel Johnson as the archetypal *akòwé*, whose male-centered writing on Yorùbá history and culture continues to define the field. In addition, I examine the way in which Johnson has been represented by contemporary historian Toyin Falola. Falola's portrayal of Johnson, both the man and his work, also become an occasion for interrogating notions of gender in the professional historian's own writing. If Johnson is enormously influential because of his pioneering role and for writing inarguably the definitive book on Yorùbá history and culture, Falola's importance cannot be overstated given the fact that he has written over a hundred books and still counting, many on Yorùbá history. A comprehensive study of Falola's work is definitely necessary, but that is not my goal in this chapter. Here my engagement with Falola is very specific and relates to his documentation and assessment of local historians or "Yorùbá Gurus"[4] as he calls them.

I will use *akòwé* in two ways: first, as a general term for literate persons, and second, to refer specifically to those who actually wrote books; in this sense, it is a synonym for author. But the term is not merely descriptive. It also carries a huge semantic load. It is an honorific. As I mentioned earlier, in the second half of the nineteenth century in colonial Yorùbáland, *akòwé* was applied to a class of people who mediated between the indigenous culture and the European culture of their employers. Initially, many of them worked for various Christian missions; indeed, many were Christian missionaries themselves, and the colonial government became the occupational destination of these newly literate colonial subjects. Literacy was undoubtedly a basis of power in a population in which lack of literacy was the social norm. But apart from their literacy and their Christian faith, the most important attribute of *akòwé* was that they were men. Despite the fact that the word *akòwé* in and of itself does not contain any gender allusions, which makes it a typical Yorùbá noun, the understanding of the meaning of the word *akòwé* was quite gender-specific.

Writing Gender into History: The Male-Only Writing Club

The prototypical *akòwé* was a male schoolteacher, a catechist, and with the establishment of the British colonial administration, a court clerk. I. B. Akinyele, who wrote one of the most respected early accounts of Ibadan history, was first a customs clerk and subsequently a council clerk working in the local government.[5] At the time, these clerks had a great sense of their own importance, which was enhanced by the prestigious positions they held. Chief Ayorinde, an *akòwé* himself, wrote that customs clerks in Ibadan at the time would wear their uniforms even when not on duty, to attend church service or to usher in the New Year, for example.[6] The uniforms were clearly a mark of social status. For historian Falola, "this uniform, the shirt and the pants, became an elite identifier. Because they were few, the uniform would be striking and would contrast with others wearing Yoruba clothes."[7]

But beyond the church and the colonial government, early chroniclers of Yorùbá history and culture were self-selected, as the example of Ẹgbẹ́ Àgbà Ò Tán (Elders still Exist Association) shows. The Ẹgbẹ́ was a group of akòwé, an elite society founded in 1913 in Ibadan by Western-educated men who perceived the need of "recording the history of the Yorùbá people for posterity."[8] The aim of the organization spelt out in its constitution was "to institute researches into all Yoruba Religions, Customs, Physiology, Medical Knowledge, Arts, Sciences, Manufactures, Poetical Cultures, Political and National Histories."[9] More important for our purposes is the third rule stated in the constitution: "That only Native Gentlemen of Yorubaland are eligible for membership."[10] They also had an elaborate initiation ceremony into what sounded like a secret cult, a fraternity in which members must be prepared to support a brother. One requirement emphasized at initiation was that members must hold "all the Secrets and Symbols of this order without divulging any of them to anyone but he who is properly initiated in this Lodge."[11] All the Ibadan aforementioned custom clerks were members of the Ẹgbẹ́, and they were akòwé in the eyes of the society. The word ẹgbẹ́ means club or group, so we can refer to the Ibadan Ẹgbẹ́ as ẹgbẹ́ akòwé (club of literates).

Given the enormity of the task the ẹgbẹ́ akòwé set for itself, and the small number of literate Yorùbá at this time, the decision to exclude women did not make sense. But the Ẹgbẹ́, like akòwé in general, operated according to a male-centered gender ideology, as is evident in the way in which they went about fulfilling their mission of creating a literature documenting Yorùbá history and culture. The organization allocated different history topics to Ẹgbẹ́ members. One of the books that emerged out of this effort was Iwe Itan Oyo-ile ati Oyo Isisiyi abi Ago-d'oyo, which translates as The History of Old and New Oyo.[12] It was one of the first town histories to be written, and its author was Moses Craig Adeyemi, who had no direct experience of Ọ̀yọ́ but whose father had been born a prince in the polity. The book was disappointing to the Ẹgbẹ́ publication committee. As Falola recounts, I. B. Akinyele, the general editor and our earlier uniformed clerk who had himself written a history of Ibadan, apologized for its brevity (and gave himself a thinly disguised compliment) in the following words: "As a matter of fact, this book is not very rich if compared with the history book of Ibadan. Meanwhile the author is trying to get more facts to make this book a voluminous one."[13] Although Akinyele mitigated his dissatisfaction with the book written by his fraternity brother by calling it a draft, there was no indication that the author saw it as such, or that he ever augmented the book in any shape or form. It is also unclear what reaction Adeyemi had to the idea that his book was not good enough or fell short of the standard set by Akinyele's book. The element of comparison and competition that the general editor's comment evoked could have had an undesirable effect on the author.

But back to the question, why was the book on Oyo commissioned by the Egbẹ́ so short given the long history of such an important polity? Falola noted that Adeyemi was known as "a man of abundant energy and enterprise, a man of indefatigable character,"[14] who subsequently wrote two books, so it could not be said that he was an indolent person. Instead, the sketchiness of the book and Adeyemi's refusal to revisit it reveal an essential problem with the way these books were commissioned, a problem related to the patriarchal ideology favored by the Egbẹ́ that I mentioned earlier Specifically, the book betrays a lack of sustained engagement with the subject matter on the part of the author. He had been selected to write a book on the history of Ọ̀yọ́ by the Egbẹ́ not because the topic interested him or that he had a desire to do so, but because his father had originated from Ọ̀yọ́. Despite the fact that he himself had been born in Ẹpẹ́ and had grown up in Oǹdó with his mother's family following the death of his father when he was only ten years old, Akinyele, the general editor, ignored the facts of Adeyemi's life and identified him with his father's town of origin. Akinyele writes that Adeyemi collected the information for his book "not from hearsay but from his father who was the son of a renowned Alafin."[15] This was an error, wishful thinking on the part of Akinyele, considering that Adeyemi's father died when he was only ten years old. Adeyemi was also his mother's child, an "Ondo man." Falola's summation of Adeyemi's life story suggests where the truth lies:

> Apart from his stints at Ọ̀yọ́ as a student and a teacher—both inevitable because of the location of the school rather than by choice—he lived all his life in Ondo as an Ondo man. His focus was the family of his mother, in which he was brought up after his father's death. Adeyemi was buried in Ondo, and his descendants claim Ondo as their hometown, alluding to Ọ̀yọ́ only with respect to their origins.[16]

Akinyele's error can be clearly traced to his (and the Egbẹ́'s) belief in an unyielding patrilineal principle that insists that children belong only with their father's family, a stance that is supported neither by the history nor by the experience of people like Adeyemi. Yorùbá kinship was bilateral, in that children could claim both their mother's and father's families and often identified with one more than the other, depending on many factors. Even in the historical reconstruction of this period, the role of the mother's family or mother's town is often alluded to in explaining historical events, suggesting that the society took matrilineal ties seriously. However, with the advent of Western education and Christian and Islamic influence on the organization of families, patrilineality was propagated and naturalized as the most important principle of Yorùbá kinship system, discounting age-old practices in which many identified with and joined the mother's family. The new practice of having surnames and taking the father's name as the family name pioneered by the missionaries, the colonial establishment, and the newly Christianized akòwé families institutionalized the patrilineal principle in concrete terms.[17]

To return to the question at hand, author Adeyemi, whose father was a prince of Ọ̀yọ́ and whose mother was the daughter of a high chief of Ondo, had grown up in his mother's family compound in Ondo, and did not know enough about Ọ̀yọ́ to write its history with any sense of authority. Falola believed that Adeyemi was probably more interested in the affairs of Ondo, his mother's town and the place where he grew up. Falola's conclusion is essentially correct that the reason that his history of Ọ̀yọ́ was so "meager" was Adeyemi's disinterest in, lack of familiarity with, and nonidentification with the town. The fact that he wrote other books and did not give up writing as a whole reinforces this line of thinking.[18]

Ironically, despite his closeness to his mother's family and the benefits that accrued to him as a result, Adeyemi decried the Ọ̀yọ́ tradition that recognized children of both male princes and female princes[19] as having equal rights to the throne. Thus, in his book, Adeyemi declared Alaafin Abiodun,[20] whom other historians had portrayed as one of the most accomplished monarchs of Ọ̀yọ́, to be an illegitimate ruler, saying, "He was not at all qualified because, his link with the royal lineage was through the female line: he was the son of a princess."[21] In spite of Adeyemi's life experiences, then, his patricentric ideology and sensibilities were no different from those of his fraternity, the club of akòwé.

Akòwé pioneered the documentation of Yorùbá history and culture and in various ways and to varying degrees wrote male dominance and female exclusion into stories of origin, historical events, language, the identity and functions of the Gods, and the nature of social institutions. Their patriarchal sensibilities on historical knowledge, who the custodians of oral traditions are, how history is passed on, and who should be writing are apparent in the following statement by Samuel Johnson, easily the dean of akòwé, who lived and worked a generation before the Egbé was formed.[22] Writing in the third person about his pioneering role in historical documentation and his aspiration for the endeavor, he hoped to stimulate among his more favored brethren the spirit of patriotism and enquiry into the histories of the less-known parts of the country. It may be that oral records are preserved in them, which are handed down from father to son.[23]

The *Ẹgbé* seemed to have taken this father-to-son relay-race type of passing on of "history" too literally, as we saw in the case of Adeyemi and his history of Ọ̀yọ́. The counterevidence right before their eyes—but apparently never seen—that inheritance passed from mother to children could not shake this misguided conviction. The exclusive language of men as the custodians of intellect and history dies very hard. J. A Atanda, historian of New Ọ̀yọ́ writing as recently as 1993 on "the intellectual life of Yorùbá people," writes:

> The society expected respectable people to have a sense of history. To learn and know the history of one's family, lineage, town or nation was therefore to be taken as civic duty. This point is embedded in one of the people's numerous proverbs and witty sayings, "'Bi omo ko mo itan yio ba awigbo." That is "Even if a young man does not know [(the whole) history [i.e., of his family or lineage, etc.] he must know the smatterings of it."[24]

What Atanda does here is to translate the gender-neutral Yorùbá word *omo* into a gender-specific English "young man" a problem that is rife in the translation of Yorùbá into English as I have repeatedly shown.[25] In so doing he abrogates the time-tested role and participation of females, most notably *Ìyá*, in passing down lineage history and family traditions especially through *oríkì*.[26]

It was not only in the beliefs and social practices of the first generations of Yorùbá local historians that male privilege and female exclusion were on stark display and being put in place. The imagination of creative writers was also a fertile ground for male aggrandizement and disparagement of women. In his seminal novel *Ogboju òde ninu igbo irunmale* (The brave hunter in the forest of thousand deities) written in Yorùbá, pioneering novelist D. O. Fagunwa is very attentive to the transition from an oral culture to literacy. He lauds literacy as progress and considers it an index of modernity. Thus in this novel, Fagunwa created a scribe—an *akòwé*, if you will—who became the vehicle for transmitting history in written form. This modern historian would surmount the past situation in which "many of the significant stories our grandfathers knew are now completely lost because they did not write those stories down."[27] But in the charmed circle of these writers, these makers of Yorùbá modernity, Fagunwa had no place for mothers and grandmothers who had important stories to tell. Literate or not, *Ìyá* were known as knowers and knowledge-makers in the culture as I showed in the previous chapter. But Fagunwa, the novelist, took *Ìyá* out of their place in the realm of knowledge and he did not include them among members of his audience whom he called *òmòràn*—knowers. In that generation, *òmòràn* is easily a synonym for *akòwé* because those who had Western education were considered knowledgeable. Wole Soyinka in his translation of the novel *Ogboju* into English had correctly translated the word *òmòràn* as "men of discerning" despite the fact that this word, like *akòwé*, is gender neutral.[28] Literary critic Olakunle George noted that *Ogboju* is oriented toward a male audience, since "the implied reader is textualized within a masculinist frame."[29] Because of the popularity and wide influence of this novel, the image of the *akòwé* as a man may have been sealed in the minds of generations of Yorùbá due to Fagunwa's depiction of the scribe and his audience. *Ogboju* became a standard textbook for the education of generations of school children.

This modern exclusion of females is more a product of androcentric representation by male *akòwé* than a reality embedded in Yorùbá culture and social practice. There were educated Yorùbá women in the historical record, though they were not perceived to be *akòwé*. The nucleus of what became the early generations of Yorùbá intelligentsia was made up of recaptives[30] and their children who returned to Yorùbáland from Sierra Leone. Among the ranks of the Saro, as they were called, were literate females. They were concentrated in Lagos and Abeokuta, although a few did settle in Ibadan. A study of marriage among the literate elite in late-nineteenth-century colonial Lagos gives us an idea of the gender composition of the group:

> Elite women were not as educated as the elite men. None received professional or university training between 1880 and 1915. Even so, all elite women had attended primary school, many had gone to secondary school in Freetown, Abeokuta or Lagos, and some had completed their education with a few years at an English girls' school.[31]

In fact, many of the male *akòwé*, especially missionaries, were married to literate women.[32] These learned women were seen as *aya akòwé* (wives of literate men), but were not defined as *akòwé* in their own right. The reason the label *akòwé* could not stick to educated women, no matter how much reading and writing they did, was that it was not extended to them as an honorific, title, or term of respect. For literate Yorùbá women, relatively speaking their education did not give them access to publicly recognized and formal roles in the missions (which saw them simply as helpmates of their husbands) and none at all in the colonial administration, because initially it had no room for female employment. In his book *Isara: A Voyage around Essay*, a tribute to his father's life and times and his cohort of pioneer

literate Yorùbá men of a small town, Nobel Laureate Wole Soyinka translates the word akòwé as "white collar workers."[33] This meaning is right on
the mark because it suggests that literacy may be a necessary but not suffi-
cient requirement to belong to that class; one must be gainfully employed in
a white-collar job. Such a reading also begins to answer the question of why
the word is narrowly used for male literates because until much later in the
colonial period, women were excluded from white-collar occupations. In
the following quotation, Soyinka's description of who akòwé were and their
attitude to the general population as they boarded the newly introduced
trains is indicative of some of the issues that are of concern in this chapter:

> The akòwé clans, complete with Madam and children and portmanteaus, all
> probably on transfer; the coat and tie, the occasional trilby hat or bowler, the
> arrogant condescending glances at the spluttering, squalling mass of "other"
> humanity.[34]

Here, it is obvious that only the man merits the name akòwé; his wife who
was also literate invited the appellation madam, which is actually a term
usually used to refer to literate women. She was more likely to be wearing
a Western-type dress than the indigenous wrapper, a garb that at the time,
distinguished her as a member of an elite group. As Adéèkó has pointed out,
Western-educated women were also known as onikaba—frock wearers—as
opposed to aroso—nonliterate, wrapper-wearing women.[35] It interesting to
note the gender nuances of the fact that literate men, akòwé, were known
for their accomplishments (literacy, writing) but literate women, onikaba,
were recognized merely by their appearance—dress.

My concern is not so much about literacy in general but more specifically the gender composition of those who pioneered historical writing. Among akòwé, there were very few females who actually wrote books.
There was undoubtedly a disparity in the educational level of literate males
and females. But this gender difference does not explain why females were
not recognized as akòwé, or more importantly, their near total absence
among indigenous documenters of history. Most of the accomplished early
chroniclers of Yorùbá history did not have more than a high school education; many had attended only primary school. In fact, in the early days, men
who had received a university education, notably in Lagos, seemed to have
gone into the professions of medicine and the law rather than authoring
books. The experience of the two brothers, Samuel and Obadiah Johnson
is instructive. Samuel Johnson, the historian who had written The History
of the Yorùbás, an accomplished and enduring book, had no more than the
equivalent of a high school education. Obadiah, his brother, had studied
medicine in England, but unlike Samuel, never set out to be a writer.[36] It is

interesting to note that M. C. Adeyemi, who had a college education, produced a less accomplished book than I. B. Akinyele, whose education concluded in high school.[37] The question, then, is, given that lack of a college
degree did not stop most of the male *akòwé* from writing books, why were
there so few women among the early Yorùbá intelligentsia?

In my book *The Invention of Women*, I exposed the huge incentive that
male wage employment represented in the decision by parents to prioritize
their sons' education over that of daughters.[38] Similarly, I would argue that
the lack of employment opportunities for literate women in the Christian
missions as well as in the various agencies of the colonial administration had
a significant effect on whether females were seen as *akòwé*, and indeed on
their ability to become authors. Being employed in the wage sector, apart
from providing a salary and opportunity to acquire experience, also gives
confidence in other areas of life. One cannot underestimate the degree to
which the customs clerk's uniforms discussed earlier boosted the self-esteem
of the men who were so employed, among other benefits. In addition, the
example of the *Ẹgbẹ́* suggests that there was no organizational infrastructure
or support that would encourage women to write, even if they had been
motivated to do so.

Writing is one thing, but publishing is a higher-stake enterprise: writers needed financial support in order to disseminate their work. Some
male writers received financial support for their writing.[39] The Church
Missionary Society (CMS) mission also played a dominant role in choosing who got published as the organization was involved in publishing both
in the colony and in England. Because CMS was a Christian mission that
defined African women as appendages of men, it is difficult to see how it
could have been an ally of a would-be female author. Henry Townsend, who
had founded the Yorùbá Mission, established a printing press at Abeokuta
to teach industrial skills and print the country's first newspaper, *Iwe Irohin*.
They subsequently established the CMS Bookshop, which published and
sold books.[40] Yet, publishing remained an uphill task. Falola discusses the
obstacles many writers faced in getting their works printed: "there are many
unpublished manuscripts simply because of the difficulty of obtaining the
resources to print."[41] I wonder how many of these unpublished manuscripts
were authored by female *akòwé*.

Writing Woman: Kemi Morgan Makes History

Academic historian Falola made the claim that among the early indigenous
Yorùbá chroniclers, as one important genre of writing, "thus far, it is only
one woman, Kemi Morgan, who has distinguished herself," that is, among
a hundred or so books and booklets that we are aware of today.[42] Falola's

phrasing—"distinguish herself"—decidedly puts the onus on the individual writer and does not seem to be aware of structural constraints that
females especially may have faced, thus giving the impression that women as
a group lacked the ability to achieve in this realm. What does the experience
of Kemi Morgan, the only "female chronicler of note and distinction,"[43] tell
us about the effects of gender division on indigenous writing during this
period? Does her experience inform us about other equally important factors that may have been at play at this time? For a start, it is important to
note that a distinguished woman local historian did not emerge until at
least half a century (1970s) after the first chronicles (1911) of Yorùbá history.[44] Even more telling is the fact that this book, titled *Akinyele's Outline
History of Ibadan*, credited to Kemi Morgan in the revised and enlarged edition (n.d.), was initially designated a "rewrite" of the first book on Ibadan
written by her uncle Chief I. B Akinyele. As Morgan herself acknowledged,
she did not set out to write a book of her own, but "intended to re-write
the old man's book."[45] In this regard, then, Morgan was no intrepid female
pioneer who set out to document the unwritten history of her ancestors, as
many of the male writers had done. Morgan may not have been personally
a member of the Old Boy's Network, but because of her pedigree, all the
resources and more of the distinguished *akòwé* and leader of the *Egbé*, I. B.
Akinyele, her uncle, had been put at her disposal. By the time she wrote,
the *Egbé* was defunct.

The original Akinyele book was written in Yorùbá and first published
in 1911, with a couple of subsequent revisions. However, because of the
pioneering nature of the work, the colonial government sought to use it as
a history text in schools. Consequently, Akinyele desired to have it translated
into English. The author himself made an attempt at translation, and in the
1940s, issued an English edition titled *Outlines of Ibadan History*. But he was
not satisfied with the quality of the English translation and promised to do
an update, a task that proved impossible for him as he became successful in
politics and took on leadership roles in the city administration. Akinyele
became *Olubadan*, the paramount ruler of Ibadan in 1955. Kemi Morgan,
the daughter of his brother Bishop Akinyele, came to the rescue and agreed
to update the English translation. She was in a very strong position to do
the job because she was highly educated: having spent many years studying
in England, she returned to Ibadan and taught English in a high school.[46]
Given the reality of female disadvantage in education and literacy, it was,
ironically Morgan's education and high competence in the English language that recommended her for the job of carrying forward her family's
legacy. As a member of the distinguished Akinyele family, as a daughter of
akòwé, an elite lineage both in the traditional and the modern sense, Morgan
reaped benefits and faced few constraints as a woman in this very specific

arena once her parents had ensured that she got a first-class education. In her own words: "I have been very, very fortunate. I can tell you that I was born among books and from very early age I had learnt to read…and again my father was a great historian may be you don't know that it was my grandfather who was one of the sources of Samuel Johnson."[47]

What motivated Morgan, and what did she achieve in this endeavor? Although she had called her book a rewrite, historian Falola, after a comparative study of the original by Akinyele, and the "revised and enlarged" edition by Morgan, came to the conclusion that she had effectively produced a new work. Essentially, she produced three volumes of what is a new work, which went above and beyond what her uncle Akinyele had written. In Falola's assessment:

> Morgan adds several new topics, expands information in Akinyele's, limits herself to the nineteenth century, and deals with causation. The differences in the work are due to a number of reasons: Akinyele was not alive to be able to influence the content of Morgan's work or to insist that she limit herself to translating his work; Morgan broadened the resource-base with evidence from oral evidence and several books.[48]

With this output of three volumes of Ibadan history, Morgan became a pioneer local historian in her own right, Falola asserts, because "by using one indigenous chronicle to write another, she has provided a unique example of African historiography."[49]

Falola's statement that Morgan is the only female writer among local historians must be qualified, first in the light of the many unpublished manuscripts whose authors remain anonymous, and second, given our discussion of the special obstacles female akòwé faced. Nevertheless, because Morgan is the only recognized female chronicler, the lone female author in the pantheon of local historians recognized by the establishment, it is pertinent to interrogate the discernible effects of gender in her biography and in the content of her work. The first thing to note is her name. Kemi Morgan was originally Kemi Akinyele, but changed her name after she married, in keeping with the new tradition that developed among the Western-educated based on the colonial marriage ordinance and Christian values they adopted. This rechristening of married women was an unfortunate development that robbed women of their immediate identification with their natal family. Our female akòwé had married Adeyinka Morgan, a lawyer who later became the chief justice of the region.[50] It is curious that despite the fact that Morgan was building on her family legacy as an Akinyele, there is no reference in the books about her motives for writing, or her ties to the Akinyele family.[51] Such information only became available

as a result of interviews in which she responded to questions posed by
Falola many years after the publication of her three volumes. One wonders
why she was reticent to mention the familial relationship in the book, especially since it was the basis of her access to this genre of writing. Did she see
her uncle as the author and herself as a mere translator? I think not, since
in the interview, she was quick to recognize herself as the writer, the author
who put her own name on the cover. Conversely, perhaps she preferred not
to allude to her family connection so as to emphasize her independence
and thus her identity as an author in her own right, although with the name
Akinyele in the title, there was no way she could have decoupled the books.
But her initial apparent reticence to claim her place in the Akinyele lineage
contrasts with her pronouncements when she was interviewed several years
after the publication of the volumes. She proudly stated, "I am part of this
history I relate. For there dwells within me a portion of the group soul of
Ibadan. For through my veins runs the blood of my sires, of Osun, Tubosun,
Bolude and Kukomi, before whose fearsome presence even he that carried
firearms would flee in terror."[52] Her language here is robustly masculinist; the choice of the word "sire" contrasts sharply with the ways in which
Yorùbá traditionally articulated procreation as more of a matricentric affair,
a fact that I discuss at length in the last chapter.

Morgan's values and sensibilities, like those of other members of the
Westernized Yorùbá elite, were shaped by the patriarchy embedded in their
English education and the faith-based female subordination of doctrinal
Christianity and the Church. Falola draws our attention to this crucial
aspect of Morgan's background when he writes:

> Both Akinyele and Morgan are Christians and educated, a circumstance that
> shows up in two ways in their books. First they are more interested in the his-
> tory of Christianity than Islam. Kemi Morgan is not just a Christian but daugh-
> ter of an Anglican priest. Chief Akinyele was no ordinary Christian either: he
> belonged to a family that was one of the earliest to be converted.[53]

The implication of this was that they must have seen themselves and family
organizations as models of Christianity. It is only against this background
that we can assess Morgan's reaction to the loss of her profession, which
she suffered when her husband Adeyinka Morgan became a judge and subsequently the chief justice of the Western region. In 1958, Mr. Morgan
was appointed a judge, and this spelled the end of Mrs. Morgan's career
as a teacher, not only because she had to follow him to his frequent post-
ings throughout the region but also because of the government regulatory
convention that insist that a judge's wife must not work outside the home
because of a possible conflict of interest. This practice effectively put an end

to Morgan's professional career.[54] The stipulation that prevented wives of judges from pursuing their own vocation is patently gender-discriminative and put paid to the career ambitions of elite women—female *akòwé*. It is no wonder, then, that such women in the first instance were regarded as helpmates and appendages of their husbands and could not be *akòwé* in their own right. In *Invention*, I pointed out the huge disadvantages for women of the newfangled nuclear family ideologies, and laws that portrayed men as the breadwinners (even when they were unemployed) and as heads of families, and women as appendages.[55] Morgan's experience underscored the cost of the convention for elite women most especially, and for families as a whole.

However, the most startling claim attributed to Morgan in an interview conducted by Falola is this:"She did not regret this early termination of her career, because it provided her with the opportunity to travel,'to reach the people, talk to them, and understand their custom.'This also was the time when she did a great deal of reading and writing."[56] Falola did not question her further in this regard, neither did he offer his own interpretation of her claim. Taking this statement at face value, Morgan did not see the loss of her profession as a negative; if anything, she wants us to believe that it was an advantage that yielded what I would call oxymoronically a "patriarchal div-idend," of which her writing was a part. From a humanist perspective that insists on the right of women to be their own persons, making their own life choices, Morgan's statement is disingenuous, since the rule forced her to stop practicing her chosen profession. From a Yorùbá perspective, Morgan was putting herself in a risky position in her marriage based on the belief that it was a monogamous one in which the couple had a joint purse. The fact that in the traditional Yorùbá marriage system, wives are expected to be financially capable and independent and that polygamy is legal and part of the social norm did not seem to have affected her perspective. Apart from the fact that the larger family made claims on the income and resources of their sons—the so-called nuclear husbands—experience showed that men could and many did take other wives both formally and informally, often rendering the "nuclear wife" destitute if she did not have her own income.[57] It was this consciousness that motivated women and informed the splitting of families that developed with male wage labor during this period. Many women followed their husbands, but some were not so eager to abandon their own vocations and move around with itinerant husbands working in the civil service or various corporations. We have to commend Morgan for creating a productive path out of her deprofessionalization by becoming a distinguished writer of both history and fiction. Morgan seemed to have turned the proverbial lemons into abundant lemonade, so to speak. It is wonderful that Morgan turned out to be a talented writer, a fact that made it possible to pursue her interest even as an amateur. If she had been a professional historian or an academic writer who required employment by, and legitimation of, an institution, there is no way she could have seen any silver lining in a rule that spelt the demise of her vocation.

Finally, on the question of gender and custodians of historical knowledge, many of the local historians and even subsequent professional historians tended to discount women as historical subjects and sources. In the early stages of writing indigenous histories, a time during which many *akòwé* relied largely on oral traditions, they did not seem to have considered women as sources of knowledge. None mentioned female informants among their sources. Even Samuel Johnson, who had relied on the *Arokin*, the male court bards, for a history of Ọ̀yọ́, seemed to have bypassed the *Akunyungba*—female court poets—whose variety of royal poetry seemed to have resisted "external influences" better than that of the male bards and have thus "remained a reliable source of material for oral historical reconstruction."[58] In the preface to his book *Yorùbá Royal Poetry*, Akintunde Akinyemi noted the male bias in the construction of history:

> Scholars of Yorùbá history have repeatedly consulted male court bards in order to recover historical information; unfortunately most of them have concentrated on materials on historical oral narratives (*itan*) which are supplied exclusively by male bards...Although, previous works make no direct reference to the relationship between gender and history, yet it was assumed that historical skills are assigned to men alone.[59]

Local historian Morgan was different on this count; she did not believe that only men could be historical subjects or had historical information and skills. She recognized women as historical actors and cited her mother in glowing terms as one of the knowledgeable informants she consulted in the writing of her books:

> My mother coming from Abeokuta also she belonged to Okeila section of Egba, who were the real actors and actresses of Egbaland. She knew everything about Egba history and she knew about Oyo because she went to school at Oyo with her uncle the late Rev. Sowande who was posted to St. Andrews College, Oyo.[60]

Here we see that Morgan's mother herself had been an *akòwé*—she had attended school and was literate. Significantly, both mother and daughter took a deep interest in history, and one wonders why the mother did not join the first generation of local historians in authoring a book of history, about which she was certainly well informed. Besides her own talents and limitations, the answer can be sought in the arguments I have made so far in this chapter about the many layers of exclusion from the world of letters that women faced. We had to wait for her daughter, Kemi Morgan, to break the mold. With the revelation of who her mother was, we have a more rounded biography of Morgan, whose interests and talents derived not only from her Akinyele pedigree but also from her matrilineal heritage. It is no wonder, then, that this female *akòwé*, this author, more than some of the much-lauded males, was prolific, writing with distinction not only as a historian but also as a creative writer.

Having examined the male *akòwé* as a group in the analysis of the Ẹgbẹ́, and pinpointing the experience of a female local historian, in the next section I spotlight Samuel Johnson as the original *akòwé*, whose book one cannot escape in any discussion of Yorùbá history and culture. In the following section, Johnson's work and Falola's representation of it, and of the man himself, invite scrutiny in our quest to understand the impact of gender on the construction of knowledge.

Writing Patriarch? Samuel Johnson

Samuel Johnson, the most influential Yorùbá writer of all time, was the archetypal *akòwé*, the pioneering nonacademic historian who wrote the monumental *History of the Yorùbás*. Since the book was published in 1921, no one writing about any aspect of the history or culture can avoid the tome. As historian Falola puts it, "In many ways, most academic works published on the Yorùbá since the 1950s have merely elaborated on the themes suggested by Johnson in *History of the Yorùbás*."[61] Beyond academics, even more significant is the fact that because Johnson is widely read among ordinary Yorùbá people, his work has been reabsorbed into the oral traditions in a feedback process, so much so that the book is often called upon to settle chieftaincy and other kinds of disputes.

From the early pages of the book, we have no doubt about Johnson's male-centered worldview. The Author's Preface to the book states that it was written so "that the history of our fatherland might not be lost in oblivion, especially as our old sires are fast dying out."[62] In my book *Invention*, I exposed the role of the reverend in creating a tradition of male-dominant history in Yorùbá discourses. I focused on the process by which he created a male-exclusive "kingship" in Old Ọ̀yọ́ from a nongender-specific list of *Ọba* (rulers) who are said to have ruled the polity from the beginning until the nineteenth century, when we begin to have some written sources. I showed that the male identity that he attributed to all but one of the rulers on his "king list" was not supported by evidence. I noted that because historically there were female rulers, and most importantly, because Yorùbá names are not gender-specific, as Johnson himself was well aware, then his claim that all but one of the monarchs on the ruler's list was a man is based on an unfounded assumption of male privilege, given that until the most recent period with confirmation by an eyewitness, there was no way of telling which *alaafin* was anamale or anafemale. I concluded that his presumptions about succession as occurring from father-to-son only, his claim that iden-tifiable anafemale monarchs were merely reigning as regents, and his general belief and representation of a patriarchal societal ethos were not supported by the evidence even in his own text.[63]

Here, I reexamine Johnson in the light of his representation as a "patri-arch" by the contemporary historian Falola. There is no doubt that Johnson wrote from a male-centered standpoint, but the question that concerns me here is this: Was he a patriarch in his family organization and life experience? I am using "patriarch" in the very specific sense of family organization in which the man is the breadwinner, the provider who also wielded author-ity as the head of the unit. Examining this question is especially significant given the traditional autonomy of Yorùbá women and their enduring role as coproviders for their families, a fact that is ignored when the Yorùbá man is named patriarch. In Western feminist discourse "patriarch" has acquired a negative connotation and is often used as an epithet. But the positive meaning attached to the word endures in the mainstream establishment in Nigeria, where the word is used as a term of honor, and an index of male accomplishment. It must have been this Nigerian context that informed Falola's naming of Johnson as patriarch. Using the word "patriarchy" in this way reduces wives and mothers to dependents, appendages, and wards of men in a culture in which such a definition of women's roles bears no resemblance to reality.

Johnson's orientation was clearly marked by his Christianity, his Western education, and an English culture, which he saw as civilized, and one that Yorùbá should emulate and adopt as the model for the transformation of their war-ravaged homeland. Granted, Johnson was also a patriot, a cul-tural nationalist who was proud of Yorùbá achievement and potential for reclaiming what he saw as lost glory. But his sensibility was deeply Victorian and male-privileging on the question of gender. We see this clearly in the way in which he introduced himself in a piece he wrote when he was being ordained as a pastor in the Anglican Church. It began, "I am the third son of my father."[64] This statement cannot be translated into Yorùbá. In the con-text of the society, it is nonsensical because in the language (even today), no one can *initiate* a conversation with *"nínú àwọn ọmọ ọkùnrin tí bàbá mi bí, èmi ni mo ṣ'ìkẹta"* (among my father's male children, I am the third one— my translation). In Yorùbá language such a statement cannot open a discus-sion or introduce a person in the manner in which Johnson did in English. In Yorùbá, if one were to make such a statement, it must be in response to a question that specifically asks how many male children your father has, because there are no single words for son or daughter in the language except the descriptive *omo ọkùnrin* (child male) or *omo obìnrin* (child female). Despite the fact that Johnson had five other siblings, Samuel saw himself only in relation to his older brothers. Johnson had four sisters, but he did not seem to reckon with them, at least in this context. His focus on the category "son" may be seen as predictable and normal in Western society, in which son is a kinship type with higher social status than daughter, and which until very recently spelt total access to a whole range of privileges in a male-dominant society. But in Yorùbá language there was no single word that made a distinction between anamale and anafemale children, a sign of the culture's rejection of body-based categories. Besides language, we also know that in Old Ọyọ́ society from which the language derived, anamales were not privileged over anafemales in matters of succession or inheritance, as evidenced by the fact that there were anafemale rulers. Johnson himself writes of an anafemale first-born of an *alaafin* "who considered the rights and privileges of the *Aremo* (crown Prince) her own."[65] But we have already seen that Johnson sets enormous store on sons, maleness, and masculinity in general. Since Johnson's statement "I am the third son of my father" was not prompted by a question about his father's male children, we can only conclude that his sensibility was thoroughly anglicized, which meant that on the question of gender, male-centered language and practices were the order of the day.[66] Johnson clearly subscribed to patriarchy in the sense that he was androcentric and females in all their guises were often invisible to him. But was he a patriarch?

An anthology on Samuel Johnson edited by Falola is titled *Pioneer, Patriot and Patriarch*. Granted, the title of the book is nicely alliterative, but I was intrigued by the word "patriarch" in the title and wondered in what way Johnson could be defined as such. Today, apart from leaders of religious orders, the most immediate arena in which the meaning of the word "patri-arch" is to be sought is in family life. Thus a patriarch is the male head of a family, a headship that rests on the assumption that he is the provider who rules the roost, and represents the unit to the outside world. Consequently, I thought that the best place to understand Falola's characterization of Johnson as patriarch was to look at his family life and domestic organiza-tion. Johnson was not open and wrote very little about his family life, but with the publication of his biography by Michel Doortmont, we are able to catch a few more glimpses of his private life.

Doortmont considered Johnson's extreme restraint in providing any details about his wives (he married twice, consecutively) or children odd, especially as he readily provided information on everyday events that did not have to do with the church.[67] I agree with Doortmont's assessment on this matter. Consider, for example, the fact that in Johnson's journal entries, he never mentioned the name of his wife, or his feelings about the marriage itself, not even on the day that he married his first wife. Here is how he described that august occasion: "Today I was coupled. May she truly prove an help meet [sic]. May we both be enabled to adorn [sic] our profession by our example, and also be enabled as long as life permits to labor in the vineyard."[68] Similarly, very little is known about Johnson's children, their birth dates, names, or how he felt about them. In his diary, he divulged the name of only one of his children, a son Geoffrey Emmanuel, who died as an infant. This was one of the rare occasions on which he expressed any personal feelings. Johnson's reticence about family relationships suggests that at the very least he derived little of his sense of self from his identity as husband and father.

Despite the masculinist orientation of his writings, his personal life does not show that he presided over a patriarchal family, at least not structurally. For instance, we know that Johnson lost his first wife, and was a widower for about eight years. During this period, his three daughters went to live with their maternal grandparents. In 1895 he married again, this time to Martha Garber, a teacher at CMS Girls' Seminary in Lagos. Following his death in 1901, the Church Financial Committee was interested in his estate because he allegedly had left a debt unpaid. They discovered that there was no money in his estate, and his wife claimed that "her husband never gave her any money. She even had to trade to get something for herself."[69] Taken at face value, Mrs. Johnson's statement suggests that the Western idea of a patriarch who was a provider and thus the head of the family did not apply to Johnson. In this regard, his family was typically Yorùbá, in that mothers were equally breadwinners and often provided more than fathers for the upkeep of themselves and children. Trade was the default occupation of the majority of Yorùbá women; in this regard Mrs. Johnson's experience was part of the norm.

Consequently, given Martha Johnson's statement, one must ask, in what way then was Johnson a patriarch, as Falola described him. I put this question to Falola, and he replied in an email, which is reproduced below

> In all the sense of it, he was a "patriarch," and I actually coined it to refer to his historic role as a "founder" of a genre…which others used and [were] forced to respond to; as a senior and the most venerable in the genealogy of non-academic historians; and for occupying an unquestionable commanding leadership in historical interpretation that has shaped subsequent narratives. Johnson virtually selected all the themes that academic historians were to follow. No one has emerged, over a hundred years later, to even move close to him in stature. His narrative is muscular, without an apology.

No one can disagree that Johnson was indeed a pioneer and founder of Yorùbá historical writing. Describing him as a patriarch,[70] however, shifts our attention to his nonpublic life. As we have seen, the term is inaccurate given his family life as we have come to know it.

Equally problematic is Falola's statement that Johnson's "narrative is muscular, without an apology," a statement that seem to reference a gender ideology. The local historian's androcentric orientation was not something he himself was aware of, because among the Western-educated classes in both his time and ours, male privilege is the "civilized" way of being, and the social norm. Thus the question of an apology did not arise for Johnson, because he did not think that he was contravening any rules. His alleged muscularity on the gender issue then is more fiction than fact.

The idea of the muscularity of Johnson's narrative may have a place, in the ways in which his writing projected Ọ̀yọ́ as the dominant Yorùbá state historically, subordinating other polities and subgroups to the "mighty" Ọ̀yọ́. But even then, it is not muscularity in the forcefulness with which he projected these ideas but in his insistence and consistency in promoting Old Ọ̀yọ́ as the center of the Yorùbá universe and the alaafin as "king of the Yorùbás." Certainly, the critique that Johnson's Yorùbá history is Ọ̀yọ́-centric has dogged his work ever since his brother Obadiah gave a lecture based on the book in Lagos in 1901. On this count, he was definitely a "son of Ọ̀yọ́," and his untiring promotion of the polity cannot be gainsaid. But the irony surrounding Johnson's close ties to Ọ̀yọ́ are that his relationship to the town is through his great grandmother; his father was born in Ilorin.[71] Johnson, like Adeyemi, whom we discussed earlier, identified closely with his matricentric ties. If we had applied the rules of the Ibadan Egbé, Johnson had no business writing about Ọ̀yọ́. He should have focused on Ilorin, his father's town of origin.[72]

But Falola's portrayal of Johnson as patriarch seems to extend beyond his writing to his personality. In addition to the academic historian's inventive description of the pioneer local historian as patriarch, he also offered some lines of oríkì (praise poetry) that he himself composed for Johnson.

Àyìnlá Ògún,
Ọkùnrin Kà, Ọkùnrin Kò,
Ọkùnrin kà kà kó kó.
Àǹ leé bọ
Ó ńlé ará wájú
Ayinla Ogun[73]
Man who does ka, man who does ko
Man who does ka ka ko ko
We are running after him
He is running after those who are ahead. (My translation)

Falola explained that the onomatopoeic "*ka ka ko ko* is militia," and it is meant to depict the subject "walking greatly like a horse (ready to charge!)." I appreciate very much Falola's creativity in this *oríkì* and his own admiration of Johnson in penning this òde to him. But who or what is Johnson charging at? It is strange that Johnson, who was known for his intellectual achievement, whose much-lauded accomplishments are in the field of writing and diplomacy, would now be represented as if he is one of those nineteenth-century Ibadan warlords about whom Falola and others have written.[74] Falola's depiction of Johnson is radically different from the way in which he appeared in contemporary accounts. Outside of Falola's characterization of the man, Johnson was described as "shy, reticent," and self-effacing, in sharp contrast to the professional historian's characterization of him as muscular, language that suggests forcefulness and chest thumping. In fact, Johnson's obituary in the *Lagos Weekly Record* in 1901 described him as "distinguished for his devotion to duty, well-known for his liberality and open-heartedness and for urbanity, self abnegation and patriotism."[75] Commenting on the fact that Johnson wrote very little or nothing about himself or family, eminent historian Jacob Ade Ajayi noted that he was "shy and reticent, he deliberately chooses to remain shadowy in the background."[76]

The description of Johnson's narrative as "muscular, without an apology" suggests rigidity, coldness, and an unyielding forcefulness. It also insinuates that Johnson must have been engaged in a heated debate, at the very least, in a contentious issue of the time. I have already drawn attention to the controversy that attended what was thought to be his advancement of Ọ̀yọ́ over other Yorùbá polities. But this debate did not involve Johnson directly, because the book was not published, and therefore his ideas on this issue were not well known until after his death. It was his brother Obadiah who bore the brunt of this contention when he presented a lecture based on *The History* to the Lagos intelligentsia in 1901. We have no evidence of unapologetic muscularity on the part of Johnson. In reality, he seemed to have shied away or failed to engage with an even more contentious issue, one that required activism and forceful advocacy: the fight against racialization and racial discrimination, which had become the policy of the colonial government in Lagos by the turn of the nineteenth century. Many members of the Yorùbá elite, including his two brothers Henry and Obadiah, were involved in challenging and resisting the racism of the colonial government.[77] Obadiah, a medical doctor, had personally experienced racial discrimination when he was bypassed for promotion and the position was given to a white man who was junior in rank to him in the colonial service.[78] Indeed, one of the most curious things about Johnson is that he did not seem to have been aware of racism, and seemed not to have paid attention to Obadiah's difficulties. Perhaps his personality caused him to shy away from conflict.

We are able to tease out more information about Johnson's personality in the debate over who was the real author of *History of Yorùbás* given its storied emergence: was it Johnson, who set out to write the original book, or his brother, Obadiah, who had midwifed its publication after Johnson's death? Falola made a forceful claim that the sole author of the book is the reverend based on the following reasoning:

> Given the hostility of Obadiah to the colonial government because of his own experience of racism—a book by him would have been far more angry in tone, perhaps condemnatory of the British, or probably reflecting his own experience of race relations. *The History of the Yorùbá* is a calm book, sympathetic to British rule and devoid of racial tension, all characteristics far more consistent with the experience and feelings of Samuel than of Obadiah.[79]

This assessment of authorship is very much in line with Obadiah's declaration that his own role was ancillary. How then do we reconcile Falola's claim that the book is "calm," a statement on the personality of the author, with his later representation of Johnson as a "charging horse" who created an unapologetically muscular narrative? On this question, consider Ajayi's own summation of the debate on authorship and the different personalities of the two brothers: "the tone in *The History* is more of the 'gentle' Samuel than of the impatient Obadiah."[80]

Beyond Johnson's writings, we must also pay attention to his conduct as we try to unravel questions about his personality. His failure to challenge white supremacy and the attendant racial discrimination, inarguably the most important issues of the time, does not lend any support to the idea that he was an assertive man, eager to articulate his ideas forcefully and unapologetically. Instead, Johnson seemed to have been missing in action on this important question. Falola is of the opinion that Johnson may not have perceived racism and did not see things as the Lagos elite did, given that he was based in the hinterland.[81] But the pioneering local historian was very much connected to Lagos society through his brothers and sisters.[82] Because his younger brother Obadiah, to whom he was very close, suffered racial discrimination and organized against it, I do not subscribe to Falola's attribution of Johnson's silence on this issue to ignorance. The question remains why Johnson chose not to see racism or why he perceived things differently than many of his contemporaries, including his two brothers.

The answer to Johnson's behavior may lie in his closeness to his white employers in the CMS mission and his single-minded focus on his writing, a mission that he saw as his supremely important work of documenting

Yorùbá history, a responsibility that could have been derailed by involvement in antiracist activities.[83] His failure to engage with, arguably, the most important question of his day, then, was most likely a pragmatic move on his part. But in terms of his personal characteristics, what this inaction shows is not his muscularity but his diffidence. I concur with Phillip Zachernuk when he noted that "Johnson could not have been ignorant of the racist sentiments permeating the Church Missionary Society (CMS) in the 1880s, which culminated in the attack on Bishop Crowther, sentiments symptomatic of a much wider trend."[84]

Johnson's phlegmatic reaction to European racism was extremely naïve, especially because that same racism cost him his life's work when the handwritten, sole copy of the manuscript on which he had labored for 20 years was lost in England by a "well-known English publisher through one of the great Missionary Societies in 1899."[85] The disastrous event was rectified only by the admirable assiduousness of his brother, Obadiah, who labored mightily to reproduce the manuscript and finally brought it to publication. Obadiah displays a well-founded skepticism in his interaction with the English when he relays the story of the loss of the original manuscript:

> The editor [Obadiah] had the occasion to visit England in 1900, and called on the publisher, but could get nothing more from him than that the manuscripts had been misplaced, that they could not be found, and that he was prepared to pay for them! This seemed to the editor and all his friends who heard of it so strange that one could not help thinking there was more to it than appeared on the surface because of other circumstances connected to the so-called loss of the manuscripts.[86]

We do not know how Johnson dealt with this monumental loss of 20 years of labor, but perhaps his reaction is encapsulated in the fact that he died the following year without any sense that the manuscript would be found or that Obadiah would be able to reproduce it. Johnson's apathetic pragmatism may have not only cost him the original manuscript, but also hastened his untimely death. One wishes that Johnson had been more conscious and forceful in his reaction against racism, so that this catastrophic "loss" could have been prevented. One wishes that Johnson had been muscular on this issue!

Falola asserted that Johnson was a "patriarch" whose narrative is "unapologetic" and "muscular." These claims have been difficult to corroborate. First, Johnson's family organization was not patriarchal, given that he was not the sole provider and seemed to have spent very little time with his wife and children. Second, his writing was in fact apologetic; he apologized in the preface to his book to anyone who may be offended by his narrative. Finally, Johnson's writing, personality, and conduct are almost the opposite of muscular or forceful. This evidence provokes two questions: What is Falola's motivation? What impels him to make these extravagant and unfounded claims about Johnson, the man?

If anything, it is Falola's language describing Johnson that is androcentric, muscular, and masculinist. His representation of Johnson as macho says more about the contemporary historian than about his subject. Falola seems to believe that the highest compliment he could pay the pioneering local historian is one couched in militarist language, no matter that the achievement is far from a literal battlefield. Military language is often used to project masculinity and male dominance. Falola as a historian is clearly Johnson's heir, given his work on the history of Ibadan, most especially. In promoting Johnson as a patriarch, Falola vaunts patriarchy, and seems to revel in the idea. His orientation is not atypical of contemporary intellectuals who continue to construct knowledge in sexist language and write as if only men were, and continue now to be, historical actors and subjects. This dangerous stance also reveals the deepening and normalization of male dominance in Nigerian society in general, even as androcentrism and male privilege are increasingly being questioned and confronted. In the next chapter, I examine the work of two scholars on Yorùbá religion in this regard.

CHAPTER 5

THE GENDER DICTATERS: MAKING GENDER
ATTRIBUTIONS IN RELIGION
AND CULTURE

A major theme of this book is the role of a diverse group of writers in creating a male-dominant Yorùbá world. In the last chapter, I concentrated on the lives and writings of first generations of local chroniclers of history, asking questions about the gender composition of the group and their gender consciousness. In this chapter, my focus shifts to the work of two contemporary social scientists who have written about religion and culture. Sociologist of religion John Peel and Jacob Olupona, a scholar of comparative religion, have both written about gender in Yorùbá culture albeit sparsely. Both scholars are very well known and are recognized for their extremely influential writings on the culture. But their bountiful scholarship contrasts sharply with the meagerness of their writing on gender, a fact that is integral to my critique of their work.

Perhaps the most troubling aspect of the role of intellectuals like Peel, Olupona, and Falola as I showed in the last chapter is their failure to recognize their own role in the patriarchalization of the culture through academic writing and mentoring of generations of scholars. In the production of knowledge on Yorùbá, Western-educated intellectuals as a group regardless of their gender or race are vectors of male dominance as they deploy various masculinist ideologies. Knowledge making is in the first instance the production of "truth." The degree to which intellectual writing is linked to power and further aggrandizement of power cannot be gainsaid. Consequently, I call these academics, gender dictaters (rhymes with "dictator") to underscore their unmitigated influence on scholarship on African religions and culture and the extent to which their claims about gender are best seen as diktats and not necessarily something that is based on evidence.

In the light of this understanding, one of the issues that concern me here is the reaction of Peel and Olupona to my thesis that gender categories in Yorùbá society must be historicized and that male dominance in the culture must be understood as a product of recent historical developments including European colonization of both society and discourse.

In academic circles, Peel is without a doubt one of the most renowned documenters of Yorùbá society and social change. A sociologist of religion, he has written numerous books and articles starting in the 1960s and continuing to the present day. His writings have spanned more than half a century, and his books are a must-read for any scholar who wants to be taken seriously on Yorùbá religion, culture, and social life. Peel's scholarship then presents an opportunity to consider the issue of gender and the role of intellectuals in portraying a culture that originally did not harbor gender divisions. The focus here is on two of his most recent writings, a paper titled "Gender in Yorùbá Religious Change" (GRC) and the tome *Religious Encounter and the Making of the Yorùbá* (REMY). In 1968, Peel wrote a colossal book on the Aladura, a sect in which a woman played a prominent founding role. He did not engage gender as a significant issue in this study. Over 45 years after the well-received *Aladura: A Religious Movement Among the Yorùbá* (1968) Peel, still, never addressed the issue of gender in any conscious or systematic way in any of his writings. The stance he took in his work, typical of many other scholars, even when gender became an issue, as feminism and gender-conscious approaches to scholarly writing gained traction in the academy, was to be silent about gender factors treating them as a nonissue in studies of society.

In a relatively more recent paper, however, Peel acknowledges this problematic state of affairs. Discussing gender and religion in Africa, he writes without irony that although "women are the mainstay of Church life throughout Africa,...the relations between religion and gender have not been given much attention. It seems that students of African religion have been interested in linking it with other variables, such as politics and ethnicity."[1] As one of the most important "students of African religion," it is disingenuous of him to make this statement at a remove, failing to recognize his own role in the debacle. As arguably the most eminent of these students of African religion to which he alludes, Peel did not explain this untoward state of affairs; neither did he recognize its implications for the validity of scholarly research, his own included. As I have shown in my book *Invention*, the lack of acknowledgment of gender factors in studies of Yorùbá religion as conducted by Peel and other gender dictaters, however, did not represent a benign omission or silence about gender issues; rather it was a systematic promotion of male gender in social and religious institutions and male dominance in everything as if this is the natural order of things. To these scholars, to notice gender difference and the male dominance that is its hallmark would be like noticing the air we breathe and the water we drink; it would be outside the normative pattern of conducting all aspects of life, including the intellectual experience. A good illustration of this surreptitious promotion of male dominance appears in Peel's earlier study of Aladura, an independent church movement I analyzed in a previous work. In his discussion of the founding of independent churches, he ignores pioneering women, making them invisible, silences them, and transfers their agency to putative males. Yet, his own data contravenes this male-dominant stance. After reviewing his study of *Aladura*, I made the following observation:

> There is a certain degree of male bias in the way questions are posed in the study…In spite of the fact that he documents a number of churches founded by women, in his analysis of the social background of church founders his major question was posed thus: "What sort of men were the founders of the *Aladura* (independent) churches in these years?" He goes on to examine various factors such as town of origin, occupation, and education.[2]

He did not mention gender as a variable that should be included in the analysis. The sociologist of religion did not take gender seriously, and did not treat it as a significant variable in the founding of churches and the organization of the movement. Because the maleness of church founders and religious leaders was taken for granted, it remained unanalyzed but was present(ed) as though male leadership and dominance are inherent. The effect of this sexist approach is to erase women's accomplishments and totally marginalize them as if indeed they were inconsequential in the society. In spite of my earlier published critique of his work, Peel refused to engage with the issue of gender in any of his writings on Yorùbá religion until he wrote the paper, "Gender in Yorùbá Religious Change,"[3] an article that followed on the heels of another monumental study, REMY, in which gender factors were still not acknowledged or brought to bear in analyzing the writings of Church Missionary Society (CMS) missionaries, most of whom were male. In GRC it would appear that Peel aims to correct the gender biases that have been a hallmark of his research and that of many other interpreters of African societies. Yet it is instructive that the late embrace of the importance of recognizing gender as a variable did not come easily to Peel. He confessed that the reason why he finally chose to address gender issues in his writing was that he had been taken to task on the gender question by a historian of gender. Accordingly, he writes, the "paper in a sense is a response to Laray Denzer's comment on a draft chapter of REMY[4] dealing with the social context of nineteenth-century Yorùbáland, that it failed to address the topic of gender in any systematic way."[5] Against this background, then, we can appreciate the importance of the paper GRC and why it must be systematically contextualized and analyzed.

It is also true that Peel's paper is a response to my thesis that gender categories appeared and became salient in Yorùbá society only recently in its history, and to my challenge to scholars to prove the existence of gender constructs and male dominance rather than assume them as the foundation of the society and, therefore, of academic studies. One refrain of my study is that in research, we cannot take for granted what indeed we are supposed to prove. Students of Yorùbá society and culture such as Peel's have taken male dominance as one of the givens in their research rather than one of the main issues to investigate. From the beginning of Peel's paper, it is clear that he had to address my work. Hence, he calls me a "gender skeptic" and proceeds, it would seem, to disprove my findings. However, the data he unearths from the CMS papers do no such thing; rather the evidence he proffers augments and reinforces my thesis on the absence of gender in Yorùbá ontology and the need to excavate masculinist ideologies in the production of knowledge by various cadres of "knowledge makers"—*babaláwo*, missionaries, sociologists, and other intellectuals. The paper GRC presents a unique opportunity for raising questions and analyzing issues that bedevil the work of many scholars of Yorùbá society and indeed many African cultures. Peel is typical in this respect.

The main problem with Peel's presentation is that he interprets Yorùbá religion, society, and people through a male-dominant gender lens without accounting for why this must be so. He approaches Yorùbá culture as a gendered and patriarchal one, deploying gender constructs, gender identities, and gender categories as if they are foundational and intrinsic to the society without providing any explanation for his assumptions. As I have argued repeatedly in much of my work, the assumption that gender constructs as ontological, natural, and present in all societies through time is a Eurocentric myth, unfounded and has to be proven, not taken as an article of faith. Since my work began to forcefully challenge the assumption that Yorùbá society was historically gendered and patriarchal, none of my critics, including Peel, have bothered to prove that the Yorùbá ethos was gendered in the first place. In fact, in their many gendered readings of institutions, their gender attributions, and imposition of gender identities, these interpreters show an inability to grasp the fact that Yorùbá epistemology differed from the Western and the Islamic ones that were being used to explain the society. If we do not assume that the Yorùbá ethos was a gendered, let alone a male-dominant one, in the first instance, then we must ask the question what was the nature of the Yorùbá world-sense, a question that must lead us to examine the wholesale imposition since the nineteenth century of a male-dominant gender system on the society by Christian missionaries (European and African), European travelers and colonizers, and Muslim clerics and intellectuals, then and now. These questions are not raised in Peel's study of CMS missionaries of the nineteenth century, despite their Christian values of male superiority, their belief in the cultural, if not racial, superiority of white people, and their own self-conscious identity as males.

In chapter 3, I demonstrated that Yorùbá society was a seniority-based system built on a matripotent ethos. In this chapter, my aim is to use the matripotent lens to explicate Yorùbá history and culture and in the process to challenge the naturalization of gender in Peel's work and that of other gender dictaters. Scholars and laymen alike have interpreted the Yorùbá world as a gendered one, having assumed gender to be natural and fundamental to human organization. This is problematic at many levels. First, it conflates gender, the social construct that societies have imposed on the body, with the sexual dimorphism of the human body. Overwhelming evidence tells us that gender systems were not universal or timeless: not all societies through time have organized themselves on the basis of a binary understanding of the human body divided into male and female in which the male is both biologically and socially dominant. True, the human body is the same everywhere, but human groups have organized themselves in myriad ways. In many scholarly writings, the inability to separate the physical appearance of the human body from meanings that have come to be ascribed to it led me to insist on new set of concepts to express the nonhierarchical and nonsocially laden Yorùbá understanding of the human body. In *Invention*, I proposed the concepts anatomic male (anamale) and anatomic female (anafemale) as translations of the Yorùbá words *ọkùnrin* and *obìnrin*, respectively. These were presented to underscore the fact that the distinction between *ọkùnrin* and *obìnrin* were superficial and did not assume social, moral, and hierarchical connotations like the English words "male/man" and "female/woman." Thus I showed that gender, which is integral to the morphology of Western societies and represented as ontological to its nature, was absent in Yorùbá world-sense and hence in its social categories. With this understanding, we are able to draw a contrast between a gendered epistemology (in which two "physical bodies are also social bodies"[6]: thus male and females are hierarchical and binarily opposed and the male is dominant) and a matrifocused epistemology in a seniority-based society. It is this gender epistemological lens that assumes that gender constructs are ontological (inherent) to all societies, including Yorùbá, and have been imposed on the culture by intellectuals such as Peel, who then proceeded to organize the Yorùbá world to fit this schema.

In contrast, I propose that the Yorùbá epistemology is a matripotent one that is distinct from the Western gender epistemology that is increasingly universalized. At the center of the matripotent understanding of the world is *Ìyá*, a singular, incomparable category that encompasses all humanity because all humans derive from them. It is not a gendered epistemology because there is no twosome here. Taking seriously the Yorùbá matripotent epistemology, I will now interrogate Peel's work and that of other gender dictaters who unthinkingly impose gender and male dominance.

In his response to my thesis that before the nineteenth century, Yorùbá did not perceive or organize their world through gender constructs, Peel calls me a "gender skeptic" and proceeds, it would seem, to disprove my findings in his paper "Gender in Yorùbá Religious Change." Commenting on my work, Peel writes:

> The virtual gender-exceptionalism that she [Oyewumi] claims for the Yorùbá is the more remarkable since they attached a very strong cultural value to the complementary physiological capacities of women and men to *bímọ* (bear/ beget children).[7]

Not only does Peel misread my thesis here, but he also misunderstands Yorùbá views on procreation and family ties. First, I do not claim gender exceptionalism for Yorùbá. In fact, I broaden my thesis beyond the Yorùbá world to argue that not all societies through time have arranged their social world based on gender constructs. In so doing, I challenge the wholesale imposition of gender(ing) on a global scale embedded in the dominant Western intellectual tradition of our time. I demonstrate that without evidence or initial research to establish what sorts of epistemologies were operational in the societies encountered by Europeans, such cultures are represented as male-dominant societies in which the social categories male and female coexist in hierarchical fashion, with men dominant and women subordinated just as they are in Europe. My study *Invention* argued that such gendered imposition is not merely an error but

> Also an obstacle to the pursuit of knowledge …The assumption of woman as a social category prevents us from asking the "right" questions about any given society, since questions are already been conceptualized *a priori*. It prevents us, as knowledge-seekers, from asking first-order, foundational questions generated from the evidence of particular societies.[8]

In essence then, my argument is not that Yorùbá society is exceptional but that other societies in Africa and worldwide have had Western gender epistemologies imposed on them before endogenous accounts of such societies have been fully grasped. Contrary to Peel's charge, I do not perceive Yorùbá people as gender exceptional. It is, however, the example under study, one that exposes the hegemonic Western gender lens that is the warp and woof of social analysis and that has been imposed on many other silenced societies whose original epistemologies we may never now get to know. Thus, my thesis is more wide ranging than the caricature of Yorùbá exceptionality would suggest. Adélékè Adéèkó's summation of my thesis is more to the point:

> Oyewumi does not claim some ahistorical exceptionalism for Yorùbá societies. Her examples show, for instance, that because a female cannot be both "ọkọ" (husband) and "aya" (wife) in her natal household, the incest taboo operates in Yorùbá societies. But the patrilocality that operated this rule in "primordial" Yorùbá publics does not invalidate the specific subjectivity or orí (inner head) of the individual that moves from one household to another. The woman who becomes "aya" (wife) in another household does not cease to be "ọkọ" (husband) in her natal household.⁹

Second, Peel's misreading of Yorùbá ideas on procreation follows directly from his failure to understand that a gendered, male-dominant social world is not the natural state of humans. If he had understood this, then he would ask more open, nongender presumptive questions about the Yorùbá social world. Hence his erroneous claim that Yorùbá posit "complementary physiological capacities for men and women to bímọ" (bear/beget children).¹⁰ The verb bí in Yorùbá means to give birth. Yorùbá do not see the reproductive physiology of Ìyá as comparable to that of fathers because it is only Ìyá who actually give birth. As I showed in the previous chapter, at the center of Yorùbá construction of the human condition is Ìyá who represents humanity. Ìyá is a singular creature who is beyond compare because they are the procreator. In Yorùbá thinking, then, Ìyá is the only one who can bímọ (birth a baby). In fact Ìyá is seen as the earthly creators of children in conjunction with the Ẹlẹ́dàá (creator). To say that fathers bímọ in Yorùbá social practice is nonsensical. The verb bí, to give birth or to birth a baby, is only applied to the anafemale who physiologically and spiritually gives birth. Fathers can indeed "ní ọmọ" (have children), as in having a claim to a child or children, but they cannot say "mo bímọ"—I gave birth. However, it is perfectly fine in Yorùbá social practice for anyone—man, woman, or child—to announce a birth on behalf of their family with the words "a bímọ" (we have given birth), underscoring the collective interest in reproduction and the role of the community in raising the child. We see this usage in Ladele et al.'s discussion of the behavior of the expectant grandmother immediately after the baby is born: "Tí ọmọ bá dé, kò ní tí ì sọ nnkankan, ó di ìgbà tí ibi ọmọ bá bọ́ kí ó tó sọ pé, 'Mo dúpé, a bímọ o."¹¹ When the baby emerges, the grandmother will not say anything; it is only after the placenta comes out that she says, "I give thanks, we have given birth." The physiological role of *bàbá*, the father, in making a child is not given prominence, if mentioned at all in the culture. For one thing, fatherhood sometimes rests on social rather than biological foundations. Thus the father of a child is not necessarily the genitor; his claim to fatherhood is based on the fact that he is the socially recognized husband of the mother of the newborn since his family gave the bridewealth to legitimate the marriage. Even when it is clear that the acknowledged father is not the genitor, the child is accepted as the child of, and a member of the *Ìyá*'s husband's family. *Ìyá*, as I have shown, is a spiritual category in ways that fatherhood is not perceived to be. Most importantly, *Ìyá* is transcendent: the category is present in all realms of existence—pre-earthly, pregestational, gestational, earthly, and forever. The relationship between *Ìyá* and child is sacred.

In her discussion of motherhood in African societies, historian Lorelle Semley takes me to task for writing eloquently and copiously on motherhood but failing to devote much time to the meaning of fatherhood.[12] But that is precisely my point: in the Yorùbá ethos that informs my work, *bàbá* and *Ìyá* are two different social categories that do not necessarily belong together. Therefore discussions of *Ìyá* does not and should not automatically invite or generate a discussion of fatherhood, as is standard in the male-privileging Western literature. To the extent that we do that, we are comparing them and making motherhood and fatherhood parallel in ways that the culture never did until recently and only in certain situations. With the understanding that in the matripotent ethos, *Ìyá* is unlike mother in the Western sense (opposite of father/female version of parent), and it is not like woman (subordinate of man) then one is able to explain some of the social occurrences that scholars have misrepresented as they translated them into gendered binary terms. Yorùbá social categories and English ones are not commensurate.

For example, Peel discussing his belief that Yorùbá people think of their particular *Òrìṣà* as a human being as a way of identifying with the god, explains:

> Now it is not easy to imagine a person in concrete terms without attributing a particular sex to them, and (in societies with gender) this in turn will inevitably become a vehicle upon which social and moral qualities will ride; or conversely, the moral qualities that one wishes to attribute to a deity may suggest its gender.[13]

First, his claim that it is difficult to imagine a person concretely but without gender is only true of societies in which gender is so embedded that it is part of the air they breathe. Contemporary societies, in Africa and world over, are almost universally gender saturated, to the extent that gender differences seem natural. But in Yorùbá society even now, and more so in the past, people routinely think about, talk to, and interact with persons without imagining them as gendered. Two anafemale traders may be having a conversation in Yorùbá in the marketplace, for example, and a young anafemale passing by may stop to greet them. One of the older traders may refer to the young anafemale as ọkọ mi (my husband) and the other woman may refer to her as ìyàwó mi (my wife) depending on their family relationship to this person. The young anafemale is both ọkọ and ìyàwó in the same body because the categories are social and not bodily based. There's nothing in such an exchange that calls for the gender binaries of Western culture that Peel unreflectingly imposes. To illustrate further, it is possible to spend 30 minutes or more in conversation telling someone about a particular person they have never met without the listener necessarily being able to discern this person's gender through the conversation. For one thing, names and pronouns that will be applied to this invisible person are nongender specific. This invisibility of gender attributes is possible in Yorùbá discourse because there are still many categories that do not allude to gender and because social and moral attributes are still largely not gender attributive. Yorùbá categories are not English categories and must not be assimilated the way Peel does. If indeed Yorùbá worshippers attribute anatomic sex to Gods, we also know that priests of Òrìṣà, whether the deity is male or female, are called ìyàwó (wives) of Òrìṣà. We also know that Òrìṣà have different anasex in different localities. Thus Òrìṣà ọkọ and Odùduwà are represented as anamale in certain localities and as anafemale in others. Peel himself was able to glimpse the fallacy of his arguments when he acknowledged that "Marc Shultz (1985)[14] found at Iganna, where what seems one of the most male of Òrìṣà, namely Ṣàngó, is locally considered 'wife' of Ara, a local thunder deity, because she came later to town."[15] So one must ask Peel, how do devotees of Ṣàngó in Igana imagine their "Lord and master" (as Ṣàngó is usually overly masculinized in androcentric academic literature).[16] Are they confused about "his gender"? Does calling Ṣàngó the wife of Ara compromise his masculinity? I ask these questions because when Peel noted that male and female devotees of "Osun, who is unusually represented as exuberantly female," are called "wife" of the Òrìṣà, it shows that even Òṣun has "male potentiality."[17] However, with the overmasculinized Ṣàngó, he did not apply the same English cultural logic and comment that Ṣàngó has "female potentiality" when he is addressed as wife of another deity. What his reasoning demonstrates is a sleight of male-dominant hand, and the inability of researchers such as Peel to let go of their imported categories and take seriously the Yorùbá categories that are staring them in the face.

To reiterate a point that I cannot repeat enough: The category *ìyàwó*, which is glossed as wife, is not about gender or the body, but rather it is a statement about seniority (who came first to a particular domicile)—a fact that speaks loudly about why researchers must first establish the meaning of local categories before they "colonize" them with prejudicial imports from other cultures. Furthermore, the fact that Yorùbá kinship categories *ọkọ* (husband), *ìyàwó* (wife), *ọmọ* (child or offspring), *ẹ̀gbọ́n* (senior sibling), and *àbúrò* (junior sibling) are seniority-based and the absence of such gender-specific kinship terms as son, daughter, brother, and sister incontrovertibly is evidence that Yorùbá did not organize their thinking and society on the basis of gender constructs. Concomitantly, we are able to see that moral and social qualities were not imprinted with gender. Thus Peel's claim that devotees of deities create gender systems by attributing gender to *Òrìṣà* is unfounded. Yes, many understand some *Òrìṣà* as having anamale or anafe-male bodies, but these do not amount to gender, which is why it is not jar-ring to discover that the same *Òrìṣà* is imagined in one way in a particular locality and in another way in a second town. Moral attributes were not gendered. I am sure that Yorùbá make all sorts of attributions to the Gods, but these attributions are gender attributions only in the eyes of Peel, the missionaries (local and foreign), intellectuals, and other gender-colonized beholders, which include many Yorùbá today. We must historicize and pay attention to social and religious change, which incidentally is Peel's spe-cialty; except that he has been very selective in the change he has chosen to see and to investigate. The changing of Yorùbá categories and increasingly the world-sense from a nongendered, seniority-based social system to a male dominant system is not a change that his research is designed to rec-ognize. Peel's attempt to discuss gender betrays his incomprehension of the concept and his lack of understanding of the nature of gender systems in the human world. Research has shown that gender systems are not naturally occurring; they are, if anything, true variables in the sense that they varied historically and socially, and that gendered societies were not universal or timeless. Clearly, he does not fully appreciate the fact that gender is variable in human organizations.

Another dimension of category confusion, to put it charitably, and the attendant epistemic violence that it generates is visible in the way in which the category *Ìyá* is interpreted in the work of gender-dictating interpret-ers of the society. A recurrent problem in authors such as Peel is that they conflate *Ìyá* with woman or wife (in the Western sense) and thereby abro-gate the matripotent ethos, in which *Ìyá* is not comparable to father and is not subordinate to anyone except the Gods. In his bid to show that Yorùbá subjects dichotomize moral attributes into male/female and then project such unto their *Òrìṣà*, Peel draws our attention to an entry in the journal of one William Allen, a Yorùbá catechist of the CMS mission who wrote about an incident in 1859, which the sociologist believes shows the process by which a Yorùbá person engages in gendering Òrìṣà and moral attributes. Summarizing Allen's journal entry, Peel writes:

One night in May 1859 a large rock crashed down from one of the hills in Abeokuta, narrowly missing children's play area. Such a forceful irruption from the wild into the settled sphere was exactly what was expected of new òrìṣà, and the local people at once recognized it as one, crying "òrìṣà ni, òrìṣà ni." And because the rock had behaved protectively towards the children, they also identified it as female—a "motherly rock," insisted one of the women at the scene.[18]

A number of assumptions are apparent in Peel's account that does not necessarily reflect the meaning of the incident from the local point of view. First the idea that only females or female Òrìṣà can act to protect their adherents is a fallacy. There is no question that one of the things that Yorùbá devotees demand of their Òrìṣà (be they male or female) is protection from the vagaries of human existence. Thus godly protection is not gendered.[19] Second, Peel takes for granted the word "motherly," present in the original journal entry, to be synonymous with female as the gendered half, and a binary opposite of male- father, thus conflating Ìyá with female. In the English cultural sense of the term, such a conflation is routine and reflects a gendered understanding of kinship categories. Peel does not tell us whether this interpretation of the "motherly" rock as a sign of femaleness is his or Allen's. Even more important, it is not clear what Yorùbá phrase Allen turned into the English "motherly rock." However, it is logical to assume that the Yorùbá phrase that was translated contained the word Ìyá. Consequently, it is likely that the woman who cried after the rock crashed down might have said not only Òrìṣà ni Òrìṣà ni (it is a deity). Because Òrìṣà, a typical Yorùbá noun, is not gender exclusive like the English god or goddess, there is no way the statement by "women at the scene" suggested gender of the deity in question. But I suspect they may have added a phrase like Ìyá ni, or abiamọ ni—it is Ìyá. As I have demonstrated at different points, Ìyá is not a gendered term in Yorùbá because Ìyá and bàbá were neither parallel nor comparable or opposites. Ìyá is singular. Thus, in this context, for example, what is the opposite of a motherly rock, a fatherly one? What would that mean? There's no such thing. Would a male Òrìṣà fail to protect worshippers by virtue of merely being male? In the matricentric Yorùbá ethos, such a phrasing would at best be meaningless if not nonsensical. There is no male counterpart of motherly! In this I go beyond nurture and speak to the spiritual pact that Ìyá are perceived to have with each of their children, an understanding that I discuss in the paragraphs that follow. The final assumption that a male Òrìṣà cannot be perceived to be protective is a fallacy. Would a male Òrìṣà not be equally protective of their devotees? Here, again I highlight and summarize the meaning and place of Ìyá in the life of their children. In his summation of social relationships as he gleaned it from the journals of the nineteenth-century Yorùbá male missioners, Peel writes:

> Close friends had an emotional importance equalled by no other relation besides a man's mother—more than fathers, wives, and brothers—and the two are brought together in a telling entry in Samuel Johnson's journal: With his own friend Oyebode, he calls to condole with a man who often attends church with a friend in deep grief over his mother's death. "To be plain," he said, "I can instance my mother's death as quite out of place. She is my backstay, and it would be better if my father had died rather than she. When I am home or about war, she takes care of my wives and children, and she is everything to me whilst my father is not."[20]

This passage from a newly Christianized Yorùbá man obviously places Ìyá and bàbá in comparative perspective, yet he emphasized the depth of his emotional ties to his Ìyá and the practical basis of his loss; however, he only hints at the spiritual armor for their children that Ìyá constitutes in the matripotent ethos when he writes, "she is my backstay." In this Yorùbá world-sense, even adult men and women are seen as more vulnerable to life's vicissitudes once they lose their Ìyá because of the understanding that Ìyá has spiritual powers that they put to no better use than to protect their progeny. For those who are still practitioners of Òrìṣà devotion, and for all those Christians and Muslims who still partake of the resources of indigenous religion, one's mother will be doing more than praying; she will be consulting babaláwo and making sacrifices on behalf of her children's well-being wherever they are. There is no greater role for Ìyá than that. It is against this background that to fall out with one's Ìyá would be seen as a suicidal move. The relationship between Ìyá and child is a bloody one, and blood is spiritually potent, even sacred. In conversation one regularly hears claims of this sort: "Ìyá put blood on your head" (referring to the passage of an infant through the birth canal). "There is no other person who did that; therefore you must revere your mother." It is in the light of such understanding of the Ìyá and their place as the progenitor of all humans that we can appreciate the Yorùbá belief that if a mother pronounces a curse on their offspring, Ìyá's metaphysical powers will make it efficacious and irreversible. No other human is perceived to have such spiritual powers over a person than their Ìyá. I discussed this understanding of the role of Ìyá earlier on in chapter 2 in regard to Yeye Ọ̀ṣun and the deity's children in the narrative of Oseetura, a chapter from the Ifá corpus.

Gendering Religious Practice

In a section of the paper on the practice of Yorùbá religion, Peel propounds a gendered practice of religion, stating first that Ifá worship is distinct from Òrìṣà worship and that from the nineteenth-century missionary records he analyzed, òrìṣà mainly claims the attention of women, and Ifá commands the attention of men.[21] Second, he noted that Yorùbá engage in the worship of two main categories of spiritual beings: ancestors and deities. He claims that ancestor worship is squarely in the realm of the men who are their descendants, but females are left to worship Òrìṣà, membership in whose cult was "associational rather than ascriptive."[22] What is the evidence for these assertions? He based this on the observations of nineteenth-century missionaries, whom he called "informed African observers," and on "statistical evidence" generated from the same source. Earlier on I have shown how problematic the use of the male-dominated, Christian, CMS archive to document Yorùbá culture is.

Gender, as I have already argued, is in the eye of the beholder. I have shown that Yorùbá categories cannot be assimilated into the gender-dichotomized and male-privileging English worldview to which the Yorùbá missionaries and Peel subscribe. Thus we cannot take their observations at face value, as Peel has done. Peel also had a lot to say about the masculinity of babaláwo and acknowledged that because "there was exceptional missionary interest in these men [babaláwo], this has yielded some of the most detailed religious case histories available to us."[23] The male-centered bias recognized here invites us to pay attention to its other side: the possible overlooking of females in certain realms, and a heightened awareness of them in other spaces when it fits the male-privileged world these African missionaries construct for their European employers and audience. Again, we see the gendered and sexist nature of their reportage when Peel remarks off-handedly that these nineteenth-century observers of Yorùbá Òrìṣà worshippers at public festivals disproportionately name women as Òrìṣà devotees: "the companies of devotees if their sex is mentioned, are nearly always said to be women."[24] One must ask then why are women the ones who are specifically mentioned in connection with Òrìṣà devotion? Why are men left out of Òrìṣà worship? Even more interesting is the fact that the only time they get gender-specific about Òrìṣà worshippers is when they want to name women as the devotees. On what basis do we conclude, as Peel does, that because they never specifically mentioned men as Òrìṣà devotees it meant that men were all but absent in this category and women were preponderant? Peel is correct to interpret the African observers in this way because as Christians they held deep prejudice toward indigenous religion, declaring it to be nothing but superstition, fit only for gullible women. Their disdain for women's intelligence is also apparent in statements such as Daniel Coker's: "The women worship Songo and Agba, they are more ignorant than the men"[25]; or in an entry from Abeokuta in 1847 that shows both the disdain for the indigenous religion and for its female devotees: "young women do not think their household furniture is complete if they have not purchased some sorts of god to worship"; or in James Johnson's dismissive remark noting the "endless prostration" of women devotees with their Òrìṣà when a house was struck by lightning in Ogbomoso in 1877.[26]

In addition, the statistical evidence Peel adduces to establish a gender-dichotomized Yorùbá religious practice, based on what he calls "concrete observation" by informed African missionaries, is erroneously presented as if gender constructs are inherent in rather than an interpretation of what is observed. The fact that one notices more anatomic female devotees of a named Òrìṣà does not in and of itself constitute gender. What it shows is that the observer has introduced a gendered lens. It may be that in that particular locality, when one notices a group of anafemales, for example, what is remarkable is that they are all wives in a lineage known to harbor important devotees of a particular Òrìṣà, a fact that the interpreter does not know because he or she is not aware of that information. To call it gender in a society whose epistemology eschewed gender consideration is a case of categoricalism, in this case gender categoricalism. Sociologist R. W. Connell explains that the categorical approach in social theory occurs when the focus is "on the category as a unit, rather than the processes by which the category is constituted, or the elements of its constituents...The social order as a whole is pictured in terms of a few major categories— usually two—related to each other by power and conflict of interest."[27] In this case a gender-differentiated practice of religion is established despite the fact that Peel himself understood that this gender dichotomous "generalization exaggerates, of course: many men were active in Òrìṣà worship and some were well known for it (like Erubami, 'a zealous idolater and a man of great note' at Ota, who became a Christian); they might be possessed by them and serve as priests—But it still fits—in [the] aggregate, that women in general were much more actively engaged in the worship of Òrìṣà than men were."[28] Whose aggregate, or better yet, who is aggregating? From this we can see that the reduction of devotees into bodies, and then the bodies sorted out into male and female, is being done by the interpreters, and their gender-specified ways of seeing are those of the interpreters (missionaries or scholars) alone, given that Yorùbá social categories did not originally mean what Peel takes them to mean. There is no evidence from

Peel's reading of the CMS papers that the Yorùbá missionaries explained to their foreign employers that males are also called "wives" of Òrìṣà. Why not? For one thing, the "men" who were active in Òrìṣà worship mentioned in the quotation are no less likely to be possessed by a particular Òrìṣà male or female, and they would be regarded as ìyàwó (wives) of the Òrìṣà just like the anafemales. What exactly is gender here?

With regard to the building of statistical categories, as I have pointed out elsewhere, "statistical categoricalism" is made that men and women are disproportionately represented in different arenas and the numbers that do not fall in the gender-designated category (which scholars or observers have set up) are then discounted, ignored, and discarded as sources of evidence. In this case the many men mentioned in the quotation, who are devotees of Òrìṣà, do not count. Equally the many women who are dedicated to Ifá or are babaláwo are not mentioned because they are not seen, and when there is a specific female that does not fit the bill, the evidence is immediately neutralized by subsuming her under a particular "husband." Here's one example in Peel's account: "The only case where a woman is reported as having her own dedicated ikin [the sacred nut for divination] concerns the wife of a famous Brazilian[29] babaláwo, Phillip Jose Meffre, but he still seems to have kept charge of it for her."[30] In a society in which there were also anafemale babaláwo as I discussed in chapters 1 and 2, I don't know how such a claim can stand. Statistics are not innocent; here they function as a vehicle for creating gender dichotomies. Statistics are collected in terms of categories that have been set up a priori by the interpreter,[31] so that statistics in and of themselves cannot prove anything other than what they are set up to prove.

Peel's own analysis contradicts the gender division he himself introduced into religious practice. In a previous paper titled "The Pastor and Babaláwo: The Interaction of Religions in Nineteenth Century Yorùbáland," he writes about the conversion of babaláwo into Christianity, detailing the conversion of three Ifá diviners. Such converts were regarded by the missionaries as "high-status converts," and the aforementioned Phillip Meffre was one such converts. Peel noted that after Yorùbá are converted, they are required to give up their òrìṣà; thus "Meffre handed over six òrìṣà: Olojo, Osu, Ogun, Ogiriyan, Osu and Ṣàngó."[32] The said Meffre—the babaláwo with the many Òrìṣà—is a man. Peel then sums up babaláwo conversion thus: "There is then a clear logic to the sequence in which babaláwo converts renounced their idols: first Èṣù, then the other òrìṣà...and finally Ifá."[33] Here he provides evidence that Ifá priests too had Òrìṣà other than Ifá. The irony of the sequence of giving up their Gods that Peel details here is its illogicality, because Ifá does not exist without Èṣù, a fact that I will explicate shortly. Given his own discussion, why then does Peel insist on his unfounded thesis that in nineteenth-century Yorùbá society there was a gender dichotomy in worship, in that men worshipped Ifa and women were devotees of Òrìṣà, whom the missionaries saw as the lesser Gods? Given the male-dominant worldview of both missionaries and scholars, it is hardly surprising that women were portrayed as inferior children of lesser Gods.

Perhaps the most egregious misapprehension of Yorùbá religion by Peel, one of the most respected analysts of the religion, is his excising of Ifá from the larger Òrìṣà worship in a bid to impose gender, a nonendogenous factor, on the religion. For Peel, Ifá is distinctive because the god Ọrúnmìlà is the only òrìṣà that does not possess its priest.[34] If this is a fact, why is this an important distinction? From the writings of CMS informers, he concludes: "The main generalization is that there was a clear gender distinction in religious practice: the Òrìṣà mainly engaging the attention of women, and Ifá of men."[35] How so? Ifá, apart from being a divination system, is itself an Òrìṣà known as Ọrúnmìlà. Second, Ifá, the divination system, is known as the "mouthpiece" of the Gods[36] because it is through Ifá divination that Yorùbá learn which is their personal deity. Ifá divination used to be a routine part of the Yorùbá journey through life. As I pointed out in chapter 1, shortly after a child is born, one of the first rituals to be engaged in universally in a pre-Christian and pre-Islamic society was to "gbo orí ọmọ" or the afesekojaye. Throughout life, especially during rites of passage, Yorùbá consulted Ifá, which led them to offer sacrifice to one òrìṣà or the other. Babaláwo were not outside the practice of the tradition, as their own divination on behalf of themselves or family members would lead them to be devotees of other òrìṣà in addition to Ọrúnmìlà. This explains why Meffre, the aforementioned babaláwo, had six "Òrìṣà to give up" after his conversion. Meffre was not atypical. Ifá is part and parcel of Òrìṣà devotion, and cannot be separate from it. The desire to separate Ifá from òrìṣà worship has to do with the reluctant recognition by Europeans missionaries, Western-educated Africans, and missionaries that Ifá divination constituted an intellectual practice in a universe they had defined as primitive and superstitious.

Besides, Ifá divination cannot exist without the collaboration of three prominent Òrìṣà: Èṣù, Ọṣun, and Orí. First, Èṣù: divinations always end with the injunction to perform sacrifice—a task that is usually carried out by a babaláwo after the client has paid for the required material. Sacrifice is the essence of òrìṣà devotion. Èṣù, the deity of uncertainty, is the receiver of the sacrifice, who is supposed to carry it to the designated òrìṣà. Èṣù is the mediator. Second, Ọṣun: the primordial Ìyá is also involved in every process of sacrifice because at the end of performance of sacrifice, the babaláwo has to invoke Ọṣun by reciting Oseetura,[37] an Odù of origin that is regarded as the deity's. How then does one think of Ifa and Òrìṣà as two separate religious systems or subsystems dichotomized by gender?

Peel's mistaken interpretation of the indigenous religion is clear in his failure to recognize the role of Orí, a third òrìṣà in the divination process. This lack of insight is compounded by his insistence that in the nineteenth century, Orí and Ifá were opposing personal cults that catered to women and men, respectively. He writes, "Men were initiated into Ifá, particularly at turning-points of early life, and received a set of dedicated palm nuts (ikin), which were kept in a small vessel and served as material icon of Ifá's protective power."[38] The question arises: what about women? Peel claims that "Ifá cult of personal security was barely open to them"; hence women relied instead on "the cult of Orí or personal destiny, whose icon was a small circular box (igba Orí) made of stiff calico and covered with cowries."[39] Given the gendered reasoning here, it is pertinent to ask whether the cult of orí was open to men? Such a question is not asked because of the assumption that men are the norm, and are the keepers of the tradition who can keep women out and away from the most important things in society. But in this masculinist approach, men are perceived to have access to all realms of religion and social institutions if they so choose. The way in which questions are posed leaves women outside of the tradition, locked out and standing at the window looking in. Peel's evidence for the supposition that Orí is a female cult is that "three quarters of the references to it in the CMS journals are expressly to its worship by women,"[40] an approach that I have already analyzed as problematic. And what about the remaining one-quarter? Why is it irrelevant in our analysis of who worshipped which deity?

In his discussion of the veneration of Ifá and orí as gender dichotomous, Peel makes a distinction between Ifá's character as a personal protective cult that he tells us was one of its most common functions in the nineteenth century. As a divination system, it was a specialized guild, whose priesthood was open to only learned men, a claim that I interrogated extensively in chapter 1. But as a protective cult, it becomes a cult that is open to all males who can be initiated without much ado. From this stance, Ifá is only open to females as clients discounting the fact that some females were also babaláwo. One cannot exaggerate how huge an error in thinking it is to assume that the elemental deity of the religion Orí can be excluded at any point from the spiritual life of a Yorùbá male or female, especially when it has to do with protection. Orí, which means head, incubates the orí-inú "inner spiritual head." Orí is elaborated as the seat of individual fate or destiny. Therefore destiny and fate are two synonyms of orí-inú. In the cosmology, the most important task facing ènìyàn (humans) in their pre-earthly guise is to choose an orí in heaven before making the journey to earth. In matters concerning human life, there is a preoccupation with choosing the right *orí* in order to have a good destiny on earth. In Ifá we also learn that *Orí* is a deity in its own right. *Orí* is thus a personal god. An *Odù* (unit of verses) tells us that the most faithful and therefore the most important divinity for any individual's well-being is his or her *orí* (personal god). Hence the injunction that the propitiation of one's *orí* should precede any entreaties to other Gods, because there is nothing that the divinities can do for an individual without the consent of *Orí*.

It is *Orí* alone
Who can accompany his devotee to any place
Without turning back
If I have money,
It is my *Orí* I will praise
My *Orí*, it is you
If I have children on earth,
It is my *Orí* to whom I will give praise
My *Orí*, it is you
All good things I have on earth,
It is *Orí*, I will praise
My *Orí*, it is you.[41]

Another Odù underscores *Orí*'s importance as mediator between the individual and other *Òrìṣà* because without *Orí*'s due sanction, no requests to other *òrìṣà* will be countenanced.

No god shall offer protection
Without sanction from *Orí*
Orí, we salute (you)
Whose protection precedes that of other *òrìṣà*
Without sanction from *Orí*
Orí, we salute (you)
Orí that is destined to live
Whosesoever sacrifice *Orí* chooses to accept,
Let him rejoice.[42]

Given the belief about *orí* and its fundamental nature in the religion and its significance for individual sense of self and well-being, I cannot imagine that the Ifá cult of personal destiny is a substitute for *Orí*; even Ifá tells us that spirituality starts with *Orí*. Furthermore, beyond Ifá as cult of personal protection, *Orí* as *Òrìṣà* is present and crucial in all divination sessions. Because the divination system is interactive, the *Orí* (subjectivity/personal *Òrìṣà*) plays an active role in leading clients of the *babaláwo* to make the choices that are appropriate to their own situation. Thus *Orí* is an integral part of Ifá. Peel himself recognized that "Ifá functions as a projective tech-nique in which the client actively contributes to the diagnosis."[43] There is a popular saying that you cannot shave someone's head in their absence: I would add that Orí is so fundamental that no part of Yorùbá religion is pos-sible without it. Thus the idea that men did not propitiate their orí makes no sense, especially if they are seeking protection. Their Ifá says "Orí, we salute (you) whose protection precedes that of other òrìṣà."[44]

No one can be excluded from the cult of Orí: it is universal and one is born with it, an inalienable and divine right. Thus the saying orí o ju orí—no head is greater than the other—expresses the basic Yorùbá notion of equality. There is no gender distinction between one Orí and another. In his analysis of the Church Missionary Society (CMS) journals, Peel draws our attention to the fact that the anxieties created by the cataclysmic disrup-tions of the nineteenth century may have heightened the need for "portable devices" for individual (spiritual) protection[45] According to Peel, women more than men relied on the "cult of Orí (literally 'head') or personal des-tiny, whose icon was a small circular box (igba Orí)." He further tells us that a Christian evangelist missionary reported that "a woman once interrupted an evangelist's outdoor preaching in Ibadan to say that even if they forsook the rest of their òrìṣà, they would still keep 'Orí the head,' for it was 'their god and maker.'"[46] Our goal here is not to document the veracity of these occurrences, but rather to explore Peel's imposition of gender on what he labels female devotion to Orí in contrast to male devotion to Ifá. In this reading, he once again fails to appreciate the colossal role of Ìyá in Yorùbá religion and the everyday life of their children, because they have not only to propitiate their own orí and protect themselves, but they also must pro-tect their children: consulting the babaláwo, offering sacrifice, propitiating orí, and constantly praying for their progeny.[47] As I showed in chapter 3, the orí of the Ìyá is a collective orí linking Ìyá, children, and ancestors in one continuous flow of blood. Ìyá is charged on a daily basis with the task of propitiating their orí and children's orí for the sake of their well-being. I dis-pute the idea that men were more conversant with Ifá than females for the same reason that it fell to the Ìyá to cater to their children's spiritual well-being. In a matripotent culture, the spiritual and sacred nature of the Ìyá-child relationship propels the Ìyá's engagements. All humans are part of the orí of their Ìyá. The orí of an adult anamale married or not is perceived to be conjoined with that of his Ìyá and ọmọọ̀yá (uterine siblings) as we saw in the case of the missionary who was grieving for his dead Ìyá. The Christian idea that in marriage a man and woman leave their parents and cleave together as one is absolutely opposed to Yorùbá world-sense regarding Ìyá's centrality to the identity and well-being of each of their birth children.

Masculinization as Elevation

Peel does not interrogate his informers. Rather, he took their prejudices and ran with them. In this regard the main concern of Peel and other nineteenth-century observers was not a conscious effort to impose gender on the religion; they took gender categories for granted and male dominance as a default position, and built on it. But it is clear that there was a conscious effort on the part of the new converts to uplift Ifá by separating it from the rest of the religion, which as newly Christianized Yorùbá they had come to see as primitive and evil. Yet African and European missionaries and even Muslim clerics all had a "grudging respect" for the Ifá divination system. From Peel's paper "Pastor and Babaláwo," we learn that after the Christian missionaries started to operate in Yorùbáland:

> The missionaries began very soon to make clear distinctions among their adversaries. Muslims apart, they differentiated sharply between "Ifá priests" and "fetish priests." The latter (i.e. *aworo*) were heaped with unalloyed contempt: corrupt and ignorant deceivers, enriching themselves through encouraging superstitious fears...It is not at all like this with *babaláwo*. Whatever the animosity, the missionaries could not but respect these mobile and sophisticated men.[48]

And yes, they were men, not because only men could be *babaláwo*, but because only the male *babaláwo* could be perceived as priests by Christian men who are steeped in the worldview of a male-centered and male-dominant religion. Even Peel is seduced by the Ifá priests. Summarizing an exchange between Gollmer, a white missionary, and a *babaláwo*, he effuses, "One admires the *babaláwo's* calm and tactful conclusion to the exchange!"[49] Clearly, there is no room for (hysterical) females here. The Muslim clerics who were increasingly a part of society especially in some towns were no less enamored of *babaláwo*. There were reports that in 1877 "individual *babaláwo* and *alufa* or Qur'anic specialists each sought out a working partner from other profession, so that they could reciprocally draw on one another's expertise in difficult matters of divination. It almost goes without saying that the Muslim *Alufa* were wholly and categorically a male profession."[50] Although it is clear that the sources of male dominance and masculinization of *babaláwo* went beyond Christian missionaries and intellectuals, the role of Islam in this regard has been little studied. That is not my focus.

At points, Peel's analysis of the missionary encounter with Yorùbá religion is insightful, as when he writes:

> The mission's strategy depended on the construction of "heathenism" as a system homologous to Christianity, in which some elements would be

retained (e.g. God, the idea of the savior or mediator, the value of "peace," *alafia*) and others replaced. Such symbolic homologies were not only aids to a more effective evangelization—they would eventually encourage a degree of mutual cognitive adaptation.[51]

But he stops short of realizing the full implications of his own analysis. One adaptation that was imposed on *òrìṣà* worship was to the patriarchal ethos of Christianity. In *Invention* I already noted that in the hands of churchmen the tenets of Yorùbá religion became masculinized: "Olódùmarè began to look like 'our Father in heaven'; the female *Òrìṣà* when they were recognized, began to look less than the male *Òrìṣà* in some nebulous way; 'our ancestors' became our forefathers."[52] In operationalizing the strategy, Peel tells us that "it is hardly surprising that it should have been the *babaláwo* who emerged on the Yorùbá side as the missionary's chief interlocutor and antagonist...it was the babaláwo...as it were pre-adapted to the encounter."[53] The use of a biological concept such as preadaptation to describe Ifá priesthood, a social institution created by humans, is instructive. It is an attempt by Peel to make it seem as though the institution was innately masculine. But social institutions have no nature in and of themselves. What they reflect are social relations of power. It is not surprising that the *babaláwo* homologized as the counterpart of Christian priests could not be anything but male, like the missionaries who were creating the correspondence. The turning of a gender-free priesthood of Ifá diviners into a Christian-type priesthood is one concrete way in which patriarchy was institutionalized and imprinted on indigenous religion.

But Peel, in creating a phallocentric distinction for Ifá, invents the evidence for *babaláwo*'s male exclusivity and self-consciously tries to obscure the role of intellectuals and interpreters in it:

> But what set Ifá apart from such oracles in several ways. Its keynote was control, not inspiration: instead of surrender to trance or possession, the *babaláwo* depended on his mastery of a technique and its accompanying corpus of knowledge. Anyone who regards this as a male stereotype will not be surprised that virtually all *babaláwo* were men. We cannot say a hundred per cent of them were, since female Ifá diviners have been noted.[54]

Again we see Peel resort to statistics, a move that immediately co-opts the counterevidence and tries to brush away the fact that female *babaláwo* exist, thereby incorporating a Yorùbá institution into the gendered world of English and Christian Europe. Control, mastery, and knowledge are stereotypes of masculinity in Western society, but this was not the case in Yorùbáland.

Parallel to this relative elevation of Ifá and its purported distinction as a male-only cult is the contrasting representation of women as more ignorant, more superstitious, and more gullible than men. The following statement was typical in the reportage of the CMS missionaries: "The women worship Ṣàngó and Agba, they are more ignorant than the men. The men do not worship any god, they hold Ifá in great reverence."[55] As I have shown repeatedly, such claims are based on a number of fallacies about Yorùbá religion and are not supported by the evidence.

Decolonizing the Intellectual: Liberating the Òrìṣà

In the next section I continue to look at the role of intellectuals in patriarchalizing religion and culture through the work of Jacob Olupona, an eminent scholar of religion. I then explore the academic setting in which these claims are produced and reproduced to show that it is a male-dominant world.

In the introduction to the anthology *African Traditions in the Study of Religion in Africa*, a book that is dedicated to Olupona, honoring him for his contributions "to method and theory in the study of religion…, change within African indigenous Religions…, indigenous religious traditions and modernity…as well as other themes" (2012:6). The scholar of religion is also rightly lauded for being a dedicated mentor who provided support for his students, a fact that underscores his influence on a new generation of scholars. The three editors of the volume, Ezra Chitando, Afe Adogame, and Bolaji Bateye, raised a number of important concerns about the academic study of religion as it relates to Africa. They pointed out that the category religion is embedded in European history and the conception of "world religions" centers Europe, portraying African religions only as "the Other."[56] Consequently, they ask a series of questions: Since African scholars are using borrowed tools, can they fashion these tools to meet their own needs? Can African scholars ensure that the study of religion in Africa reflect African issues, concerns, and approaches? The editors of the anthology leave no doubt that the study of religion in Africa requires no less than intellectual decolonization, in the process, moving Africa to the center. They argue that dismantling Eurocentrism "is the challenge facing African scholars of religion in postcolonial Africa."[57]

Does Olupona meet up to this challenge in his writings on gender? To answer this question, I interrogate his major paper on the subject titled "Imagining the Goddess: Gender in Yorùbá Religious Traditions and Modernity." The fact that Olupona does not reckon with indigenous categories from the get go is glaring given the title of his paper, "Imagining the Goddess." In Yorùbá, there are no Gods and Goddesses; there is only the nongendered word *Òrìṣà* that is used to name all deities. In a paper on gender such as this one, the writer should, at the very least, start by explaining his conceptual choices and the rationale for why he chose to impose Western gender categories such as "goddess" on Yorùbá. His naming of a Yorùbá deity as "goddess" by diktat immediately imposes an alien worldview, erases Yorùbá ontology that eschews gender constructs, and obliterates the culture's epistemology. We are then not surprised that Olupona had to look to studies of European society in order to find "evidence" for gender in Yorùbá culture. Or how are we to understand his use of the following quotation by Riches and Salih, taken from their book *Gender and Holiness*, a study of gender categories in medieval Europe. In his discussion of religious ritual, without presenting any evidence for gender in the Yorùbá religious system, he writes:

> There is a clear indication of gender fluidity in Yorùbá religious traditions, and religious discourse is framed in a manner that may be entirely unfamiliar to Western audiences. On many occasions, Yorùbá society authorizes males to take on appearances perceived and valued as female.[58]

He then quotes European medievalists to validate this claim:

> As Riches and Salis point to in another cultural context, "the boundaries between 'maleness' and 'femaleness' are permeable and individuals could move on occasion (especially on occasions of ritual and festival) between gender or adopt the attributes of another gender."[59]

First, given that Riches and Salih's statement is made about a "different cultural context," which Olupona acknowledged, what makes it applicable to the Yorùbá religious tradition? Olupona does not say. On examination of the cited European study on the perception of saints, we find that the editors of the volume argued for "the representation of St. George as a transgendered martyr and suggest that Margery Kempe may have drawn on both male and female saintly exemplars in her performance of apostolicism" in medieval Europe.[60] Because the European culture on which their study was based had been proven to be indisputably gendered, these scholars recognize that certain moral attributes and religious experiences in the society exhibited a gendered pattern and therefore their claims about gender boundaries and how they could be breached make sense. But Yorùbá society was different and did not exhibit any of the gender patterns that would make it comparable to European societies on this question of gender and its meaning. Thus the first thing required of Olupona, the scholar of Yorùbá indigenous tradition, is to prove the existence of gender constructs in Yorùbá world-sense and then explain how social categories express such a putative gendered epistemology. Unlike in the Yorùbá world, medieval or contemporary European societies did not represent a god as the wife of another deity (male or female), they did not call male and female devotees of Gods wives of the god, they did not regard ordinary women as husbands of wives, in their society, neither could females become priests to cite a few examples. The reason that a person with a male or female body can be a "wife," or "husband" in Yorùbá society is not because the boundaries are permeable but that the categories ọkọ and ìyàwó are not gendered in the first place, and therefore do not carry gender boundaries related to the anatomy. Yes, ọkọ and ìyàwó express boundaries not of the body (gender), but of the relationship of an individual to a particular space, a family dwelling, or shrine of Òrìṣà. Male and female Òrìṣà do not have distinctive social and moral attributes; their endowments and functions are not differentiated in that regard, and thus there are no boundaries to cross one way or the other. How then can the claims of the scholars of medieval Europe, which are correct for the culture they were studying, be used to make sense of Yorùbá religion, which is grounded in a totally different epistemology and ethos? In an earlier paper, Olupona had correctly noted that:

> While the primary hermeneutical concern of the history of religions would be to "understand" the religious character, qualities and meaning of African religion, one cannot draw any hard and fast line between religion and the culture through which it is expressed...The thrust of the discourse would in fact be sustained by evidence from the cultural life of the people.[61]

This is an excellent statement of purpose, but he does not follow his own advice in the paper "Imagining the Goddess"; he all but disregards the evidence of Yorùbá culture for explaining its religious traditions, appealing instead to Europe.

Taken together, Olupona's statements about gender show that he does not understand the meaning of the concept in the first instance. He needs to explain his usage of male, female, masculine, feminine, and gender itself. His assumption is based on the idea that "physical bodies are social bodies,"[62] making gender automatically a function of biology. But this is not the case, because decades of research have shown that gender is a social construction in that gender categories were not present in every society, and even in places where one found gender systems there is huge variation. Riches and Salis, the two scholars he quotes approvingly, acknowledge this development in the field of gender studies when they state in the introduction to their anthology, "We are writing from the constructionist view of gender which can now be said to be consensual."[63]

More specifically, Yorùbá social categories show that gender must be understood as a social, and not biological, arrangement. Yorùbá categories are not based on anatomic sex. Literary scholar Adéẹ̀kọ́, in an autobiographical piece responding to my thesis that Yorùbá culture is not gendered in its origins, eloquently captured the confusion involved in assimilating Yorùbá categories into English (as Olupona has done), and underscored the gap between the languages even as English categories have become central to the ways in which many Yorùbá think about themselves. Let me quote him at some length:

> In my youth, I was taught both in school and at church to accept the following: (i) the English word "man" means "ọkùnrin" in Yorùbá; (ii) "woman" means "obìnrin"; (iii) husband means "ọkọ"; (iv) wife means "aya" or "ìyàwó"; (v) father means "baba"; (vi) mother means "ìyá" or "mama"; female means "abo"; (viii) male means "akọ" and (ix) child means "ọmọ." At home, my mother either called me by my given name or addressed me as "ọkọ mi" (my husband). When describing me to others, then I was "ọmọ" ("child"). *At* 72, my mother still calls me her "ọkọ" (husband). I cannot remember her referring to my father directly as "ọkọ mi" ("my husband"). He is always "Iba Leke" (Leke's father) to her, and she was always "Iye Leke" (Leke's mother) to him...Táíwò [my wife] like many other Yorùbá women I know in Colorado [where they now live] calls our children, including girls "ọkọ mi" (my husband). When I asked our American born children if they were puzzled by the term, they just smiled. I am not sure my explanations made sense to them.[64]

Adéẹ̀kọ́ concluded, "Oyewumi's argument in *Invention* gives us the intellectual framework for discovering the logic that underlies these terms. I learned from this book that these are not Yorùbá metaphoric terms for gender universals but meaningful articulations of social relationships as they are organized by that society."[65] By assimilating Yorùbá categories into the Western mode, Olupona shows that he does not recognize the integrity, independence, and validity of the Yorùbá world-sense on which social relationships are imagined and organized. If Olupona takes Yorùbá categories seriously, then he will have to explain the meaning of gender, and what exactly are male and female gender attributes in the tradition. Gender in the first instance is a cultural category only intelligible in relation to the societal ethos.

The paper "Imagining the Goddess" is an intervention in a debate about gender provoked by my thesis that gender is not ontological to Yorùbá society and as such its emergence must be understood as historical. Olupona, like Peel, postulates gender as a natural category that is inherent in the culture. Many of the claims made by him are similar to Peel's in that from the get go he assumes gender to be natural and therefore require no evidence or proof of how it came to be. In the introduction to his paper, he tells us that Ifá should constitute an important source of knowledge on Yorùbá thought and practices and thus he

> is convinced that the Ifá divination texts and forms of Yorùbá oral tradition constitute important primary sources for understanding the wide spectrum of women's religious experiences and gender issues in Yorùbá traditional society. Second, Ifá divination poems are largely the product of the imagination of male diviners. In many instances, they outline publicly visible roles for women and varieties of gender issues that reflect my own central thesis.[66]

In the first two chapters of this book, I challenged the idea of treating Ifá knowledge as a canonical source of evidence for Yorùbá society because many Ifá texts have been imprinted by sundry scholars and diviners, with gender constructs and significantly male superiority. Despite Olupona's claim of using a hermeneutical approach,[67] his representation of Ifá here is as a pristine, untouched body of knowledge that is handed down without any interpretation. The direction of his thesis is already clear when he declared that Ifá was created by "male diviners" and he virtually ignores female babaláwo thereby imposing a male-dominant interpretation on the knowledge system.[68] In previous chapters of this book, I have dealt with the question of Ifá authorship and many other issues arising from the gendering of the genre. Given this inaccurate foundation for Olupona's thesis, much of the claims he makes on Ifá have little merit. Ifá, which he assumes provides evidence of gender, needs to be approached with the awareness that it too has been subjected to interpretation and this fact must be taken into account in any study of the content. At a time in history in which patriarchy dominates human interactions, it is predictable that it has infected large aspects of society including knowledge systems, social institutions, representations of history, and the knowledge producers themselves. This observation should not come as a surprise to Olupona because in an earlier publication, commenting on the work of Joseph Omoyajowo, who had written on the role of women in traditional Yorùbá religion, Olupona writes, "Omoyajowo shows that some of the Yorùbá Deities who were originally conceived as females have since changed into males, perhaps as a result of the changing social system of the Yorùbá people."[69] Although in the paper he goes on to acknowledge the important role of Òrìṣà Òṣun as depicted in Ifá (which I discussed in chapter 2), his overall stance is to assume males to be the norm in the society and to take male superiority as an article of faith rather than a function of history and social change.

Furthermore, Olupona explained, "deities exhibit ambiguity in gender, and gender may vary from region to region. Odùduwà, who is God, cultural hero, and progenitor of Yorùbá people, appears male in southwestern Yorùbá. However, Odùduwà appears female in Ekiti, in Northeastern Yorùbá."[70] Given the conceptual confusion that is a mark of this paper, it is necessary for the scholar of religion to explain what he means by ambiguity of gender. Elsewhere I drew attention to the multiple representations of Odùduwà in different Yorùbá regions. I demonstrated that the reason why it is possible to imagine deities as either anatomically male or female is precisely that their biology was incidental to their identity and functions in the society.[71] Moreover *obìnrin* (anafemale) and *okùnrin* (anamale) are terms that were not infused with gendered social or moral attributes: thus the female deity Oya is regarded as destructive and fearsome like Ṣàngó the thunder god because strength, authority, violence, and destruction are not stereotyped and attributed to only anamales. Similarly, devotees of *Òrìṣà*—both anamale and anafemale—look to their *Òrìṣà* as sources of all kinds of blessings including children, the ultimate good. The fiery Ṣàngó is also seen by his devotees as benevolent, just like Òṣun the great *Ìyá*. Thus Olupona's use of the term "gender ambiguity" here is incorrect because Odùduwà is not intersexed, which is the only way the deity can express ambiguity in a culture such as Yorùbá in which social attributes were not stereotyped as belonging to male or female. In summing up my discussion of Yorùbá social categories, I wrote, "Yorùbá genderlessness is not to be read as androgyny or ambiguity of gender. It is not genderless in terms of a presence of both male and female attributes. Instead it is genderless because human attributes are not gender-specific."[72]

Olupona has indeed made contributions to "method and theory in the study of religion..., [and] change within the African Indigenous Religions...," but on gender, religion, and culture, his intervention leaves much to be desired. His laudable contributions to the field notwithstanding, his paper "*Imagining the Goddess: Gender in Yorùbá Religious Traditions and Modernity*" is certainly not a good example of the decolonizing of religion or knowledge. This paper reinscribes Eurocentrism by universalizing its cultural practices and imposing them on Yorùbá religion, an approach that obliterates its ethos.

I want to suggest that this failure in his writing is very much tied to his lack of understanding of gender as a concept and an inadequate recognition of gender studies as an important academic field. This is not peculiar to him; we have seen the same incomprehension with Peel. Their oblivious stance may be a cultivated ignorance having to do with these men's dismissal of gender as an important variable in social life and their sense that the field of gender studies is not to be taken seriously. Nevertheless, their lack of understanding of gender as a field of discourse should not preclude their understanding and appreciation of their own privileged place as males in the academy surrounded by other males and picking and choosing what is worth studying and what is not.

Gender in the Academy and Beyond[73]

In March 2008, Olupona convened the Harvard Conference on Ifá (HCI) titled "Sacred Knowledge, Sacred Power and Performance: Ifá Divination in West Africa and the African Diaspora."[74] The HCI was a well-attended, particularly interesting meeting because of the ways in which it bridged the variety of gaps between town and gown, intellectuals and practitioners of divination, Africa and Diaspora, sovereigns and their subjects, performers and academics. The yawning chasm that remained was between Yorùbá oral traditions and the interpretations of Western-educated scholars. Much of this gap was a gender disparity, and it is this that I wish to address in this section. On the opening day especially, the conference was a microcosm of a Yorùbá community, with the presence of ten traditional Yorùbá rulers (ọba) from Nigeria and many prominent Yorùbá personalities, including the governor of Ọṣun state of Nigeria, eminent scholars, drummers, singers, and dancers.

The conference at Harvard was an occasion for elucidating issues of gendering, male dominance, and fraternity in the Yorùbá intellectual community. Olupona, who now teaches at Harvard, like many of the scholars in attendance, used to be on the faculty at the University of Ife in Nigeria, which was the center of Yorùbá Studies. Quite a number of the younger scholars at the conference were students of the older ones. Most of the native-speaking Yorùbá scholars received their PhDs from North American universities in disciplines like English, literary studies, philosophy, anthropology, history, and religion. Most of them today are tenured faculty in North American universities, including Harvard. Wande Abimbola, the most prominent and prolific Ifá scholar, one of the persons to whom the conference was dedicated, had not only spent his academic career at Ife, but he had also become the vice chancellor (president) of the university in the 1980s.

As a Yorùbá and a student of the culture, I thought that the conference would be a wonderful opportunity to directly address many of the scholars who have been in the forefront of interpreting Yorùbá religious and cultural traditions. My long-standing research on the continuing imposition of male dominance through language and translation, on the introduction of male privilege on institutions and practices that do not in and of themselves embrace gender exclusivity or male privilege, and on the promotion of values that denigrate females made it imperative to address gender issues. My goal was to pose to the assembled scholars the question of why male dominance and gender exclusivity continue to mark scholarship on Yorùbá religious and cultural traditions despite the fact that patriarchy is not rooted in the oral traditions these writings purport to be interpreting. I thought the question of which language Ifá speaks and what its implications are for our understanding of contemporary gender inequality was an appropriate one to address at this conference. With these ideas in mind, I accepted the invitation to the conference and submitted an abstract for a paper titled "Ifá Speaks: Gender(ing) Epistemologies in Yorùbá Divination Discourses, History and Social Practices." My abstract expressed the following ideas:

> Given my thesis that gender is a colonial category and therefore not ontological to Yorùbá religious and cultural practices, and given that Ifá is a hugely important system of knowledge and wisdom in Yorùbá traditions, it is the logical source to go to make enquiries about particular developments in Yorùbá society. Thus, my goal in this paper is to investigate what Ifá can tell us about gender. In the classic interrogation mode used to consult Ifá, I want to ask *kíni Ifá wí nípa jéńdà?* At the same time, how gender is implicated in Ifá as knowledge system, as social and ritual practice, and as cultural institution in a changing world will engage our attention.

As soon as I saw the conference program, it was clear that very little if any attention would be devoted to addressing questions of gender whether in the languages in play, or the gender of the diviners, the gendering of forms of divination, the assigning of sex to the Òrìṣà, or even the gender of intellectuals who have chosen for themselves the role of interpreters of Ifá to the world. Despite panel titles like "Epistemology and Ifá," "Ifá in the Americas," and "Ifá and Aesthetics," these sessions contained no papers that sought to address gender questions. Not surprisingly, my paper, whose main subject is epistemology, was not included in the panel on epistemology, but was ghettoized, with another paper under a panel titled "Women and Gender in Ifá," scheduled to take place from 6:45 to 7:45 p.m. at the end of a full day of "conferencing." The panel was the only two-person panel of the whole conference, or shall I say two-woman panel. On further examination of the program, I knew there was "gender trouble" ahead.

On the first full day of the conference, the third panel of the day titled "Ifá in Comparative Perspective" was assembled. Olupona presented a paper on Islamic tradition in Ifá. A very interesting paper, it also spoke to the historical reception of Islam in Yorùbá society. In this presentation, the scholar reiterated a claim that Yorùbá people and indeed many African communities were receptive to Islam when it was brought into their communities because of the convergence between Islamic culture and African cultures. I raised my hand and made the observation that despite the fact that this statement about the similarity between Islamic and African cultures has become so accepted as to become a cliché, I question the veracity of such a broad and unqualified claim. With regard to Yorùbá society, I pointed out, there is an absolute gulf between the way in which Islamic cultures insist on removing women from public spaces and the contrasting Yorùbá social organization in which females are hypervisible (from the Western and Islamic perspective) in the most public spaces such as the streets and the markets. I then posed the following question: From the perspective of which gender is there a convergence between Islamic and Yorùbá traditions and why? Olupona refused to entertain my question, saying that he could not understand why I chose to bring gender into the discussion. Furthermore, he said, I had no business bringing up gender questions since the gender panel was not until six o'clock! We were not going to "do gender" until then! I was shocked by his response not merely because of the level of abject sexism and ignorance it displayed, but because of how comfortable he was in exhibiting such sexism and ignorance so publicly. In short, he felt that he was among "friends" who shared his views on gender. And he was right, because no one else raised further questions.

My interpretation of his retort is that as far as he was concerned, gender issues were irrelevant to the conference and were only pertinent during the discussion of what he termed the role of women in Ifá. The implication was that my question was out of place, and that I seemed ungrateful, considering that the organizers of the conference had been generous enough to allocate space—a panel—to women to discuss the "role of women in Ifá." But what about the role of men like the professor himself in Ifá? Are men not a gender category? The professor promptly dismissed my questions and went on with what he considered the important business of discussing Ifá, and was determined not to be distracted either by real, live women or female Gods and the reaction of the audience were not out of place at Harvard, given that a couple of years ago Larry Summers, the former president of the college, had questioned women's inherent ability to do science.[75]

Perhaps the most troubling aspect of the role of the akòwé like Peel, Olupona, or even Omoyajowo is their failure to recognize their own role in the patriarchalization of religion, and the fact that they themselves, as akòwé, are vectors of male dominance. Discussing women in studies of Africa is treated as if it is a supplement to the study of men, since men exist as the default category. Men have a gender too, and it is time we examine the role of masculinity in scholarship, which is what I have been attempting to do in this chapter. But it is more than scholarship, because a significant question raised by the series of events at the Harvard conference is the embeddedness of male dominance in the culture of the academic community. In the next section, I cite two instances of conduct that expose other facets of sexism in the academy. The first one pertains to the University of Ife, a premier institution in Nigeria, which had been the home of Olupona earlier in his career, indeed and that of many of the Yorùbá conference panelists including Wande Abimbola, one of the honorees, the Ifá scholar whose writings I took to task in the first chapters of this book.

Beyond Scholarship: What Manner of Community?

In his inaugural lecture titled "*Àjọbí* and *Àjọgbé*: Variations on the Theme of Sociation," delivered at the University of Ife, Nigeria, in 1980, Nigerian sociologist Akinsola Akiwowo presents a number of sociological concepts, which he derived from Ifá.[76] He then proposes the use of these concepts in analyzing human society and the different forms it may take. Akiwowo goes on to discuss the inherent nature of social conflict and social change in society, the role of intellectuals, and the need to use knowledge to remake our problem-ridden world. More interesting is his identification of five social rights to which each human being is entitled. Human society is only meaningful, he says, if these values are consciously sought as common goals. His findings are significant but here, my interest in Akiwowo's sociology lies elsewhere in his lecture but not unrelated to his concern about solving social problems.

In the preamble to the lecture Akiwowo gives us a portrait of his home department, the Sociology Department at the University of Ife, which he spent his career building as the founding chairman. The statement is striking for its gender explicitness and for what it reveals about the university community in which he was writing at the time, as well as Akiwowo's own views of male dominance in contemporary Nigerian life:

> The Department has become known in the faculty as the department in which the female teaching staff members have outnumbered the males by one. *In a male-dominated society, it is a credit to the male staff that the social organizational structure of the Department has not been irreparably shredded by conflicts. It is also a clear evidence of the fine sensibility of our female colleagues that they maintain their own as intellectual equals without fuss.*[77]

This statement is sexist and patronizing of women, and because it invokes a number of stereotypes about them, it is prejudicial at a number of levels:

1. Akiwowo expected all hell to break loose because there were more females than male faculty in the Sociology Department, which he sees as an unnatural state of affairs. Male dominance to him is the norm, which is demonstrated by the rest of the departments in the university.

2. Akiwowo gives credit to the male staff (faculty) for tolerating the presence of a high number of females who have upended the natural order of things. In a sense he is saying that the females are out of place and the males have been nice enough to live within this unnatural state. In essence, he claims that the social organization of the department has not been irreparably damaged by conflict between the males and females, who are the interlopers; hence his recognition of the magnanimity of the men in the department.

3. At another level, he may have been thanking the males for keeping the department viable in spite of the females, whose very presence and behavior have been stereotyped as conflict generating and quarrelsome. In the second sense, conflict among the women has not damaged the social organization of the department because the males have done a good job of holding up the department in spite of the quarrelsome females.

4. Akiwowo assumes the intellectual inferiority of women; hence his surprise that "*our female colleagues…maintain their own as intellectual equals without fuss.*" He then proceeds to compliment them on their fine sensibility.

5. The implication of this multilayered gender stereotyping and discrimination is that the male faculty (Akiwowo included) in the Department of Sociology at the University of Ife is doing society a favor by tolerating the overwhelming number of females.

Akiwowo's statement leads one to ask what the quality of sociality in his department and the University of Ife was like. Explicating Ifá texts in the lecture, he writes[78]:

Human society provides for each member who makes it up, five categories of inalienable social values which constitute the goal of human collectivities. These are:
 a. *Ire àìkú* (the value of good health till old age)
 b. *Ire-owó* (financial security)
 c. *Ire ọkọ-aya* (the value of intimate companionship and love)
 d. *Ire ọmọ* (the value of parenthood)
 e. *Ire aborí ọtá* (the value of assured self-actualization)

Since the ultimate aim of Akiwowo is to create a society in which all members have access to *ire gbogbo*, the five basic social rights he derives from Ifá, was the professor aware of the fact that male dominance has a direct impact on whether the female faculty and indeed females in society realize their own *ire gbogbo*? Given the much-lauded male dominance in both the department and university, what was the quality of "sociality" for the female faculty and indeed all females at the university?

Some of the answers to these questions lie in the way in which scholars relate to one another and create social networks that facilitate scholarly work. Conferences are good opportunities to observe the role gender plays in social interactions. For a gender scholar, Yorùbá scholarship, along with the academic community and society, provides an unusual opportunity for witnessing the systematic way in which male dominance is constructed. With regard to the institution of language, the process is easier to see, and it is being done one concept at a time, one word at a time, right before our eyes.

My experience and observations at these meetings are instructive enough. When two Yorùbá scholars meet at conferences anywhere in the world, as soon as we recognize each other as Yorùbá we are more likely than not to speak the language to each other. If one does not speak the language after initial introductions, it is a sign that one does not understand the language or that one wants to maintain a distance, for whatever reason. Once we start addressing one another in the language, the choice of pronoun and the appellation we call each other display each person's understanding of our place in the hierarchy of seniority that Yorùbá pronouns encapsulate. Yorùbá pronouns do not denote gender but they do express age hierarchy. For one thing, a junior person in the hierarchy cannot (if the social intercourse is to remain civil) address the senior by name. I have noticed that there is a difference between the ways in which quite a number of junior Yorùbá colleagues address senior female Yorùbá colleagues in contrast to senior male scholars. This kind of behavior suggests a certain disregard for the accomplishments of females. On several occasions I have had to call my junior colleagues to order because they addressed me as àǹtí, a Yorùbá reworking of the English word "aunty" to mean older female relative. My objection to this appellation is that these colleagues are persons that I hardly knew, and, sometimes, I am just meeting for the first time at a professional conference, and they promptly show their "respect" for my age by naming me àǹtí. In contrast, they never address their senior male colleagues as uncle or bùrọ̀dá (another Yorùbá variation on the English word "brother" meant to signify older male relative). Herein lies a double standard biased against females. When I asked a male junior colleague not to call me àǹtí, he was shocked and distressed that he had offended me (which was not his intention) and could not understand why àǹtí was inappropriate or offensive to me. But as soon as I asked him what he called senior male colleagues who were my peers, he got the picture, telling me that he referred to his senior male colleagues as ẹ̀gbọ́n if they were a few years older than he, or Prof. (as in Professor) if they were much older. I then asked him why he could not use either term to refer to me in this fluid Yorùbá dance of hierarchy. He got my point and subsequently calls me Prof., the same way he, as well as I, refer to senior Yorùbá colleagues, male or female. Ẹgbọ́n is the Yorùbá kinship term for senior relation or friend, and it is not gender specific in everyday Yorùbá usage. However, today in some circles, the way in which this word is increasingly used to refer only to males calls for resistance of this gendering at the most micro level. I am not the only one who has noticed the shift in language. I have heard other female colleagues complain of the same kind of untoward treatment from both junior male and female colleagues alike. It is a case of gendering of authority to the detriment of females in a world where this had not been the case historically and linguistically. I want to reiterate the point I made more than a decade ago: "We can begin to talk about the linguistic genderization of authority in Yorùbá life. This is happening through the adoption of English-derived words and through the genderization of Yorùbá words that were once non-gender-specific."[79]

Intellectuals, academic institutions, and the process of knowledge production are very much embedded in society molding as well as expressing relations of power. Knowledge production is among other things the production of "truth," certain "truths" that largely reflect the interests of those whose charge it is to do research, analyze history and society, inform the public and public policy. What we see in Yorùbá society since the colonial period is the subversion of endogenous epistemologies, promotion of male dominance through masculinist concerns and perspectives, conscious subordination of matripotency, the eclipse of females as knowledge-makers, and the challenge to the matripotent ethos. What is remarkable is that scholars like Peel and Olupona, indeed academics in general, have not paid enough attention, if at all, to their own role in the creation and reproduction male dominance, a virulent disease of our time.

CHAPTER 6

TOWARD A GENEALOGY OF GENDER, GENDERED NAMES, AND NAMING PRACTICES

The nineteenth century was a revolutionary period in Yorùbá history, producing great social changes that we are still trying to understand. The historical transformations that were to have this huge impact were documented by historian B. Agiri among others. They include:

> First, the disintegration of the old Ọ̀yọ́ Empire and the emergence of a new political order; second, the collapse of the maritime slave trade and the growth of new exports,...the arrival of Christian missionaries and the establishment of the British at Lagos, followed by the spread of British influence inland. For the average Yorùbá citizen, it was a century of confusion and chaos when the old traditions were questioned. Some customs were modified, while others were reinforced or discarded.[1]

What needs to be added to his list is that Islam, which had been present in some parts of Yorùbá communities before this time, was not only putting down deeper roots but was also expanding with noticeable impact on the society. In this chapter, my focus is on new customs, new institutions, new social practices, and most significantly new names that emerged in this period. Seemingly gendered names, gendered practices, and gendered institutions appeared, particularly in Ibadan and Abeokuta, two new polities that absorbed the fleeing refugees of internecine wars attending the fallen Ọ̀yọ́ empire. The emergence of new names and novel naming practices was certainly a notable development. It is impossible to exaggerate the importance of names to Yorùbá people and therefore it is a useful window to their thinking, social practices, and social change. Naming systems are by definition knowledge systems given the epistemic value of names.

Traditionally, Yorùbá names are not gender-specific in that both males and females bore the same names. Yorùbá names and naming are no different

from their other social institution all of which expose an epistemology that
does not construct gender. Hence, as I have established in various writings
and in earlier chapters of this book, there were no gendered moral and
social attributes in the cultural ethos, and so notions of masculinity or femininity are alien. However, in the nineteenth century, *oríkì* or personal praise
names, a particular kind of name that appear to be gendered, came into use.
Such names seem to be gender specific in the sense that today in popular
understanding a particular set of *oríkì* are associated with the anafemale
body and another parallel group are anamale identified. Gendered names
at any level do not fit in with the already existing variety of names, neither
did they conform to the logic of Yorùbá naming practices, world-sense,
and social institutions. The apparent identification of a set of praise names
with one body type, and another group of *oríkì* with the other body type,
then, becomes a curiosity, a puzzle that need to be explained. In my book
Invention, I showed that gender constructs are a recent historical development in the society, emerging in the nineteenth century. Following from
this thesis then, I surmised/hypothesize that personal praise names must be
of relatively recent origin even though they seem deeply rooted in the current social structure, as if they have been in use from time immemorial.

My objective in the next three chapters, which are intertwined, is to
investigate the origin of *oríkì* and its relationship to the convulsions that
engulfed Òyó-Yorùbá society following the disintegration of the empire.
Second, I will examine the links between the use of praise names and the
newly emerging Christian and Muslim convert communities. Despite the
fact that female *oríkì* and male *oríkì* are thought of as a gender field of the
same phenomenon, analysis of the meanings of the names suggest the two
sets of names developed differently. My investigation will not take the gendered nature of personal praise names for granted recognizing that their
apparent use today in a gendered fashion may be a result of change over
time. Theoretically, the question of whether a particular practice or institution is gendered can be apprehended at two levels: first, gender is routinely
invoked when the phenomenon under study is seen to superficially attach
to male and female bodies differently, and in a binary way. The second level
of gendering is more fundamental in that it speaks to the gender division
of social and moral attributes that is embedded in the ethos, which is then
expressed in social practices throughout. In Western societies, whose mores
and values overly inform academic discussions of gender, the two levels are
conflated because of the degree to which gender "doings" have become
the warp and woof of the culture. However, in Yorùbá society because gender as a construct is not ontological to the ethos, and since any articulation of gender is a new development historically, the multilevel process of
understanding gender becomes obvious. Thus a study of gendering in this

society affords scholars the opportunity to understand the process by which institutions and practices become gendered. Does the presence of the first level, that is, the superficial naming of male bodies and female bodies differently automatically signal the presence in the society of gendered moral and social attributes? The evidence from Yorùbá society does not support this line of thinking because social and moral attributes are still not universally understood to inhere in males and females differently. A second question is whether the first level of gendering expressed in the naming of social phenomena as male or female is a sign that a society has embarked on a process of gender differentiation, classifying males and females differently, if not unequally. A third level is how to make sense of societies in which gender constructs were originally absent but have now been imposed through colonial processes of incorporation of such societies into the Western cultural gendered ethos. That is my task in this chapter.

My analysis of names here is really a vehicle for raising questions about where apparent distinctions between female and male character that is suggested by different sets of names come from. The ultimate question in any discussion of origins of gender constructs in Yorùbá society really is not whether Yorùbá thought recognizes differences between male and female bodies but whether it recognizes social and moral attributes as feminine or masculine and has as a result organized social facts to express such a belief. I am also interested in praise names for what they can tell us about social change, particularly in relation to gender. One of the most fascinating things about indigenous names is what one scholar calls their record-keeping function, a fact that has bearing on how names have come to encapsulate elements of social change. According to anthropologist Niyi Akinnaso:

> Yorùbá personal names serve as an open diary by providing a system through which information is symbolically stored and retrieved. The diary is open because personal names are public, being the primary mode of address among the Yorùbá. However, the nature and range of information stored in a given personal name may not be known to every member of the community. Since personal names are used several times a day in the normal course of an individual's life routine, this diary-keeping function is particularly effective in serving as a reminder of those dominant social values, important personal concerns, and other special events that are reflected in personal names.[2]

Yorùbá names can be literally read for information and it is this archival function that attracted me to the idea of using such to probe gender issues. Although a number of scholars[3] have demonstrated the value of oríkì poetry as a source of historical data, and a few linguists have analyzed oríkì names linguistically, many of the questions I am asking in this chapter have never been asked before in studies of Yorùbá culture. Consequently, the task of establishing the origin of praise names, whether they are gendered or not, is a multifaceted process that will draw in many other institutions and practices across three centuries. Investigating these questions requires a detailed examination of social practices and institutions that may at times appear to be far from the subject of gender, but this is not the case because in order to establish the genealogy of gender, this comprehensive excursion is necessary.

Naming Names: Putting *Oríkì* Names in Social Context

The word *oríkì* refers to a verbal genre popularly described as praise poetry. However, there are a number of subgenres of *oríkì* poetry: *oríkì orílè* (lineage *oríkì* extolling the characteristics of particular lineages), *oríkì ìlú* (dealing with the foundation of towns), and *oríkì bòròkìnní* (*oríkì* of notable personalities). But *oríkì* can also refer to a personal name that is one among many names given to a child after birth. *Oríkì* names are distinctive and recognizable; they generally cannot be easily confused with any other names. In Yorùbáland, when one is asked about one's *oríkì*, it is clear that the expected response is the single word personal name and not the long poetic verses referring to the lineage, town, or important people, since very few people today know the longer versions of their lineage *oríkì*. My primary interest here is in the *oríkì* personal name, the one-word, single names that are recognized as appellations, designed to flatter and praise someone, bolstering that person's self-esteem. I will also refer to *oríkì* names as praise names, which the vast majority of them are, although a few are not as clear in meaning.

To situate praise names in the culture, we must look at the overall naming system. There are many different types of indigenous names, but they fall into two broad categories, namely, *àmútòrunwá* (literally a name that the infant brings from the Otherworld) and *àbíso* (the primary names given after the birth of a child). *Àmútòrunwá* are very specific names, few in number (probably not more than ten), whose chief distinction is that they are based on the observed biological facts attending the birth of that child. For example, the names Táíwò and Kẹ́hìndé are names of twins, and Ige is the name of a baby who emerges from the birth canal feet first. For Yorùbá people, babies who generate *àmútòrunwá* names enter the world already armed with their own name. Being born with a name is interesting and significant because in the culture, there is a reluctance to name an infant until a week or so after birth. The *ìkómọjáde* (literally exposing of the infant to the public, coupled with a naming ceremony) is supposed to be the occasion when the child is formally presented to nonfamily members, and the time when the name of the infant is announced by parents. Not so for *àmútòrunwá* babies, because these children preempt the elders and literally name themselves through the way in which they come into the world. These babies have already acquired a name, an identity long before the *ìkómọjáde*. These children seem to forcefully insert themselves into society as they are born. It is important to note that *àmútọ̀runwá* names are not gender specific. The second broad category of names, *àbísọ*, encompasses all other name types, the distinguishing feature being that these are names given after birth. The majority of the names in the *àbísọ* category are primary given names that are simply called *àbísọ*. Literally, "to born and name." When one is asked "*kíni orúkọ rẹ?*" (What is your name?), an *àbísọ* is usually the expected answer. Equally significant is the fact that *àbísọ* names are given to newborns due to the circumstances surrounding their birth, ranging from what the family might be going through to what the birth of the child entailed for the mother or the political and social climate of the time. Samuel Johnson, the pioneering Yorùbá local historian and ethnographer, identified different sets of circumstances of the family that will lead to particular *àbísọ*:

> Names having reference to the child itself directly or indirectly to the family e.g. Ayodele (Joy enters the house); Names having reference to the family directly or indirectly to the child: Kurumi (Death has impoverished me); names compounded of prefixes such as Ade [crown], Ola [honor], Olú [chieftaincy], For example Oyeyemi (title becomes me).[4]

Praise names also fall under the broader category of *àbísọ*, if we follow the Yorùbá categorization scheme, because they are names given after birth, in contrast to *àmútọ̀runwá*, which are tied to the birthing process itself. Nevertheless, in usage, the distinctiveness of *oríkì* as a particular kind of *àbísọ* is recognized. To illustrate further, a praise name unlike any other *àbísọ*, is not a primary name; it is not a name you answer to all the time. Rather, *oríkì* are intended for particular moments. Such an occasion can occur as many times in the day as the older person in an interaction finds necessary to address a younger person, or not at all.[5] The point is that the names are designed to perform a specific function: to praise, to flatter, to exhort the subject, and to raise self-esteem. They are especially effective because they are not overused unlike the regular *àbísọ* that is used at all times. Whenever one is called by one's personal *oríkì*, it is a sign of affection, and is associated with times when one is basking in favorable light.[6] *Oríkì*, then, are terms of endearment. It is for these reasons that Ọ̀yọ́ Yorùbá people express consternation[7] when they find such names being used as the primary name for identification, as is increasingly common today. The ability of *oríkì* to elevate the subject psychologically has to do with its association with especially positive moments in one's life. When they are used as everyday, all-the-time given names, then they lose their luster and can no longer fulfill this function.

Oríkì are designed to flatter and praise and when coupled with the longer lineage oríkì poetry, their effect is to puff up the person being named. Socially, when the oríkì name is invoked, it is accompanied by the orílè, which is the totem of the family. My own oríkì is Àníkẹ́ and my family totem is Ọ̀kín. When my oríkì is used by my parents or an older person who wishes to extol me, they usually say Àníkẹ́ Ọ̀kín. Generally speaking the totemic name is derived from one's father's lineage of origin, and married women's totem remains that of their natal homes.

Linguist Olasope Oyelaran has compared the function of oríkì coupled with the family totem to the United States' Social Security Number system: "a lè sọ pé bí nọ́mbà ti jẹ́ sí àwọn ará Amẹ́ríkà, bẹ́ẹ̀ ni orúkọ, oríkì, àti orílẹ̀ jẹ́ sí àwọn Yorùbá. Ní ilẹ̀ Amẹ́ríkà, tí o bá ti mọ nọ́mbà ètó eese ìfẹ̀yìntì [Social Security Number] ènìyàn, tí o sì mọ nọ́mbà láńsẹ́ẹ̀sì àti ti tẹlifóònù rẹ, o ti mọ̀ ọ́n tán. Bẹ́ẹ̀ ni ti orúkọ, oríkì, ati orílẹ̀ jẹ́ láàrin àwa Yorùbá" (We can say what numbers are to Americans is the same with oríkì among Yorùbá. In the United States of America, when you know the Social Security Number of a person, know the license and telephone numbers, you can identify them absolutely. That is how oríkì coupled with orílẹ̀ among Yorùbá [my translation]).[8] He makes the claim that oríkì in combination with the primary name and orílẹ̀ are as unique to the individual as the United States' Social Security Number.

The comparison of oríkì to Social Security Number is baffling at a number of levels, and its veracity cannot be sustained for a couple of reasons. First, oríkì names are limited in number. According to Akintunde Akinyemi, a scholar who has studied the social uses of the oríkì genre, "personal oríkì are few in number unlike other types of personal names…the total number of both male and female personal oríkì found among the Yorùbá is still under one hundred (100)."[9] He also explains, "There is no way that we can coin or create new personal oríkì despite their unique phonological uniformity and systematical grammatical structure."[10] My own research concurs with this finding that oríkì names are few in number; as a matter of fact one hundred is a generous figure. Consequently, oríkì are invariably duplicated, especially in large households, which is the characteristic Ọ̀yọ́-Yorùbá family settlement pattern. Many lineages have more than a hundred, two hundred, or even three hundred members. Thus, within one lineage compound, it is common to have names duplicated among cousins, uncles, and aunts of the same or different generations. Because they are all members of the same family, the totem names accompanying the oríkì are also the same. Even primary names are duplicated, given that the circumstances of birth that these particular appellations rest on can and do repeat themselves. Similarly, àmútọ̀runwá names, like twin names, are repeated within a lineage, as a family could have many sets of twins and they would all be expected to bear the same names, since these names are set in ritual concrete emanating from the biological fact of how the babies came into the world. In a particular household, then, you could have two cousins called Àlàkẹ́, and because their family totem name is Òpó, then they would both be addressed as Àlàkẹ́ Òpó and finally, they could both have been given Olúrẹ̀mílẹ́kún (the lord has comforted me because they were born after painful happenings in the family) as their àbísọ names. Thus you have two persons in the same family with exactly the same three names. Because of the size of families, and because they are segmented within, parents—name-givers—often do not realize these duplications until much later. Since oríkì names are occasional (as in a special occasion or momentary) names, a person's oríkì is rarely at the tip of the tongue of their many family members, much less of strangers. As a result, one frequent question in social interactions is: "what is your oríkì?" Or, whenever a senior person in an interaction wants to laud the junior one, they are likely to start with "remind me of your oríkì." A visitor to a home is not guaranteed to learn a person's oríkì indirectly (unlike the primary name), because it's use is strategic, being invoked for a particular purpose not necessarily just for identification. The best way to know a person's oríkì is to ask. Duplication of oríkì is not seen as a problem and has no effect on its primary purpose as a flattering device in that the oríkì is uttered directly and addressed to a particular subject who knows that s/he, and s/he alone, is being addressed at that moment in time. Oyelaran mistakenly deduces oríkì use from contemporary fragments of lineages that are trying to mimic the tiny Western nuclear family size, which is a legacy of Christian and colonial notions of acceptable family configuration. Oríkì are truly personal names but totally nonexclusive even in the family.

Oríkì are not universal to all Yorùbá subgroups. Despite the wide distribution and prevalence of Oríkì poetry as a defining institution in Yorùbá society, personal praise names are particular to Ọ̀yọ́-Yorùbá and are not prevalent among other Yorùbá subgroups such as Ìjẹ̀bú, Èkìtì, Ìjẹ̀sà, and so on. According to Ladele et al:

Ní ilẹ̀ Yorùbá, pàápàá láàrin àwọn Ọ̀yọ́, bí a bá ti sọ ọmọ ní orúkọ ní ọjọ́ kẹjọ ni a o fún ọmọ náà ní oríkì ṣókí tí a ó máa fi kì í…Nínú ìwadìí tí a ṣe, a rí i dájú pé púpọ̀ nínú àwọn Èkìtì, Oǹdó, Ìlàjẹ, Ìjẹ̀bú àti Ìkálẹ̀ ni kò ní oríkì ṣókí. Àwọn díẹ̀ tí ó ní ni ó jẹ́ pé bàbá tàbí ìyá wọn jẹ́ ẹ̀yà Yorùbá tí ó máa ń fún ọmọ wọn l'oríkì. (Inú wa yóò dùn bí a bá lè ri ẹni fihàn wá pé àwọn ẹ̀ya Yorùbá tí a ní wọn kì í ní oríkì máa ń ni. Ṣùgbọ́n gbogbo ẹ̀ya Yorùbá Ọ̀yọ́ l'ó ń ní oríkì.[11]

(Among the Yorùbá, especially the Ọ̀yọ́, newborns are given brief oríkì (praise names) when they are named on the seventh day after birth. We found in the course of our research that a good number of other Yorùbá groups—Ekiti, Ondo, Ijebu, and Ikale—do not have the brief *oríkì* [praise names] tradition. The few among them that do are often descendants of Yorùbá groups that give such appellations. [We shall be happy to entertain information to the contrary. The entire Ọyọ-Yorùbá region certainly gives brief praise names].)

My own research bears out the finding that the use of *oríkì* is specific to Ọyọ-Yorùbá and not universal to the whole ethnonationality.[12] But this statement needs some qualification, because following the wars that tore Yorùbá polities apart and reconstituted them and created new polities in the nineteenth century, different groups of Yorùbá were scattered to many parts of the region. Thus there are Ọyọ groups today that make their hometown in originally non-Ọyọ spaces. Hence one does find families in Ekiti, for example, who give *oríkì* to their children. Polities like Ibadan, Abeokuta, and Lagos are amalgamations of people originating from different Yorùbá towns and beyond. Nevertheless, the Ọyọ Yorùbá proudly distinguish themselves from other subgroups by claiming that the other groups do not have personal *oríkì*, as if to say they are uncultured. In my experience and research, I find that in my generation many persons of Ọyọ origin readily proffer an *oríkì* as soon as you ask the question, "What is your *oríkì*?" In contrast, many non-Ọyọ Yorùbá often do not even know that such names exist or that they are distinct from primary names since use of these names is not part of their family experience.

In my own Ọyọ-steeped family, each and every one of us has an *oríkì*, which is one of the names we are given on the eight day during the naming ceremony. Because of the importance of these names in our family interactions, I, in turn, have given praise names to my children, even those born in the United States—the meaning of which they have come to appreciate even more deeply when they visit their grandparents in Nigeria. Knowing the significance of the genre, I did not think twice before giving my children, born outside of Nigeria, *oríkì* names in addition to their other names. One cannot do without it, because it is required that parents and seniors use it to greet, praise, comfort, and motivate family members. The first thing one does when one marries a "foreigner" (non-Ọyọ) is to give him or her an *oríkì*. Àjọkẹ (one to be loved by all) is an extremely popular *oriki* that is given to in-marrying non-Ọyọ brides who do not come with their own *oríkì*. The experience of the anthropologist Barber with *oríkì* in Okuku an Ọyọ Yorùbá town is rich and telling. "I stayed three years in Okuku...I was given *oríkì* myself: the *oríkì* of the royal family, because I was 'adopted' by the ọba. Everyday I would hear the same phrases...Àjíkẹ Ọkín, child of the owner of the morning!"[13] Ajike (one who wakes up to be cherished) was Barber's *oríkì*. In Ọyọ Yorùbá communities, *oríkì* are central to identity and are treated as if they have been part of the culture from time immemorial, a belief that I am calling into question.

Many more issues arise regarding exactly when *oríkì* emerged as another set of personal names given to a child at the naming ceremony (*isomoloruko*), a week or so after birth. The first documentation of the existence of *oríkì* name is Johnson's which meant that such names were already in existence by the mid-nineteenth century. Despite the certitude with which Johnson discussed them, I am suggesting that *oríkì* have not always existed as another type of name that was given after birth. They are not primordial. Perhaps I should point out that the question is not merely about whether one can identify a name or two as praise names in an earlier period[14]; the issue is when did such a name become distinctly recognizable as its own category and more significantly, when did two distinct sets of names become coupled, and developed identities as belonging exclusively to males or females.

Examining the historical record, we find that the first bishop of the Niger, Samuel Ajayi Crowther, who was born in Oṣogun, an Ọ̀yọ́ town in 1806, was never associated with any *oríkì* name; his only indigenous name Ajayi is an *àmútòrunwá*, a name that the child brought from the other-world. The name Ajayi is given a child born face down. None of the names listed for his parents and siblings is an *oríkì*.[15] A study of Johnson's dynastic list of Ọ̀yọ́ rulers through time until the nineteenth century yields no praise names.[16] The local historian Johnson and his brother Obadiah had *oríkì* placed with their family totem in the author's and editor's prefaces of the book *The History of Yorùbás*. But what is not clear is when and how they acquired the names, given that they were born in the Yorùbá diaspora in Sierra Leone. (I will discuss the Johnson family history and naming practices later.) In Johnson's time, such names must have already become institutionalized in places like Ibadan, where he grew up, New Ọ̀yọ́ and Ogbomoso. But older historical documents, such as Johnson's ruler's list, and oral traditions, whether *Ìtàn* or larger *oríkì orílè*, rarely contained names that one would readily recognize as *oríkì*. It seems logical to look at histori-cal documents for *oríkì* names. However, it is important to note that the fact that we cannot find such a name for a particular person does not necessarily mean that they did not have one since *oríkì* are not everyday names that are used to identify a subject. Accounting for the gender specificity of *oríkì* looms large: and the answer to the gender question may lie in the origin of the name type.

To Gender, or Not to Gender? Making Sense of Praise Names

Unlike any other indigenous name type, *oríkì* are today gender specific in that male and female names seem to be distinguishable. No other Yorùbá

names, whether the primary names, or *àmútòrunwá*, have gender associations. The seniority-based system of social hierarchy is manifested in the
naming of twins. The names Táíwò for the twin who is born first, and
Kẹ́hìndé for the second born, are given regardless of sex. As I pointed out
earlier, names for twins is the archetypal *àmútòrunwá*, and the assignment of
names reflects the seniority principle encapsulated in Yorùbá kinship terms
àbúrò (junior sibling) and *ẹ̀gbọ́n* (older sibling). The expression of seniority in
naming twins also demonstrates the daily practice of hierarchy among siblings, in that Táíwò, who actually comes out of the mother first, is regarded
as the junior. "The idea is that the first born was sent forward to announce
the coming of the latter, and he[17] is considered the younger of the two."[18]
Yorùbá do not distinguish between fraternal or identical twins, nor do they
make a distinction among whether there are two boys, two girls, or mixed-
sex twins. Twins are regarded as special kind of children with metaphysical
powers, and their mothers must perform certain rituals in order for them
to continue to survive. The same rituals are performed for twins regardless
of their anatomies. I go to this length to explain Yorùbá names and naming
practices in order to show how unusual the *oríkì* is in its apparent gender
specificity. Are they in this regard, then, the exception that proves the rule
that Yorùbá did not originally dichotomize their social world by using gender constructs? Given the gender-free nature of names, kinship categories,
political titles, moral attributes, and the nongendering of social and political
institutions before the nineteenth century, I am curious as to how and why
oríkì are gender specific at least in current usage and what this can tell us
about the coming of gender paradigms in the culture.

Against this background what is the origin of the praise name? Why are
they seemingly gender specific? What do these names tell us about social
change? What do these names tell us about gender processes? Johnson had
much to say about names. Writing from the middle of the nineteenth century, he observed the nongender specificity of Yorùbá names but made
exception of personal *oríkì* declaring them to be gender divided. But he did
not seem to think that such an unusual characteristic demanded an explanation. In fact, he builds on the gendered aspect of the name type:

> Oríkì or cognomen or pet name: this is an attributive name, expressing what
> the child is, or what he or she is hoped to become. If a male it is always
> expressive of something heroic, brave or strong: if a female, it is a term of
> endearment or of praise. In either case it is intended to have a stimulating
> effect on the individual.[19]

Although Johnson's unconscious gendering of experience through the use
of English pronouns is a problem, I agree with him that female-identified

oríkì are praise names intended to stimulate the individual and to express the love of parents for their children. But such sentiments are not limited to anafemale children; it is what parents anywhere desire for all their children. My point here is that female *oríkì* are stock names, and despite their apparent gender specificity in usage, they do not encapsulate any notion of femininity because moral and social attributes are not feminized or masculinized in the Yorùbá ethos; the sentiments they express are interchangeable from one child to the other, male or female. Thus the meanings of Àníké, Àsàké, Àdùké, Àsàbí, Àwèró, Àmòpé, Àjoké, Àbèbí—all female-identified *oríkì*—are similar or one and the same, emphasizing the preciousness of the child and the need to love, cherish, and pamper the offspring. Again, they are terms that express affection. What is the hope of the parents of Àdùké? That everyone the individual encounters should compete to cherish them. Is this not the hope of parents for all children, male and female? A cursory look at female-identified names will show that most of them end in "*ké*," a verb meaning to love or cherish. On the basis of such inventory one might conclude that the verb to "*ké*" has been feminized. Such thinking would be an error because there are many primary names that also contain the verb "*ke*," which are not limited to males or females. For example, Adekemi, Obafunke and Ikepo like contain the verb and are not gender identified.

With regard to the meaning of male-associated *oríkì*, however, a different scenario becomes apparent. Unlike the female ones, the meanings of male names are varied, and seem more often to include verbs of agency, for example, Àjàmú (one who fights and triumphs) and Àjàní (one who fights and gets what he is fighting for). With regard to the female-identified *oríkì* the names suggest what others should do for the child. But in regard to male *oríkì* we are told that these have more to do with characteristics of the child. Johnson's claim that the names express parents' gendered expectations for children is not borne out when we analyze the meanings of the names (more on this topic later). Like Johnson, few scholars of *oríkì* such as Oyelaran, T. A Ladele et al., Barber, A. Oyetade, and Akintunde Akinyemi never asked any questions as to why *oríkì* names appear to be gendered even though all other types of Yorùbá names are not. My guess is that contemporary writers are living in an age dominated by a Western, Judeo-Christian, and Islamic cultures in which gendered names are normative. Steeped in Western intellectual theories, many Yorùbá scholars are not attuned to Yorùbá traditional norms and some may have a certain investment in the male superiority of present-day global culture. As far as I know, I am the first person to raise questions as to why *oríkì* are gender specific in a universe of Yorùbá names that do not encode gender.

Deconstructing the meanings of the names and discovering that there is nothing intrinsic in them that expresses femininity or masculinity immediately suggests that the gender associations are tied to usage. In fact, the parental desires they express are equally applicable to females and males. K. Yusuf[20] seems to be the exception in that he addressed the issue of gender and *oríkì* in his writing. I cannot agree more with this linguist who concluded "that there is nothing in the linguistic and semantic structures of *oríkì àbísọ*[21] that distinguish it as feminine and masculine, that *oríkì àbísọ* acquire gender associations from usage alone among the Yorùbá."[22] Two scholars disagree with this finding, and I will discuss them later. Of course accounting for why oríkì came to be used in a gendered fashion is part of the question. What is also obvious from the analysis of the pattern and meanings of the names is that female *oríkì* and male *oríkì* are so different that they appear not to have the same origin, which suggest that they may have developed for dissimilar purposes. It is my contention, therefore, that despite the fact that the female and male *oríkì* have become coupled in everyday use, and are treated as if they emerged together by most scholars, I aver that they have different histories and may have had nothing to do with each other originally. The majority of names in the genre are associated with females. Because the female *oríkì* names are truly praise names and define the category, I believe that the female ones emerged first as a distinct name category. Female *oríkì*, despite their numbers and apparent variety, all express the same thing: the desire that a child be cherished by all. Strictly speaking, not all male *oríkì* are praise names; they are truly varied in meaning, and do not necessarily refer to the characteristic of the child so named. We will discover that oftentimes, the name indicates a characteristic of the mother or father or conditions under which the child was conceived and not necessarily a personal quality of the child. In this sense, it is truly like other *àbísọ*, which are associated with the circumstance of birth or what the family, mother, or father are going through.

Disciplinary Debates: What Do Linguists Have to Say?

As may have become apparent from earlier sections, since Johnson, the most consistent scholars who have studied *oríkì* are linguists. Despite the technicality of their research, I believe it is important to interrogate their findings on this subject. Undoubtedly, many important issues come to the fore when these names are analyzed from that disciplinary perspective. In a paper on tones in *oríkì*, B. A. Oyetade defined an *oríkì* as "a nominalized tri-syllabic" word.[23] From this perspective, tones on syllables are important, since in Yorùbá, a tonal language, "tonal information is part of the lexical representation of words and morphemes."[24] That is, the tones on Yorùbá words (indicating sound) are inherent in the structure of words and therefore are part and parcel of their meaning. Oyetade posited that of the 27 possibilities that tonal patterns can take in tri-syllabic Yorùbá words (such as *oríkì*), only 3 are utilized in these names. The majority of *oríkì*—both male and female—follow a predominant LLH (referring to low tone, low tone, and high tone).[25] The second pattern LHH is fewer in occurrence and is found only in female *oríkì*. He writes, "I have not found a single male *oríkì àbísọ* with the LHH pattern."[26] Finally, Oyetade presents a third pattern, LMH (low, medium, high), in only a single *oríkì*: the female name Ajoke.[27] What are the implications of this finding and what sense do we make of it in relation to gender? Oyetade does not say, but Olanike Orie, another linguist, has considered some of these findings in the light of her own research.

Paying close attention to Oyetade's finding that the LLH tonal pattern is the predominant one in *oríkì* names, in contrast to the LHH patterned names, which are fewer in number, Orie then asked the question, "Is this asymmetry in frequency an accidental gap, or does it follow from any principle of grammar?"[28] She believes that it is not accidental, given that there's "a systematic robust pattern" that cannot be dismissed as insignificant.[29] What then is this pattern that Orie sees that follows from a principle of grammar? Oyetade had made the observation that the predominant LLH pattern in *oríkì* names occur in both female and male appellations, giving us a list of 22 female and male names in this category. Second, he observed that the other, less predominant tonal pattern LHH occurs only in female names, giving us a list of 11 names. He concluded emphatically that he has not found a single male name exhibiting this tonal pattern.[30] Orie does not challenge any of these findings; she agrees with them. The problem to be unraveled from her viewpoint is not an asymmetry in the frequency of one set of toned-patterned names over the other; the asymmetry that she sees here is a gender asymmetry. Despite the fact that as many female names as male names occur in the predominant LLH tonal pattern, Orie labels it the male pattern. She then contrasts it with the LHH pattern, which contains exclusively female names as the female half. By doing so, she has introduced a gender binary where there was none. Orie then concludes that the explanation for the asymmetry in the occurrence of the LLH patterned names and the LHH patterned names is explained by a grammatical rule about "markedness distinctions" in which the male category is seen as unmarked, generic, and universalized to cover both males and females, and the female category is limited, restricted only to things female.[31] She explains,

> The LLH pattern is more common than the LHH pattern because both male and female names are formed from it is explained if the LLH pattern is the unmarked form—the universal generic form that may have both masculine and feminine referents. The LHH pattern is less common because it is

the marked form, the form reserved exclusively for creating feminine praise names.[32]

There are many questions to ask regarding Orie's claims. First, how does a nongender-specific category, LLH tonal patterned names, become transformed into a male-only category? Most fundamentally, what is the grammatical rule that overrides the presence of females and excludes them so totally in the definition of the category? There is no such rule, grammatical or otherwise, in Yorùbá. Orie had to go outside of Yorùbá language and culture to find such a male-dominant, gender-discriminating rule, and she found it in European languages and imports it to explain a Yorùbá sociolingual phenomenon.[33] She writes:

> In languages such as English and French, masculine pronouns are sometimes used as universal signifiers that may have masculine or feminine referents. For example, in French, *elles* "they" is used when all referents are feminine. However if one of the referents is masculine, *ils*, "they" is adopted. Since the masculine form can be used for reference to both sexes, it is considered to be the unmarked form.[34]

But Yorùbá is not English, French, or even another romance language, its cousin. The most basic reaction to Orie's subterfuge is to point out that Yorùbá language has its own third-person pronoun, "*wọn*," which has no gender associations whatsoever. Furthermore, Yorùbá categories, whether in grammar or in social reality, do not contain any gender rules. Yorùbá pronouns, names, and kinship categories are not gender specific, and therefore the idea of a male generic does not arise. For example, the problem in English of the "ultimate generic" man used to designate male and female human beings does not arise in Yorùbá because humans are designated by the gender-neutral word *ènìyàn* (humans). The following is how I express this fact about Yorùbá culture in a previous work:

> There is no conception here of an original human type against which the other variety had to be measured. *Eniyan* is the non-gender specific word for humans. In contrast, "man" the word labeling humans in general in English that supposedly encompasses males and females, actually privileges males...Marilyn Frye captures the essence of this privileging in Western thought when she writes, "The word 'woman' was supposed to mean *female of the species* but the name of the species was 'Man.'"[35]

Why then does Orie disregard everything she knows about Yorùbá grammar and culture to impose a European system on the language and its naming practices? Orie herself had noted at the beginning of her paper, "Although gender is marked in many languages, some languages do not classify nouns or pronouns in terms of gender. Yorùbá is considered an example of such a language; it classifies pronouns in terms of person and number, but not on the basis of gender."[36]

According to linguists, because Yorùbá is a tonal language, tones are an intrinsic part of the structure and meaning of a word. This means that if the LLH patterned names contain both male and female *oríkì*, then these tone combination cannot be said to be gender discriminatory. The gender discrimination that Orie is alleging is extrinsic to the names and is clearly of her own making. The imposition by Orie of English- and French-language rules on Yorùbá is a colonial move if there ever was one, an archetypal disregard and erasure of the indigenous episteme. At a time when Western feminists are seeking to make their languages more gender inclusive, like Yorùbá and many other African languages, it is unfortunate that Orie would move in the opposite direction. If it were that easy, many Western feminists would be happy to impose the rules of Yorùbá grammar on English and French. Can we by analogy impose the nongendered rules of Yorùbá grammar and dispose of "he" and "she" in English? Can we because of our love for French start referring to a table as "she" in the English language?

Thus far, it is clear that the gendered nature of *oríkì* is more apparent than real, in that there is nothing inherent in the so-called male-associated names or female-identified names that makes them so, other than perception or convention. To put it another way, female names do not display any kind of femininity, neither do male names encapsulate heroism as one assumed mark of masculinity. The unfortunate thing is that scholars conflate female with femininity and male with masculinity. For example, Orie used female and femininity interchangeably. In a section of her paper titled "Femininity and Aesthetics," she reports that

> one of her research subjects said that the *oríkì* "names Àgbékẹ́ and Àbákẹ́ were chosen for her daughters because they sound more feminine and attractive than names such as Àdùkẹ́ or Awekẹ́. In essence, this speaker views LHH names as displaying femininity and aesthetics, factors that may explain why LHH names are exclusively feminine."[37]

What Orie means to say here is that LHH names are exclusively female; we all know that because it would appear that all persons bearing the names are anatomically female. But what is feminine? And what is feminine in Yorùbá culture, since masculinity and femininity are cultural constructions, if ever and whenever they are constructed. What is the evidence of femininity in female *oríkì* names whose meanings are interchangeable? If it is true that LHH names are exclusively female and attractive to parents because they are feminine, why then are they so few? The answer of course is that such an analysis is incorrect. There is nothing in Àgbékẹ́ (one who is carried to be petted/pampered) that distinguishes it from Àdùkẹ́ (one whom we all fall over ourselves to pet/pamper) to suggest any level of femininity in either name. As I noted earlier, what is remarkable about female oríkì is the uniformity in their meanings and sentiment expressed in these names. Both examples of "feminine" and less "feminine" names that Orie proffers contain the verb kẹ́—to love, pamper, pet, nurture, or cherish—typical of most female praise names. Orie herself had pointed out that "feminine names contain verbs reflecting themes involving nurturing."[38] She also mentions that for most parents, the overriding choice of name is in the "semantics," that is, the meaning of the name.[39] In truth with regard to female oríkì, they are more or less interchangeable, because they virtually mean the same thing.

Another dimension of imposing gender on these names is apparent in the work of Akinyemi, who questions K. Yusuf's accurate findings that there is nothing in the structures of oríkì names that distinguishes them as feminine or masculine, and that they acquire gender associations from usage alone. Akinyemi claims that oríkì names are not "gender neutral," and that

> all the personal oríkì that are peculiar to female are feminine and cannot be given under any circumstances to male children in the Yorùbá tradition. Likewise, some personal oríkì are peculiar to males and such personal oríkì are masculine too and cannot be given to female children. This is not a taboo but it is not practiced in the society.[40]

Akinyemi's argument that the names are feminine because they are female is tautological. At the very least, he needs to explain his usage of the terms. Female and feminine are not synonyms, and similarly male and masculine have different meanings. The terms "female" and "male" refer to the biological distinction of sex, which all human societies recognize, although in Western societies these terms already have social connotations. However, "feminine" and "masculine" more explicitly refer to distinct social expectations that some societies attribute to anatomic females and anatomic males, respectively. Though societies universally make anatomic sex distinctions for procreation purposes, not all have attributed social and moral attributes on the basis of distinct anatomies. Masculine and feminine categories are gender categories that carry social baggage, but anamale and anafemale categories are strictly bionatural. However, in societies like the West where gender thinking and practices are so ingrained, it is near impossible to separate the biological and social. In societies like Yorùbá, biological sex distinction did not carry any social or moral attributes and hence there was no gender. Perhaps, I should remind the reader that this is precisely why I coined the term "anasex" to underscore the fact that the Yorùbá biodistinctive categories (ọkùnrin and obìnrin) are not gender divisions. Consequently, Akinyemi's claim that names are masculine and feminine in Yorùbá and are not interchangeable is simply incorrect because Yorùbá given names (àbísọ and àmútọ̀runwá), which form the vast majority of names, have no gender associations. If Yorùbá people had established notions of masculinity and femininity, then àbísọ, which are the everyday names by which individuals are identified, would be gender specific. They are not. It is also a fact that there are oríkì such as Àbèfé and Akoki that are given to both males and females; such oríkì names reflect the Yorùbá norm in which names are not gender associated. Third, Akinyemi does not define masculine or feminine in Yorùbá society; therefore it is difficult to know what he means by "female names are feminine" in a society in which these terms have not been defined. From the perspective of gender studies, he conflates male with masculine and female with feminine, a grave error, since male and female are often used to denote the biological anatomy, but masculine and feminine are social constructions that impute certain moral and social attributes to bodies.

Like Orie in the preceding section, Akinyemi divides female-associated oríkì into two fields: "those depicting the tender nature of women" and "those depicting the beauty and the complete set of fundamental virtues in women."[41] Names like Àníké, Àṣàké, and Àbíké, all containing the verb to pet, pamper, cherish, he puts in the first category. As I pointed out earlier, concurring with Oyetade, these verbs point to the desire to cherish a child—there's nothing that says it is only a female child who must be cared for. But Akintunde writes that the verbs bè (to beg) and ké (to cherish) in the names refer to "the tender care that would be given to the female child."[42] Because there is nothing semantically in these names to indicate male or female, we are left with no explanation for Akinyemi's quirky and erroneous interpretation. Why should male children be excluded from care? He does not say.[43] We also know that in Yorùbá society both male and female children are cared for and celebrated. With regard to the second category of oríkì names that he delineated, Akinyemi posits that they express "the complete set of fundamental virtues of the female child"; these include Àmọ̀pé, Àṣàké, Àrìnpé, and Àbèní.[44] Thus for him the verbs ṣà, "select carefully," and pé "to be complete," among others, speak to the "fundamental virtues of beauty that will make the child stand out" and presumably therefore attributes only relevant to the female.[45] Again, Akinyemi's interpretation is unfounded and goes beyond the semantics of the name. What I hear in his coupling of female and virtues are echoes of the biblical virtuous woman,[46] a far cry from the nongender-discriminatory traditional understanding of social virtue. Moreover, the notion that beauty in Yorùbá culture is gendered female is problematic. The most basic notion of beauty (ẹwà) links it to character (ìwà); thus ìwàlẹwà—character is beauty. The true mark of an ọmọlúàbí—a virtuous person—is his or her ìwà (character), which is truly the essence of beauty (ẹwà). Males too are supposed to have ìwà and ẹwà—two inseparable virtues. It is character that beautifies. If anything, the oríkì names that are said to be explicitly about beauty are expressing the same thing as the other praise names—that this child is one who must be loved because it possesses attributes that one cannot but cherish. Thus female-associated oríkì names are testimonies about the good character of the subject, that is, a child, an attribute that compels love, care, and pampering. A Yorùbá primary name like Ọmọlẹwà (child is beauty) or Arẹwà (the beautiful one) is given to both males and females.

Oyetade, Akinyemi, Yusuf, and Orie have all paid close attention to the issue of gender in oríkì, and they must be lauded for having generated a debate in the field because for a long time, very little analysis of these names was done. They have certainly advanced the discourse. Nevertheless, the uncritical reflection of many scholars, especially linguists, on the gendered nature of oríkì names is perplexing, because they take it for granted even in the face of its unusualness. Perhaps because linguists are so focused on the mechanics of words and treat these names as merely words as if they do not occur in social context. Names are the product of a language, society, and culture. If Orie and Akinyemi had taken seriously the idea that gendered praise names are an exception to Yorùbá cultural norms, in that names, pronouns, kinship categories, and social institutions are originally nongendered, then it would have been clearer to the scholars that they need to provide evidence for their claims. Why is it that up till now, the exceptionality of oríkì as gendered names has not attracted much scholarly attention? It is this question of the apparent gender exceptionality of oríkì that led me to this investigation.

It would appear that some of the points of debate with the linguists are tied to disciplinary orientation in regard to what constitutes an anomaly, what it is based on, and how to resolve it. I cannot disagree with linguists that tones constitute part of the meaning of a Yorùbá word; therefore if LHH toned names are associated with only one category of a thing—in this case female names—then it must implicate "something." I do not disagree that this occurrence must be accounted for, but where does one look in order to do this accounting. Tone pattern can indeed alert us that something is amiss but it cannot tell us what exactly is going on. As a student of society as a whole, I am suggesting that in order to understand why the LHH names are only found on names given to females, but do not encapsulate all female names that are present in a second category of gender-inclusive *oríkì*, we must go beyond the narrow confines of the discipline and look to other sources of evidence. Akintunde who is a literary critic does try to use other sources, but his claim that using female *oríkì* names for males is not a taboo but is not just done cannot be sustained. If something is not a taboo and is not presented as such, the only reason why it is female or what we say it is is because of convention. Convention by definition is arbitrary and time sensitive. To restate the point, without a clear statement that a particular practice is forbidden, and without an established rule undergirding a specific social practice, movement in time or space could immediately falsify a claim. In essence the claim of genderness or nongenderness is not merely about prevalence at the time of observation, but must incorporate something more. The idea that there is nothing intrinsic in the so-called female *oríkì* that preclude their use for males is borne out by the fourth set of *oríkì* that have been identified as unisex.[47] These names include Àkànkẹ́, Àdùfẹ́, Àkòkí, Àmọ̀rí, Àyọ̀fẹ́, Àpèfẹ́, and Àṣàfẹ́. Although these names are unisex, they seem to be closer in meaning to female-associated *oríkì* in that they contain the verbs *kẹ́* and *fẹ́*. Also, a good number of them are terms of endearment that sound as if they emerged out of a highly sexualized situation. Even more so then, it is interesting that they are not gender discriminatory. With this example, it is difficult to sustain Akinyemi's argument that *oríkì* for some unstated reason are gender specific and betray masculine and feminine traits.

Indeed, the three tonal patterns and their distribution may indicate something is amiss although they do not specifically point to what distinctions they encapsulate. I would suggest that what the distinctions in tonal patterns of LLH and LHH may represent is a difference in provenance. That is a difference in the time period during which they were composed. Even the third type that contains only a single name—Àjọkẹ́—that so far has not been factored into the linguist's analysis should be explained. The debate about tones can be framed differently. Why is it that female-associated names come in a variety of tone combinations but male-identified names come in only one tone pattern? The answer to this question may lie in the fact that the female *oríkì* pioneered the genre. In keeping with the principle that there is more variety at the original source of social and biological phenomena, I believe that the female-associated *oríkì* came first. What the tone debate suggests is that a certain cluster of *oríkì* must have come into being at a different time than others. My conclusion is that the LHH tonal names that are said to be exclusively female may have originated first and defined the genre. The meaning and significance of female-associated *oríkì* does not lie in individual names, but in the origins of the category as a whole, a development that will be my focus in the next chapter.

CHAPTER 7

THE POETRY OF WEEPING BRIDES: THE ROLE AND IMPACT OF MARRIAGE RESIDENCE IN THE MAKING OF PRAISE NAMES

I n the previous chapter, I mentioned the profound historical changes that were under way in Ọ̀yọ́ Yorùbá society in the wake of the demise of the empire and the rise of new polities such as Ibadan and Abeokuta. My interest in these developments has to do with the emergence of not only new towns and new practices, but most especially new names such as the personal *oríkì*. My objective in this chapter is to determine whether *oríkì*, unlike other Yorùbá name types, is truly gender-specific and in so doing, interrogate what this search can tell us about the evolution of gender as a social division in Yorùbá society. In examining the meanings of praise names, I joined debates with a group of scholars, most notably linguists, who had written about the nature of *oríkì* names and the question of gender division in usage. The driving question in the present chapter is: What are the origins of both male and female personal *oríkì*?

In deconstructing the meanings of *oríkì*, it became clear that the female-associated set of names and the male-identified group of names are so different as to suggest different origins. Earlier on, I pointed out that the most important question to ask may be how the two sets of names became coupled rather than whether they expressed gender specificity originally. Because it is the coupling of the two sets of names rather than anything else that lead to the idea that they are gender-specific names. The preponderant number of *oríkì* are female-associated. Male-identified names are much fewer. Thus it became important to examine the origin of each set of names separately. Because the female personal *oríkì* are truly praise names in that they laud the bearer, it is obvious then that they define the genre.

Consequently, we must consider their history first before we attend to the male-identified names.

It is my contention therefore that female *oríkì* are a product of the turbulent times and the social earthquake that followed the disintegration of Old Ọ̀yọ́ in the nineteenth century. As such, they are relatively recent additions to the universe of Yorùbá names. I do not mean that individual names are necessarily all newly composed; rather what I am suggesting here is that the practice of giving each child a personal *oríkì* after a number of other names have been presented at *ìsọmọlórúkọ* (the child naming ceremony) appears to be a late historical development associated with the disruptions and subsequent regrouping attending the fall of Ọ̀yọ́, the rise of Ibadan, and the troubles of the nineteenth century. I believe that *oríkì* developed as part of a new genre of poetry called *Ẹkún Ìyàwó*[1] or *rárà ìyàwó*, a bridal chant performed on the eve of the bride's departure to join her husband's family. These names were originally a result of self-naming: they are one "nickname" in a constellation of appellations that brides gave themselves when they performed the *ẹkún ìyàwó* as they prepared to move to the husband's family compound at the completion of marriage rites. The *ẹkún ìyàwó* performance is a study in lamentation that borrows liberally from *oríkì orílè* (lineage poetry) in order to make its point. The bridal chant just like personal *oríkì* name are particular to Ọ̀yọ́ Yorùbá; the fact that they occur together is evidence that *oríkì* names are part and parcel of *ẹkún ìyàwó*. You do not find *oríkì* names in places without *ẹkún ìyàwó*, and vice versa.

Because the names are terms of endearment as Johnson puts it,[2] they seem to be designed to comfort, pacify, soothe, and elevate the mood of the subject. In a sense they are also prayers in a spiritually based culture. They are invocations to the personal god—Orí—a religious practice I discussed in previous chapters. Such self-naming expresses the general belief in the concept of "àpèmọ́raẹni ni à ńpe tèmídire," which translates as "good luck or good fortune must start with the (desiring) self." The names were also *àlàjé* in their original incarnation. What is *àlàjé*? According to Ladele et al., "*èyí ni oríkì tí èèyàn tìkararẹ̀ lè fún ara rẹ̀, yálà nítorí bíbí ire nítorí agbára tí ó rò pé òún ní, tàbí nítorí ọgbón-orí rẹ̀*" (Àlàjé is the name that one gives one self, because of honorable birth, perceived strength, or intelligence that one possesses).[3] What is clear is that these are names designed to augment one's sense of self or self-importance, one's noble ancestry, and probably underscoring free status at a time when domestic slavery had become widespread and institutionalized.

As I discussed earlier, linguist Oyetade suggested that we should not assume that there is a difference in meaning between *oríkì* that contain the verb *kẹ́*—to care for, to cherish—which is the predominant form of these names, and those that do not. He writes, "even if the issue of care is not mentioned in the verbs as can be seen in Arinpe, Amope, Aweni, Ayoka, Alari etc, the good luck of the child in being born into that particular home cannot be denied."[4] I cannot agree more with his analysis that these are names about caring for, and nurturance. Where we differ is in reference to the home that is alluded to in the names. Notwithstanding Oyetade's reiteration of current practice that *oríkì* names are "given to a child at birth alongside its first and other names,"[5] his explication of the meaning of female *oríkì*, rather than contradicting my claim that female praise names originated in the transition of brides from one family home (natal) to another (marital family), actually inadvertently sheds light on the fact that these names were not initially given at birth. The home being referenced in the *oríkì*, where the caring is expected to take place, is the anticipated marital home. Thus, I conclude that these names were not given at birth, but were originally taken by brides at the time of marriage. How so? Why one must ask, given the uniform meaning of these praise names, are prayers being uttered for only the female child to have the good luck of being associated with a specific family home, a sentiment that is repeatedly expressed in the meaning of female personal *oríkì*? The answer is that when these names originated, they were not given in infancy, and therefore the home being referred to is not the home into which the bride is born, but her marital home to which she is moving. This is a marriage residence which the bride is anticipating with anxiety, hoping and praying that it will be a new home in which she will be as loved, cherished, and cared for as she had been in her own mother's bosom, in her natal home. Even more interesting are *oríkì* like Àpèké or Àṣàké, which speak to the purposeful way in which the child has been chosen, called to join and be cherished in the particular family. Indeed these names express the developing process of marriage for females at the time, and today: they are selected, chosen, nay carried by the grooms' family into the marital homes. Thus *ìgbeyàwó* (carrying of the bride) describes what the groom's family is said to be doing when they marry a wife for their male offspring.

As a bride performs the *ẹkún ìyàwó*, her distress is palpable: she questions why she must make the transition from her natal home to her husband's home. This lamentation of the bride is a daylong performance, often accompanied with weeping, that the young woman stages on the day before she is to leave her natal compound for her husband's house. The purpose is to express her feelings about this impending change of state from child to adult, and most significantly to a prospective mother, from a permanent *ọmọ ilé* (member of the family) to *aya ilé* (aya or *obìnrin ilé* of another family) living among "strangers." The impending change of residence from her natal lineage to her husband's fills her with anxiety, uncertainty, anticipation, joy. and sorrow, and all these themes are registered in the content of *ẹkún ìyàwó*.

The genre has been studied by a number of academics, most notably Dejo Faniyi and Karin Barber. Here are samples of some of the themes expressed in the lamentation. The first set of verses are from the Faniyi[6]:

> The bride addresses her parents:
> My father, thank you for petting me,
> My mother, thank you for making me comfortable,
> Thank you for robing me with wisdom which is more important than
>   robing me with clothes.
> Slaves will care for you.
> Servants will be your helpers.

> Children which I shall bear, will take minister unto you.[7]
> In anticipation of the natal home and husband's family: she prays:
> That my would-be father-in-law
> May not be my slanderer;
> That my would-be mother-in-law
> May not be my undoing.
> That the co-wife[8] that I shall meet
> May not be an antagonist.[9]

> How does one prevent being disgraced,
> Child of Lalonpe?
> How does one guard against making mistakes,
> When one gets to the husband's house?
> How does one guard against making mistakes?
> So that one behaves like an adult?[10]

Questions, and more anxiety-ridden questions: the anxiety and uncertainty are a result of the fact that the bride is moving from a known and predictable home in the bosom of loving parents into an unknown world of "strangers," who remain unpredictable, and maybe even hostile.

Excerpts from Karin Barber's study of the oríkì genre that also included ẹkún ìyàwó, which she collected in the 1970s, highlight other themes. The following verse expresses "what she hopes for in the marriage"[11]:

> I'm going to my new home now
> I'm going to my new home to have money
> I'm going to my new home now
> I'm going to my new home to bear children
> If you say your good luck will escort me
> It will escort me right to my room
> May good luck attend me today.[12]
> She also bids farewell to her youth and her friends:

I am not yet tired of young girl's games
A towering head-tie is not big enough for me to wear to the market
Cloth of a pound a yard is not enough to wind round my head
But now I've left that time behind
"Laughing Teeth,"[13] Thanks to my father's standing
May good luck attend me today.[14]

In his classic work *Sociology of the Yorùbá*, N. A. Fadipe sums up the situation of the bride as she goes through the marriage rituals:

> It constitutes no less a mental than a physical wrench for a girl to be asked to exchange the familiar physical and social environment of twenty years or more for an almost totally unfamiliar surrounding environment on leaving for her husband's home.[15]

But the day of the staging of the *ẹkún ìyàwó* can also be seen as something more joyful, because the bride is anticipating motherhood as we saw in one of the verses earlier. Barber writing about the town of Okuku in the twentieth century tells us that the day is known as "*Fààjì Ìyàwó*—the bride's enjoyment," a day in which she is the center of attention.[16] It is a day in which the bride calls attention to herself and resituates her identity as a member of her natal lineage, reaffirms her relationship to her parents, and expresses her hopes and prayers for the future. Affirmation and reaffirmation of her birth lineage identity is underscored by the fact that "when she goes on her parade, she carries in her hand an emblem of her *ilé*."[17]

To reiterate my argument, female *oríkì* originated as names that brides gave themselves as they made the transition from their natal home to their marital home, at a time in which patrilocality (moving into the husband's family home) became institutionalized as the dominant mode of marriage residence in Ọ̀yọ́ Yorùbá society. Thus I submit that *oríkì* were originally names taken by brides as they anticipated the change in residence from their natal to marital home—a change that in many cases involved movement to a different town. In the next section, I examine the changing nature of marriage residence.

Naming and the Changing Institution of Marriage

The *ẹkún ìyàwó* performance encapsulates the meaning of marriage. Today, the defining characteristic of Yorùbá marriage for females is closely tied to the marriage residence, the house/compound—the *ilé*—and this invariably shows up in the vocabulary of marriage. To be married is expressed as to "*wà ní ilé ọkọ*"—to be in the husband's house—and so a married woman is an *abileko*. Similarly, to be divorced is to have left the husband's house (*kúrò nílé okọ*). Interestingly, *adélébọ̀* (one who has gone to the *ilé* and returned) is the word for a woman of a certain age or one close to or past menopause. What *adélébọ̀* demonstrates is the practice of mature women returning to their natal compounds as *ilémọṣú*[18] after many years of marriage. This vocabulary is very much tied to patrilocality—the fact that upon marriage a bride moves into the residence of the husband and his family. In the past, however, patrilocality was not the norm, given the fact that Ọ̀yọ́ Yorùbá towns were large and most people did not have to leave town to find brides or grooms. Hence couples could both be in the same town but live in different residences. The rules of marriage residence were more fluid, especially for brides of affluent and "honorable" backgrounds. For example, Johnson writes that "some girls of noble birth will marry below their rank, but would have their children brought up in their own home, and among their father's children and adopt his totem."[19] Females could not do that effectively unless they remained in their natal home. Johnson's observation here also reflects a popular and current saying that females from affluent backgrounds cannot stay in the husband's house, presumably uttered as a cautionary note to prospective grooms and their families. More recently, Barber noted in her Okuku study that "some women even maintained a working arrangement with their husbands, where they continued to have children for him but lived at home with their parents."[20]

By the nineteenth century, patrilocality became more deep-rooted in the culture, with many more brides not only leaving home but also leaving hometowns to marry further afield. In my view, this is the immediate context in which the personal female praise name emerged. The reason for this shift was the widespread dispersal of Ọ̀yọ́ Yorùbá people following the fall of the Ọ̀yọ́ empire and its capital; its reconstitution and the rise of new polities, most notably Ibadan. Many of the Ọ̀yọ́ Yorùbá towns, both old, such as Ogbomoso, and new, such as Ibadan, became settlements for large numbers of refugees originating from different places. The dispersal due to decades of war, coupled with the developing presence of Islam, Christian missionaries, trade with Europeans, and the occupation of Lagos by the British, opened up society in such a way that original residents of towns and members of families were no longer contained in one place. The implication of this was that finding marriage partners became as much a long-distance, intertown affair as it was local. Because Ibadan was at the center of these historic developments and was for a time the source of the wars that were visited on all sorts of large and small towns further afield, it is illuminating to focus briefly on the city.

By 1860, the newly founded "city on a hill" had settled down and out of its initial class of war chiefs had developed a civil administration that was distinctly Ibadan—republican, unlike the traditional monarchical system of older polities from which most Ibadan people originated. Ibadan was a slave society whose economy depended on domestic slave labor. Its political structure composed of a group of war chiefs presiding over large compounds, who enhanced their political status vis-à-vis their rivals by going to war and proving their prowess on the battlefield. Consequently, Ibadan was constantly at war and embedded in the town praise poetry is the line: "*A kìí wáyé ká má'larùn kan lára, Ìjàgboro lárùn Ìbàdàn*" (It is impossible for any being in this world not to have a defect, Ibadan's blemish is its constant civil war).[21] For our purposes, the most important part of this story is the type of social structure that developed as a result of the demographic movement. Ibadan had become a place of refuge for large numbers of refugees and adventurers; the city was in this incarnation what I would call a diaspora of towns (not just of people), since its *agbo ilé* (compounds) contained people from many older Yorùbá towns. Falola, a historian of Ibadan, paints a detailed picture of this process:

> Once a stranger came to Ibadan and succeeded in founding his own compound, becoming prosperous and famous, some of his townsmen, whether they had any relationship with him or not, would come to settle in his compound and, in the course of time, would become permanent members…During the period under consideration, strangers from Ọ̀yọ́ would go to *Ile* Iba, those from Iwo could go to Ile Ogunmola and after 1870 also to that of Ali Iwo at Agodi. Those coming from Ogbomoso, Ilora, Agberi and Ofa were welcomed in the compounds of Ope Agbe and Ibikunle, Latosa, Oderinlo and Alesinloye respectively.[22]

The reference to "strangers" here as in much of historical writing refer to males. But all these men, captives and free, required wives at some point in their lives. For the free men of stature and accomplishment, they often looked to their towns of origin for wives.

What was inside these *agbo ilé* (compounds) was equally significant. According to Falola, many of them were heterogeneous, not only in terms of ancestry and origins, but in the variety of social statuses and relationships that bound the persons within them together. In any compound, there was a dominant *ìdílé* (lineage), usually of the founders, forming the core of the house, and its members known as *ọmọ ilé*. But there were also *ará ilé*, who are not blood relations but may have joined the compound because they were from the same town of origin as the core members or they befriended the powerful leader of the compound. Also in residence were *iwòfà* (bondsmen) and *ẹrú-ilé* (enslaved persons) claimed by the core members of the compound. "By the late nineteenth century, Oroge estimates that there were about 100 great households in Ibadan, averaging 500 slaves each. The slave population in the city far outnumbered the free"[23] and within households, "female slaves could be taken as second-class wives to increase the population of his household."[24] It is against this background that we can appreciate the origin of ẹkún ìyàwó, the development of female oríkì names, their meanings, function, and subsequent institutionalization.

Given these social and political developments, there was a marriage pool of warrior chiefs, not to mention the many young men who were their retainers. Many of these men looked to their hometowns and other places for wives. Since this was a time of great flux, for newly established warriors, many of whom were of "lowly" origins, there must have been a desire to improve their status by marrying "girls of noble birth" from the older Yorùbá towns. It is from this class of prospective brides and their mothers that the ẹkún ìyàwó must have developed as a swan song, the final public act of a bride leaving town to marry and become an adult (mother). Ẹkún ìyàwó is performed only once, because a Yorùbá female can remarry, but she can "sèyàwó"—be a bride—only once. It is standard for performers of Yorùbá oral genre to make self-referential allusions, and I hypothesize that it was during such a performance that the first innovating bride gave herself a new name to match the occasion. Thus, I submit that oríkì name originated from the rite of passage called marriage rather than a name given immediately after birth. My thesis is that originally, personal oríkì names were bridal names, but subsequently they became institutionalized as names given shortly after birth, like other àbísọ.

What was the path of evolution of these names from bridal to àbísọ? The reason for the institutionalization of oríkì names is not difficult to imagine. The fact that within the performance, the bride insists on drawing attention to her pedigree may explain why praise names are usually coupled with the family's totemic name. The habit of brides of calling attention to their background during the performance may speak to the scourge of domestic slavery, in which many female captives had been turned into "wives" so that within any lineage, you have two types of aya (wives), captive and free who would be the mothers of the lineage children. It thus became imperative for females of relatively free birth to hold on to marks of distinction. Captive women could not be ìyàwó (bride) because unlike free females, they were not spoken for, no prestations were paid on their behalf, and they would not go through the long process of marriage, including the rite of ẹkún ìyàwó, which served to establish the unburdened pedigree of noncaptive brides. In short, the bridal chant, from which these names originated, became a signal of "noble" identity and served to distinguish these brides from the captive women who had "no people" and had been taken as disvalued wives, since by being enslaved, they had been dispossessed of family that would demand prestations from the prospective groom's family. Enslaved women had no grooms but owners who sexually exploited them. Yorùbá marriage was an interfamily arrangement not just one between the couple that cemented relations between two or more lineages. The enslaved woman who became a wife, however, had no people, no relations who would stand up for her. The free bride felt the need to establish the fact that she had people who would influence the way in which she would be treated in the husband's house. The females who became brides, and who staged the ẹkún ìyàwó, were those for whom prestations were made and gifts exchanged.

Sociologist Fadipe points out that of the different forms of marriage that existed in late nineteenth and early twentieth century when both Islam and Christianity had introduced new marriage forms:

> The one with the distinguishing feature of an elaborate system of gifts and services is the most favored as being typical and preferred. It has come to be closely identified with freemen, in which the kinsmen of both sides of the man and woman are joined together with the two principal parties, whose members are both witnesses and guarantors of the permanence of the union.[25]

Currently, the predominant word for "wife" is ìyàwó as opposed to aya. The word ìyàwó originally meant "bride"; it is a name applied to females who have "ṣe ìyàwó"—been made into brides by their families or conversely have been "gbé ní ìyàwó"—carried as brides by the husband's family. The carrying here refers literally to the rite of carrying the bride into the husband's family compound by other wives of the lineage. I wonder whether the preference for ìyàwó, now democratized to all and sundry, no matter how they entered the husband's house, may also speak to the desire of women to claim status and thereby avoid discrimination at a time in which matrimony was being used to rank women. Wives, just like husbands, were never equal. A captive woman could not be ìyàwó, but she was an aya, and enlarged the family with her progeny, who were born free.[26] Many of these themes resonate with historian Kristin Mann's study of Yorùbá marriage in colonial Lagos. She quotes from Reverend James Campbell, who wrote to a local newspaper on the state of marriage at a time when the institution was in a state of flux and the way in which people married indicated their "grade" in society. But even more so for women, he explained, as "there are three kinds of wives in native polygamous life The Dowry wife. The Gift Wife. And the Slave Wife."[27] Some chiefs "distinguished between wives called ìyàwó and aya and concubines called àlè."[28] The "top of the line" woman was the one who went from youthfulness to bride (ìyàwó), and then aya (wife).

It is within the context of concerns about domestic slavery, change in marriage residence and the new marriage respectability that ẹkún ìyàwó and oríkì names first emerged. Making wives of captive women had financial benefits for the prominent self-made men who already owned them. As we have pointed out already, it did not require any outlay of goods or services to the woman's family, which was a standard requirement from the bride's family. However, a "slave wife" could not be the main or only wife of a "big man," notwithstanding the fact that her children did not inherit her slave status. Writing about social stratification in nineteenth-century Ibadan, Falola tells us that "the people of Ibadan made clear-cut distinction among the poor (*talika, olosi, akuse*), a rich person (*olowo*), a propertied person (*oloro* or *olola*) and a man of honour (*olola*)."[29] The warriors, the notables, who took sexual advantage of female enslavement were "self-aggrandizers," to use Barber's term, who not only wanted to be recognized as *olowo* (rich) but also as *olola* (honorable), and some of that honor came from whose daughters they were allowed to marry.[30] The wives of a man and his affines are as much part of his status and self-definition as any other markers of distinction. As Barber has shown, one way in which the longer personal *oríkì* poetry works to enhance the subject is to demonstrate his or her "wealth" in people by piling on relationships such as husband of so and so, and father of so and so—standard lines in such chants.[31] And the *oríkì* poetry chanter could borrow liberally from the praise poetry of the lineage of the wife of the subject to elevate him. The man could exhibit his riches by pointing out the sheer numbers of captives that he owned, but he could not name an enslaved woman who has been turned into wife as a mark of accomplishment. Barber's argument that at the height of Ibadan militarism and the emergence of self-made, self-aggrandizing warriors, the style and content of personal *oríkì* poetry concentrated on naming them for their deeds and not their relationships is extremely persuasive.[32] Many of these warriors during what turned out to be a very short historical phase did not have many edifying relationships to speak of. It was not only brides who had to "marry well," to use Kristin Mann's apt phrase, but also bridegrooms. It is not surprising, then, that as Ibadan settled down to a certain measure of civility, and privilege became more entrenched, the old style of *oríkì* extolling social relationships resurged.

Oríkì names anticipated the challenges of modernity when many people—male and female—had to leave original homes for marriage, work, school, and the like and all could use an *oríkì* name like Àdùkẹ́, Àníkẹ́, or Àṣàkẹ́—an invocation that suggests that even when one is among strangers, one should be loved and cared for. In that sense, then, even males could use the so-called female *oríkì*. It may be that the creative brides who first gave such names to themselves extended praise names to their children given the beauty and the wonderful sentiments expressed by the names. What is not to like? Oríkì names are beautifully appealing. Lineage *oríkì* performed by Ìyá constituted lullaby for children, and it would not be surprising in that context that they spread these beautiful names that spoke of love and caring. It is also plausible that once it became institutionalized as one of the names given at the naming ceremony, seven or eight days after birth, it was extended to male children, and that is why indeed "unisex" *oríkì* like Akoke and Àdùfẹ́ may not be exceptional but a reflection of a period during which these names were given to both male and female children. There would be nothing unusual about this, since the vast majority of Yorùbá names were never gender associated and still remain gender neutral to this day. All this is a testament to the fact that the sentiments expressed in these names are universal, a sign that social and moral attributes still largely betray no gender associations. In the next section I focus on male personal *oríkì*.

Naming and Lauding Masculinity

Male *oríkì* originated differently and probably at a later date than female ones. I believe that unlike female *oríkì*, male praise names are not a product of self-naming but must have emerged out of naming practices of lineage wives. In an earlier chapter, I pointed out that a major role of wives and *Ìyá* of the family is to recite the *oríkì orílẹ̀* to affirm and esteem their collective *husbands*, namely, members of their marital family, including their own children. As part of the rules of family relations, lineage wives do not address by name any members of their marital family who preceded them (by birth) into the lineage because wives are considered junior in the family hierarchy. Hence one of the immediate task confronting a newlywed bride, for example, is what creative names she is going to invent to address the various relatives of her husband. Thus an important function of lineage wives is to name family members by giving nicknames. I propose that this is the context in which the male *oríkì* emerged. The varied names that became institutionalized as male personal *oríkì* must have been first articulated as nicknames given by a wife of the lineage. Earlier, I drew attention to the fact that a number of male *oríkì* contain the verb "*ja,*" to fight, to struggle, which is a word that spells agency. *Oríkì* names such as Àjàmú (one who fights and triumphs) and Àjàní (one who fights and gets what he is fighting for) strike me as the kind of a nickname that an *aya ilé* will use to tease one of her husbands. It is this context of origin that explains the agentic verb. Like the female *oríkì* that speaks to context of origin rather than a putative notion of femininity, there is nothing in the male *oríkì* that expresses some intrinsic notion of masculinity. Yet a chorus of writers and scholars have made the claim that male-identified praise names express masculinity. Following Johnson, who said male *oríkì* is always "expressive of something heroic, brave, and strong,"[33] a number of writers have expressed the same idea. Ladele et al. wrote, "*oríkì tí àwọn ọkùnrin ń jẹ́, a ó ríi pé púpọ̀ nínú rẹ̀ l'ó ń fi ìwà akin àti ìgboyà tàbí agbára hàn"* (many of male *oríkì* names express masculine character, bravery and strength [my translation]).[34] And Oyetade writes, "Usually the verbs refer to acts of bravery, manliness, specialty etc."[35] There certainly seems to be a masculinist ideology at work in the representation of these names by interpreters of the culture who by their conduct reinforce this line of thinking. Indeed, this has been the dominant theme of previous chapters of this book: the role of intellectuals in creating a masculinist ethos.

Even if the names express strength, heroism, bravery, and courage, the idea that these attributes are male-exclusive in Yorùbá culture cannot be taken at face value but need to be accounted for given the nongender-exclusive nature of these values. But first, what exactly is manhood or manliness? What is masculinity? In an anthology *Men and Masculinities in Africa*, historian Stephan Miescher writes that masculinity "refers to a cluster of norms, values, and behavioral patterns expressing explicit and implicit expectations of how men should act and represent themselves to others. Ideologies of masculinity—like those of femininity—are culturally and historically constructed."[36] Despite the fact that this definition recognizes that masculinity is contingent on history and culture, Miescher and his contributors seem to take the construction of masculinity for granted as an inevitable fact of life in African societies throughout history—precolonial and modern. But the evidence from Yorùbá society does not support the idea that there were gender constructs in the past, of which masculine identity was a part. Prior to the nineteenth century, cultural norms, patterns, and behaviors did not support the notion that there was an ideology of masculinity. Ideas about self-respectability and maintaining the dignity of persons did not devolve into a gender binary.

Miescher is equally clear that masculinity must be distinguished from manhood, which is a notion "explicitly related to male physiology, often recognized in terms of male adulthood."[37] It is certainly necessary and useful to distinguish between the two. Scholarship on gender has established that we cannot make an assumption that males as individual bodies possess an intrinsic masculinity that is always already there bursting to be expressed. The fact that male and female bodies are a biological fact of existence does not necessarily mean that all societies are organized based on gender constructs, which emanate from ideas about the morphology of the human body. Many European societies whose experiences have been the template for our intellectual theories have been constructing gender as a dichotomous and oppositional category for centuries. Sociologist of masculinity R. W. Connell makes two important points: first, that the conception of masculinity in the modern age "presupposes a belief in individual difference and personal agency. In that sense it is built on the conception of *individuality* that developed in early-modern Europe,"[38] and second, that in Western culture "the physical sense of maleness and femaleness is central to the cultural interpretation of gender. Masculine gender is (among other things) a certain feel to the skin, certain muscular shapes and tensions, certain postures and ways of moving and certain possibilities in sex."[39] Such a notion of individuality and physicality of the body was not something that Yorùbá people organized around in traditional society. If anything, human persons rarely behaved or were treated or imagined as individuals. But this is not to say that there was no notion of the self or that individuals did not exist. Rather, the conception of *orí* (destiny, individual fate), which I explicated at length in chapter 3, makes it abundantly clear that persons exist as discrete individuals in the Yorùbá world and are endowed with individual fate, life being its unfolding, albeit as part of a collectivity. We must remember, however, that even the individual *orí* of a person is thought of as being linked to the *Ìyá's orí*, a belief that undergirded what I have described as a matripotent ethos.

Social expectations were predicated on the idea that each person in the first instance was part of a collectivity, and behavior by and toward anyone was hinged on collective identities, most notably lineage membership and within it segments of *ọmọọ̀yá* (uterine siblings). As I demonstrated in the previous section, this orientation started to change in the nineteenth century, and we can see the manifestation of some of these developments in the Ibadan warriors. If traditional Yorùbá society had been based on a gendered ontology in which notions of masculinity and femininity were constructed, then it would have been impossible to imagine that the social categories *ọkọ* (husband) and *ìyàwó* (wife) would not have been gendered. These categories are not based on body type; each one of them is inclusive of both males and females and therefore not predicated on any conception of gender. As evidence, consider postcolonial interpretations of Ṣàngó the Thundergod—a dominant *òrìṣà* of Ọ̀yọ́ Yorùbá, which is constructed as hypermasculine, with his elaborate powers being wrapped up in his manhood. The irony of this latter-day construction of manhood is that in another Yorùbá locality, Ṣàngó is regarded as the *ìyàwó* of Àrá, another deity who could herself be female.[40] The gender dichotomy that current writers impose on the *òrìṣà* falls flat in the face of traditional representations of both male and female *òrìṣà* using the same language of courage, bravery, and fierceness that the interpreters of male *oríkì* seem to claim just for men. In her study of *òrìṣà* devotees in Okuku, Barber makes the relevant point:

> The *òrìṣà* are differentiated in *oríkì*. Ṣòpọ̀nnón the deity of smallpox, and Ṣàngó, the god of lightning, are evoked as gigantic and terrifying figures

commanding cosmic forces of sun and fire, ruthless and implacable; while
Ọ̀ṣun and Ọ̀tìn are evoked as predominantly mild, cool figures, associated
with child-giving and curative powers of water. What is less well known is
that in *oríkì*, Sonponnon and Ṣàngó are also praised for their curative powers
and the ability to give children, while Ọ̀ṣun, Ọ̀tìn and Esile are also represented as tough, ferocious and dangerous. Each *òrìṣà* is credited with both sets
of qualities though in different proportions.[41]

The point is that anamale or anafemale *òrìṣà* are not dichotomized on the
basis of character attributes. It is for this reason that in my previous work
I rejected a term like "goddess" and insisted on the Yorùbá nongendered
practice in which *òrìṣà* is *òrìṣà* regardless of sex, and therefore use god to
refer to all of the deities, no matter their body type. Significantly, despite
the fact that water is associated with coolness and healing, Ọya the female
river god is portrayed as one of the fiercest *òrìṣà*, as ruthless as her husband
Ṣàngó, who is also Ọ̀ṣun's husband. The deity represents terrifying weather
events such as storm, hurricanes, and tornadoes. The fact that Ṣàngó, who
is often depicted as the hypermasculine husband of many wives in current
accounts, is found to be represented as an *ìyàwó* of Ara, a deity in another
Yorùbá community, troubles the dominant Western notions of masculinity.
What is masculinity here?

In the light of the foregoing, I would reiterate the point that there was
no institutionalized endogenous notion of masculinity in Ọ̀yọ́ Yorùbá
society before the fall of Old Ọ̀yọ́. Yet many scholars continue to take for
granted the idea that there was a Yorùbá notion of manliness. A number
of writers locate "manliness" in the institution of marriage. Sociologist
Peel's example is typical of how current interpreters tend to think of
masculinity in African societies. Peel is very clear on this question: he
argued that in the nineteenth century, the newly Christian Yorùbá men
were persuaded "to go to war,[42] against their pastor's injunctions, on
account of frequent charges of cowardice and *womanliness* from heathens"
(his emphasis), because he asserts that Christianity was seen as a wom-
anly religion, in contrast to Islam.[43] Peel concludes that some of these
Christians repudiated the religion and embraced Islam instead, "which
was much more compatible with *Yorùbá values of manliness*."[44] What are
these Yorùbá values of manliness? Peel does not explain, but his next sentence on polygamy betrays what must have been on his mind. He high-
lights the experience of David Kukomi, an Ibadan warlord and leader of
one of the notable lineages, as prototypical of the sacrifice a male convert
had to make, since he had to renounce all but 1 of his 17 wives on conversion to Christianity.[45] Presumably, he was sacrificing his "masculinity" in this singular act. Kukomi's 17-wife polygamy was pretty unusual
being a specific phenomenon of the flagrant polygamy of Ibadan warrior

slaveholders of the nineteenth century. Based on a Western gender ideology, Peel interprets polygamy as an act of sexuality (hypersexuality)
rather than of social accumulation of people as wealth that it represented
in the life, conduct, and imagination of Yorùbá people as in the saying ènìyàn lasọ mi (people are my cloth/wealth). Marriage among other
things represented an important mode of expanding the lineage and did
not necessarily amount to sexual prowess. The irony of predicating masculinity on marriage is that in the culture, the first time a man married,
it was his parents who "married the wife for him" to put it in local par-
lance. It was the responsibility of parents and other family members to
provide the gifts for securing a bride from her family. Imagine the implications of this fact in terms of lines of power, responsibility, authority, and
obligations within the family.

Equally important is the function of marriage in extending lineage
influence through the relationship's lineages contract with their affines—
lineages of wives they have married. The reduction of indigenous polygamy to manliness and sexual prowess represents the view of the outsider
imposed on a different culture; or views propagating masculinist ideologies at a time of ascending male dominance riding on the backs of
the new religions: Islam and Christianity. For one thing, in Yorùbá culture, even impotent or infertile men could marry and father children
through other men in the family or from outside of the family without
this compromising their standing. Remember that fatherhood was fundamentally a social construct, not only in a metaphoric manner but also
due to the fact that the absence of the father's DNA in a child did not
nullify his claim as the father. Legal fatherhood of a child was secured by
the gifts and prestations offered to the lineage of the bride. It was this
exchange that legitimated the marriage of the ìyàwó to the husband's
lineage. Furthermore, it was not unusual for men who were advanced
in age and sometimes impotent to marry younger women. Presumably,
then, it is not illogical to suppose that there were impotent polygamous
Yorùbá men who could offer ìdána (bridewealth) for multiple women;
some of whom preferred to join large illustrious lineages (ilé ọlọlá) even
if they had prior knowledge that the prospective husband would not be
able to copulate with them. They were assured of becoming mothers and
giving birth to children through other males in or out of the lineage, by
arrangement. These practices may seem outlandish and un-Christian, un-
Islamic, and "primitive" from the point of view of many contemporary
Yorùbá people and intellectuals, but we must remember that not every
one share current biases and these practices may not have been uncommon and exotic as our postcolonial "civilized" selves may see it today.
Indeed, consider a recent report in a Lagos newspaper, which suggests

that such practices have not been left entirely behind as the cultural reformist would prefer:

> A housewife, Mrs. Seinab Adebayo, yesterday told an Ijebu-Òde Customary Court Grade "A" that her husband, Adewale, was not the biological father of their three children. Adebayo, who is pregnant with the fourth child, also told the court that her husband was not responsible for the pregnancy. The husband, Adewale, who was the plaintiff had early this month, dragged his wife to court for packing out of the house with the three children without his consent. He urged the court to order his wife to return his three children to him. But the wife said she packed out of the house because her husband, who, she said, she married 12 years ago, was not the biological father of the children and was not responsible for the pregnancy. Adebayo told the court that she was made to swore [sic] an oath to keep the secret that her husband was not the biological father of the children, adding that it was a deal between the two of them. She said her husband had been married for 10 years without an issue before she got married to him.[46]

What we must appreciate is that traditionally, Yorùbá marriage was not formulated as a union between an individual "manly man" and a "feminine woman" (whatever that means); marriage in Yorùbá society was imagined, conducted, and experienced as a collective act. Thus the normal idiom of marriage is polygamous not because of the fact that many men had more than one wife but because all the wives of the males in the lineage are seen as wives of the family and relate to each other in a seniority hierarchy that treats them as if they are married to one and the same man. They are cowives because they married men who belong to the same lineage, not necessarily because they share the same individual husband. It is also because of the collective nature of marriage that the wives of the family are not only wives to the males of the house; they are also wives to the females of the house. Husband and wife in the first instance are social not necessarily sexual categories. No one prevented the female members of the lineage from exercising the obligations and privileges of husbandhood even if they had no penises with which to copulate with the wives in order to produce children, because the defining part of such privileges for one individual, are social not sexual. Elsewhere, I have written about forms of Yorùbá and other African marriages that did not involve sexual consummation between individual parties involved.[47] To go back to the question at hand, where and what is the meaning of manliness in such a cultural context? Given the foregoing, is it correct to assume that manliness and marriage were incontrovertibly linked for individual men? The fact that the category husband, along with its responsibilities and benefits, was not limited to male members of the lineage speaks loudly to the fact that Yorùbá categories are not English or biblical ones that can be easily converted or assimilated. The questions remain: What is the masculinity that male personal *oríkì* are said to express? What is the origin of this masculinity? How do we understand it against the background of a society in which originally such gender consciousness and dichotomizing did not exist?

Indeed, in the nineteenth century, by the time Kukomi was renouncing his 17 wives, many changes had already taken place in the society. The fact that Kukomi had 17 wives was a function of the particular historical period in which many of the Ibadan so called "big men," warriors, had made wives of captive women. Kukomi was one of the "big men." The fact that he could willfully get rid of his wives without consulting anyone, including the wives themselves, suggests how he acquired these wives and shows how significantly things had changed. Yorùbá society at this time was not an Islamized society in which when marriage is contracted under sharia law, all that a displeased husband needs to do to divorce his wife is utter "I divorce thee" three times. In Yorùbáland, a wife for whom *ìdána* was exchanged and who performed the *ẹkún ìyàwó* could not be as easily dispensed with because that marriage was a union of lineages. It is clear that gendered practices if not identities appeared in tandem with ideologies of masculinity. The sources of gendering were fivefold: Islamic teachings and practices; Christian missionary activities, teachings, and practices; European gender notions; the increasing process of individuation emanating from a rapidly changing social structure; and a militaristic culture. The emergence of gender constructs with a recognizable ideology of masculinity was the product of a constellation of processes.

In the previous section, I mentioned Barber's work on the transformation of personal *oríkì* poetry (appellations accumulated by men and women during the course of their lives) from a genre that made an art of locating notable men in their family relationships to one that glorified their individual, often "dastardly deeds." Let us revisit her arguments more fully. Personal *oríkì* are composed by wives of the lineage and by professional *asunrárà* (praise singers) who sought to salute, applaud, and enhance what Barber called "big men" in a culture in which warmongering and slavery had become the coin of the realm. Barber focused on the personal *oríkì* poetry to document the ideological changes that followed the sociopolitical changes of the nineteenth century. She concluded that "the violence and masculinist values that were beginning to take hold were imprinted in the performance of personal praise poetry, as the reputation of 'big men' was no longer enhanced by their relationships, but by the dastardly acts that became the hallmark of the era."[48] Barber contrasts the style of praise poetry of notables in the pre-Ibadan Ọ̀yọ́ Yorùbá society with that of the leaders of the new polity Ibadan and comes to the conclusion that the new notables

were measured by their deeds rather than by their relationships. A stanza of
the personal *oríkì* of Ibikunle, the founder of Ibadan, goes:

> He made war on Alake, he killed the Alake's child
> He made war on Igbein, Ibikunle became a terror in captivity
> He struck at Somuyi, He struck at Apati
> He took out a cudgel and chased Alola around
> Without effort, he got the better of the Elba
> He killed Alola who sent them to war
> He kept on winning every case.[49]

For contrast, Barber offers the personal *oríkì* of an Oba of Okuku, who
reigned before the nineteenth century.[50] Pre-Ibadan *oríkì* of notables
emphasized their relationship, underscoring their wealth in people.

> Akani, there is no shortage of money for adornment
> …
> Oriare, one whose dance whirls around the circle of onlookers
> …
> Husband of Ojisabola
> with his jutting velvet cap, father of Sunoye
> Father of Buola is one who has more than other people
> He sees the new moon early from his courtyard, father of Jolasun

From these lines, we can see the emphasis on the web relationships in which
Akani is enmeshed quite apart from his own wonderful personal attributes
of being a good dancer.

The wives of the lineage of such men must have had ample opportunity
to spotlight their prowess and invent appropriate nicknames to express the
fact. Thus I aver that females—brides and wives who became *Ìyá*—are the
authors of male praise names. It is not surprising then that many of these
male names—Àjàgbé (one who fights to carry), Àjàmú (one who fights
to take hold)—contain the verb *jà*—to fight, to struggle, to war. Ibadan
was a militarist state that engaged in predatory wars. The warriors who
attracted a new name were the inheritors of a new dispensation following
the devastation of Ọ̀yọ́, its reconstitution, and the development of Ibadan
and Abeokuta in what came to be known as the Ibadan era. It is plausible
that the many wars that were fought by men fed into emerging notions
defining maleness through the antics of warriors, fighters who attracted
adjectives like brave, courageous, and heroic; hence the association of these
attributes with masculinity.[51] Paradoxically, some women too went to war, a
fact that suggests that the coupling of masculinity and war did not preclude
other possibilities.

But the idea that male *oríkì* express the fighting spirit is not the whole story. The meanings of male *oríkì* unlike the female ones were more eclectic. In deconstructing male *oríkì* names, we see that notions of heroism, courage, or bravery are not expressed in many of them. Thus a name like Àkànní or Àkànbí—"one who is purposefully given birth to"—or Àjàní, "a child conceived after a fight by the parents," invites us to focus on the parents rather than on the child. One must ask the question why a male child is so named. Is it only a male child who can be conceived after a fight? Is it only a male child who is born purposefully? I think not. What this suggests is that the interpretation of these names as masculine is ideological. It could be that only a couple of names were produced by the masculinist ideology and over time because of the convention of already existing *oríkì* names borne predominantly by females given their bridal origins, male-associated names developed and were universalized in a society that was increasingly imbued with a gender ideology of male superiority and emerging spheres of male advantage.

In contrast to female *oríkì*, male *oríkì* names do not boast uniformity in meaning and express diverse sentiments, which suggests that they had different origin. As I pointed out earlier, I believe it was the wives of the lineage of these men who first came up with male *oríkì* to appreciate their husbands. Additionally, a second generation of *oríkì* names must also have been given at birth by *Ìyá* to their male children after the practice had already become institutionalized for female children. I am suggesting that male *oríkì* had multiple origins rather than a specific occasion such as the wedding from which female names emerged.[52]

Despite the chorus of current writers who claim that male *oríkì* names encapsulate masculinity, they actually express different meanings that may or may not have anything to do with masculinity. Linguist Oyetade points out that the meaning of a number of the male *oríkì* such as Àmọ̀ọ́, Àrẹ̀ó, Àlàó cannot readily be deciphered (there is one female *oríkì* Àbẹ̀ó that also falls into this group).[53] But more importantly, he notes that some of the verbs used in male *oríkì* have multiple meanings. "For instance, 'kàn' translated as 'purposefully' here can equally mean to 'take in turn.' In which case the name [Àkànní] expresses the fact that 'I have given birth to this (child) when it is my turn.'"[54] The "I" in the previous sentence obviously refers to the mother and may be an expression of the practice in polygamous marriages in which wives have to take turns to have sexual relations with their husbands. I also wondered whether the need to proclaim that one has not jumped the queue suggests some Islamic influence, given that for Muslims, it is unethical for husbands to copulate with a particular wife when it is not her turn to be intimate with the husband. Some popular interpretations of this principle propound that a child born when it is not the mother's turn to be intimate

with the husband is regarded as illegitimate.[55] Àkànní then becomes a proc-
lamation of the "legitimacy" of the child, an interesting development in a
culture where children are never considered to be illegitimate and a married
woman's children could never be fatherless. Oyetade also tells us that the verb
"kàn' can also mean "knock" as in the case of knocking a door, or "knock"
as in the case of two goats or rams locking horns in a fight."[56] Would this
be what lends the name "Àkànní" an air of masculinity? T. A. Ladele and
his coauthors seem to think so. They explain the meaning of Àkànbí and
Àkàndé, two male *oríkì* that also contain the verb *kàn* as "*omokùnrin tí ó jé
pé èèkan péré ni a súnmó ìyá rè tí ó fi lóyún rè*"[57]—a male child that is born as
a result of one single act of copulation with his mother. They then add the
reason for naming a child as such "*nítorí ìgboyà tí ó ní*"—because of the courage or bravery he displays. As in the previous rendering of the verb *kàn*, even
this meaning shifts our focus from the child to the mother, who would be
the only possible source of the information that the pregnancy resulted from
only one act of copulation. But then Ladele et al. immediately tell us that it
is actually the behavior of the child—his bravery—that motivates such an
attribution. It is difficult to reconcile how the idea of a child resulting from a
single act of copulation means that the child is courageous or brave. Perhaps
the belief that children already exist in the other world just waiting to come
to earth means that Àkànní was determined, purposeful, and courageous, and
that is how he could facilitate his own birth without much "sexual work"
on the part of his parents. But why he and not she? Why is it only a male
child that can be self-making in this way? The answer to this question lies
not in some intrinsic masculinity in the name but rather in the masculinist
ideologies of the beholder. Or perhaps Àkànní is a wife's salute to her husband, who was able to effect a much-desired pregnancy in a single sex act.
Obviously, there is nothing in the name that makes it male-exclusive other
than a new custom in a society where names are not customarily gendered.
Interestingly enough, if we accept that the names speak of the son and not
the father, as Ladele et al. seem to suggest, then *oríkì* names such as Àkànní,
Àkàngbé, and Àkànbí seem more like *àmútòrunwá*—names brought from the
otherworld—than names given after birth (*àbísọ*). The paradox is that unlike
other *àmútòrunwá* births, like those of twins, the name is not obvious until
we "watch" the child's behavior or until the mother reveals those details of
intimacy. And then unlike traditional *àmútòrunwá* the new names contain a
gender distinction.

Summary and Conclusion

Oríkì names as a recognizable category of names probably emerged in
the nineteenth century in the wake of the upheavals that resulted in the

dispersal of Ọ̀yọ́ Yorùbá following the fall of Ọ̀yọ́, its reconstitution, and the emergence of new polities like Ibadan and Abeokuta. The dispersal, coupled with the developing presence of Islam, Christian missionaries, trade with Europeans, and the occupation of Lagos by the British opened up society in such a way that people realized that members of their town and families were no longer contained in one town or one place. The implication of this was that finding marriage partners became increasingly a long-distance multitown affair. Because marriage residence, which was never universally patrilocal or virilocal, became more so, marriage for brides became fraught with all sorts of anxieties. This apprehension was expressed by brides in a new genre of poetry among Ọ̀yọ́ Yorùbá called ẹkún ìyàwó or rárà ìyàwó. It was in the performance of bridal chants on the eve of the bride's move to the husband's lineage compound that the female oríkì names emerged: it was a name that the bride gave herself. In essence, the name was a prayer, a statement of hope, but also an affirmation that since the bride is worthy of love, she will inevitably attract in the marital home the kind of love that she has enjoyed in her family of origin. The fact that ẹkún ìyàwó and oríkì name co-occur only among the Ọ̀yọ́ Yorùbá reinforces the idea that they were attached and linked to the upheavals of the nineteenth century, because the Ọ̀yọ́ were at the center of these cataclysmic events. The fact that all female oríkì names have more or less the same meaning supports the idea that they contained a specific message that articulated what should happen in the bride's new home. Because there is more variety in the female oríkì, variety in number and tone combinations show that female oríkì are the original set of names that inaugurated the genre.

Female oríkì are truly praise names and therefore define the genre that is known as praise names. There is nothing intrinsically feminine about them, their "femaleness" has to do with the fact that they came into being in a marriage situation in which it is the bride who moves and is expected to make a home among strangers. With regard to male oríkì, I suggest that they developed later, and the initial names must have been names given by wives to lineage husbands or by Ìyá to male children. On close examination, we discover that these names, unlike female oríkì, have varied meanings and many did not express masculinity, as has commonly been assumed. But because the period in which these names developed was under a militarist state with a warrior culture, a masculinist ethos developed in conjunction with ideas of male superiority emanating from Westernization, Islam, and Christianity, which were rapidly gaining converts in Yorùbáland. The idea that male oríkì names were masculine became an article of faith at least among writers, akòwé. The personal oríkì of notable warriors—oríkì bòròkìnní—in Ibadan, for example, contained many of these names, and the genre not only expanded in its soaring affirmation of the terrible conduct of these warriors but actually came into its own during this period as society became more oriented toward individualism. Throughout my discussion in the previous two chapters, I allude to the growing influence of Islam and Christianity on a number of institutions and practices. In the final chapter, I will systematically look at the impact of these new religions on names, naming practices, and *oríkì* names in particular.

CHAPTER 8

CHANGING NAMES: THE ROLES OF CHRISTIANITY AND ISLAM IN MAKING YORÙBÁ NAMES KOSHER FOR THE MODERN WORLD

According to anthropologist Niyi Akinnaso, Yorùbá names fulfill a record-keeping purpose in that they "serve as an open diary by providing a system through which information is symbolically stored and retrieved."[1] One type of knowledge that Yorùbá names betray is the extent to which the society has integrated the new religions of Islam and Christianity. We already got an inkling of that function in the last chapter when we considered the idea that some male praise names may have been influenced by marriage practices that are associated with Islam. In this chapter, I aim to investigate the role of Christianity and Islam on the emergence of new names and naming practices, and the impact of the world religions in the modification of, and proliferation of, different kinds of Yorùbá-language names particularly in terms of gender divisions. The story that I have been telling in the last two chapters is about the development of praise names and the meaning of current gender-specific associations. The evolution of personal *oríkì* name, however, is merely one part of the changes in name and naming practices that overtook Yorùbá society in the nineteenth century. Other names and new practices also emerged during this period, and they influenced the usage of *oríkì* constructing its gendered associations.

The Reverend Johnson, the pioneering local historian and ethnographer, was the first to document the noticeable changes that were underfoot in the nineteenth century, drawing attention to the adoption of Christian and Islamic names by new converts. For the Christians, even English, Dutch, and German names had become popular in lieu of biblical names, all signaling conversion to Christianity. Johnson also pointed out the development of surnames and the universal adoption of Islamic names as *àbísọ* (primary names) by new Yorùbá Muslims.[2] The reverend himself is the poster child of Yorùbá name change: despite his cultural nationalism and his deep appreciation of the significance of names and naming in Yorùbá society, it is curious that he and other members of his family never fully embraced indigenous names for themselves. The fact that he was born of Yorùbá parentage in Sierra Leone and not Yorùbáland does not constitute an acceptable explanation for his choices given the fact that his Saro compatriots usually signal their full return to Yorùbá identity by adopting or rediscovering their Yorùbá names.[3] On researching the Johnson family, one discovers that the father of the reverend, Henry Johnson, was said to have been born sometime in the nineteenth century in Ilorin, a relatively new Ọ̀yọ́ Yorùbá town, became a captive, was subsequently freed, and became a member of the recaptive[4] community in Sierra Leone. In 1858, Henry came back to Yorùbáland with his family, settling in Ibadan where he had come to work with the English missionary David Hinderer in building the CMS church. The family consisted of his wife Sara, a Yorùbá woman who like him was a recaptive, three sons, and three daughters. We learn that Henry arrived in Ibadan with six children (because his eldest son Henry Jr. was already an adult), among them twelve-year-old Samuel who became the Reverend Johnson. Henry worked as a scripture reader until his death in 1865.[5] There was never any indication that Henry, like some of his Saro compatriots, had tried to change his name or cared to pick up his Yorùbá given names, which he must have answered to before he became a victim of the slave trade. We are told that his àbísọ was Erugun and he was a descendant of "one Otubokun."[6] Neither Henry Johnson nor his children ever answered to either Yorùbá name in any shape or form. This information about his original name only came into the historical record as a result of a letter written by Henry Junior, his eldest son, who while visiting Ilorin in 1877 divulged the information that his father had been born there. Indeed, if we compare Henry Johnson to Bishop Samuel Ajayi Crowther, his more highly educated Saro compatriot and contemporary, the contrast is striking, namewise. Although Crowther, as a Christian and pioneer church leader, kept his Christian first name and English last name, he still insisted on his Yorùbá given name—Ajayi[7]—which is an àmútọ̀runwá, an indigenous name that is not immediately associated with religion but expresses the biological presentation of the baby at birth. Johnson in his younger days as the son of Henry Johnson, went to school in Ibadan and Abeokuta, emerged well educated (for the time), and garnered coveted posts as catechist, school master, and subsequently diplomat and accomplished historian.[8]

Although many Saro did reject their English and Christian names for indigenous names, it is reasonable not to expect Johnson to change any of his names, especially his last name, so long as his father was alive, if the father did not subscribe to such a practice. Following his father's death and his own rise to prominence in war-torn Yorùbáland, however, we do not have any evidence that Johnson had any inclination to drop his foreign names. But then, as he himself observed even as Yorùbá converts tried to move away from wholesale adoption of foreign names by Christian communities: "nothing sticks so fast as a name, and nothing more difficult to eradicate."[9] Names are difficult to change, and more so if they confer a certain desirable identity and status and are regarded as a "mark of enlightenment" as Christian names came to represent at the time.[10] I am suggesting that for Henry Johnson's family, their identities as committed Christians, church workers, "enlightened" and Western-educated persons meant more to them than a putative Yorùbá identity. Recognizing also that names are difficult to change even when one so desires leads me to look to the next generation, focusing instead on the reverend's own branch of the family. He was well versed in Yorùbá names and naming practices and wrote eloquently about the sociology of names, but when it was his turn to name his children, did he avail himself of indigenous names? Reverend Johnson was reticent to talk about his personal and family life, and therefore very little is known about his wives (he became a widower and married a second time) and six children. His biographer Michael Doortmont, noting this reticence, writes:

> The silence about his married life extended to the birth of Johnson's children. We know that his first child, a daughter, was born in Kudeti on 6 December 1875, but that was only because his wife's labour pains prevented him from attending a missionary meeting.[11]

So we are unlikely to find a long disquisition on his children, their names, and why he gave them those names, as is standard with Yorùbá parents. However, we have one clue that gave us an indication of his name preference. In October 1879 he lost his one-year-old son, and according to Doortmont, "the passage in which Johnson described the death of his son is one of the rare occasions he showed some personal feelings; he even gave the name of the child: Geoffrey Emmanuel."[12] There you have it: Johnson gave a German/Christian names to his son. We also find a daughter with an English name: The *Lagos Weekly Record* of December 14, 1912, carried the following marriage announcement: "The marriage of the Rev. Michael S. Cole, principal of Abeokuta Grammar School, with Miss Adelaide Johnson, youngest daughter the late Rev. Samuel Johnson of Ọ̀yọ́."

Christian first names were the standard for Yorùbá committed Christians in the nineteenth and early twentieth century, but what is astonishing is that the first name the reverend gave his son is Germanic and not Christian in the biblical sense and the second name Emmanuel is biblical, which makes both names non-Yorùbá. His daughter's name also was English and not straight out of the Bible. The only reason one is raising this question is because of Reverend Johnson's Yorùbá nationalism and his deep awareness of the culture and the significance of names. He had lamented the fact that among Christians who claim European names because of their faith, biblical names were not being given "but in British West African colonies, Yorùbá and other tribes with Christian names include English, Scotch, Irish, Welsh, German and Dutch names."[13] What is jaw-dropping is the contradiction between his words and his deeds. He had written about the wholesale adoption of European names as uninformed, and had predicted correctly that such practices would change: "educated Yorùbás cannot see why Philip Jones or Geoffrey Williams should be more Christian than Adewale or Ibiyemi."[14] Why the enlightened, cultured, and well-informed Johnson did not take his own advice in naming his children can be seen either as a puzzle or as the height of hypocrisy. But then he had already explained the difficulty of the Western-educated converts leaving European names behind since they considered European names and practices to be symbols of their superiority, and regarded themselves more civilized than "their pagan brethren."[15]

Having said that, it is interesting however, that Johnson and his similarly accomplished younger brother Dr. Obadiah Johnson, unlike their father Henry, answered to recognizable Yorùbá names recorded in the author's and editor's prefaces to the famous book *The History of the Yorùbás*. Both names are male-associated *oríkì*. It is not clear how they came to acquire these names. Johnson's *oríkì* was Ànlá—a standard contraction of Àyìnlá—which means one who is worthy of praise, and his brother Obadiah's was Àjàgbé, which means one who fights and carries away the prize. Both names as they presented it are accompanied by their family totem Ògún, which is the standard way personal *oríkì* name is rendered. There is no record that their three sisters and two brothers also had praise names or Yorùbá given names for that matter—all we have are their Christian names. It is doubtful for a number of reasons that Johnson and Obadiah got these praise names from their parents because: first, their father had shown no inclination to recognize any local name for himself or his children; and second, because all the children were born in Sierra Leone, where despite the fact that some Yorùbá were reverting to their indigenous names, while others were newly claiming Yorùbá names, there does not seem to be even one *oríkì* name in the pool of names circulating in the Saro community at the time. Though Henry and Sara Johnson had been born in Yorùbáland early in the nineteenth century, they may not have known that *oríkì* names existed because as these names were far from known or institutionalized until later in the century. Where and how did Samuel and Obadiah acquire their *oríkì*? I believe that like the bridal originators of the *oríkì* genre, Johnson and Obadiah must have taken stock of their personal circumstances and lauded themselves by using the names. The two *oríkì* names, which speak of struggle and accomplishment, seem to capture the narratives of their lives, especially in light of the story of the writing and publication of *The History of the Yorùbás* (1921) which I discussed in chapter 4, and Obadiah's struggle against racism in the colonial Civil Service. Because of the brothers' shared love for the history and culture and their deep appreciation of the meaning of *oríkì*, it is not surprising that they picked up *oríkì* names despite the fact that neither Johnson nor Obadiah had Yorùbá given names. The two brothers understood themselves to be strivers if not achievers, but it is not obvious at what point in their adult lives they self-named. They both became highly accomplished at a very difficult time in history, and they were well aware of the laudatory function of *oríkì*. Johnson was a catechist, pastor, and an effective diplomat, historian, and writer. Obadiah was a medical doctor trained in Scotland and was also a writer. But where did Ògún, the family totem, come from? Perhaps from their deep roots in Ọ̀yọ́ through their paternal grandmother. We are told that the reverend's interest in the history of Ọ̀yọ́ and his unwavering promotion of that polity over others may have had a personal aspect to it, given that his father Henry was a grandson of Alafin Abiodun through his mother.[16] Could it be that Johnson's observation that some children take their mother's totem "where the father has lost his, or more usually when the mother's indicate a higher or nobler rank"[17] expressed his own personal experience of adopting Ògún, a totem from his paternal grandmother, who was an Ọ̀yọ́ princess? To be sure, his Ọ̀yọ́ roots were much easier to embrace than his Ilorin antecedents, because that city represented to him the evil Islamized polity that had brought down his idealized, unified Yorùbá homeland. If my suggestion that the two brothers gave themselves praise names is correct, the irony is that they came by the appellations in the same way that the pioneering brides who invented the genre got theirs: self-naming. These names show that Johnson and Obadiah had a strong sense of themselves and their own accomplishments. This is not surprising, given what we already know about the lengths to which they went in order to publish *The History*. The two brothers had a profound interest in Yorùbá history and culture, as demonstrated by the fact that Obadiah contributed to the rewriting and publication of Johnson's master work, assembling notes and writing parts of it when the manuscript that took 20 years of labor went missing in the hands of the would-be publishers in England.

What about Bishop Ajayi Crowther, who was of Henry Johnson's generation? What can the experience of the pioneer missionary, intellectual, and first bishop of the Niger tell us about names, naming, and social change in nineteenth century Yorùbáland? Crowther was born in 1806 and lived a relatively long life; he died in 1891. Like Henry Johnson, Crowther had been born in an Ọ̀yọ́ town—Oshogun—in 1806, was captured and sold into slavery, and ended up a recaptive in Sierra Leone. He converted to Christianity and received his education in both Sierra Leone and England under the tutelage of the Church of England, in which he became a bishop: the first African and black man to achieve that status.[18] Unlike the Johnsons, however, Crowther had a recognizable Yorùbá given name: Ajayi. This indigenous name remained his middle name throughout his life. Despite the fact that he was as old as Henry Johnson, we know much more about Crowther's family history and most importantly for our purposes, the names of all his family members. His father Aiyemi and mother Afala had four children: Ajayi was the son and three daughters were named Bola, Lanre, and Amosa.[19] None of these primary names are oríkì, perhaps because oríkì are never first names. It was standard for Yorùbá Christians to adopt Christian names when they were baptized and then to give such names to their children at birth. I have not seen any of Crowther's writing in which he made his views known about naming practices one way or the other. However, his children all had Christian names. Crowther wife's name was Susan Asano Crowther, their children's names were Samuel Junior, Abigail, Susan, Josiah, Julianah, and Dandeson.[20]

In the nineteenth century, Muslim and Christian converts were eager to drop their Yorùbá names in favor of Christian, European, and Arabic names. The singular motivating factor was the fact that Yorùbá names were considered pagan. As Johnson noted, "The early missionaries, notably those of Sierra Leone, abolished native names wholesale, considering them 'heathenish,' and substituted English names instead: such names are naturally transmitted to their children anglice."[21] The reason for the supposed heathenishness of indigenous names has to do with the fact that many Yorùbá names venerate the Òrìṣà worshipped by the parents or to whom the child is dedicated. Thus a child whose father is a devotee of the god Ògún will have a name such as Ògúnníyì (Ògún is honorable), or a child whose mother is an Ifá diviner could be named Awóbùnmi or Ifábùnmi (Ifá has given me this child), and you can substitute many Òrìṣà as the prefixes of these names. Thus the initial strategy for the new Yorùbá converts was to reject such names and all indigenous names wholesale except if they were family names, which proved more difficult to give up. But with more discernment and reflection, it became clear that not all Yorùbá names and prefixes encapsulated an ode to an Òrìṣà. For example, the much celebrated Yorùbá language novelist Daniel Oróówọlé Fagunwa dropped his given name Orowole, which contains an allusion to spiritual beings for a newly minted Yorùbá-language Christian name—Ọlọ́runfẹ́mi (God loves me). It is not that the name 'Fẹ́mi did not exist before; previously it could be

Sangofemi (the god Sango loves me) or Ọṣúnfẹ́mi (Oṣun loves me). The new development was that for Christians, who had embraced what they saw as a monotheistic tradition, Olú or Olúwa or Ọlọ́run became the name for the Christian God. It is not also the case that Olú did not exist before as a name prefix; it is that the meaning of the term Olú shifted and came to be singularly associated with Christianity in certain quarters. Consequently, names with Olú/Olúwa proliferated in Yorùbá society and continue to do so. But Olú was not the only acceptable prefix for Yorùbá who had adopted Christianity. They realized that they could still use old-time prefixes such as Adé (crown); thus Adéfẹ́mi is the crown loves me. Another still acceptable prefix is Ọlá (honor); thus Ọládùnni (it is good to be honorable). Ìbí (birth, kinship) was another one; thus Ìbíyẹmí (the birth of the child becomes me; kinship honors me). A final example is Ọmọ (child), thus Ọmọlayọ̀ (a child is joy). But that was not all: àmútọ̀runwá names too became very popular among Yorùbá Christian converts, as they were not seen as paganish. Perhaps these names were accepted because the biological facts of such unusual births suggest the actions of a Supreme Being.[22] Names of twins such as Táíwò and Kẹ́hìndé, Àjàyí, Ìgè, and so on started to be used as surnames, a development that Johnson saw as highly irregular, culturally speaking. "Some ridiculous results have thereby been obtained e.g. a woman is called Mrs. Táíwò, who was not twin-born, and probably her husband was not either."[23] I would venture to say that Bishop Crowther retained his indigenous Àjàyí without any modification because it is an àmútọ̀runwá. Thus far, I have been explaining the different strategies used by Christian converts to make indigenous names that they saw as "heathenish" compliant with their newfound religion. Initially they had rejected all indigenous names embracing biblical and European names as first names. But as they became more discerning, they realized that they could have local names and still be Christian, since not all native names paid homage to the Òrìṣà. Among acceptable secular names were those starting with the prefixes Adé (crown), Oyè (royal title), Ọlá (honor), Ọmọ (child), and Ìbí (birth). Most importantly, they composed what we now understand to be Christian Yorùbá names such as Olúfẹ́mi and Olúwaṣeun, names prefixed by Olú or Olúwa, which had come to be adopted as the name for the monotheistic Christian God in Yorùbá. This was easily done with first names; family names were much more difficult. Many of them were clearly marked by the names of Òrìṣà that the parents or lineage venerated. Surnames were introduced to the society at mission schools, and children were sent to schools at which they had to present a first name and a last name just like the families of the Saro who had come to settle in towns such as Lagos, Abeokuta, and Ibadan.[24]

The story I have been telling about the transformation of names is so far one about Christian converts. But what about Muslims? The Muslim community did not tolerate substituting Yorùbá names for Islamic[25] names if converts want to be regarded as true Muslims. In places like Ibadan, Ọ̀yọ́, and Lagos, where there were recognizable communities of Muslims, the adoption of Islamic names as first names became standard and universal. These names were specifically called *suna* (meaning name in Hausa), a new word introduced into the Yorùbá lexicon. Thus when children were born, they were given *suna* names in lieu of or in conjunction with *àbísọ* names. In Yorùbá Muslim communities, a standard question was "*kíni súná ọmọ*" (what is the child's Islamic name), as distinct from "*kíni orúkọ ọmọ*" (what is the child's name referring to *àbísọ*). But this kind of distinction between *orúkọ* and *súná* was made only in communities where Islam had not been totally assimilated. In highly Islamized communities like Ilorin,[26] *súná* became *àbísọ* in that it was the primary and only name recognized as significant for the individual. Islamic names are gender specific. These names were mandatory for Muslims because of the belief that on the day of heavenly judgment (*ijọ́ ìgbénOde al-Qiyāmah*), this was the name by which each and every individual would be recognized and raised from the dead. Because Muslim converts as much as Christians saw indigenous names as "paganish," they did not need much motivation to move away from them. But like Christian converts, Muslims soon discovered secular Yorùbá names, but a different set than those the Christians were using. For Muslims it was the personal *oríkì* that had the quality of not being tied to indigenous spirituality. The fact that it was Muslims and not Christians who first started to use *oríkì* names for secular reasons buttress the idea that *oríkì* names are more an Ọ̀yọ́-Yorùbá invention because Islam domiciled relatively much earlier in Northern Yorùbá communities. Thus Muslims availed themselves of an existing genre of names that was not available to Christian communities whose core settlements were in Abeokuta, Badagry, and Lagos further south.

Muslims discovered that *oríkì* are absolutely secular in that they make no reference to the Gods. *Oríkì* became very popular as first names, middle names, and surnames. Indeed in established Yorùbá Muslim communities in Lagos and Ilorin, *oríkì* names are common as ordinary names and not as specialized praise names. A saying among Yorùbá in places like Ibadan and Ogbomoso is "awon ara Eko to nfi oriki j"oruko"—people of Lagos who (mis)use praise names as primary names. As I pointed earlier, when *oríkì* are used as primary names, they lose their luster and can no longer perform their primary function of lauding and puffing up the addressee.

Even in towns where they did not reinvent *oríkì* as primary name, it is standard among Ọ̀yọ́ Yorùbá Muslims to give *oríkì* to children alongside *suna*. The following story sheds some light on the impact of Islam on names. One Friday in July 2008, I was in the palace in Ogbomoso and witnessed the installation of Shittu Mustafa as the Pàràkòyí of Muslims in Ogbomoso by Ọba Oladunni Oyewumi. The names Shittu and Mustafa are names of Arabic origin. The fact that there was a chieftaincy for the leader of the Muslim community in Ogbomoso indicates that Islam had become sufficiently deeply rooted to be part of the civil organization of the town. At the installation ceremony, it became a source of curiosity that an 80-something-year-old Ogbomoso-born man did not seem to have an indigenous name. The monarch asked him what his àbísọ (given name) was. He seemed puzzled by the question and asked for clarification of what àbísọ (an indigenous name given after birth) means. After the meaning was explained to Mustafa, he replied that Àjàgbé was his Yorùbá name. The Ọba and a number of the chiefs in attendance were taken aback and chorused that Àjàgbé is an oríkì, not an àbísọ, making a distinction between the two. Traditionally oríkì are never primary names. This difference was lost on Mustafa, or shall I say the distinctions between oríkì, àbísọ, and suna had started to look anachronistic if we take into consideration the changing landscape of religion and names in the society. The ceremony proceeded. After the event, Mustafa was not available for an interview, but fortunately his daughter, a woman in her forties, was present. I approached her and said it seemed unusual that her father did not have any Yorùbá appellations other than oríkì, especially given his age. The woman, who introduced herself to me as Kudiratu (an Arabic name for girls popular among Yorùbá Muslims), explained that in their family tradition neither she nor her siblings had been given Yorùbá names. The Islamic names represented for them their real names. Furthermore, she pointed out that Islamic traditions had deep roots in their family, as even her grandfather had been a devout Muslim. In Ilorin and some Lagos and Ibadan communities in which Islam had become deeply rooted, there would have been no curiosity about Mustafa's names because the other people in attendance would also have names such as Abibu, Tajudeen Oseni, and Akeem Ramoni—all Muslim names but often rendered in Yorùbá idiom. The gendered use of oríkì would seem natural to this community since Muslim names are gender specified. Apart from the fact that names in Arabia are gender specific, another factor that may have reinforced the male-dominance and gender division of names has to do with the fact that Prophet Muhammad presented what has come to be known as the 99 names of Allah. These names are all male identified and are the preferred appellations among Yorùbá Muslims. They are prefixed with Abdul, which means "servant of Allah." Some examples of these names are Abdul Rasheed and Abdul Lateef. However, Yorùbá rarely if ever attached the prefix Abdul to such names in everyday life. The 99[27] names of Allah are truly Islamic names in that they came into being as a result of the founding of the faith. Islamic names are distinctive from Arabic names that already existed in the

culture before Islam was founded. There are no female names with the prefix Abdul. Logically then, there are more male Islamic names than female
ones. Additional female names were created by adding "at," the feminine
suffix in Arabic, to male names. Yorùbá Muslims also partook of this tradition adding a "u" to the Arabic "at" to reflect Yorùbá pronunciation. Thus
female names like Rashidatu from Abdul Rashid, Latifatu from Abdul Latif,
Basiratu from Bashir, and Shakiratu from Shakir are popular among them.

    Islam influenced Yorùbá names and naming practices in other ways as
well. The pilgrimage to Mecca, which is one of the five Pillars of Islam, has
also generated a number of Yorùbá-language names, of which two are particularly striking: Àbọ̀lọrẹ and Àbídèmí-Mecca. Àbọ̀lọrẹ is a name given to the
first female child born after the mother returns from hajj—the pilgrimage
to Mecca. Apparently, this is a female-identified name and there is no male
counterpart. Àbídèmí is a Yorùbá name used to name boys or girl whose
fathers were away from home when they were born. Àbídèmí means a child
born while the family await my (the father's) return. Yorùbá Muslims added
a twist to the name when they specified where the father had gone—in
this case on a pilgrimage to Mecca—hence Àbídèmí-Mecca. Thus it would
not be surprising to find a Yorùbá child named Àbídèmí-London, adding
London another popular destination of Yorùbá travel to a traditional name.

    Another name deriving from the encounter with Islam is the male name
Jimoh, which gained currency among Muslims. Jimoh is a Yorùbá rendering of Jumat, the holy day of Muslim worship given to a son born on
Friday. There do not seem to be girls named Jimoh even though girls are
also born on Fridays! But in Hausa communities, girls born on Friday are
often named Jummai and boys, Danjuma. The Yorùbá boy Jimoh could also
be named Ojóńlá—important day—to express the fact that he was born
on a day special to Muslims. It is interesting that Abọ́sẹ̀dé or Abíọ́sẹ̀ (child
that comes with the week) is its Yorùbá Christian counterpart, given to
children (male and female) born on Sunday as that day became recognized
as the first day of the week among the Yorùbá literate and Westernized
elite. Unlike the Akan of Ghana or Hausa of Northern Nigeria, who had
traditions of naming people for the day they are born, before the advent
Christianity and Islam, there were few if any "day names" among them. The
only day names present today are associated with these religions and probably Hausa, Borgu, and Fulani influences.

    Even more significant is that the emergence of surnames, which were a
new development, provided an impetus for gendering names and propagating certain kinds of names. I have already discussed how many Christians
modified existing names by dropping the reference to Òrìṣà and insert-
ing Olú or Olúwa (monotheistic God) in its place, or using more secular
prefixes like Ọlá, Oyè, Ọmọ, Ìbí, and Adé instead of the names of Òrìṣà like

Ọṣun, Ògún, Ṣàngó, Ọya, Ifá, and so on. In Yorùbá Muslim communities, many started to use *oríkì* as surnames. Names like Àlàgbé, Àkànní, and Àtàndá became recognizable surnames among the Ọ̀yọ́ Yorùbá. Shittu Mustapha, whom we encountered earlier at his chieftaincy installation, could have introduced himself as Shittu Àjàgbé. The following example is a good illustration of the phenomenon. In the summer of 2010, I was invited by the Department of Cultural Studies to give a lecture at Obafemi Awolowo University in Ile-Ife. During the lecture I discussed some of my research findings on *oríkì* and the influence of Islam on Yorùbá naming. After the lecture, during the question-and-answer session, Professor Akínkúnmi Àlàó, my host and the departmental chair, shared his family's experience. He said that his experience mirrored my findings in that his father was the first in their village outside of Ibadan to become a Muslim, as a result of which he immediately adopted his *oríkì* Àlàó as their family name, which set them apart from the rest of the lineage. Mr. Àlàó senior subsequently changed his religion and converted to Christianity, but he did not have to change his name again because Àlàó was already an acceptable name even for a Christian. Àlàó was not perceived to be paganish.

Thus, I am suggesting that there is a relationship between Islam and the intensification of use of male praise names; recall that one meaning usually attributed to the male *oríkì* Àkànní makes sense only in relation to an Islamic practice. The least we can say is that Islam intensified the use of already existing *oríkì* and may have facilitated the introduction of a few more, although male *oríkì* became recognized and used as surnames as the practice of using surnames was institutionalized in the newly established colonial and missionary schools (both Christian and Islamic). Because of the practice of each individual having multiple names, many Yorùbá who have highly gender-specific Islamic names bear such names alongside their indigenous nongender-specific *àbísọ*, a fact that does not seem to produce any gender anxiety for them.

It is interesting that Christians also introduced *àmútòrunwá* names as surname despite the fact that these names are not exclusively male identified.[28] This orientation parallels the practice among non-Westernized Yorùbá women (and men), whose personal *oríkì* were used as part of self-identification in ways that suggested a surname. For women, this practice is striking because female associated *oríkì* functioned like surnames. Many women would introduce themselves with their *suna* (Islamic name) or *àbísọ* as first name and their female *oríkì* as last name, for example, Sínọtù Àbáké, Sàlámọ̀tù Àgbèké, Sàríyù Àbèní, and Súbèdátù Àlàké, Kíkélọmọ Àmọ̀ké, Adékẹmi Àdùfẹ, Mórénikẹ Àṣàbí, and Lásùmbọ̀ Àbíkẹ. Such an approach to naming and identification continues to occur wherever women want to identify themselves eschewing Western practices of imposing father's or husband's name as their last name. In fact, the examples I have used here were taken from a list of members of Mrs. Funmilayo Ransome Kuti's Abeokuta Women's Club in 1944. Ninety-five percent of the names on this list follow the practice of using their personal female *oríkì* as last names. Similarly, Salawat Abeni and Batili Alake, two current popular Yorùbá female musician, exhibit this pattern of female *oríkì* as surname. Especially interesting here is that most of the first names on this list are Islamic names. I will discuss the significance of this later.

Writer K. Yusuf advocated that women should use their *oríkì* as last name and that this would be "an effective way of desexing surnames."[29] another scholar, Akinyemi, challenged this idea by raising several objections to what he saw as Yusuf's feminist stance. His most significant disagreement is that *oríkì* names are so few that they cannot successfully be used for that purpose.[30] The point that seems to be lost in this academic debate is that earlier, in the twentieth century and continuing until today, many non-Westernized married women already use their *oríkì* as their last name. So do some Yorùbá men; it is just not as visible as that of women. Hence at one level, the relative paucity of *oríkì* has not been a deterrent to this practice. There are many possibilities of developing a whole series of female *oríkì*-based names by hyphenating them with other names. One informant told me about a woman whose last name is Abeni-Oye. Abeni is a female-associated *oríkì*. Beyond the superficial issue of numbers is a larger issue to which the debaters have been able to draw attention: why in the first place surnames for everyone in society must be the father's name, and for women the husband's name. Johnson in regard to the new custom of women taking their husbands last name stated categorically "neither Christianity nor civilization requires a man's name to be given to his wife or children, considering the purpose for which children are named amongst the Yorùbás."[31] In fact, Islam enjoins that women must bear their father's name and not the husband's. But alas, it was increasingly not a matter of choice: the problem is that anyone who operates in the expanding civic public that derives from colonization is forced to declare their father's name or husband's name as surname, a practice that started to take hold among Christians by the middle of the nineteenth century. As Adélékè Adéèkó explained: the first lesson children learned in Christian missionary and then government schools is that they must have a surname, and that name must be the father's name.[32] Furthermore, Adéèkó alerted us to the social divide between women in the civic public originating from the colonial experience and those in the primordial public, who are more grounded in indigenous tradition. Drawing attention to Soyinka's expression of the division in Aké, his home community, Adéèkó writes: "women of the civic public used to be called '*oníkaba*' (frock wearers [like European women]) and those of the primordial public '*aróṣọ*' (wrapper wearers)."[33] It is these "*aróṣọ*" women who operate largely in the primordial public that have been using their *oríkì* as their last name; many members of Abeokuta Women's Union in 1944 were "*aróṣọ*." What is notable is that most of the members of the club who used their *oríkì* as surname were Muslims, given their Islamic first name, a fact that underscores the degree to which Christianity and Western cultural practices like privileging male names are linked. Christianized Yorùbá embraced fully that the man was the head of the family and in this instance meant that wife/ wives and children were to be branded with his name.[34] With regard to the paucity of *oríkì* names, there are many places in the world, including large swaths of West Africa, in which last names are very few because they designate huge clans of people. This has not stopped the people from bearing surnames and names that are duplicated again and again. Ultimately, the issue of last names has more to do with the freedom with which anyone is allowed to choose a name or even create a new one. Making the taking of certain names compulsory and backing this gender discrimination with the force of law is the problem. Even husbands should be able to take their wife's father's name if the couple so wish. The irony is that Yorùbá names by their very nature do not need to be "desexed," since there is nothing intrinsic in each name that alludes to gender-dichotomized social and moral attributes. Consequently, many Yorùbá with indigenous names like mine can easily reverse their first name and last name without much ado. But then why do that since surnames do not have to be male or female-identified, but just a name!

Another naming practice that came out of Yorùbá Muslim communities is the use of nicknames, especially as last names. Nicknames are *orúkọ ìnagijẹ*, which are:

orúkọ tí à ń jẹ́ léhìn tí a bá ti dàgbà ni a lè pè l'orúkọ kejì ẹni...A lè fún ara ẹni ní ìnagijẹ tí yóò dùn ún gbọ́ létí tí yóò bu'yì kún ọmọlúàbí ènìyàn...Bákan náà ẹwẹ̀, àwọn ènìyàn, ọ̀rẹ́, aládùúgbò, ẹgbé àti ọgbà le fún ènìyàn ní orúkọ ìnagijẹ.[35]

Names given when one is already an adult, we may call them second names. One can give oneself such a name because it is music to the ears and may boost ones self esteem. Similarly, such names may come from friends, neighbors, fellow club members, all can give one a nickname.

Many of these nicknames became surnames of prominent families, in Ibadan most notably, names like Aríṣekọ́lá, Alébíoṣù, Arẹ́gbẹ́ṣọlá, Ajélonbáwí, Ajídàgbà, Ajọ̀màle, Adáranímọ̀le, Ajíṣafẹ̀, Ajéwálé, Owónifáàrí, Arówólò, Owódùnúnní, and the like. Like Yorùbá Christians who invented new names and recomposed old ones, the idea was to find new names that did not implicate the Gods, since many Ibadan had converted to Islam.

An equally interesting phenomenon developed in regard to Arabic names and nicknames among Yorùbá Muslims. According to Ladele et al.:

Nígbà tí ẹ̀sìn Mùsùlùmí dé ilẹ̀ Yorùbá, àwọn tí wọ́n bá kọ òrìṣà wọn sílẹ̀ láti gba "àdíínì" máa ń pa orúkọ wọn dà sí ti orúkọ Lárúbáàwá. Àwọn Yorùbá wá fún orúkọ Lárúbáwà wọ̀nyí ní orúkọ àpèjé kọọkan, irú orúkọ báyìí fẹ́rẹ̀ fi ara jọ oríkì; àwọn onílù a sì máa fi í ki àwọn tí ń jẹ́ ẹ.

When Islam came to Yorùbáland, converts who want to lay down their Òrìṣà and accept the Islamic faith changed their names to Arab ones. Yorùbá people then attached to these Arabic names single appellations; such names resemble *oríkì*. In fact performers (praise singers) use them as such.

They look like *oríkì* because they start with the vowel "a" and quite a number of them are trisyllabic. Some of these Arabic names with their Yorùbá appellations are:

Sànúsí	Àká (Alákàá—oní Àká)
Sàlàmí	Agbájé (Agbájélọlá)
Wàhábì	Alárápé
Láwàní	Amúbíẹyá
Húmọ̀ání	Alaga
Rájí	Alákànṣe (a-wọ̀-ẹwú-àrán-re-kóòtù)
Gbàdàmọ́sí	Aíbùkí (Ariwó-ọlá).[36]

Today we have many families who use these Yorùbá appellations especially as last names without any awareness that originally such a name had an Arabic pair.[37] What the origin of this practice is unclear. However, a linguist alerted me to the fact that this pairing of local names with Arabic ones is not just a Yorùbá phenomenon: it has also been identified in Fulbe and Wolof communities in Senegal and in Hausa communities in Nigeria.[38] The practice may have been more widespread at the beginning of the incorporation of Islam into these African communities but may have tapered off as Islam deepened. It requires further research and in the context of this study, to determine if there are any gender associations in the way the process evolved. The aforementioned list of names includes names of men and women. Perhaps, I should note that in the past 25 years or so, with the deepening of Arabic knowledge and the spread influence of wahabism—a fundamentalist ideology originating from Saudi Arabia, many Yorùbá muslims have embraced Islamic and Arabic names as both first names and last names. They are increasingly rejecting any Yorùbá-language names, be they *oríkì* or not. They are also streamlining the spellings to fit exactly the original Arabic. They have dropped the ubiquitous ending vowel in Yorùbá female Islamic names such that Sherifatu is now Sherifat, Basiratu is now Basira, and Latifatu is now Latifat. One striking change is the Yorùbá Muslim male name Buremo—it is now faithfully rendered as the Arabic , Ibrahim. Yorùbá are also now insisting on the Abdul prefix that is part of male names like Lateef and Rasheed, which are drawn from the 99 names of Allah.

Despite the fact that I have emphasized the distinctly different processes by which Yorùbá Christians and Muslims modified existing names, minted new ones, and created new pairings to express their new religious identities, the two faith communities were not separate but rather quite intertwined. Because of a tradition of religious tolerance emanating from the multiplicity of Òrìṣà,[39] and the relatively peaceful way in which Islam and Christianity spread in Yorùbáland, families tended to include persons of both Abrahamic faiths, as well as members who still venerated the Òrìṣà. What the experience of Professor Àlàó shows is that one religious group may have originally favored certain names over others, but over time, due to reconversion and intermarriage, last names have become generally mixed up. One will find both Muslim and Christian Yorùbá with oríkì last names. It is also interesting that one would also find Yorùbá with Islamic last names like Shittu, Disu (Idris), Salau, and Salami, who are practicing Christians—a sign of conversion and reconversion that is a continuing hallmark of such a religiously plural and tolerant society.

The process of making Yorùbá names Kosher clearly had gender elements in it in a number of ways. First, the direct adoption of English, German, Arabic, and biblical names following their usage in the cultures of origin meant that Yorùbá also used them in a gender-specific fashion. For example, Johnson named his son Geoffrey and not his daughter, despite his awareness that Yorùbá did not use àbíṣọ in a gender-specific way. Second, in the case of Islamic names, there was an added layer of gender specificity when converts realized the specialness of certain male-identified names because they are regarded as the names of Allah. The fact that none of the 99 names of Allah is associated with a female at the very least gives the impression that Allah is male and having a male name especially glorified him. Although Muslims have created female versions of many of the names. I wonder whether the Yorùbá nongendered understanding of names may have provided an impetus to create female versions of what in Arabic were male exclusive names. Third, the emergence of surnames, which came to mean father's name, introduced another dimension of gendering. To boot, the increasing use of male-identified oríkì as last name reinforced the idea that oríkì are inherently gender specific with male ones being passed along as surnames to children. Despite the fact that some women started to use their personal oríkì in a way akin to a surname, they could not pass it on to their schoolchildren as such institutions started to ask for father's names for identification.

Having said that, framing the question as one in which nongendered Yorùbá names and naming practices started to show signs of a gender division, the question could easily be reframed as to why have many Yorùbá names remained ungendered despite the massive external shocks to the world-sense? Apart from the existing stock of traditional nongendered àbísọ, it is interesting that many newly minted àbísọ emanating from Christian communities today are not gender specific. With the contemporary Pentecostal movement, in the past two decades, we see a rash of new Yorùbá Christian names, a process akin to that of the nineteenth century first generation of Christians. Many of the popular current names are focused on what are regarded as Christian concepts such as love, hope, grace, and the like, with Olúwa, the preferred Yorùbá Christian name for God. Thus we have Ìfẹ́olúwa, Olúdára, Olúwadámilọ́lá, Ọrẹolúwa, Ìrètíolúwa, Ọlọ́runtóbi, and some new names substituting Jesus for Olúwa such as in Jéésùbunmi. What is remarkable about this new generation of Christianity-induced Yorùbá names is that both males and females bear these names; therefore they are not gender specific. Clearly, in any discussion of names over long periods of time there are many trends and ideological shifts in the choices that parents make and I do not want to minimize those. Still the nongenderness of the stock of basic abiso names old and newly invented is striking. Today, the process of inventing new Yorùbá-language names is largely driven by Yorùbá Christians. For Yorùbá Muslims, adoption of Islamic names and Arabic language names more extensively rendered faithfully in the original language, has become the norm. When they include Yoruba language names as part of the tradition of having multiple names, such appellations are likely to be "old school" and distinct from the ones preferred (and newly coined) by Christians. Their Yoruba names remain non-gendered unlike the favored Arabic names. It seems as though Yoruba muslims have transferred their creativity in naming to Arabic language names, some of which are said to be non-existent in Arabia. An empirical study of current names and naming practices will do much to answer the many questions this study has raised.

What Is Not in a Name?

In my exposition of Yorùbá names and naming practices, I began with the question of whether to gender or not to gender oríkì names. Such a question is clearly informed by colonization: why must anything be gendered, given that gender division is a social contrivance with nothing inherent about it, as Yorùbá culture shows. When we say a social practice or institution is gendered, we tend to think of it as "his" or "hers" and assume that it was gendered at its point of origin. Such an assumption works in a society where gender constructs are routine and the norm. In the Yorùbá world, this is not the case, and therefore the apparent gender of *oríkì* does not constitute gender per se—the difference between current female-associated names and male-associated ones reflects a difference in the origins of each set, and not in the nature of the names or the function that they perform. The fact that ordinary (non-oriki) Yorùbá-language names continue to be used in a nongendered manner even in a postcolonial society would support the argument that *oríkì* names are intrinsically not gendered. Although the Yorùbá have been pushed and pulled in many directions over three hundred years of history, creativity and the rejection of gender categories remains an enduring aspect of their episteme.

As I have shown in the last three chapters, Yorùbá names are varied and various, encapsulating a myriad of values and performing different functions. For this reason, instead of asking the question "What's in a name?" one might better ask, "What is *not* in a name?" The answer to this question with regard to Yorùbá is "gender."[40]

This study also raises questions about how we use gender as an analytical category. On what basis is gender attribution made to institutions and social practices? Is it possible to think about gendering as a multilayered process taking into account its varied depth in time among other variables? In many societies gender categories remain epiphenomenal,[41] even in the face of the current Euro/American-led, male-dominant global system. I am wondering about the extent to which the taken-for-grantedness of gender typing, and stereotyping globally, reifies and promote gender binaries with all their negative power dynamics.

CONCLUSION

MOTHERHOOD IN THE QUEST FOR SOCIAL TRANSFORMATION

In this conclusion, my goal is to explore the ways in which understanding the institution of motherhood and its unique position in Yorùbá society can aid in the struggle to transform the lives of all Africans, but especially the lives of African women and children. Specifically, I will focus on the relationship between motherhood and leadership as it has emerged in a variety of social and political contexts from the colonial period to the present. As I have demonstrated throughout the book, the dominance of the West threatens to obliterate matripotent values, institutions, and episteme. Thus I will begin by considering the implications for Africans of Western feminist dominance in the construction of motherhood.

As I reflected on the institution of motherhood in this book, I have returned to the transformations that have taken place in Yorùbá society post colonization, and hence the changes in the construction of motherhood, many of them to negative effect. In chapter 3, I drew attention to how aspects of the *Ìyá* as a category has been demonized as new religions and new values have come to dominate the lives and imaginations of people. In chapter 8, I showed how even as we recognize the persistence of gender-free Yorùbá-language names in the society, we cannot ignore the fact that the focus of meaning-making in many Yorùbá names today seem to have shifted from the *Òrìṣà* to Jesus and the Christian God (*Oluwa*) or to Arabic names as first and last names. These have implications for what values we hold dear and who authorizes them.

More disturbing than current naming practices is the high rate of maternal mortality, a bane of many African countries and a sign of the depth of the continent's predicament. There is no question, then, that another transformation is necessary. From the perspective of a society grounded on a matripotent ethos, there is nothing worse than the death of a mother in childbirth, which, as I pointed out in chapter 3, portends all sorts of misfortune. According to Ladele et al., such a death has for centuries called for elaborate and costly cleansing rituals.[1] But today, we have become so inured to the loss of women in childbirth that cleansing rituals rarely, if ever, take place, even among those few who still worship the Gods who demand them.

Feminism and Motherhood

Let me start with an anecdote. On Mother's Day 2014, I went out to dinner in New York City, on the Upper West Side, not far from my apartment. After dinner, I decided to walk home, and on my way I stopped at a small grocery store to buy some fruit. As I entered the store, the owner greeted me with the words "Happy Holidays." From his accent, I surmised that he was an immigrant. I immediately asked him where he was from, and he said Egypt. I then asked him why he did not know that the appropriate rendering of the greeting for that special day was "Happy Mother's Day." He laughed and then he tilted his head toward me in a conspiratorial manner, even though we were the only two in the store, and said that I would not believe how many times women who had come into the store on that day had registered strong objections to the greeting, "Happy Mother's Day." They said they were not mothers, would never consider becoming mothers, and felt insulted by being addressed as such. The storekeeper said that as a result, he stopped using the greeting, but felt that he still had to acknowledge that the day was special. His solution to the dilemma was "Happy Holidays," a greeting that has its own controversy in the United States when it is used during the Christmas season as a standard greeting, to accommodate those who do not identify as Christian.

I was not surprised by the story recounted by the grocer. It confirmed much recent research concerning Western feminism and motherhood, some of which I have responded to in my own work.[2] It seems as if in many circles in the United States, motherhood is a four-letter word, as it is blamed for women's troubles however they are defined. At the time that I had the Mother's Day encounter in New York,[3] the reigning book on the *New York Times* best-seller list was by Sheryl Sandberg, the chief operations officer (COO) of Facebook. In this book, *Lean In: Women, Work, and the Will to Lead*, Sandberg laments the absence of women in leadership positions in all sectors of society, especially in the corporate world, an absence she attributes to the fact that many women have no "will to lead":

> We hold ourselves back in ways both big and small, by lacking self-confidence, by not raising our hands, by pulling back when we should be leaning

in. We internalize negative messages throughout our lives—the messages that say it is wrong to be outspoken, aggressive, and more powerful than men. We internalize the negative messages we get throughout our lives...We compromise our career goals to make room for children who may not yet exist...This book makes a case for leaning in, for being ambitious in our pursuits.[4]

In her view, then, becoming a mother is not only unambitious, it is antiambition.

Although Sandberg's is not a scholarly book, its message on motherhood recalls that of many academics.[5] The central theme in white feminist theorization of motherhood in the United States is matrophobia, which Adrienne Rich defines as "the fear not of one's mother or motherhood but of *becoming one's mother*."[6] Although Rich did not coin the word "matrophobia," she reintroduced it into the discourse in her classic book *Of Woman Born: Motherhood as Experience and Institution*. The reason she offers for white feminist matrophobia (and it is indeed specific to white women in the United States)[7] is the fact of the patriarchal conditions under which motherhood takes place in their society. Rich explains, "The mother stands for the victim in ourselves, the unfree woman, the martyr. Our personalities seem dangerously to blur with our mothers; and in a desperate attempt to know where mother ends and daughter begins, we perform radical surgery."[8] D. Lynn Hallstein argues for the purging of matrophobia from white feminism because this malady is partly to blame for the persistent claim that feminism is antimotherhood.[9] Significantly, she explains, "It is clear to me that, if we want to understand fully both contemporary feminism and maternity and the relationship that exists today between the two, then, we must finally purge matrophobia from our analyses."[10] Hallstein's book *White Feminists and Contemporary Maternity: Purging Matrophobia* explores the construction of motherhood, white feminist analysis of mothering, and the history of the malady called "matrophobia." She also noted that the preference for sisterhood over motherhood as a term of solidarity among women is also tied to matrophobia.[11] In earlier work, questioning the wholesale globalization of sisterhood, a concept that emerged from a specifically white cultural experience, I observed:

In the nuclear family, the gender identification of children with their mothers underscores the fact that the mother is first and foremost (even to [her] children) the patriarch's wife. The gender-based division of labor in the family permanently cast the mother in the powerless role of victim. It is not surprising then that motherhood never ranked high in the kin role to which middle-class white feminists aspired. They could, on the other hand, identify with their sisters, who not only grew up under the terrifying shadow of the patriarchal father but shared the same difficult gender identification with the powerless mother.[12]

In earlier writings,[13] I have made a case that dominant Western feminist accounts of motherhood reduce it to a gender category. As such, a mother is represented as a woman first and foremost, a category that is perceived to be subordinated, disadvantaged, and oppressed because women are subordinate to males, who are the privileged group. The gendering of the institution of motherhood leads to its patriarchalization. In turn, because of the privileging of males, reproductive processes like parturition, gestation, and childbirth, which have no male equivalents, are erased from many feminist accounts of motherhood. Within this patriarchalizing model, motherhood cannot be understood in and of itself, but only through the lens of women's oppression. With this approach, powerlessness and lack of agency attach by definition to motherhood.

Given this history and the fact that the contemporary capitalist industrialized societies in which white feminists are located are structured to disregard motherhood as well as the biological fact that it is a necessary institution and process if humanity is to survive, many feminists have bought into the idea that to progress (whatever that means), women must discount, minimize, nay eschew motherhood in their lives. Hence we have terms such as "childfree" being deployed to suggest a conscious emancipation from motherhood. I suppose the idea is that men are powerful and liberated because they are "childfree." It is curious that many feminists are wary of motherhood because of the perceived patriarchal nature of the nuclear family in which it is embedded, and yet they embrace the role of wife in the same kind of family.

In the light of the coloniality of power and the attendant unequal power relationships within the global system, the West represents the beacon and model for emancipated women. For Africans, even more significant is the West's role in trying to "fix" Africa, a continent that has come to be portrayed as the poster child of human misery and victimization of women. The development establishment set up to "fix" an Africa that is constantly depicted as an "orphaned continent" that has become the ward of the international system is an industry—a growth industry—providing jobs for many foreign and some African personnel. African academics are hired both as staff of NGOs and as consultants to conduct what has come to be known as donor-driven research, which addresses the interests and facilitates the work of the donors, in this case foreign governments and international organizations. The costs are very high for Africa. One keen observer writes about the impact on Africa of donor-driven research:

> Given the ideological nature of development policies in Africa that are often driven by neo-liberal agenda and the dictates of globalization, the research agenda on gender tends to be determined by external priorities and policy

orientations that reinforce recolonization of African social science. Donor-driven research can also undermine academic programs if the faculty is motivated by the pursuit of funds for research, especially in the light of the economic difficulties of the continent and the low salaries of faculty.[14]

Most pertinent to our focus here, external interests overdetermine gender research on the continent, to the extent that the only African woman who is of interest to many international organizations is the victimized, the mutilated, and the "poorest of the world's poor," to use some of the favored jargon. There is no room to imagine African women who can help themselves, or African cultures poised to teach the world important lessons, including the benefits of matripotency.

It is not surprising, then, that there is very little feminist research on the continent that can tell us about endogenous constructions of motherhood, because our scholars take their funds, concepts, and cues from Western feminist research. For example, in an otherwise informative article on the restructuring of local government councils in Uganda in order to include more women in the drive for gender equity, political scientist Josephine Ahikire writes:

> At a general level, women are said to be more inclined to development *owing to their role in society as mothers,* but we need to go beyond these *essentialising assertions* to a more critical analysis of what is going on. Views on the appropriateness of putting women in charge of finance signified *essentialised notions of womanhood.*[15]

Ahikire seems to have missed an opportunity to investigate and analyze why mothers and women are thought of in these very positive and enabling terms in Uganda. Instead she dismisses such constructions with a Western feminist flourish of essentialism. What exactly is essentialist about mothers taking on responsibility to provide for their children? Equally significant is the question of whether what is regarded as essentialist in the United States is similarly essentialist in Uganda. These issues merit analysis from the local perspective, not dismissal. Ahikire correctly calls for critical analysis, but the feminist cry of essentialism that she utters is a strategy of co-optation and should itself be subjected to critical analysis. In the Yorùbá matripotent ethos that I have articulated and analyzed in this book as one case study, there is no room to cry essentialism, because *Ìyá* is first and foremost a spiritual category and has no binary counterpart. The concept of gender essentialism is fundamentally a biological one emerging out of the Western biologic. Matripotency emerges out of Yorùbá society's spiritual logic. As a result, the matrophobia of white feminists, which calls for disidentification with mother, has no place in the matripotent ethos, considering that the *ori* (destiny) of mothers and that of their children, regardless of anatomy, are perceived to be spiritually conjoined.

Coupling Motherhood and Leadership in the African Experience

It is in the arena of grassroots activism that African constructions of motherhood are revealed in all their variety. Studies on African women and leadership have exposed strong connections between motherhood and leadership. Filomina Steady is easily the foremost scholar on African women and leadership. In her recent empirical study of African women in four West African countries, *Women and Leadership in Africa: Mothering the Nation, Humanizing the State*, motherhood retains a positive connection with leadership because Africans understand that the fundamental role of mothers goes "beyond reproductive and nurturing roles in households, but reflects the normative values and humanistic ideologies that embrace notions of preservation of past, present and future generations; prosperity and well being of society as a whole; and the promotion of equality, peace, and justice. It is also viewed as a metaphor for humanizing the state."[16]

In my own research on motherhood, I found that mother is the name many African women choose to call themselves: they revel in the role-identity, and it is often an impetus to activism. A central theme in much discussion of motherhood is that it is inherently the practice of leadership.[17] As leaders, mothers are also visionaries, as they must constantly project into the future for the benefit of their children. Indeed, as has been well documented, maternal ideology is central to communal identity and leadership in many African cultures, where conceptions of motherhood diverge sharply from the gendered motherhood found in the Western nuclear families described by Euro/American feminist scholars. Nzegwu writes about maternal ideology in Igbo society:

> The ideology of motherhood extends to all mothers and constituted the basis for compelling obedience from everyone who gestated in a womb. Its power covers a range of activities that continues long after birth of the child, the most important of which is establishing the moral parameters of belongingness and loyalty.[18]

We can see the basis of the maternal ideology in stories of origin and creation in a number of African societies. In chapter 2, I discussed Oseetura, a Yorùbá story of origin that names Yèyé Ọ̀ṣun as *Ìyá* the founder of human society. Among the Kikuyu of Kenya, Mumbi is the founding mother, and her nine daughters represent the nine clans of the ethnic group[19]. In Mireille

Rabenoro's discussion of motherhood in Malagasy, we find parallels with Yorùbá ideas and indeed those of other African societies. She writes that in the legends of indigenous Malagasy society "emerges an image of women existing among the elements (the air, the water), long before the appearance of men, of whom they are the source, the spring—the Mother."[20] Similarly, as the Akan proverb declares, even the king has a mother, highlighting the fact that motherhood antedates the king and therefore cannot be subordinated to any social institution. The maternal ideology tells us that motherhood is the originary source—the fountainhead of the social. *Ìyá* is the source of life and the base on which social order rests.

Steady tells us further that "regardless of indigenous notions that also equate men with leadership in Africa, a nuanced Afro-centric perspective reveals a different reality, where the image of motherhood can have political resonance and be linked to leadership in a real way." This was apparent in many political campaigns involving women. For instance, she writes about Jeredine Williams of Sierra Leone, who ran for the presidency in 1996 under the Coalition for Progress Party, "which was commonly referred to as Kombra Party, meaning Mothers Party. Although she did not win, participation in the electoral process reinforced the connection between motherhood and leadership."[21] Steady also noted that:

> in a previous field study of the Women's Congress, then the women's wing of the ruling All People's Congress (APC) in Sierra Leone, Nancy Steele, secretary-general of the Women's Congress, manipulated the symbol of motherhood and protection to mobilize support, get out the vote, and intimidate the opposition. Her speeches consistently evoked this symbol. "Women give birth to men; therefore we own them. Women are the natural leaders."[22]

Similarly, Sylvia Tamale,[23] writing about women in politics in Uganda, documents the experience of Betty Bigombe, who was named peace negotiator and had to meet numerous times with the murderous rebel leader Joseph Kony.[24] In Tamale's account, Bigombe chronicles the evolution of her relationship with the rebels, explaining that she knew she had made a breakthrough when the rebels started addressing her as mother: "I graduated from being a girl to being a woman until eventually everybody started referring to me as mother. It signified trust and respect." Even Kony started to call her "mummy Bigombe."[25]

In recent times, the centrality of motherhood in African societies has come to the fore because of the emergence of three female presidents[26] and a female-majority legislature in Rwanda.[27] Female politicians and leaders in Africa do not hesitate to use the label of mother as a positive and enabling one, given the meaning of motherhood in many African cultures.

For example, Liberia's president Ellen Johnson-Sirleaf came to power on a huge surge of support from women voters. Sirleaf of Liberia is perceived, and perceives herself, as mother of the nation.

> The symbolism of motherhood, as a tool of mobilization, offers an opportunity for rebirth and renewal. As "Ma Ellen," Sirleaf was viewed as a mother who could heal her ailing nation, devastated and traumatized by a 14-year civil war. This was all the more poignant because her opponent, George Weah, a football hero, was young enough to be her son.[28]

The point I am emphasizing here is that unlike in Europe and America, being called a mother in politics is welcome, because the role is associated with leadership and responsibility, and thus has the potential to garner votes. What this suggests is that our research on Africa must start with African realities, and that we must not lose sight of our own traditions by hiding under the skirts of our feminist "senior sisters" from Europe and America.

Motherhood as enabling identity is equally apparent in social movements across the continent. In Nobel Laureate Wangari Maathai's Green Belt Movement and the Liberian Peace Movement, we see that ordinary women are motivated by the ideology of motherhood, which propels their activism and leadership. The focus on motherhood is not a reification of biology or biological motherhood, but a recognition that mothers in raising children create and sustain the future. Motherhood is by definition visionary. As Maathai puts it, "Women…have a capacity to care for others, to see beyond personal gain. Many women, I believe, are at their happiest and best when they are serving. I myself am at my happiest and my best when I am serving. There is nothing wrong with women serving, for service exemplifies the noble ideal of giving oneself to the community to better the lot of all."[29] Mothers see themselves as custodians of society: Leymah Gbowee, another Nobel Laureate, the leader of the Liberian peace movement, explains women's motivation in confronting Charles Taylor, the warmongering president, in these words:

> We are tired of war. We are tired of running. We are tired of begging for bulgur wheat. We are tired of our children being raped. We are now taking this stand, to secure the future of our children. *Because we believe, as custodians of society, tomorrow our children will ask us, "Mama, what was your role during the crisis?"*[30]

The story I have been telling so far is real enough, but there is also the reality of the world we live in today. We live in a Eurocentric universe—Africans are no longer self-authorizing. Globalization has made Africans wards or children of the international system, in other words, the West. On the continent, the problem that has plagued Africans in the past three centuries, at least, is that resources are not in the hands of those who want to serve, but in the clutches of a rapacious male-dominant elite of kleptocrats. Mothers have all the responsibilities but few of the resources required to nurture and build society and the future.

We look to the West for all our solutions, even though Western exploitation has created privileges for some and some fundamentally unresolvable problems given the capitalist, racist, and patriarchal models under which women are supposed to lean in. Why is the West, which has pathologized motherhood, and African motherhood even more, our model for liberation or for any kind of transformation? Studies of globalization draw attention to the stratification of mothers and the privileges that accrue to a tiny minority at the expense of the majority:

> Affluent career women increasingly earn their status not through leisure as they might have a century ago, but by apparently "doing it all"—producing a full time career, thriving children, a contented spouse, and a well-managed home. In order to preserve this illusion, domestic workers and nannies make the house hotel-room perfect, feed and bathe the children, cook, clean up—and magically fade from sight. The lifestyles of the First World are made possible by a global transfer of the services associated with a wife's traditional role—child care, homemaking, and sex—from poor countries to rich ones.[31]

Black feminist Audre Lorde understood this many decades before globalization was part of the discourse:

> Poor women and women of Color know there is a difference between the daily manifestations of marital slavery and prostitution because it is our daughters who line 42nd Street. If white American feminist theory need not deal with the differences between us, and the resulting difference in our oppressions, then how do you deal with the fact that the women who clean your houses and tend your children while you attend conferences on feminist theory are, for the most part, poor women and women of Color? What is the theory behind racist feminism?[32]

Today, the process of exploiting poorer women to augment the lives of class-privileged women is not limited to whites or the West; in the Global south, privileged women of all colors owe their well-ordered lives to the sacrifice of poor women.

It is clear that few of us can lean into anything when someone is standing on top of our heads. The ideology that informs "lean in," like all Western ideologies emanating from a racist capitalist patriarchal system, prizes the sort of individualism that preserves white privilege and male privilege. As such, it is unsustainable.

In contrast, indigenous African maternal ideologies are community-oriented. How can we bring this to bear in social transformation? Steady writes about "the socio-centric ethos of African feminism in which the advancement and well being of society is central rather than groups as groups, based on gender or special interest agendas, or the advancement of individuals."[33] Motherhood in African contexts is a collective rather than an individually constructed category. Consequently, I believe, the maternal ideology should be the basis of our activism; it is enabling, ennobling, and inclusive.

Leaning into career, as Sandberg and many feminists are advocating, is unsustainable because most mothers do not have opportunities for careers; rather, in a capitalist world, where jobs are few and far between, they labor at starvation wages to feed their children. Children, in turn, are perceived to be the private responsibility of their parents (particularly mothers), although in reality what they represent is a human necessity and a collective good.

Humanity cannot reproduce itself without motherhood. Therefore the institution and everyday practices of mothering humanity must be a collective act, impelled by communal will. The challenge then is how to convince society that motherhood should not be the responsibility of just one woman or just one nuclear family but should be the bedrock on which society is built and the way in which we organize our lives. Our insistence on using the white man as the model of freedom and white male privilege as the ideal that should inform social transformation ignores the fact that white privilege, specifically white male privilege, is a pathology. We need not build anything on it. Rather, we need to tear it down. In the brilliant and wise words of Audre Lorde:

> The master's tools will never dismantle the master's house. They may allow us temporarily to beat him at his own game, but they will never enable us to bring about genuine change. And this fact is only threatening to those women who still define the master's house as their only source of support.[34]

In a world of possibilities for all who are born of Ìyá, the maternal ideology, which is community oriented, all-inclusive, life giving, life sustaining, and life preserving can provide the vision and the foundation for political action and necessary social transformation.

NOTES

Introduction: Exhuming Subjugated Knowledge and Liberating Marginalized Epistemes

1. Anibal Quijano, "Coloniality and Modernity/Rationality," *Cultural Studies* 21, no. 2/3 (March/May 2007): 169.
2. Maria Lugones, "Hetrosexualism and the Colonial Modern Gender System," *Hypatia* 22, no. 1 (Winter 2007): 186.
3. Dipesh Chakrabarty, *Provincializing Europe Postcolonial Thought and Historical Difference* (Princeton, NJ: Princeton University Press, 2000).
4. Sabelo Ndlovu-Gatsheni, *Coloniality of Power in Postcolonial Africa. Myths of Decolonization* (Dakar, Sengal: Codesria, 2013), 52.
5. Ibid., 16.
6. *New York Times*, February 3, 2015.
7. Ifi Amadiume, *Re-inventing Africa Matriarchy, Religion, and Culture* (London: Zed Books, 1997), 23.
8. Maxwell Owusu, "Toward an African Critique of African Ethnography: The Usefulness of the Useless," in *Reclaiming the Human Sciences and Humanities through African Perspectives*, ed. H. Lauer and Kofi Anyidoho (Accra, Ghana: Sub-Saharan Publishers), 90.

1 Divining Knowledge: The Man Question in *Ifá*

1. Throughout the text, although I refer to Yorùbá people, my primary focus is on the history and culture Ọ̀yọ́-Yorùbá, which is a dominant subgroup of the nationality. That said, it should be noted that those cultural specificities were more pronounced before the sweeping changes that occurred in civil war and in the post-nineteenth-century periods. Language is also central to this study, and my engagement is with standard Yorùbá language, which is said to have privileged the Ọ̀yọ́ dialect. The term "Ọ̀yọ́-Yorùbá" covers many towns and communities that were at the center of Ọ̀yọ́ Empire. Today many of those towns are spread through many Yorùbá states in Nigeria. They include Ibadan, Ọ̀yọ́, Ogbomoso, Iwo, Iseyin, Ilorin Offa, Osogbo, Okuku, and Ejigbo.

2. See Oyèrónké Oyěwùmí, *The Invention of Women: Making an African Sense of Western Gender Discourses* (Minneapolis: University of Minnesota Press, 1997).

3. Adefisoye Oyesakin, "The Image of Women in Ifá Literary Corpus," *Nigeria Magazine* 141 (1982).

4. Wande Abimbola, "Images of Women in the Ifá Literary Corpus," *Annals of the New York Academy of Science* 810, no. 1 (1997).

5. Some Western feminist scholars such as Nancy Dowd have used the concept "man question" to analyze aspects of male disadvantage in the United States. N. E. Dowd, *The Man Question: Male Subordination and Privilege* (New York: New York University Press, 2010). But my own usage here is to encapsulate ideas of male dominance and male privilege that have come to define societies around the globe especially following European and American conquest. Thus in a comparative frame, the question in the "woman question" is one of subordination; the question in man question as I apply it to Yorùbá society and discourses is one of dominance.

6. Indeed today notions of masculinity and femininity exist in the society but they are legitimated by quotations from the Bible or Q'uran without any awareness that these religions did not originate from the society.

7. Oyěwùmí, *The Invention of Women*.

8. Adélékè Adéèkó, "'Writing' and 'Reference' in Ifá Divination Chants," *Oral Tradition* 25, no. 2 (2010): 284.

9. See Karin Barber, *I Could Speak until Tomorrow: Oríkì, Women, and the Past in a Yorùbá Town* (Edinburgh: Edinburgh University Press, 1991); Adéèkó, "'Writing' and 'Reference' in Ifá Divination Chants." For example, argument made that the elevation of Ifá over other kinds of divination is tied up with male privilege and the perception that it is a male province.

10. William R. Bascom, *Sixteen Cowries: Yorùbá Divination from Africa to the New World* (Bloomington: Indiana University Press, 1993), 10.

11. Abimbola, "Images of Women in the Ifá Literary Corpus," 86.

12. This section includes excerpts from my chapter "Decolonizing the Intellectual and the Quotidian," in *Gender Epistemologies in Africa: Gendering Traditions, Spaces, Social Institutions and Identities* (Palgrave, 2011).

13. The remaining polities such as Ajase fell under French jurisdiction and became part of the French colony of Dahomey.

14. See Oyěwùmí, *The Invention of Women*, Chapter 4 for a detailed account of male dominant colonial policies and practices.

15. See Abimbola, "Images of Women in the Ifá Literary Corpus."

16. Wande Abimbola, *Ifá: An Exposition of Ifá Literary Corpus* (Ibadan: Oxford University Press, 1976), 61.

17. Ibid.

18. Ibid., 242.

19. Argument made that the elevation of Ifá over other kinds of divination is tied up with male privilege and the perception that it is a male province.

20. William R. Bascom, *Ifá Divination: Communication between Gods and Men in West Africa* (Bloomington: Indiana University Press, 1991), 81.

21. See Michelle and Louise Lamphere Rosaldo, eds., *Women, Culture, and Society* (Stanford: Stanford University Press, 1974).

22. Bascom, *Ifá Divination*, 91.

23. Cited in ibid.

24. See Oyěwùmí, *The Invention of Women*, 76.

25. J. D. Y. Peel, "Gender in Yorùbá Religious Change," *Journal of Religion in Africa* 32, no. 2 (2002): 149.

26. Bascom, *Sixteen Cowries*, 3. In this regard also, it is important to note that Bertha, Bascom's wife, was born and raised in Cuba.

27. Quoted in Bascom, *Ifá Divination*, 13.

28. P. B. Bouche, *Sept Ans En Afrique Occidentale: La Côte Des Esclaves Et Le Dahomey* (Paris: E. Plon Nourrit, 1885), 120.

29. Malidoma Patrice Somé, *Of Water and the Spirit: Ritual, Magic and Initiation in the Life of an African Shaman* (New York: Penguin, 1995), 163.

30. Adéèkó, "'Writing' and 'Reference' in Ifá Divination Chants," 284.

31. Peel, "Gender in Yorùbá Religious Change," 147.

32. Oyeronke Olajubu, *Women in the Yorùbá Religious Sphere* (Albany: State University Press of New York, 2003), 119.

33. Ibid.

34. Bascom, *Sixteen Cowries*, 12.

35. Adéèkó, "'Writing' and 'Reference' in Ifá Divination Chants," 287.

36. Barber, *I Could Speak until Tomorrow*, 289.

37. Abimbola, *Ifá: An Exposition of Ifá Literary Corpus*, 14.

38. Wande Abimbola and I. Miller, *Ifá Will Mend Our Broken World: Thoughts on Yorùbá Religion and Culture in Africa and the Diaspora* (Roxbury: Aim Books, 1997), 86–87.

39. Bernard Maupoil, *La Géomancie À L'ancienne Côte Des Esclaves* (Paris: Institut d'ethnologie, 1943), 153–154.

40. Barber, *I Could Speak until Tomorrow*, 103.

41. Olajubu, *Women in the Yorùbá Religious Sphere*, 115.

42. Interview of Chief Akalaifa, babalawo in Ogbomoso, on July 17, 2008. Her name was Ajeje and her story was well known in the town. Ajeje is said to have originated in Ilorin, which is 35 miles from Ogbomoso. She had settled in the town in the 1960s following a Muslim-inspired violent purge of identifiable practitioners of indigenous religion who were regarded as heathens and were not going to be tolerated in a town that sought to inscribe a Muslim identity. I have not seen any documentation in scholarship or popular press on religious riots in Ilorin that may have led to the fleeing of such diviners from the town.

43. See a discussion of the gendering of Yorùbá language and its implications in Oyěwùmí, *The Invention of Women*, Chapter 5.

44. Barber, *I Could Speak until Tomorrow*, 289.

45. T. J. Bowen, *Central Africa: Adventures and Missionary Labors in Several Countries in the Interior of Africa, from 1849 to 1856* (Charleston, SC: Southern Baptist Publication Society, 1857), 317.

46. Bascom, *Ifá Divination*, 23.

47. Ibid.
48. Oyěwùmí, *The Invention of Women*; Oyèrónkẹ́ Oyěwùmí, "Colonizing Bodies and Minds: Gender and Colonialism," in *Postcolonialisms: An Anthology of Cultural Theory and Criticism*, ed. Gaurav and Supriya Nair Desai (New Jersey: Rutgers University Press, 2005).
49. D. O. Ogungbile, "ÉÉRìndínlógún: The Seeing Eyes of Sacred Shells and Stones," in *Ọ̀ṢUn across the Waters: A YorùBá Goddess in Africa and the Americas*, ed. Joseph M. and Mei-Mei Sanford Murphy (Bloomington: Indiana University Press, 2001).
50. Bascom, *Sixteen Cowries*, 3.
51. Ibid., 4.
52. Ibid., 3.
53. Ogungbile, "ÉÉRìndínlógún," 191.
54. Ibid., 196.
55. Bascom, *Sixteen Cowries*, 10.
56. Ibid., 21.
57. What is sacrifice? See Omosade J. Awolalu, *Yorùbá Beliefs and Sacrificial Rites* (London: Longman, 1979).
58. Bascom, *Sixteen Cowries*, 11.
59. Niyi. F. Akinnaso, "Bourdieu and the Diviner: Knowledge and Symbolic Power in Yorùbá Divination," in *The Pursuit of Certainty: Religious and Cultural Formulations*, ed. Wendy James (London: Routledge, 1995), 238.
60. Wande Abimbola, "The Bag of Wisdom: Ọ̀ṢUn and the Origins of Ifá Divination," in *Ọ̀Ṣun across the Waters: A Yorùbá Goddess in Africa and the Americans*, ed. Joseph M. and Mei-Mei Sanford Murphy (Bloomington: Indiana University Press, 2001), 150.
61. On July 20, 2009.
62. Ogungbile, "ÉÉRìndínlógún," 96.
63. Abimbola, "The Bag of Wisdom," 141; my emphasis.
64. Robert Sydney Smith, "Alaafin in Exile: A Study of the Igboho Period in Ọ̀YỌ́ History," *Journal of African History* 6, no. 1 (1865): 68.
65. Akalaifa interviews: July 21, 2008.
66. Bascom, *Ifá Divination*, 11.
67. T. G. O Gbadamosi, "Odù Imale. Islam in Ifá Divination and the Case of Predestined Muslims," *Journal of the Historical Society of Nigeria* 8, no. 4 (1977).
68. Akinnaso, "Bourdieu and the Diviner," 244.

2 (Re)Casting the Yorùbá World: *Ifá*, *Ìyá*, and the Signification of Difference

1. At the conference at Harvard in 2006, I asked Professor Wande Abimbola why in his writings he translates Yorùbá gender-neutral pronouns, for example, into English gendered pronouns that immediately translates the language and world into a male one. He acknowledged the problem but asked

that we pay attention to his more recent writings, which have become more gender sensitive and are attempting to correct past mistakes. It is this claim that led me to call his more recent writings the "later Abimbola."

2. Oyeronke Olajubu, "Seeing through a Woman's Eye: Yorùbá Religious Tradition and Gender Relations," *Journal of Feminist Studies in Religion* 20, no. 1 (2004): 43.

3. The curiosity is that very few Yorùbá people today know that Odùduwà is also portrayed as *Ìyá* in the traditions. In my research, when I asked ordinary Yorùbá individuals about the representation of Odùduwà as female in some oral traditions, they were shocked, although many know the story of Odùduwà as the founding father.

4. In chapter 5, I do an extensive historical sociology of Yorùbá names and what informs them.

5. Olajubu, "Seeing through a Woman's Eye," 54–55.

6. Ibid., 55.

7. Ibid., 57–58.

8. For a discussion of the role of Ato, a female official in the egungun cult, see S. O. Babayemi, *Egungun among the Ọ̀yọ́ Yorùbá* (Ibadan: Board Publication Limited, 1980).

9. Oyèrónkẹ́ Oyěwùmí, *The Invention of Women: Making an African Sense of Western Gender Discourses* (Minneapolis: University of Minnesota Press, 1997).

10. Wande Abimbola, *Ifá: An Exposition of Ifá Literary Corpus* (Ibadan: Oxford University Press, 1976), 27.

11. I use female god instead of goddess because *òrìṣà*, the indigenous category, is gender neutral and does not draw attention to the anatomy of the entity so named.

12. Although many of the scholars I interrogated easily used the gender pronoun she to refer to Ọ̀ṣun the female god, I will use the collective pronoun "they" to refer to Ọ̀ṣun in order to be faithful to the Yorùbá nongender specificity. The pronoun they in one move expresses both gender neutrality and senior status of the deity among the Irúnmọlẹ̀.

13. Rowland Abiodun, "Hidden Power: Ọ̀sun, the Seventeenth Odù," in *Ọ̀Ṣun across the Waters: A Yorùbá Goddess in Africa and the Americas*, ed. Joseph M. and Mei-Mei Sanford Murphy (Bloomington: Indiana University Press, 2001), 16–17.

14. Ibid., 17.

15. Diedre Badejo, *Ọ̀Ṣun Seegesi: The Elegant Deity of Wealth, Power, and Femininity* (Trenton: Africa World Press, 1996), 79.

16. Abiodun, "Hidden Power," 16–18.

17. Ibid., 19.

18. Ibid., 18.

19. Ibid., 19.

20. Ibid., 18.

21. D. O. Ogungbile, "ÉÉRìndínlógún: The Seeing Eyes of Sacred Shells and Stones," in *Ọ̀Ṣun across the Waters: A Yorùbá Goddess in Africa and the Americas*,

ed. Joseph M. and Mei-Mei Sanford Murphy (Bloomington: Indiana University Press, 2001), 193–194.

22. Ibid.
23. Ibid., 190.
24. Ibid., 191.
25. Ibid., 194.
26. C. O. Adepegba. "Osun and Brass: An Insight into Yoruba Religious Symbology," in Osun Across the waters, p. 107.
27. Ogungbile, "Ẹ́Ẹ́Rìndínlógún," 193.
28. Abiodun, "Hidden Power," 17.
29. Ibid.
30. Ogungbile, "Ẹ́Ẹ́Rìndínlógún," 193.
31. Oyeronke Olajubu, Women in the Yorùbá Religious Sphere (Albany: State University Press of New York, 2003), 80.
32. Abiodun, "Hidden Power," 16–17.
33. Ibid., 17.
34. Ibid., 18.
35. Ogungbile, "Ẹ́Ẹ́Rìndínlógún," 189.
36. Abiodun, "Hidden Power," 19.
37. Olajubu, Women in the Yorùbá Religious Sphere, 80.
38. Badejo, Ọ̀Ṣun Seegesi, 78.
39. Abiodun, "Hidden Power," 28.
40. Similar ideas have also been expressed in other African societies such as Asante, where it is said that even the king has a mother (Emmanuel Akyeampong and Pashington Obeng, "Spirituality, Gender, and Power in Asante History," in African Gender Studies: A Reader, ed. Oyèrónkẹ́ Oyěwùmí [New York: Palgrave Macmillan, 2005]); and Igbo society, where it is said that Nnneka—mother is supreme (Nkiru Uwechia Nzegwu, Family Matters: Feminist Concepts in African Philosophy of Culture [New York: State University of New York Press, 2006]).
41. Ogungbile, "Ẹ́Ẹ́Rìndínlógún," 193.
42. Abiodun, "Hidden Power," 28.
43. Adélékè Adéẹ̀kọ́, "'Writing' and 'Reference' in Ifá Divination Chants," Oral Tradition 25, no. 2 (2010), 280.
44. G. C. Bond and A. Gilliam, eds., Social Construction of the Past: Representation as Power (New York: Routledge, 1994), 8.
45. T. M. Aluko, One Man One Wife (London: Heinemann, 1959), 59.

3 Matripotency: Ìyá in Philosophical Concepts and Sociopolitical Institutions

★Parts of this chapter have been published before and can be found in the following publications: "Abiyamo: Theorizing African Motherhood," in Jenda: A Journal of Gender and African Women's Studies, Issue 4, 1 (2003); "Conceptualizing Gender: The Eurocentric Foundations of Feminist Concepts and the Challenge of African Epistemologies," in Jenda: A Journal of Gender and African Women's Studies 2, no. 1 (2002); "Beyond Gendercentric Models: Restoring Motherhood to discourses of African art and Aesthetics," in *Gender Epistemologies in Africa.* and "Decolonizing the Intellectual and Quotidian: Yoruba Scholar(ship) and in *Gender Epistemologies in Africa.*

1. I collected this verse from Chief Olagoke Akanni, Araba Oluawo Ogbomoso, on July 7, 2008.

2. Rowland Abiodun, "Verbal and Visual Metaphors: Mythical Allusions in Yorùbá Ritualistic Art of Orí," *Word and Image* 3, no. 3 (1987): 266.

3. Ibid., 267.

4. Segun Gbadegesin, "Toward a Theory of Destiny," in *A Companion to African Philosophy*, ed. Kwasi Wiredu (Oxford: Blackwell Publishing Ltd, 2007), 318.

5. Babatunde Lawal, "Aworan: Representing the Self and Its Metaphysical Other in Yorùbá Art," *The Art Bulletin* 83, no. 3 (2001): 523.

6. The filmmaker Adeyemi Afolayan explored the theme of ritual begging in his 1984 film, *Ìyá Ni Wura* (Mother is Gold). The movie featured scenes of mothers dancing with their twins in the market as a required sacrifice for their children. Also see Lawal, "Aworan," 85.

7. Lawal, "Aworan," 512.

8. Rowland Abiodun, "Woman in Yorùbá Religious Images," *Journal of African Cultural Studies* 2, no. 1 (1989): 13–14.

9. T. A. A. Ladele et al., *Iwadii Ijinle Asa Yorùbá* (Ibadan: Macmillan, 1986), 139.

10. I thank my colleague Professor Olufemi Taiwo for this translation.

11. See ibid., 229–30.

12. T. M. Aluko, *One Man, One Wife* (London: Heinemann, 1959), 107–108.

13. Rowland Abiodun, "Understanding Yorùbá Art and Aesthetics: The Concept of Àṣẹ," *African Arts* 27, no. 3 (1994): 72.

14. John III Pemberton and Funso S. Afolayan, *Yorùbá Sacred Kingship: A Power Like That of the Gods* (Washington and London: Smithsonian Institution, 1996), 92.

15. J. D. Y. Peel, "Gender in Yorùbá Religious Change," *Journal of Religion in Africa* 32, no. 2 (2002): 150.

16. Ibid.

17. Lawal, "Aworan," 500.

18. Ibid.

19. Abiodun, "Woman in Yorùbá Religious Images," 14.

20. Joan A. Westcott and Peter Morton-Williams, "The Festival of Iyamapo," *Nigeria Magazine* (1958): 220–224.

21. Karin Barber, *I Could Speak until Tomorrow: Oríkì, Women, and the Past in a Yorùbá Town* (Edinburgh: Edinburgh University Press, 1991), 16.

22. Ibid.

23. Ibid., 75.

24. Nkiru Uwechia Nzegwu, *Family Matters: Feminist Concepts in African Philosophy of Culture* (New York: State University of New York Press, 2006); Niara Sudarkasa, *The Strength of Our Mothers: African & African American Women and Families. Essays and Speeches* (Trenton, NJ: Africa World Press, 1986); Ifi Amadiume, *Afrikan Matriarchal Foundations: The Igbo Case* (Red Sea Press, 2000); Cheikh Anta Diop, *The Cultural Unity of Black Africa: The*

Domains of Patriarchy and Matriarchy in Classical Antiquity (Chicago: Third World Press, 1978); Filimena Steady, *Women and Collective Action in Africa* (New York: Palgrave, 2006); Filomina Steady, *Women and Leadership in Africa: Mothering the Nation, Humanizing the State* (New York: Palgrave/Macmillan, 2013).

25. Oyèrónké Oyěwùmí, "Introduction. Feminism, Sisterhood, and Other Foreign Relations," in *African Women and Feminism: Reflecting on the Politics of Sisterhood*, ed. Oyèrónké Oyěwùmí (New Jersey: Africa World Press, 2003).

26. The European nuclear family system that privileges marriage ties and in so doing promotes male dominance has been "sold" as the natural and universal system. But this is clearly an imperial imposition totally at odds with the way in which African kinship ties were socially constituted.

27. Jomo Kenyatta, *Facing Mount Kenya: The Tribal Life of the Gikuyu* (London: Heinemann Group of Publishers, 1962), 5.

28. Akyeampong, "Spirituality, Gender, and Power in Asante History," in *African Gender Studies: A Reader*, ed. Oyèrónké Oyěwùmí (New York: Palgrave Macmillan, 2005), 23.

29. Today, *ìyàwó* has become the preferred term for denoting wife, where originally it meant bride. See discussion in chapter 6.

30. Oyěwùmí, *The Invention of Women: Making an African Sense of Western Gender Discourses* (Minneapolis: University of Minnesota Press, 1997), 45.

31. Babatunde Lawal, "A Ya Gbo, a Ya To: New Perspectives on Edan Ogboni," *African Arts* 28, no. 1 (1995): 38.

32. Nzegwu, *Family Matters*, 54.

33. Oyěwùmí, "Introduction. Feminism, Sisterhood, and Other Foreign Relations."

34. Dierde Badejo, *Ọ̀Ṣun Seegesi: The Elegant Deity of Wealth, Power, and Femininity* (Trenton: Africa World Press, 1996).

35. Westcott and Morton-Williams, "The Festival of Iyamapo," 220.

36. See Toyin Falola, "Gender, Business and Space Control: Yorùbá Market Women and Power," in *African Market Women's Economic Power: The Role of Women in African Economic Development*, ed. Bessie House-Midamba and Felik K. Ekechi (Westport, CT: Greenwood Press, 1995).

37. Oyěwùmí, *The Invention of Women*, 67.

38. Ibid.

39. Jamie Bruce Lockhart and Paul E. Lovejoy, eds., *Hugh Clapperton into the Interior of Africa: Records of the Second Expedition 1825–1827* (Leiden and Boston: Brill, Clapperton, Hugh), 117.

40. Oyěwùmí, *The Invention of Women*, 58.

41. Kola Abimbola, "Images of Women in the Ifá Literary Corpus," *Annals of the New York Academy of Science* 810, no. 1 (1997): 137–139.

42. Jacob Olupona, "ỌRÌṢÀ ỌṢun: Yorùbá Sacred Kingship and Civil Religion in Oṣogbo, Nigeria," in *ỌṢun across the Waters: A Yorùbá Goddess in Africa and the Americans*, ed. Joseph M. and Mei-Mei Sanford Murphy (Bloomington: Indiana University Press, 2001), 5.

43. I discussed this issue at length in Chapter 3 of *Invention*.
44. Oyeronke Olajubu, *Women in the Yorùbá Religious Sphere* (Albany: State University Press of New York, 2003), 26.
45. E. Bolaji Idowu, *Olodumare: God in Yoruba Belief* (London: Longman. 1962), 27.
46. John III Pemberton and Funso S. Afolayan, *Yorùbá Sacred Kingship: A Power Like That of the Gods* (Washington and London: Smithsonian Institution, 1996), 92.
47. Samuel Johnson and Obadiah Johnson, *The History of the Yorubas: From the Earliest Times to the Beginning of the British Protectorate* (Westport, CT: Negro University Press, 1921), 77.
48. Ibid., 64.
49. Olajubu, *Women in the Yorùbá Religious Sphere*.
50. Bolanle Awe, "The Iyalode in the Traditional Yoruba Political System," in *Readings in Gender in Africa*, ed. Andrea Cornwall (Bloomington: Indiana University Press, 2005), 196.
51. Ibid.
52. Ibid.
53. Ibid., 196.
54. Oyěwùmí, *The Invention of Women*, 111.
55. Bolanle Awe, "The Rise of Ibadan as a Yorùbá Power, 1851–1893" (PhD dissertation, Oxford University, 1964).
56. Awe, "The Iyalode in the Traditional Yoruba Political System," 196.
57. Oyěwùmí, *The Invention of Women*, 108; Ruth Watson, *Civil Disorder Is the Disease of Ibadan: Chieftaincy & Civic Culture in a Yorùbá City* (Oxford: James Currey Publishers, 2003).
58. Watson, *Civil Disorder Is the Disease of Ibadan*, 21.
59. Awe, "The Iyalode in the Traditional Yoruba Political System," 196.
60. This raises even more fundamental question about the much touted Ibadan Republicanism (ibid.).
61. Ibid., 197.
62. Ibid., 196.
63. Samuel Johnson and Obadiah Johnson, *The History of the Yorubas: From the Earliest Times to the Beginning of the British Protectorate* (Westport, CT: Negro University Press, 1921), 77.
64. Adeleke Adéèkó. Efunsetan Aniwura 2011 #366@44}
65. I wish to thank Adéléké Adéèkó for drawing my attention to the existence of an Ìyálóde square in Abeokuta.
66. It is interesting to note that many of the gender claims being made about the Ìyálóde title comes from missionary Anna Hinderer's memoir about life in nineteenth-century Ibadan (Anna Hinderer, *17 Years in Yoruba Country. Memorials of Anna Hinderer* [London: Seeley, Jackson and Halliday, 1877]).
67. Rowland Abiodun, "Hidden Power: Ọsun, the Seventeenth Odù," in *Ọsun across the Waters: A Yorùbá Goddess in Africa and the Americans*, ed. Joseph M. and Mei-Mei Sanford Murphy (Bloomington: Indiana University Press, 2001), 16, 25.

68. Ibid.

69. A (date) Yorùbá-language film titled *Maami* (my mother), produced and directed by award-winning film maker Tunde Kelani, captures very well the shock value of this statement in a scene where the young boy Kashimawo is reading *Ogboju Òde* to his illiterate mother. As soon as he read those lines, the mother exclaims "haa" with great alarm. This characterization of *ìyá* most certainly produces great anxiety especially among females.

70. D. O. Fagunwa, *Forest of a Thousand Daemons: A Hunter's Saga*, trans. Wole Soyinka (New York: Random House, 1982), 2.

71. Olakunle George, *Relocating Agency: Modernity and African Letters* (New York: State University of New York Press, 2012), 121.

72. Ibid.

73. Afolabi Olabimtan, "Religion as Theme in Fagunwa's Novels," *Odù* 11 (1975): 107.

74. Ibid., 102.

75. Rudo B. Gaidzanwa, *Images of Women in Zimbabwean Literature* (Harare: College Press, 1997), 48.

76. One wonders whether the misfortunes that befell Johnson's manuscripts would have occurred if he had had their support. The original manuscript got lost in the hands of the publisher in London.

77. Olabimtan, "Religion as Theme in Fagunwa's Novels," 111.

78. D. O. Fagunwa, *Ogboju Ọdẹ Ninu Igbo Irunmalẹ* (1986), 3.

79. Fagunwa, *Forest of a Thousand Daemons: A Hunter's Saga*, 2.

80. Ibid., 51.

81. Some of the text in the following pages were originally published in "Decolonizing the Intellectual and the Quotidian," in *Gender Epistemologies in Africa* (Palgrave, 2011).

82. Wande Abimbola, *Ifá: An Exposition of Ifá Literary Corpus* (Ibadan: Oxford University Press, 1976), 152.

83. Abimbola, "Images of Women in the Ifá Literary Corpus," 403.

84. Making sacrifice to appease the gods is central to Òrìṣà worship.

85. Abimbola, *Ifá: An Exposition of Ifá Literary Corpus*, 165.

86. Ibid., 167.

87. Kola Abimbola, *Yorùbá Culture: A Philosophical Account* (Great Britain: Iroko Academic Publishers, 2006), 64.

88. Abimbola, *Ifá: An Exposition of Ifá Literary Corpus*, 177.

89. Abimbola, *Yorùbá Culture*, 50.

90. George Olusola Ajibade, *Negotiating Performance: Ọ̀ṣun in the Verbal and Visual Metaphors*, vol. 4, Bayreuth African Studies Working Papers (Bayreuth: Institute of African Studies, 2005), 93.

91. Abimbola, "Images of Women in the Ifá Literary Corpus," 404.

92. Babaláwo Akalaifa, personal Interview, July 21, 2008.

93. B. Hallen and J. O. Sodipo, *Knowledge, Belief and Witchcraft: Analytic Experiments in African Philosophy* (London: Ethnographica Ltd., 1986).

94. Ibid., 103.

95. Ibid., 117.

NOTES 231

4   Writing and Gendering the Past: *Akòwé* and the
    Endogenous Production of History

1. See J. F. Ade Ajayi, "How Yorùbá Was Reduced to Writing," *Odù* 8 (1960).
2. Oyèrónké Oyěwùmí, "Making History, Creating Gender: Some Methodological and Interpretive Questions in the Writing of Oyo Oral Traditions," *History in Africa* 25 (1998).
3. In Yorùbá society, Arabic script literacy predated the one in Roman letters. Persons literate in Arabic letters are called *akewu* (one who chants Qur'anic verses), and if they are also lettered in the Roman Script, they are called *akewu-kewe*. The verb to *ke* means to vocalize, to chant, and is associated with oral delivery, an understanding that is also apparent in *akewi* or oral poets. The fact that the verb *ko*—to write—is not associated with Islamic literacy may have had to do with the rote learning, memorization, and chanting of Qur'anic verses that was the hallmark of such learning. What is remarkable however is the fact that even when Muslim clerics were known to be literate in both scripts and in three languages—Yorùbá, English, and Arabic—their practice is not defined by their writing but by chanting. Thus they are *akewu-kewe* not *akòwé*. In conversation with linguist Oyesope Oyelaran (May 19, 2013), he pointed out that Quranic reading was associated with voicing of the script and not silent reading that came to define Roman script literacy. Isaac Ogunbiyi, writing about the tensions among Yorùbá literates around the choice of a Romanized Yorùbá script over the Yorùbá Arabic script in 1875, captures the displeasure of the Muslims thus: "In spite of this seeming fait accompli status of Romanized Yorùbá orthography, a subdued feeling of resentment persisted among Muslim scholars, especially those of them who were not immersed in the Western education promoted by missionary enterprise. This subterranean feeling surfaced time and again in form of direct and indirect attacks on the superimposition of Christian/British colonial education over Arabic, the primary tool of Muslim education, which preceded the entry of Christianity into Yorùbáland" (Isaac Ogunbiyi, "The Search for Yoruba Orthography since the 1840s: Obstacles to the Choice of the Arabic Script," *Sudanic Africa* 14 [2003]: 77).
4. Toyin Falola, *Yorùbá Gurus: Indigenous Production of Knowledge in Africa* (Trenton: Africa World Press, 1999).
5. Ibid.
6. Ibid.
7. Ibid. Also see *Aroso* and *Onikaba*.
8. M. R. Doortmont, "Recapturing the Past: Samuel Johnson and the Construction of the History of the Yorùbá" (PhD dissertation, Erasmus University, 1994), 121.
9. Ibid., 160.
10. Ibid.
11. Ibid., 161.
12. Falola, *Yorùbá Gurus*, 55.
13. Ibid.

14. Ibid., 76.
15. Ibid., 57.
16. Ibid., 76.
17. See Adélékè Adéékó, "'Kò Sóhun tí Mbẹ tí ò Nítàn' (Nothing Is That Lacks a [Hi]story): On Oyèrónkẹ Òyéwùmí's *The Invention of Women*," in *African Gender Studies: A Reader*, ed. Oyèrónkẹ Òyéwùmí (New York: Palgrave Macmillan, 2005).
18. Falola, *Yorùbá Gurus*, 76.
19. Because *omo-ọba* (prince) is not gender specific in Yorùbá, I have translated it as prince and qualify it with the anasex since gender is important to the discussion.
20. Alaafin Abiodun was Samuel Johnson's matrilateral great grandfather.
21. Falola, *Yorùbá Gurus*, 59.
22. His brother Obadiah Johnson was one of the patrons of the *Ẹgbẹ́*. See M. R. Doortmont, "Samuel Johnson (1846–1901): Missionary, Diplomat, and Historian," in *YorùBá Historiography*, ed. Toyin Falola (Madison: University of Wisconsin, 1991), 177.
23. Samuel Johnson and Obadiah Johnson, *The History of the Yorubas: From the Earliest Times to the Beginning of the British Protectorate* (Westport, CT: Negro University Press, 1921), vii.
24. J. A. Atanda, "Samuel Johnson on the Intellectual Life of the Yorùbá People," in *Pioneer, Patriot, and Patriarchy: Samuel Johnson and the Yorùbá People*, ed. Toyin Falola (Madison: University of Wisconsin, 1993), 81.
25. Oyèrónkẹ Oyěwùmí, *The Invention of Women: Making an African Sense of Western Gender Discourses* (Minneapolis: University of Minnesota Press, 1997).
26. A verbal genre popularly called praise poetry, which I have already alluded to in chapter 3 as a main province through which *Ìyá* nurture, esteem, and educate members of the family.
27. Olakunle George, *Relocating Agency: Modernity and African Letters* (New York: State University of New York Press, 2003), 118.
28. D. O. Fagunwa, *Forest of a Thousand Daemons: A Hunter's Saga*, trans. Wole Soyinka (New York: Random House, 1982), 120.
29. Ibid., 121.
30. Recaptives were Africans who had been captured into slavery and were already being shipped to the Americas when these ships were taken over by the British squadron, which was attempting to abolish slavery on the West African coast in the nineteenth century. The enslaved persons were rescued and taken to Freetown, a newly created colony for freed Africans.
31. Kristin Mann, *Marrying Well: Marriage, Status, and Social Change among the Educated Elite in Colonial Lagos* (Cambridge: Cambridge University Press, 1985), 26.
32. Neither was there an absence of European female fashion that conferred social status on literate females the way in which our earlier custom clerks in Ibadan had derived status from their uniform. In actuality Western-educated

Yorùbá women came to be distinguished as *onikaba* (frock wearers) from their wrapper wearing (*aroso*) nonliterate counterparts (Adéẹ̀kọ́, *African Gender Studies Reader*, ed. Oyeronke Oyewumi [Palgrave: New York, 2005], 124). The *akọ̀wé* preferred to marry *onikaba*.

33. Wole Soyinka, *Isara: A Voyage around Essay* (Ibadan: Fountain Publications, 1989), 15.

34. Ibid.

35. Adéẹ̀kọ́, *African Gender Studies Reader*.

36. Although he had written a dissertation, see Doortmont, "Recapturing the Past," 29.

37. To boot famous Yorùbá literary writers such as D. O. Fagunwa and Amos Tutuola did not attend college. Amos Tutuola, the author of Palmwine Drinkard, is in a class by himself; he had only a primary school level education. Literary scholar Olakunle George writing about the educational attainment of Yorùbá writers pointed out that in the first half of the twentieth century, the acquisition of primary school certificate "was enough to make anyone who possessed it part of a distinct local elite" (George, *Relocating Agency*, 139).

38. Oyěwùmí, *The Invention of Women*, 133–134.

39. Falola, *Yorùbá Gurus*, 24.

40. Ibid., 23–24.

41. Ibid., 24.

42. Ibid., 133.

43. Ibid.

44. By the 1960s professional historians had emerged in Yorùbáland with at least one woman, Professor Bolanle Awe, present in their ranks.

45. Falola, *Yorùbá Gurus*, 133.

46. Ibid., 134–135.

47. Ibid., 147.

48. Ibid., 153.

49. Ibid.

50. Ibid., 134.

51. Ibid., 146.

52. Ibid.

53. Ibid., 137–138.

54. Ibid., 134–135.

55. Not even the nonelite woman seemed to have been spared from the privileging of male employment and the constant deploying of government workers, as we see in this example of one Madam Bankole, a subject in an ethnographic study of Yorùbá migrants: In 1949, she married another Ijebu man who was a supervisor in the telegraph office and had recently been widowed. He was transferred frequently from place to place, and she went with him, changing her trade each time. From Warri in the Western Niger Delta she transported palm oil to Ibadan and re-sold it there to retailers. Then from Jos to Kano she sent rice and beans to the woman to whom who sublet her Dugbe stall…From 1949 to 1962 she moved

around with him. D. R. Aronson, *The City Is Our Farm: Seven Migrant Ijebu Yorùbá Families* (Cambridge: Schenkman Publishing Company, 1978), 128–129.

56. Falola, *Yorùbá Gurus*, 135.
57. See Mann, *Marrying Well*, Chapter 4.
58. A. Akinyemi, *Yorùbá Royal Poetry: A Socio-Historical Exposition and Annotated Translation* (Bayreuth: Pia Thielmann and Eckhard Breitinger, 2004), 45.
59. Ibid., 4.
60. Falola, *Yorùbá Gurus*, 147.
61. Toyin Falola, ed., *Pioneer, Patriot, and Patriarchy: Samuel Johnson and the Yorùbá People* (Madison: University of Wisconsin, 1993), 1.
62. Johnson and Johnson, *The History of the Yorubas*, vii.
63. Oyěwùmí, *The Invention of Women*, 86–91.
64. Doortmont, "Recapturing the Past," 153.
65. Johnson and Johnson, *The History of the Yorubas*, 173.
66. Similarly, his older brother Nathaniel who had been ordained ahead of him started his own self-introduction: "I am the 2nd son of my lamented father Henry Johnson" (Doortmont, "Recapturing the Past," 152). Did Johnson borrow this language from him?
67. Ibid., 22.
68. Ibid.
69. Ibid., 27.
70. Johnson himself had used the word "patriarch" to describe one of his informants. See Johnson and Johnson, *The History of the Yorubas*, 173, vii.
71. Doortmont, "Recapturing the Past," 19.
72. In chapter 6, I speculate on why he could not identify with Ilorin.
73. This is Johnson's *oríkì* name, a particular genre of names that I analyze in chapter 5.
74. Johnson was no David Kukomi, one of his informants, who had been an Ibadan warlord with 17 wives. J. D. Y. Peel, "Gender in Yorùbá Religious Change," *Journal of Religion in Africa* 32, no. 2 (2002): 157. Incidentally, Johnson had called Kukomi a patriarch. See Johnson and Johnson, *The History of the Yorubas*, vii.
75. J. F. Ade Ajayi, "Samuel Johnson: Historian of the Yorùbá," in *Pioneer, Patriot, and Patriarchy: Samuel Johnson and the Yorùbá People*, ed. Toyin Falola (Madison: University of Wisconsin, 1993), 31.
76. Ibid.
77. Doortmont, "Recapturing the Past," 31.
78. Falola, *Pioneer, Patriot, and Patriarchy*, 38.
79. Falola, *Yorùbá Gurus*, 38; my emphasis.
80. Ibid., 36.
81. Ibid., 33.
82. He even found his second wife in Lagos!
83. And benefit of hindsight, he may have been right that writing "The History" was a good strategy for countering racist images of Africans most especially the insult that Africans are people's without history.

84. S. Phillip Zachernuk, "Johnson and the Victorian Image of the Yorùbá," in *Pioneer, Patriot, and Patriarchy: Samuel Johnson and the Yorùbá People*, ed. Toyin Falola (Madison: University of Wisconsin, 1993), 33.

85. Johnson and Johnson, *The History of the Yorubas*, ix.

86. Ibid.

5   The Gender Dictaters: Making Gender Attributions in Religion and Culture

1. J. D. Y. Peel, "Gender in Yorùbá Religious Change," *Journal of Religion in Africa* 32, no. 2 (2002): 136.

2. Oyèrónkẹ́ Oyěwùmí, *The Invention of Women: Making an African Sense of Western Gender Discourses* (Minneapolis: University of Minnesota Press, 1997), 139.

3. Peel, "Gender in Yorùbá Religious Change."

4. J. D. Y. Peel, *Religious Encounter and the Making of the Yorùbá* (Bloomington: Indiana University Press, 2000).

5. Ibid., 162, note 1.

6. Judith Lorber, *Paradoxes of Gender* (New Haven: Yale University Press, 1994).

7. Peel, "Gender in Yorùbá Religious Change," 138.

8. Oyěwùmí, *The Invention of Women*, 176.

9. Adélékè Adéèkọ́, "'Kò Sóhun tí M̀bẹ tí ò Nítàn' (Nothing Is that Lacks a [Hi]story): On Oyèrónkẹ́ Òyéwùmí's *The Invention of Women*," in *African Gender Studies: A Reader*, ed. Oyèrónkẹ́ Òyéwùmí (New York: Palgrave Macmillan, 2005).

10. Peel, "Gender in Yorùbá Religious Change," 138.

11. Ladele et al., *Iwadii Ijinle Asa Yorùbá* (Ibadan: Macmillan, 1986), 139.

12. Lorelle D. Semley, *Mother Is Gold, Father Is Glass: Gender and Colonialism in a Yorùbá Town* (Bloomington: Indiana University Press, 2011), 10.

13. Peel, "Gender in Yorùbá Religious Change," 140.

14. Quoted in ibid.

15. Ibid.

16. John Pemberton, "The Ọ̀Yọ́ Empire," in *Yorùbá: Nine Centuries of Art and Thought*, ed. Henry Drewal et al. (New York: Center for African Art in Association with H. N Abram, 1989).

17. Peel, "Gender in Yorùbá Religious Change," 141.

18. Ibid., 140.

19. This expectation of protection from a deity is not unique to indigenous tradition, even adherents of the so-called world religions of Christianity and Islam expect to be protected by the God they believe in.

20. Peel, *Religious Encounter and the Making of the Yorùbá*, 54.

21. Peel, "Gender in Yorùbá Religious Change," 147.

22. Ibid., 148.

23. J. D. Y. "The Pastor and the "Babaláwo: The Interaction of Religions in Nineteenth-Century Yorùbáland," *Africa: Journal of the International African Institute* 60, no. 3 (1990): 350.

24. Peel, "Gender in Yorùbá Religious Change," 148.
25. Ibid., 147.
26. Peel, "The Pastor and the "Babaláwo," 343.
27. R. W. Connell, *Masculinities* (Los Angeles: University of California Press, 1995).
28. Peel, "Gender in Yorùbá Religious Change," 147.
29. Peel, "The Pastor and the "Babaláwo."
30. Peel, "Gender in Yorùbá Religious Change," 149; my emphasis.
31. Oyěwùmí, *The Invention of Women*, 76.
32. Peel, "The Pastor and the "Babaláwo," 353.
33. Ibid., 355.
34. Ibid., 344.
35. Peel, "Gender in Yorùbá Religious Change," 147.
36. Wande Abimbola, *Ifá: An Exposition of Ifá Literary Corpus* (Ibadan: Oxford University Press, 1976), 115.
37. I analyzed this Odù in chapter 2.
38. Peel, "Gender in Yorùbá Religious Change," 149.
39. Ibid., 150.
40. Ibid.
41. Rowland Abiodun, "Verbal and Visual Metaphors: Mythical Allusions in Yorùbá Ritualistic Art of Orí," *Word and Image* 3, no. 3 (1987): 266.
42. Ibid., 267.
43. Peel, "The Pastor and the "Babaláwo," 340.
44. Abiodun, "Verbal and Visual Metaphors," 267.
45. Peel, "Gender in Yorùbá Religious Change," 150.
46. Ibid.
47. Ibid., 148.
48. Peel, "The Pastor and the "Babaláwo," 345–346.
49. Peel, "Gender in Yorùbá Religious Change," 346.
50. Ibid., 149.
51. Peel, "The Pastor and the "Babaláwo," 347.
52. Oyěwùmí, *The Invention of Women*, 141.
53. Ibid., 347.
54. Peel, "Gender in Yorùbá Religious Change," 148–149.
55. Peel, "The Pastor and the "Babaláwo."
56. Ibid., 1.
57. Ibid., 2.
58. Jacob Olupona, "Imagining the Goddess: Gender in Yorùbá Religious Traditions and Modernity," *Dialogue and Alliance* 18, no. 1 (2004/2005): 73.
59. Ibid.
60. S. Riches and S. Salih, eds., *Gender and Holiness: Men, Women and Saints in Late Medieval Europe* (London and New York: Routledge, 2002), 4.
61. "Introduction," in *African Traditional Religions in Contemporary Society*, ed. Jacob Olupona (New York. Paragon House, 1991).
62. See Lorber, *Paradoxes of Gender*.
63. Riches and Salih, *Gender and Holiness*, 4.

64. Adéléke Adéèkó, "'Kò Sóhun tí Mbe tí ò Nítàn' (Nothing Is That Lacks a [Hi]story): On Oyèrónké Òyéwùmí's *The Invention of Women*," in *African Gender Studies: A Reader*, ed. Oyèrónké Òyéwùmí (New York: Palgrave Macmillan, 2005), 121–26.

65. Ibid.

66. Olupona, "Imagining the Goddess," 73.

67. Ibid., 72.

68. Ibid., 73.

69. "Introduction," in *African Traditional Religions in Contemporary Society*, ed. Jacob Olupona (New York: Paragon House, 1991).

70. Olupona, "Imagining the Goddess," 76.

71. Oyěwùmí, *The Invention of Women*, 174.

72. Ibid.

73. This section to the end of the chapter has been published in Decolonizing the Intellectual and the Quotidian, in Gender Epistemologies.

74. This section and the next are excerpted from my paper "Decolonizing the Intellectual and the Quotidian," in *Gender Epistemologies in Africa* (Palgrave, 2011).

75. At an economics conference in 2005, Harvard President Larry H. Summers triggered controversy when he suggested that the relative paucity of women in science and engineering professions is due in part to "innate differences" between men and women.

76. Akinsola Akiwowo, *Ajobi and Ajogbe: Variations on the Theme of Sociation* (Ile-Ife: University of Ife Press, 1983),

77. Ibid., 7; my emphasis.

78. Ibid.

79. Oyěwùmí, *The Invention of Women*, 163.

6 Toward a Genealogy of Gender, Gendered Names, and Naming Practices

1. B. Agiri, "Slavery in Yorùbá Society in the 19th Century," in *The Ideology of Slavery in Africa, Ed. Lovejoy, Paul E.*, ed. Paul E. Lovejoy (Beverly Hills: Sage Publications, 1981), 123.

2. Niyi F. Akinnaso, "The Sociolinguistic Basis of Yorùbá Personal Names," *Anthropological Linguistics* 22, no. 7 (1980): 279.

3. Following historian Bolanle Awe (1974), who showed us how *oríkì* (praise poetry) can be used as a source of historical evidence, literary anthropologist Karin Barber (1981), in a paper documenting the changes in the performance of *oríkì* (praise poetry), insightfully shows how the tone, content, and style of performance itself can illuminate the changes that took place in a particular epoch that led to social transformation.

4. Samuel Johnson and Obadiah Johnson, *The History of the Yorubas: From the Earliest Times to the Beginning of the British Protectorate* (Westport, CT: Negro University Press, 1921), 82.

5. It is rude to address an older person by name or worse their *oríkì* except of course if you are a performer.

6. Because *oríkì* are said to encapsulate the essence of a person, they are also useful in times of personal crisis, for example, when a person is in a coma or distressed in any way.

7. One common saying I have heard about *oríkì* in Ibadan and Ogbomoso marvels at why Yorùbá people from Lagos tend to use *oríkì* as their primary names: "*Awon ara Eko ti won f'oríkì je oruko.*"

8. Oyesope Oyelaran and Lawrence Adewole, *Isenbaye Ati Ilo Ede Yorùbá* (South Africa: Center for Advanced Studies of African Society, 2007), 144–145.

9. A. Akinyemi, "On the Meaning of Yorùbá Female Personal Oríkì (Oríkì Àbísọ)—A Literary Appraisal," *Research in Yorùbá Language and Literature* 4 (1993): 82.

10. Ibid.

11. Ladele et al., *Iwadii Ijinle Asa Yorùbá* (Ibadan: Macmillan, 1986), 164–165.

12. Ibid., 165.

13. Karin Barber, *I Could Speak until Tomorrow: Oríkì, Women, and the Past in a Yorùbá Town* (Edinburgh: Edinburgh University Press, 1991), 17.

14. A nonauthoritative and disputed source claims Ayinla as the founder of Ilorin before the closing years of the eighteenth century. H. O. Danmole, "Samuel Johnson and the History of Ilorin," in *Pioneer, Patriot, and Patriarchy: Samuel Johnson and the Yorùbá People*, ed. Toyin Falola (Madison: University of Wisconsin, 1993), 140. Ayinla is an *oríkì*.

15. J. F. Ade Ajayi, *A Patriot to the Core: Bishop Ajayi Crowther* (Ibadan: Spectrum Books, 2001), 21. One of Crowther's sisters is named Amosa, a name that resembles an *oríkì* linguistically. I cannot ascertain whether this is an *oríkì* because it is also not common today.

16. Oyèrónkẹ́ Oyěwùmí, *The Invention of Women: Making an African Sense of Western Gender Discourses* (Minneapolis: University of Minnesota Press, 1997), 88.

17. Johnson's use of the gendered pronoun "he" inadvertently adds gender to the seniority-based universe. Significantly, there are no gender distinctions made in whether the twins are two females, two males, or mixed sex.

18. Johnson and Johnson, *The History of the Yorubas*, 80.

19. Ibid., 85.

20. As cited in Akinyemi, "On the Meaning of Yorùbá Female Personal Oríkì (Oríkì Àbísọ)."

21. Some scholars such as Oyelaran refer to praise name as *oríkì àbísọ* and one finds this usage in the writings of linguists, many his former students.

22. As cited in Akinyemi, "On the Meaning of Yorùbá Female Personal Oríkì (Oríkì Àbísọ)."

23. B. A. Oyetade, "Tones in the Yorùbá Personal Praise Names: Oríkì Àbísọ," *Research in Yorùbá Language and Literature* 1 (1991): 55.

24. Ibid., 56.

25. Ibid., 58.

26. Ibid., 59.

27. Ibid.
28. Ọla Ọlanike Orie, "Yorùbá Names and Gender Marking," *Anthropological Linguistics* 44, no. 2 (2002): 134.
29. Ibid.
30. Oyetade, "Tones in the Yorùbá Personal Praise Names: Oríkì Àbísọ," 59.
31. Orie, "Yorùbá Names and Gender Marking," 134.
32. Ibid.
33. Reference to Euro/America social norms in order to explain Africa is not unusual among African scholars, a legacy of colonial thinking and the fact that intellectual categories are insufficiently decolonized and remain Eurocentric. In chapter 4, I have already drawn attention to such a problem in the work of Jacob Olupona, scholar of religion.
34. Ibid., 134.
35. Oyěwùmí, *The Invention of Women*, 33.
36. Orie, "Yorùbá Names and Gender Marking," 115.
37. Ibid., 135.
38. Ibid., 115.
39. Ibid.
40. Akinyemi, "On the Meaning of Yorùbá Female Personal Oríkì (Oríkì Àbísọ)," 79.
41. Ibid., 80.
42. Ibid.
43. The irony is that in some cultures around the world the neglect and lack of care of the so-called girl child often resulting in infanticide has been one of the focal points of feminist activism around the globe.
44. Akinyemi, "On the Meaning of Yorùbá Female Personal Oríkì (Oríkì Àbísọ)," 81.
45. Ibid.
46. "Who can find a virtuous woman? For her price is far above rubies" (King James Version; Proverb 31:10).
47. Orie, "Yorùbá Names and Gender Marking," 136–137.

7 The Poetry of Weeping Brides: The Role and Impact of Marriage Residence in the Making of Praise Names

1. See Dejo Faniyi, "Ẹ̀KÚn Ìyàwó: A Traditional Yorùbá Nuptial Chant," in *Yorùbá Oral Tradition: Selections from the Papers Presented at the Seminar on Yorùbá Oral Tradition: Poetry in Music, Dance, and Drama No. 1*, ed. Wande Abimbola (Ile-Ife: University of Ifẹ, 1975); Karin Barber, *I Could Speak until Tomorrow: Oríkì, Women, and the Past in a Yorùbá Town* (Edinburgh: Edinburgh University Press, 1991);
2. Samuel Johnson and Obadiah Johnson, *The History of the Yorubas: From the Earliest Times to the Beginning of the British Protectorate* (Westport, CT: Negro University Press, 1921).
3. Ladele et al., *Iwadii Ijinle Asa Yorùbá* (Ibadan: Macmillan, 1986), 167.

4. B. A. Oyetade, "Tones in the Yorùbá Personal Praise Names: Oríkì Àbísọ," *Research in Yorùbá Language and Literature* 1 (1991): 62.

5. Ibid., 55.

6. Faniyi, "Ẹ̀Kún Ìyàwó.

7. Ibid., 680.

8. The reference to cowife does not immediately mean that she is marrying a man who has a wife already. What this reference speaks to is what I call the polygamous and collective ethos of Yorùbá marriage in which all the wives of the males in the family are seen as cowives and are ranked in the seniority hierarchy as if they are married to one man. What the bride is expressing here remains a standard prayer for the bride during Yorùbá weddings that she will be well-received into the marital family.

9. Faniyi, "Ẹ̀Kún Ìyàwó," 681.

10. Ibid., 684.

11. Barber, *I Could Speak until Tomorrow*, 110.

12. Ibid.

13. This reference is to her own nickname is interesting. It looks like one of the names that an "*ìyàwó*" (wife of a male relation) of her family must have given to her, a practice that I explain later.

14. Barber, *I Could Speak until Tomorrow*, 111.

15. N. A. Fadipe, *The Sociology of the Yorùbá* (Ibadan: Ibadan University Press, 1970), 81.

16. Barber, *I Could Speak until Tomorrow*, 108.

17. Ibid., 115.

18. Today, this practice of returning to their birth homes of married women is increasingly stigmatized given the Christian faith-based ideas that a woman must be married "till death do us part." But most significantly, the hostility to daughters who stay or return home is new and expresses the anxiety of their brothers about inheritance and property and who has a claim to it. Traditionally all males and females have equal rights to their lineage inheritance and property, a practice that is increasingly challenged in the newfangled patriarchy of a postcolonial society.

19. Johnson and Johnson, *The History of the Yorubas*, 86.

20. Barber, *I Could Speak until Tomorrow*, 109.

21. For a history of Ibadan, see Bolanle Awe, "The Rise of Ibadan as a Yorùbá Power, 1851–1893" (PhD dissertation, Oxford University, 1964). See Toyin Falola, *The Political Economy of a Pre-Colonial African State* (Ile-Ife: University of Ife Press, 1984) for a documentation of its slave economy. See Ruth Watson, *Civil Disorder Is the Disease of Ibadan: Chieftaincy & Civic Culture in a Yorùbá City* (Oxford: James Currey Publishers, 2003), for a sustained probe of the implications of warmongering and civil strife and the "disease of Ibadan."

22. Falola, *The Political Economy of a Pre-Colonial African State*, 45.

23. Barber, *I Could Speak until Tomorrow*, 42.

24. Ibid.

25. Fadipe, *The Sociology of the Yorùbá*.

26. See Ruth Watson, "What Is Our Intelligence, Our School Going and Our Reading of Books without Getting Money? Akinpelu Obisesan and His Diary," in *African Hidden Histories: Everyday Literacy and the Making of the Self*, ed. Karin Barber (Bloomington: Indiana University Press, 2006).

27. Kristin Mann, *Marrying Well: Marriage, Status, and Social Change among the Educated Elite in Colonial Lagos* (Cambridge: Cambridge University Press, 1985), 42.

28. Ibid.

29. Falola, *The Political Economy of a Pre-Colonial African State*, 71.

30. Karin Barber, "Documenting Social and Ideological Change through Yoruba Oriki: A Stylistic Analysis," *Journal of the Historical Society of Nigeria* 10, no. 4 (June 1981): 39–52, 40.

31. Ibid.

32. Ibid., 49.

33. Johnson and Johnson, *The History of the Yorubas*, 85.

34. Ladele et al., *Iwadii Ijinle Asa Yorùbá*.

35. Oyetade, "Tones in the Yorùbá Personal Praise Names," 58.

36. Lisa A. Lindsay and Stephan Miescher, eds., *Men and Masculinities in Modern Africa* (Portsmouth, NH: Heinemann, 2003), 4.

37. Ibid., 5.

38. R. W. Connell, *Masculinities* (Los Angeles: University of California Press, 1995), 68; my emphasis.

39. Ibid., 53.

40. J. D. Y. Peel, "Gender in Yorùbá Religious Change," *Journal of Religion in Africa* 32, no. 2 (2002).

41. Karin Barber, "Oríkì, Women and the Proliferation and Merging of Òrìṣà," *Africa* 60, no. 03b (1990): 320.

42. Yorùbá women went to war. See Watson, *Civil Disorder Is the Disease of Ibadan*, 46.

43. Peel, "Gender in Yorùbá Religious Change," 157.

44. Ibid.; my emphasis.

45. Ibid.

46. *The Sun Publishing*, Friday, March 23, 2012.

47. Oyèrónkẹ́ Oyěwùmí, "Introduction. Feminism, Sisterhood, and Other Foreign Relations," in *African Women and Feminism: Reflecting on the Politics of Sisterhood*, ed. Oyèrónkẹ́ Oyěwùmí (New Jersey: Africa World Press, 2003).

48. Barber, "Documenting Social and Ideological Change through Yoruba Oriki."

49. Ibid., 49.

50. Barber's collection of *okuku* lineage poetry contains male *oríkì* names.

51. See Ade Ajayi and Robert Smith, *Yoruba Warfare in the Nineteenth Century* (University Press in association with the Institute of African Studies, University of Ibadan), for a study of Yorùbá wars.

52. Barber presents a number of personal *oríkì* of notables that are said to be pre-nineteenth century, which contains male-identified *oríkì* names like Akanni, mentioned in the verse earlier. Given my supposition that female

oríkì appeared first, two thoughts come to my mind. First, that we have to question the chronology of these *oríkì* poetry from Okuku. Second, perhaps the issue is not the presence of one or two male or female *oríkì*-sounding names in earlier periods but that they became *oríkì* names, a recognizable category of their own in the nineteenth century.

53. Oyetade, "Tones in the Yorùbá Personal Praise Names," 62.
54. Ibid.
55. Such a harsh judgment rife among women suggests that this may have been a mode of control not only of the husband's behavior but of a wife who may be usurping another one's position.
56. Ibid.
57. Ladele et al., *Iwadii Ijinle Asa Yorùbá*, 164.

8   Changing Names: The Roles of Christianity and Islam in Making Yorùbá Names Kosher for the Modern World

1. Niyi F. Akinnaso, "The Sociolinguistic Basis of YorùBá Personal Names," *Anthropological Linguistics* 22, no. 7 (1980): 279.
2. Samuel Johnson and Obadiah Johnson, *The History of the Yorubas: From the Earliest Times to the Beginning of the British Protectorate* (Westport, CT: Negro University Press, 1921), 88–89.
3. In his book *The Krio of Sierra Leone: An Interpretive History* (London: C. Hurst and Company, 1989), 9, Akintola Wyse said the following regarding changes of names by recaptives: "When the Liberated Africans arrived in Sierra Leone, they were forced by circumstances to take European names...But many also retained or adopted an African first name such as Akintola, Bimbola, Femi, Kehinde, Kojo, Shola and Taiwo."
4. The Saro, also called Akus and Recaptives, were enslaved persons who had been liberated and settled in the British Colony of Sierra Leone. Many originated from Yorùbáland, were kidnapped and sold during the Atlantic Slave Trade, but were rescued on the West African coast by the British Squadron. In 1843, after being Christianized and Westernized, they started to emigrate back to Yorùbáland and were to play a decisive role in the propagation of Western values and goods among Yorùbá people. By late nineteenth century, they had become an elite group in Lagos and Abeokuta. Bishop Ajayi Crowther and the Reverend Samuel Johnson were prominent and influential Saro.
5. M. R. Doortmont, "Recapturing the Past: Samuel Johnson and the Construction of the History of the Yorùbá" (PhD dissertation, Erasmus University, 1994), 18–19.
6. Ibid., 19.
7. Meaning of Ajayi.
8. Doortmont, "Recapturing the Past," 18–28.
9. Johnson and Johnson, *The History of the Yorubas*, 87.
10. Ibid., 88.

11. M.R.Doortmont,"Samuel Johnson (1846–1901):Missionary,Diplomat,and Historian," in *YorùBá Historiography*, ed.Toyin Falola (Madison: University of Wisconsin, 1991), 170.

12. Ibid., 171.

13. Johnson and Johnson, *The History of the Yorubas*, 88.

14. Ibid., 87.

15. Ibid., 88.

16. Doortmont, "Samuel Johnson (1846–1901)," 176.

17. Johnson and Johnson, *The History of the Yorubas*, 86.

18. J. F. Ade Ajayi, *Patriot to the Core: Bishop Ajayi Crowther* (Ibadan: Spectrum Books, 2001).

19. Amosa resembles *oríkì* in form but the name is uncommon and an outlier given the meaning of female-associated *oríkì* names.

20. Ibid., 56.

21. Johnson and Johnson, *The History of the Yorubas*, 87.

22. Incidentally, there is another shift in naming ideology in that today, in the latest phase of Pentecostal evangelization, many Yorùbá believe that *àmútòrunwá* names too are fetishtic. For example, some Christian families now refuse to give twins the standard indigenous name associated with that kind of birth.

23. Johnson and Johnson, *The History of the Yorubas*, 89.

24. Adéléké Adéèkó, "Kò Sóhun tí Ḿbẹ tí ò Nítàn" (Nothing Is that Lacks a [Hi]story): On Oyèrónké Òyéwùmí's *The Invention of Women*," in *African Gender Studies: A Reader*, ed. Oyèrónké Òyéwùmí (New York: Palgrave Macmillan, 2005).

25. Distinction between Arabic and Islamic names.

26. Iorin and Islamization—see Muhammad's note.

27. This section has benefitted from my discussion with Farooq Kperogi who freely shared his insights on Islamic names and their usage among Yorùbá and Hausa in Nigeria.

28. Bolaji Idowu changed family name.

29. Quoted in A. Akinyemi, "On the Meaning of Yorùbá Female Personal Oríkì (Oríkì Àbísọ)—A Literary Appraisal," *Research in Yorùbá Language and Literature* 4 (1993): 79.

30. Johnson and Johnson, *The History of the Yorubas*, 79.

31. Ibid., 89.

32. "Kò Sóhun tí Ḿbẹ tí ò Nítàn."

33. Ibid.

34. Contradictions of having two wives-Madame Camara. 1 & 2—see Camara Laye, *The African Child by Camara Laye*, trans. James Kirkup (Fontana Bks, 1959), 160.

35. Ladele et al., *Iwadii Ijinle Asa Yorùbá* (Ibadan: Macmillan, 1986), 161.

36. Ibid., 162.

37. Ibid.

38. Personal communication with Dr. Maryam Sy, who gave the example of Soda as a name that is paired with Mayam in Senegal. I happen to also know another

Senegalese Mariam whose middle or other name is Soda. Dr. Muhammad Shakir Balogun also confirmed the practice among Hausa in Nigeria: Yusuf pairs with Maitama, Halima with Duhu, Hauwa with Kulu, Umaru with Sanda, and Aliyu with Sambo. These include male and female names.

39. Four hundred and one Gods.

40. Compare anthropologist Igor Kopytoff's arguments about existential and immanent features of gender in "Women's Roles and Existential Identities," in ed. Oyeronke Oyewumi (2005).

Conclusion: Motherhood in the Quest for Social Transformation

1. Ladele et al., *Iwadii Ijinle Asa Yorùbá* (Ibadan: Macmillan, 1986), 229–230.

2. Oyèrónké Oyěwùmí, "Introduction. Feminism, Sisterhood, and Other Foreign Relations," in *African Women and Feminism: Reflecting on the Politics of Sisterhood*, ed. Oyèrónké Oyěwùmí (New Jersey: Africa World Press, 2003).

3. It could be argued that the distancing away from motherhood is more acute in a global city like New York, in which, for most women, the challenge of raising children, procuring childcare, and just making a living is well near impossible. Nevertheless, it should be noted that the women who seem to resent motherhood the most are middle-class and upper-class women.

4. Sheryl and Nell Scovell Sandberg, *Lean In: Women, Work, and the Will to Lead*. (New York: Alfred A. Knopf, 2013), 8, 10.

5. Nancy Chodorow, for example, made a strong case that it is the fact of the "women mother" that is responsible for their subordination. Hence her solution is for men too to share mothering. However, she does not address how men can also participate in gestation. Nancy Chodorow, *The Reproduction of Mothering: Psychoanalysis and the Sociology of Gender* (Berkeley: University of California Press, 1978).

6. Adrienne Rich, *Of Woman Born: Motherhood as Experience and Institution* (New York: Norton, 1986); emphasis in the original.

7. Halstein, following Benita Roth, points out that we must acknowledge that "second wave feminisms were organized along racial/ethnic lines." D. Lynn O'Brien Hallstein, *White Feminists and Contemporary Maternity: Purging Matrophobia* (New York: Palgrave Macmillan, 2010), 13.

8. Rich, *Of Woman Born*, 237.

9. Hallstein, *White Feminists and Contemporary Maternity*, 6–10.

10. Ibid., 11.

11. Ibid., 10.

12. Oyěwùmí, "Introduction. Feminism, Sisterhood, and Other Foreign Relations," 8.

13. Oyèrónké Oyěwùmí, *The Invention of Women: Making an African Sense of Western Gender Discourses* (Minneapolis: University of Minnesota Press, 1997); "Making History, Creating Gender: Some Methodological and Interpretive Questions in the Writing of Oyo Oral Traditions," *History in*

Africa 25 (1998); "Introduction. Feminism, Sisterhood, and Other Foreign Relations." "Family Bonds/Conceptual Binds: African Notes on Feminist Epistemologies *Feminism's at a Millennium*," in *Signs: Journal of Women in Culture and Society* 25 (1), no. 4 (1) (Summer 2000).

14. Ama Mazama, *Africa in the 21st Century: Toward a New Future* (New York: Routledge, 2007), x.
15. Josephine Ahikire, in *No Shortcuts to Power: African Women in Politics and Policy Making*, ed. Shireen Hassim and Anne Marie Gouws (Zed Books, 2003), 231; my emphasis.
16. Filomena Chioma Steady, *Women and Leadership in West Africa: Mothering the Nation and Humanizing the State* (New York: Palgrave Macmillan, 2011), 22.
17. Oyewumi, "Family bonds/Conceptual Binds."
18. Nkiru Uwechia Nzegwu, *Family Matters: Feminist Concepts in African Philosophy of Culture* (New York: State University of New York Press, 2006), 53.
19. Personal communication with Professor Wairimu Njambi.
20. Mireille Rabenoro, "Motherhood in Malagasy Society: A Major Component in the Tradition vs. Modernity Conflict," *Jenda*, Issue 4 (2003): 1.
21. Filomena Steady, *Women and Leadership in Africa: Mothering the Nation, Humanizing the State*. New York: Palgrave/Macmillan, 2013), 23.
22. Ibid.
23. Sylvia Rosila Tamale, *When Hens Begin to Crow: Gender and Parliamentary Politics in Uganda* (Boulder, CO: Westview Press, 2000).
24. Joseph Kony is the leader of the Lord's Resistance Army (LRA), a guerrilla group that operated in Uganda for decades. In 2005, Kony was indicted by the International Criminal Court in the Hague following allegations that he abducted children and used them as child soldiers and sex slaves. He remains at large.
25. Tamale, *When Hens Begin to Crow*, 50.
26. In 2014, the female presidents in three African countries were Ellen Johnson-Sirleaf of Liberia, Joyce Banda of Malawi, and Catherine Samba-Panza of Central African Republic. In 2015, the only one left in office is Johnson-Sirleaf.
27. Gretchen Bauer and Hannah Evelyn Britton, *Women in African Parliaments* (Boulder, CO: Lynne Rienner Publishers, 2006).
28. Steady, *Women and Leadership in Africa* (2013), 23.
29. Wangari Maathai, *The Green Belt Movement Manual* (Nairobi, Kenya: W. Maathai, 1991), 55.
30. Leymah Gbowee, *Mighty Be Our Powers: How Sisterhood, Prayer, and Sex Changed a Nation at War. A Memoir* (New York: Beast Books, 2013), 141; my emphasis.
31. Barbara Ehrenreich and Arlie Russell Hochschild, eds., *Global Woman: Nannies, Maids, and Sex Workers in the New Economy* (New York: Henry Holt and Company, 2004), 4.
32. Audre Lorde, *Sister Outsider: Essays and Speeches*, The Crossing Press Feminist Series (CA: The Crossing Press/Freedom, 1984), 115.
33. Steady, *Women and Leadership in Africa*, 11.
34. Lorde, *Sister Outsider: Essays and Speeches*.

GLOSSARY

ààfin	Ọba's palace
abiléko	married woman
àbíso	the primary names given after the birth of a child
Abiyamo	birth mother
Abo	female of animals
aboyún	pregnant female
àbúrò	younger sibling
adé	crown
adelébò	one who has gone to the *ile* and returned; woman of a certain age or one close to or past menopause
agbo ilé	compounds
àjé	spiritually gifted
ajogun	purveyors of doom
akéwì	oral poets
akéwú	one who chants koranic verses
àkosèjáyé	the ritual of consulting *Ifa* when a child is born, to see what *Òrìsà* presides over their fate
akòwé	one who writes or writer, author
Àkúnlèyàn	the pre-earthly act of kneeling before the Creator to choose one's *destiny*
akùnyùngbà	female court poets
aláàfin	monarch of Oyo Empire or Oyo town
Aláfíà	peace
àlàjé	a name that one gives one's self
alè	concubine, intimate relationship between two married people
Àlùfá	Qur'anic specialist
àmútòrunwá	a name that the infant brings from the Otherworld
àǹtí	Aunty
ará ilé	compound members
ará òkè	rustic

àrẹ̀mọ	crown prince or first born
arẹwà	the beautiful one
arókin	indigenous custodians of history
àròsọ	wrapper wearing
àṣẹ	power of the word/authority
asunràrá	praise singers
àwo	diviners
awolórìṣà	the divination generalist
àwọn ìyá	plural of ìyá
àwòrò	Priests
Aya	wife
aya ilé	wife of the house
Baálẹ̀	small town head
Bàbá	expertise
bàbá	father
Babaláwo	Ifá diviner/divination specialist
bùrọ̀dá	brother
ẹbọ	ritual
eégún	ancestral cult
Ẹ́érìndínlógún	Ifá divination system
ẹgbẹ́	age-mate/group
ẹ̀gbọ́n	older sibling
ẹ̀kú	costume
ẹkún Ìyàwó/rárà ìyàwó	bridal chant
ènìyàn	humans
ẹrú-ilé	enslaved persons
ẹwà	beauty
fàájì Ìyàwó	the bride's enjoyment
iba	father
ìbí	birth
ìdána	bridewealth
ìdílé	lineage
ifese	the first rituals performed after the birth of a child
igbá orí	small circular box
ìgbéyàwó	carrying of the bride
ìjọba	the monarch's community
ikin	sixteen ritually blessed palm nuts
ìkómọjáde	a naming ceremony
ìkúnlẹ̀	kneeling
ìkúnlẹ̀ abiyamọ	the kneeling of an Ìyá in the pains of labor; day of kneeling in labor

ilé	lineage household
ilé ọkọ	husband's house
ilé ọlọ́lá	illustrious lineages
ilémọṣú	an institution of female offspring who return to their families of birth after years of marriage
ìlú	urban settlements
ire aborí ọ̀tá	the value of assured self-actualization
ire àìkú	the value of good health till old age
ire gbogbo	whole value
ire ọkọ-aya	the value of intimate companionship and love
ire ọmọ	the value of parenthood
ire-owó	financial security
irúnmọlẹ̀	primordial deities
ìsálayé	earth
iṣẹ́	work
ìsọmọlórúkọ	the child naming ceremony
ìtàn	history
ìwà	character
ìwàlẹwà	character is beauty
ìwọ̀fà	bondsmen
Ìyá	domination
Ìyá	procreator
ìyálẹwà	mother makes beauty
ìyámàpó	a deity, another name for vagina
Ìyàmi	a cult of powerful females
ìyánífá	expert in Ifá
ìyàwó	bride
iye / Yèyé	the one who laid me like an egg
Ọba	monarch
Obìnrin	anafemale, female
obìnrin ilé	lineage wives
odù	unit of verses, chapter
odù Ìmàle	*Ifá* verses about the coming of Islam to Yorùbáland
ọ̀gbèrì	novice/lay people
ọ̀já	sash used to strap the baby on the back
ọjà	the market space
ọjọ́ ìkúnlẹ̀	day of birth
oko	farmlands
ọkọ	husband
ọkùnrin	anamale, male
ọlá	honor
Olódùmarè	the supreme being

ọlọ́lá	honorable
olówo	rich
omi	water
ọmọ ilé	member of the family
ọmọ obìnrin	child female
ọmọ ọkùnrin	child male
ọmọlẹwà	child is beauty
ọmọlúwàbí	virtuous character
ọmọòyá	the ultimate term of solidarity within and without the family; children of the mother
òmọ̀ràn	knowers
ọnàyíyà	making art
oníkaba	frock wearers
Opa	grove
òpẹ̀lẹ̀	a divining chain
orí	agency/head/personal god
orí-inu	inner head
orí-òde	outer head
oríkì	headpraise
oríkì bọ̀rọ̀kìnní	praise poetry of notable personalities
oríkì ìlú	poetry dealing with the foundation of towns
oríkì orílẹ̀	praise poetry extolling the characteristics of particular lineages
oríkì orílẹ̀	lineage poetry
orílẹ̀	lineage
Òrìṣà	gods
oro ìyá	maternal bonds
òrun	otherworld
òtá	enemy
Ọwọ́ Ifá kan	one hand of *Ifá*
oyè	royal title
rìkíṣí	intriguers
súná	meaning name in Arabic
tálíkà/olòṣì/akúṣẹ́ẹ́	poor

BIBLIOGRAPHY

Abimbola, Kola. *Yorùbá Culture: A Philosophical Account.* Great Britain: Iroko Academic Publishers, 2006.

Abimbola, Wande. "The Bag of Wisdom: ỌṢUn and the Origins of Ifá Divination." In *Oṣun across the Waters: A Yorùbá Goddess in Africa and the Americas,* edited by Joseph M. and Mei-Mei Sanford Murphy, 141–154. Bloomington: Indiana University Press, 2001.

———. *Ifá: An Exposition of Ifá Literary Corpus.* Ibadan: Oxford University Press, 1976.

———. "Images of Women in the Ifá Literary Corpus." *Annals of the New York Academy of Science* 810, no. 1 (1997): 401–413.

Abimbola, Wande, and I. Miller. *Ifá Will Mend Our Broken World: Thoughts on Yorùbá Religion and Culture in Africa and the Diaspora.* Roxbury: Aim Books, 1997.

Abiodun, Rowland. "Hidden Power: ỌṢUn, the Seventeenth Odù." In *Oṣun across the Waters: A Yorùbá Goddess in Africa and the Americas,* edited by Joseph M. and Mei-Mei Sanford Murphy, 10–33. Bloomington: Indiana University Press, 2001.

———. "Understanding Yorùbá Art and Aesthetics: The Concept of ÀṣE." *African Arts* 27, no. 3 (1994): 68–103.

———. "Verbal and Visual Metaphors: Mythical Allusions in Yorùbá Ritualistic Art of Orí." *Word and Image* 3, no. 3 (1987): 252–270.

———. "Woman in Yorùbá Religious Images." *Journal of African Cultural Studies* 2, no. 1 (1989): 1–18.

Ade Ajayi, J. F. "How YorùBá Was Reduced to Writing." *Odù* 8 (1960): 49–58.

———. *A Patriot to the Core: Bishop Ajayi Crowther.* Ibadan: Spectrum Books, 2001.

———. "Samuel Johnson: Historian of the Yorùbá." In *Pioneer, Patriot, and Patriarchy: Samuel Johnson and the Yorùbá People,* edited by Toyin Falola, 27–32. Madison: University of Wisconsin, 1993.

Ade Ajayi, J. F., and Robert Smith. *Yoruba Warfare in the Nineteenth Century.* University Press in association with the Institute of African Studies, University of Ibadan, 1971.

Adepegba, C. O. "Osun and Brass: An Insight into Yoruba Religious Symbology," in *Osun Across the waters,* p. 107.

Adéẹ̀kọ́, Adélékè. "'Kò Sóhun tí M̀bẹ tí ò Nítàn' (Nothing Is That Lacks a [Hi]story): On Oyèrónkẹ́ Òyéwùmí's *The Invention of Women,*" in *African Gender Studies: A Reader,* edited by Oyèrónkẹ́ Òyéwùmí, 121–26. New York: Palgrave Macmillan, 2005.

————. "'Writing' and 'Reference' in Ifá Divination Chants." *Oral Tradition* 25, no. 2 (2010): 283–303.

————, ed. *Gender in Translation: Efunsetan Aninwura in Gender Epistemologies in Africa: Gendering Traditions, Spaces, Social Institutions and Identities.* Palgrave, 2011.

Agiri, B. "Slavery in Yorùbá Society in the 19th Century." In *The Ideology of Slavery in Africa*, edited by Paul E. Lovejoy, 123–148. Beverly Hills: Sage Publications, 1981.

Ajibade, George Olusola. *Negotiating Performance: Oṣun in the Verbal and Visual Metaphors.* Bayreuth African Studies Working Papers. Vol. 4, Bayreuth: Institute of African Studies, 2005.

Akinnaso, Niyi F. "Bourdieu and the Diviner: Knowledge and Symbolic Power in Yorùbá Divination." In *The Pursuit of Certainty: Religious and Cultural Formulations*, edited by Wendy James, 235–258. London: Routledge, 1995.

————. "The Sociolinguistic Basis of Yorùbá Personal Names." *Anthropological Linguistics* 22, no. 7 (1980): 275–304.

Akintola, Wyse. *The Krio of Sierra Leone: An Interpretive History.* London: C. Hurst and Company, 1989.

Akinyemi, A. "On the Meaning of Yorùbá Female Personal Oríkì (Oríkì Àbísọ)—a Literary Appraisal." *Research in Yorùbá Language and Literature* 4 (1993): 78–82.

————. *Yorùbá Royal Poetry: A Socio-historical Exposition and Annotated Translation.* Bayreuth: Pia Thielmann and Eckhard Breitinger, 2004.

Akiwowo, Akinsola. *Ajobi and Ajogbe: Variations on the Theme of Sociation.* Ile-Ife: University of Ife Press, 1983.

Akyeampong, Emmanuel, and Pashington Obeng. "Spirituality, Gender, and Power in Asante History." In *African Gender Studies: A Reader*, edited by Oyèrónké Oyěwùmí, 23–48. New York: Palgrave Macmillan, 2005.

Aluko, T. M. *One Man, One Wife.* London: Heinemann, 1959.

Amadiume, Ifi. *Afrikan Matriarchal Foundations: The Igbo Case.* Red Sea Press, 2000.

————. *Re-inventing Africa Matriarchy, Religion, and Culture.* London: Zed Books, 1997.

Aronson, D. R. *The City Is Our Farm: Seven Migrant Ijebu Yorùbá Families.* Cambridge: Schenkman Publishing Company, 1978.

Atanda, J. A. "Samuel Johnson on the Intellectual Life of the Yorùbá People." In *Pioneer, Patriot, and Patriarchy: Samuel Johnson and the Yorùbá People*, edited by Toyin Falola, 77–86. Madison: University of Wisconsin, 1993.

Awe, Bolanle. "The Iyalode in the Traditional Yoruba Political System." In *Readings in Gender in Africa*, edited by Andrea Cornwall, 196–200. Bloomington: Indiana University Press, 2005.

————. "The Rise of Ibadan as a Yorùbá Power, 1851–1893." PhD Dissertation, Oxford University, 1964.

Awolalu, Omosade J. *Yorùbá Beliefs and Sacrificial Rites.* London: Longman, 1979.

Babayemi, S. O. *Egungun among the Ọ̀yọ́ Yorùbá.* Ibadan: Board Publication Limited, 1980.

Badejo, Diedre. *Oṣun Seegesi: The Elegant Deity of Wealth, Power, and Femininity.* Trenton: Africa World Press, 1996.

Barber, Karin. "Documenting Social and Ideological Change through Yoruba Oriki: A Stylistic Analysis." *Journal of the Historical Society of Nigeria* 10, no. 4 (June 1981): 39–52.

———. *I Could Speak until Tomorrow: Oríkì, Women, and the Past in a Yorùbá Town*. Edinburgh: Edinburgh University Press, 1991.

———. "Oríkì, Women and the Proliferation and Merging of Òrìṣà." *Africa* 60, no. 03b (1990): 313–337.

Bascom, William R. *Ifá Divination: Communication between Gods and Men in West Africa*. Bloomington: Indiana University Press, 1991.

———. *Sixteen Cowries: Yorùbá Divination from Africa to the New World*. Bloomington: Indiana University Press, 1993.

Bauer, Gretchen, and Hannah Evelyn Britton. *Women in African Parliaments*. Boulder, CO: Lynne Rienner Publishers, 2006.

Bond, G. C., and A. Gilliam, eds. *Social Construction of the Past: Representation as Power*. New York: Routledge, 1994.

Bouche, P. B. *Sept Ans En Afrique Occidentale: La Côte Des Esclaves Et Le Dahomey*. Paris: E. Plon Nourrit, 1885.

Bowen, T. J. *Central Africa: Adventures and Missionary Labors in Several Countries in the Interior of Africa, from 1849 to 1856* [in English]. Charleston, SC: Southern Baptist Publication Society, 1857.

Chakrabarty, Dipesh. *Provincializing Europe Postcolonial Thought and Historical Difference*. Princeton, NJ: Princeton University Press, 2000.

Chodorow, Nancy. *The Reproduction of Mothering: Psychoanalysis and the Sociology of Gender*. Berkeley: University of California Press, 1978.

Clapperton, Hugh. *Journal of the 2nd Expedition into the Interior of Africa*. Philadelphia: Carey, Lea, and Carey, 1829.

Connell, R. W. *Masculinities*. Los Angeles: University of California Press, 1995.

Danmole, H. O. "Samuel Johnson and the History of Ilorin." In *Pioneer, Patriot, and Patriarchy: Samuel Johnson and the Yorùbá People*, edited by Toyin Falola, 139–149. Madison: University of Wisconsin, 1993.

Diop, Cheikh Anta. *The Cultural Unity of Black Africa: The Domains of Patrairchy and Matriarchy in Classical Antiquity*. Chicago: Third World Press, 1978.

Doortmont, M. R. "Recapturing the Past: Samuel Johnson and the Construction of the History of the Yorùbá." PhD Dissertation, Erasmus University, 1994.

———. "Samuel Johnson (1846–1901): Missionary, Diplomat, and Historian." In *YorùBá Historiography*, edited by Toyin Falola, 167–182. Madison: University of Wisconsin, 1991.

Dowd, N. E. *The Man Question: Male Subordination and Privilege*. New York: New York University Press, 2010.

Ehrenreich, Barbara, and Arlie Russell Hochschild, eds. *Global Woman: Nannies, Maids, and Sex Workers in the New Economy*. New York: Henry Holt and Company, 2004.

Emmanuel. *Abosede—Odun Ifa: Ifa Festival*. West African Book Publishers, 1978.

Epega, Afolabi. *The Sacred Ifa Oracle*. Harper Collins, 1995.

Fadipe, N. A. *The Sociology of the Yorùbá*. Ibadan: Ibadan University Press, 1970.

Fagunwa, D. O. *Forest of a Thousand Daemons: A Hunter's Saga.* Translated by Wole Soyinka. New York: Random House, 1982.

———. *Ogboju Ọdẹ Ninu Igbo Irunmalẹ.* Nelson Publishers, 2005.

Falola, Toyin. "Gender, Business and Space Control: Yorùbá Market Women and Power." In *African Market Women's Economic Power: The Role of Women in African Economic Development,* edited by Bessie House-Midamba and Felik K. Ekechi, 23–40. Westport, CT: Greenwood Press, 1995.

———, ed. *Pioneer, Patriot, and Patriarchy: Samuel Johnson and the Yorùbá People.* Madison: University of Wisconsin, 1993.

———. *The Political Economy of a Pre-Colonial African State.* Ile-Ife: University of Ife Press, 1984.

———. *Yorùbá Gurus: Indigenous Production of Knowledge in Africa.* Trenton: Africa World Press, 1999.

Faniyi, Dejo. "ẸKún Ìyàwó: A Traditional Yorùbá Nuptial Chant." In *Yorùbá Oral Tradition: Selections from the Papers Presented at the Seminar on Yorùbá Oral Tradition: Poetry in Music, Dance, and Drama No. 1,* edited by Wande Abimbola. Ile-Ife: University of Ifẹ, 1975.

Gaidzanwa, Rudo B. *Images of Women in Zimbabwean Literature.* Harare: College Press, 1997.

Gbadamosi, T. G. O. "Odù Imale. Islam in Ifá Divination and the Case of Predestined Muslims." *Journal of the Historical Society of Nigeria* 8, no. 4 (1977): 77–93.

Gbadegesin, Segun. "Toward a Theory of Destiny." In *A Companion to African Philosophy,* edited by Kwasi Wiredu, 313–323. Oxford: Blackwell Publishing Ltd, 2007.

Gbowee, Leymah. *Mighty Be Our Powers: How Sisterhood, Prayer, and Sex Changed a Nation at War. A Memoir.* New York: Beast Books, 2013.

George, Olakunle. *Relocating Agency: Modernity and African Letters.* New York: State University of New York Press, 2012.

Hallen, B., and J. O. Sodipo. *Knowledge, Belief and Witchcraft: Analytic Experiments in African Philosophy.* London: Ethnographica Ltd., 1986.

Hallstein, D. Lynn O'Brien. *White Feminists and Contemporary Maternity: Purging Matrophobia.* New York: Palgrave Macmillan, 2010.

Johnson, Samuel, and Obadiah Johnson. *The History of the Yorubas: From the Earliest Times to the Beginning of the British Protectorate.* Westport, CT: Negro University Press, 1921.

Kenyatta, Jomo. *Facing Mount Kenya: The Tribal Life of the Gikuyu.* London: Heinemann Group of Publishers, 1962.

Ladele, T. A. A., O. Mustapha, I. A. Aworinde, O. Oyerinde, and O. Akojopo Oladapo. *Iwadii Ijinle Asa Yorùbá.* Ibadan: Macmillan, 1986.

Laye, Camara. *The African Child by Camara Laye.* Translated by James Kirkup. Fontana Bks, 1959.

Lawal, Babatunde. "A Ya Gbo, a Ya To: New Perspectives on Edan Ogboni." *African Arts* 28, no. 1 (1995): 37–100.

———. "Aworan: Representing the Self and Its Metaphysical Other in Yorùbá Art." *The Art Bulletin* 83, no. 3 (2001): 498–526.

Lindsay, Lisa A., and Stephan Miescher, eds. *Men and Masculinities in Modern Africa.* Portsmouth, NH: Heinemann, 2003.

Lorber, Judith. *Paradoxes of Gender.* New Haven: Yale University Press, 1994.

Lugones, Maria. "Hetrosexualism and the Colonial Modern Gender System." *Hypatia* 22, no. 1 (Winter 2007).

Maathai, Wangari. *The Green Belt Movement Manual.* Nairobi, Kenya: W. Maathai, 1991.

Mann, Kristin. *Marrying Well: Marriage, Status, and Social Change among the Educated Elite in Colonial Lagos.* Cambridge: Cambridge University Press, 1985.

Maupoil, Bernard. *La Géomancie À L'ancienne Côte Des Esclaves.* Paris: Institut d'ethnologie, 1943.

Mazama, Ama. *Africa in the 21st Century: Toward a New Future.* New York: Routledge, 2007.

Ndlovu-Gatsheni, Sabelo. *Coloniality of Power in Postcolonial Africa. Myths of Decolonizatiion.* Dakar, Sengal: Codesria, 2013.

New York Times, February 3, 2015.

Nzegwu, Nkiru Uwechia. *Family Matters: Feminist Concepts in African Philosophy of Culture.* New York: State University of New York Press, 2006.

Ogungbile, D. O. "ẸẸRìndínlógún: The Seeing Eyes of Sacred Shells and Stones." In *ỌṢUn across the Waters: A YorùBá Goddess in Africa and the Americas,* edited by Joseph M. and Mei-Mei Sanford Murphy, 189–212. Bloomington: Indiana University Press, 2001.

Olabimtan, Afolabi. "Religion as Theme in Fagunwa's Novels." *Odù* 11 (1975): 101–114.

Olajubu, Oyeronke. "Seeing through a Woman's Eye: Yorùbá Religious Tradition and Gender Relations." *Journal of Feminist Studies in Religion* 20, no. 1 (2004): 41–60.

———. *Women in the Yorùbá Religious Sphere.* Albany: State University Press of New York, 2003.

Olupona, Jacob. "Imagining the Goddess: Gender in Yorùbá Religious Traditions and Modernity." *Dialogue and Alliance* 18, no. 1 (2004/2005): 71–86.

———. "ÒRìsà ỌṢun: Yorùbá Sacred Kingship and Civil Religion in Oṣogbo, Nigeria." In *ỌṢun across the Waters: A Yorùbá Goddess in Africa and the Americas,* edited by Joseph M. and Mei-Mei Sanford Murphy, 46–67. Bloomington: Indiana University Press, 2001.

Orie, Ọla Ọlanike. "Yorùbá Names and Gender Marking." *Anthropological Linguistics* 44, no. 2 (2002): 115–142.

Owusu, Maxwell. "Toward an African Critique of African Ethnography: The Usefulness of the Useless." In *Reclaiming the Human Sciences and Humanities through African Perspectives,* edited by H. Lauer and Kofi Anyidoho, 77–104. Accra, Ghana: Sub-Saharan Publishers, 2012.

Oyelaran, Oyesope, and Lawrence Adewole. *Isenbaye Ati Ilo Ede Yorùbá.* South Africa: Center for Advanced Studies of African Society, 2007.

Oyesakin, Adefisoye. "The Image of Women in Ifá Literary Corpus." *Nigeria Magazine* 141 (1982): 16–23.

Oyetade, B. A. "Tones in the Yorùbá Personal Praise Names: Oríkì Àbísọ." *Research in Yorùbá Language and Literature* 1 (1991): 55–62.

Oyěwùmí, Oyèrónké. "Colonizing Bodies and Minds: Gender and Colonialism." In *Postconialisms: An Anthology of Cultural Theory and Criticism*, edited by Gaurav and Supriya Nair Desai, 1–24. New Jersey: Rutgers University Press, 2005.

———. "Introduction. Feminism, Sisterhood, and Other Foreign Relations." In *African Women and Feminism: Reflecting on the Politics of Sisterhood*, edited by Oyèrónké Oyěwùmí, 1–24. New Jersey: Africa World Press, 2003.

———. *The Invention of Women: Making an African Sense of Western Gender Discourses.* Minneapolis: University of Minnesota Press, 1997.

———. "Making History, Creating Gender: Some Methodological and Interpretive Questions in the Writing of Oyo Oral Traditions." *History in Africa* 25 (1998): 263–305.

Peel, J. D. Y. "Gender in Yorùbá Religious Change." *Journal of Religion in Africa* 32, no. 2 (2002): 136–166.

———. "The Pastor and the 'Babaláwo':The Interaction of Religions in Nineteenth-Century Yorùbáland." *Africa: Journal of the International African Institute* 60, no. 3 (1990): 338–369.

———. *Religious Encounter and the Making of the Yorùbá.* Bloomington: Indiana University Press, 2000.

Pemberton, John. "The Ọ̀Yọ́ Empire." In *Yorùbá: Nine Centuries of Art and Thought*, edited by Henry Drewal, John Pemberton, Rowland Abiodun, and Allen Wardwell. New York: Center for African Art in Association with H. N Abram, 1989.

Pemberton, John III, and Funso S. Afolayan. *Yorùbá Sacred Kingship: A Power Like That of the Gods.* Washington and London: Smithsonian Institution, 1996.

Quijano, Anibal. "Coloniality and Modernity/Rationality." *Cultural Studies* 21, no. 2/3 (March/May 2007): 168–178.

Rich, Adrienne. *Of Woman Born: Motherhood as Experience and Institution.* New York: Norton, 1986.

Riches, S., and S. Salih, eds. *Gender and Holiness: Men, Women and Saints in Late Medieval Europe.* London and New York: Routledge, 2002.

Rosaldo, Michelle, and Louise Lamphere, eds. *Women, Culture, and Society.* Stanford: Stanford University Press, 1974.

Salami, Ayo. *Ifa: A Complete Divination.* Unknown Binding, 2009.

Sandberg, Sheryl, and Nell Scovell. *Lean In: Women, Work, and the Will to Lead.* New York: Alfred A. Knopf, 2013.

Semley, Lorelle D. *Mother Is Gold, Father Is Glass: Gender and Colonialism in a Yorùbá Town.* Bloomington: Indiana University Press, 2011.

Smith, Robert Sydney. "Alaafin in Exile: A Study of the Igboho Period in Ọ̀YỌ́ History." *Journal of African History* 6, no. 1 (1865): 57–77.

Somé, Malidoma Patrice. *Of Water and the Spirit: Ritual, Magic and Initiation in the Life of an African Shaman.* New York: Penguin, 1995.

Soyinka, Wole. *Isara: A Voyage around Essay.* Ibadan: Fountain Publications, 1989.

Steady, Filimena. *Women and Collective Action in Africa.* New York: Palgrave, 2006.

———. *Women and Leadership in Africa: Mothering the Nation, Humanizing the State.* New York: Palgrave/Macmillan, 2013.

Sudarkasa, Niara. *The Strength of Our Mothers: African & African American Women and Families. Essays and Speeches.* Trenton, NJ: Africa World Press, 1986.

Tamale, Sylvia Rosila. *When Hens Begin to Crow: Gender and Parliamentary Politics in Uganda.* Boulder, CO: Westview Press, 2000.

Watson, Ruth. *Civil Disorder Is the Disease of Ibadan: Chieftaincy & Civic Culture in a Yorùbá City.* Oxford: James Currey Publishers, 2003.

———. "What Is Our Intelligence, Our School Going and Our Reading of Books without Getting Money? Akinpelu Obisesan and His Diary." In *African Hidden Histories: Everyday Literacy and the Making of the Self,* edited by Karin Barber, 52–77. Bloomington: Indiana University Press, 2006.

Westcott, Joan A., and Peter Morton-Williams. "The Festival of Iyamapo." *Nigeria Magazine* (1958): 212–224.

Zachernuk, S. Phillip. "Johnson and the Victorian Image of the Yorùbá." In *Pioneer, Patriot, and Patriarchy: Samuel Johnson and the Yorùbá People,* edited by Toyin Falola, 33–46. Madison: University of Wisconsin, 1993.

INDEX

Abimbola, Kola, 88, 89, 228, 230
Abimbola, Wande, 14, 15, 23, 35, 86, 89, 144, 147, 222–5, 230, 236, 239, 254
Abiodun, Rowland, 43, 225–7, 229, 236, 256
academy, 118, 144, 146
Ade Ajayi, J., 112, 231, 234, 238, 241, 243
Adeeko, Adeleke, 229
Adepegba, C. O., 26
Adogame, Afe, 138
Afolayan, Adeyemi, 227
Agiri, B., 151, 237, 252
Ahikire, Josephine, 215, 245
Ajibade, Olusola, 230
Akan, 202, 217
akewu-kewe, 231
Akinnaso, Niyi, 28, 33, 153, 193
Akinyele, I. B, 95, 101, 102
Akinyemi, Akintunde, ix, 106, 156, 161
Akiwowo, Akinsola, 147, 237
Akòwé, 231
Akyeampong, Emmanuel, 226
Alaafin Abiodun, 97, 232
Allen, William, 127
Aluko, T. M., 55, 64, 226, 227
Amadiume, Ifi, 6, 221, 227
anafemale, 11, 24, 30, 50, 59, 68, 71, 72, 75, 76, 79, 108, 109, 121, 123, 125, 131, 143, 152, 161, 166, 184, 249
anamale, 11, 13, 16, 59, 68, 71, 108, 109, 121, 125, 126, 135, 143, 152, 166, 184, 249
Anta Diop, Cheikh, 227

Arabic script, 93, 231
Aronson, Daniel, 234, 252
Atanda, J. A., 98, 232
Atlantic Slave Trade, 242
Awe, Bolanle, 79, 229, 233, 237, 240
Awolalu, J. O., 224, 252
Ayorinde, E. A., 94

Badejo, Deidre, 42, 49
Banda, Joyce, 245
Barber, Karin, 23, 68, 174, 222, 227, 237–9, 241, 257
Bascom, William, 13, 35
Bateye, Bolaji, 138
Bond, George, 54
Bouche, Pierre, 20
Bowen, T. J., 20, 25
brides, 9, 158, 171–3, 175–81, 183, 185, 187, 189, 191, 197, 239

capitalism, 214, 220
Chakrabarty, Dipesh, 4, 221
Chitando, Ezra, 138
Christianity, 13, 18, 19, 22, 33, 34, 66, 84, 85, 104, 108, 131, 136, 137, 179, 184, 185, 191–3, 198, 199, 202–5, 207, 231, 235, 242
    influence on naming, 84, 191, 193, 198, 199, 202–4, 207, 208
Christianity and Names, 84, 191, 193, 198, 199, 202–4, 207, 208
Church Missionary Society, 19, 65, 85, 101, 114, 119, 135
Clapperton, Hugh, 228
Coker, Daniel, 21, 130

colonialism, 3–6, 12, 224, 235, 256
coloniality of knowledge, 2
coloniality of power, 2, 3, 214, 221, 255
colonization, 1, 2, 4, 7, 11, 12, 14, 92,
    118, 204, 208, 211
Connell, R.W., 130, 182, 236, 241
Craig, M.A., 95
Crowther, Samuel Ajayi, 159, 194, 197,
    238, 242, 243, 251

Danmole, Hakeem, 238, 253
Denzer, Laray, 119
diviners, 1, 13, 14, 17–20, 22–36, 39, 40,
    42, 50, 131, 137, 142, 145, 223, 248
    of eerindinlogun, 26, 30
    of Ifa, 13, 18, 20, 22, 23, 24, 28, 31–6,
    40, 42, 131, 137, 142
Doortmont, Michel, 109
Dowd, Nancy, 222

Egbe Agba O Tan, 95–8, 101, 102, 107,
    111
ẹkún ìyàwó, 172–5, 178, 179, 185, 191,
    239, 248
Emmanuel, Abosede, 14
English language, 6, 12, 14, 16, 32, 50,
    102, 165
    problem of translation, 11, 14, 15,
    16, 20, 31, 42, 57, 65–6, 77, 91, 98,
    102, 108, 144
    role in colonization, 6, 12, 14, 16, 32
Epega, Afolabi, 14, 253
epistemicide, 4

Fadipe, N.A., 175, 240
Fagunwa, D.O., 83, 98, 230, 232, 233
Falola, Toyin, x, 94, 228, 231, 232, 234,
    235, 238, 240, 243, 251–3, 257
Faniyi, Dejo, 174, 239
fatherhood, 61, 66, 124, 185
feminist theory, 219
feminist writings, 12
Fulani, 77, 202

Gaidzanwa, Rudo, 84
Gbadamosi, G., 224, 254

Gbadegesin, Segun, 60, 227
Gbowee, Leymah, 218, 245
gender, i–iv, 1–12, 14–24, 26–42,
    44–50, 52, 54, 58, 60, 62, 64, 66,
    68, 70–2, 74–6, 78–82, 84, 86,
    88–90, 92, 94–6, 98–100, 102–4,
    106–12, 114, 117–56, 158–69,
    171, 172, 174, 176, 178, 180–90,
    192–4, 196, 198, 200–9, 212–16,
    218, 220–39, 241, 243–5, 251–7
    as category, 34
    as factor of social organization, 34
    as source of identity, 34
gender attribution, 209
gender binary, 163, 182
gender complementarity, 38, 50
gender dichotomy, 46, 50, 89, 132, 183
gender division, 20, 29, 39, 40, 78, 102,
    131, 152, 171, 201, 208
gender subordination, 12
genderism, 32, 42
George, Olakunle, ix, 83, 99, 230, 232, 233
Gilliam, Angela, 54
Gods and gender, 138–40

Hallen, Barry, 91
Harvard Conference, 144, 146
Hausa, ix, 200, 202, 206, 243, 244
Hinderer, Anna, 229

Ibadan, ix, 1, 33, 65, 79–82, 94, 95,
    99, 102–4, 111, 112, 115, 135,
    151, 158, 159, 171, 172, 176, 177,
    180, 183, 184, 187, 188, 191, 194,
    199–201, 203, 205, 221, 222, 225,
    227, 229, 230, 232–6, 238–41, 243,
    244, 251–4, 256, 257
Igbo, 73, 83, 98, 216, 226, 227, 230,
    252, 254
importance of sacrifice, 28, 32, 65, 87,
    88, 132, 135
intellectuals and colonization, 126
Islam, ix, 13, 18, 19, 22, 33, 34, 40, 104, 136,
    145, 151, 176, 179, 184, 185, 191–3,
    200–7, 224, 235, 242, 249, 254
    impact on names, 193, 202, 205, 207

CPSIA information can be obtained
at www.ICGtesting.com
Printed in the USA
LVHW021735011220
673044LV00016B/506